They and We

They and We

Racial and Ethnic Relations in the United States and Beyond

Seventh Edition

FIFTIETH ANNIVERSARY YEAR

Peter I. Rose

Routledge

Taylor & Francis Group

LONDON AND NEW YORK

First published 2014 by Paradigm Publishers

Published 2016 by Routledge
2 Park Square, Milton Park, Abingdon, Oxon OX14 4RN
711 Third Avenue, New York, NY 10017, USA

Routledge is an imprint of the Taylor & Francis Group, an informa business

Copyright © 2014, Taylor & Francis.

Library of Congress Cataloging-in-Publication Data

Rose, Peter Isaac, 1933–
    They and we : racial and ethnic relations in the United States and beyond / Peter I. Rose. — Seventh
edition, Fiftieth anniversary year.
        pages cm
    Includes bibliographical references and index.
    ISBN 978-1-61205-660-9 (pbk. : acid-free paper) — ISBN 978-1-61205-635-7 (consumer
ebook)
    1. Minorities—United States.   2. Discrimination—United States.   3. United States—Race
relations.   4. United States—Ethnic relations.   I. Title.
    E184.A1R72 2014
    305.800973—dc23

                                                                                            2014005891

Designed and typeset by Straight Creek Bookmakers.

ISBN 13: 978-1-61205-660-9 (pbk)

For Hedy

Contents

Preface

The first edition of *They and We* was completed in 1963, the year the Civil Rights Movement reached its zenith. "Black Power" was but a hushed whisper then. Few who listened to Reverend Martin Luther King Jr. address a quarter of a million black and white Americans assembled on the Mall in front of the Lincoln Memorial in Washington, DC, on August 28, 1963, realized that he, his people, and their allies in the struggle—and their enemies—were about to enter a new era. The whisper was to become a roar.

Those days now seem light-years away. In the period immediately before the March on Washington for Jobs and Freedom, thousands had participated in a crusade of radical pacifism, a campaign involving a variety of nonviolent direct action tactics—marches, boycotts, sit-ins, and freedom rides—seeking to force the country to honor its own vaunted ideals and win for all the rights most white Americans took for granted. It was a difficult and uphill struggle. Although the costs were considerable, there were a number of significant victories. But several events that occurred a few months after the March on Washington led to a dramatic change in the tone, the temper, and the orientation of the movement.

The mounting frustration of militant blacks and many others confined to inner-city ghettos became painfully apparent to all members of society. Anger was expressed in a variety of contexts. Riots broke out in some cities. Within the civil rights organizations, many whites who had played key roles as organizers or foot soldiers were eased or pushed from positions of leadership; many African Americans (and Asian Americans and Latinos and Native Americans in their own fashions) foreswore the rhetoric of integration for the rhetoric of revolution.

In many ways the rhetoric was reified. In a real sense there was a revolution.

First, the members of the dominant white majority were told over and over that they, all of them, and not just "the southern bigots," were racists. A spate of new books hammered home the theme. Many black people who, for any number of reasons, had not organized themselves before began to add action to their verbal attacks. Demands were made, met, escalated, and often made again. A new litany began to be heard. Watchwords like "Freedom, Now" and "We Shall Overcome" were replaced by various new slogans that reflected the view tersely expressed in the warning, "Look out, whitey, black power gon' get your momma," and the self-asserting statement, "Black is beautiful." Then there came a call for recompense. Ultimately, in what many saw as justified and others saw as a kind of racism-in-reverse, the pleas for admission and fairness became a call for special treatment to help those handicapped by the stigma of inferiority to improve their chances to run an equal race.

As the demands, particularly of college students, were beginning to be responded to by frightened faculties and baffled administrations (often liberal and therefore particularly susceptible to the accusations of the protesters), more conservative organizations began making their own concessions. For example, large industries increased the level of tokenism to include more African American and Latino workers, especially in places where they would be seen. Television networks and local stations began to employ them, too. In the beginning most of the new hires were assigned to do race-based "Minority Reports." (It would be several more years before they would begin to move more directly into mainline positions.)

The pressure tactics were quite successful. It was a revelation to some to see how many qualified "people of color" were actually available as potential students for Ivy League colleges, as workers in various Fortune 500 companies, as TV announcers and print media commentators when the threat of disruption loomed on the immediate horizon.

As disaffected members of the old civil rights movement were beginning to rally their troops for new assaults on the academy and the factory, the people on the street became involved, too. Some did it in organized fashion, others more spontaneously. Dozens of urban disturbances flared up in cities as different as New York, Detroit, Cleveland, and Los Angeles as poor folks joined in the burning and looting in a frenzied expression of frustration and bitterness and, for some, the sheer thrill of revenge.

Other people engaged in more carefully planned political activities, many of them centered on the issue of local or community control, particularly of schools. Still others simply took renewed pride in who they were, if not where they found themselves.

All this—the rhetoric, the organizing, the calculated attacks on the system, and the spontaneous outbursts—shook the entire nation. Many white Americans reeled in disbelief and then, in a variety of ways, they reacted.

Part of the response came from traditional reactionaries whose predominant theme was "We told you so." But more significant, and far greater in the numbers involved, was the response of those in two significant cohorts: white, Protestant, lower-middle-class, and small-town "middle Americans"; and working-class, predominantly Catholic, and urban "white ethnics." The latter group, often but a generation or two from ghetto living themselves, began to feel that they, in particular, were being asked to pay for the sins of other peoples' fathers and mothers.

Backlash became a reality, though, save for widespread reaction to forced school busing, it was far less vicious than many had predicted. Even so, by the early 1970s the bookstores had another section to add to the one that shelved volumes by Maya Angelou, James Baldwin, Eldridge Cleaver, Angela Davis, Ralph Ellison, Frantz Fanon, and on through the rest of an alphabetical list of black writers and writers on black subjects. The new shelf, not yet so long, included books with telling titles like Murray Friedman's *Overcoming Middle Class Rage,* Nathan Glazer's *Affirmative Discrimination,* Andrew M. Greeley's *Why Can't They Be Like Us?,* Louise Howe's *The White Majority,* Michael Novak's *The Rise of the Unmeltable Ethnics,* Peter Shrag's *Out of Place in America,* and many more with similar themes. That list was to grow much longer, especially in the 1990s and in the first decade of the new millennium. It would include two especially hard-hitting critiques: Arthur M. Schlesinger's *The Disuniting of America,* published in 1991, and Samuel P. Huntington's *Who Are We?,* published in 2004.

Parallel to the growing resistance to the pressures being exerted by black and brown and other minority Americans was a reexamination of their own places in the society, and their own histories as well. A new cadre of African American writers appeared. Many of them would form the vanguard of a powerful group of articulate activists, college professors, public figures, and celebrity intellectuals who began to have a heavy impact well beyond the confines of their base communities. In fact, the leaders and spokespeople for the Black Power movement and their emphasis on ethnic consciousness were largely responsible for identity politics and communalism becoming legitimized, then institutionalized in what would later be known as "multiculturalism"—in a manner unprecedented in our history.

The period from 1964 to 1974 was quite a volatile one on the ethnic front. Yet, by the middle of the 1970s "race" was no longer a central issue, nor was American involvement in Vietnam, the war having ended in 1975. From that time through the rest of the decade, economics and energy concerns took center stage, dominating foreign affairs and also domestic debates.

This is not to say everything was settled in the realm of racial and ethnic relations. It wasn't. In fact, the energy crisis served to accentuate the plight of the poor who had the most to lose from rising prices and increasing shortages of fuel, to say nothing of the growing scourge of unemployment as the economy slowed and layoffs became the order of the day.

At the same time, the general economic downturn led increasing numbers of middle Americans and white ethnics to take even more conservative stances regarding bread-and-butter issues. Concerned about where tax dollars were going, they railed against "giveaways" to "welfare chiselers," whom some styled "the undeserving poor." Many voiced the opinion that minorities seemed to get too much of the public funds and too many of the private positions and jobs. Court decisions gave additional support to those opposed to affirmative action and quotas, however "benign" they were claimed to be.

By the end of the 1970s, the strains of economic and political problems were deeply etched in the face of America. Unemployment reached a forty-year high and, as always, nonwhites bore the brunt of the burden. Riots in Miami, Orlando, and Chattanooga in the summer of 1980 were an ugly reminder of the depth of hostility still extant in urban ghettos.

International conflicts influenced many domestic debates as well, and many began choosing sides over US policies in southern Africa and the Middle East. Moreover, increasing numbers of citizens expressed resentment over the influx of hundreds of thousands of Cubans, Soviet Jews, and Southeast Asians who were seen not just as refugees from communism but as potential usurpers of jobs and benefits of Americans.

With the depressed economic situation, the increase in racial tension, the rising tide of political conservatism, and a dearth of strong civil rights leadership, many feared that the gains made by minorities in the 1960s and 1970s would prove to be Pyrrhic victories. They were not far off the mark. One reason is that, for all the changes, including the implementation of affirmative action programs during the years of the Nixon administration, certain underlying structural characteristics of our society remained relatively constant. Among the most enduring of a long list of seemingly endemic traits was that of a nation that remained hierarchically divided in terms of social class.

While it is true that those in the upper echelons were better off than ever before (this was a time when a new and colorful term, *yuppies*—young, urban profession-als—took on special meaning) and increasing numbers of minority-group members were able to join the ranks of the middle class, often as the result of special efforts to assist them, many black and brown as well as white working-class Americans found they were treading water just to stay afloat in a highly turbulent economic sea. This was also true of the hundreds of thousands of resident aliens who, thanks to the Immigration Reform Act of 1965, had entered the country as immigrants looking for chances to benefit from the still widely regarded promise of the "Ameri-can Dream." Like the many refugees being resettled in the United States, they also often found themselves perceived of as interlopers poised to take jobs of those who claimed them almost as their birthright. Often the legal immigrants and the political refugees were grouped with illegal migrants or "undocumented aliens." In many circles, as it had been in the late nineteenth and early twentieth century, "immigrant" was once again becoming a pejorative word.

Then there were those others who came to be known in the press and in the sociology classroom by the generic label "underclass"—many of them members of nonwhite minorities—who were found to be falling further and further behind. The social profiles of such truly disadvantaged African, Hispanic, and Native American people belied any claims, even by the most optimistic of political lead-ers, that dramatic progress had been made in dealing with one of the most basic domestic problems in our society.

The Reagan years, which began in 1980, were extended with the presidency of George H. W. Bush. Despite assurances that he would be a "kinder and gentler leader," Bush adhered to many of the policies that had turned away from the pro-gressive activities of the 1960s and 1970s, favoring instead a faith in "voluntarism." But even the attempt to ignite "a thousand points of light," Bush's expression for private initiatives, could not stem the tide of decay in the most devastated parts of society. Consequently, during the waning years of his one-term occupancy of the White House, the country was plagued with renewed calls for governmental action to address the needs of those most disadvantaged by past and continuing discrimination.

Bush was defeated. But it was not because of his racial policies—or lack thereof. Still, there was hope in the old civil rights circles that the new president, Bill Clinton, would be more sympathetic to the plight of the poor and the dispossessed, especially when he so pointedly selected cabinet members with liberal agendas, individuals who also, for the first time in history, did, as Clinton himself said, "look like America."

While some attempts were made to address the persisting grievances of minorities, women, and homosexuals, as well as poor whites, the constant sniping of the old centrist groups (those middle Americans and white ethnics) led to considerable equivocation and, eventually, retreat on many fronts. But even such acquiescence was not enough. In 1994, hundreds of Republicans were swept into office and took control of both houses of Congress, riding to power on the concerns of many who still opposed "welfarism" and "special treatment" of certain minorities, and who were firmly opposed to what they called "governmental interventionism." At the time of their victorious routing of the liberals, many of whom had been specifically targeted, the United States was still a deeply divided nation, separate and unequal in many quarters. The depth of the division became most clearly apparent in the fall of 1995 when, after a lengthy televised trial, African American former football star O. J. Simpson was found innocent of charges of murdering his ex-wife, Nicole, and her friend, Ronald Goldman. Both of the victims were white.

Poll data after the verdict was handed down revealed what those who had hoped for a color-blind assessment of the case most feared: opinion about the correctness of the jury's decision was directly correlated with "color." An overwhelming majority of African Americans thought the decision was justified. As for whether it was just, some claimed that "Whatever the truth, this was clearly a victory over a traditionally biased system of criminal justice." Most whites disagreed with both the verdict and the sentiment, some quite vehemently.

Almost immediately on the heels of the Simpson trial came both corroboration and contradiction. The "Million Man March" in Washington in 1995, organized and led by the Muslim leader Louis Farrakhan, provoked reaction that, while far more nuanced than those in response to the Simpson verdict, further pointed to a seemingly deepening chasm cleaving two major communities and influencing the general perceptions of white and black Americans. Yet there was mounting evidence that that may only be one side of the story.

Until he withdrew from consideration on November 8, 1995, former chief of staff of the armed forces, General Colin Powell, a black moderate and self-professed Republican, was the most popular challenger to Bill Clinton, who was gearing up to run for a second term in the Oval Office. Some argued that Powell, whose support was almost as strong among whites as it was among African Americans, was seen so favorably because it was felt that only someone like him could begin to bring the clearly estranged communities together.

Colin Powell did not run for president, but he did become the secretary of state in the cabinet of the man who won the election of 2000, George W. Bush. A conservative by every measure but in his seemingly color-blind selection of high-ranking officials in his first administration, the second President Bush, like Ronald Reagan and like his father, did little to address the continuing needs of minority communities. Indeed, in many ways he and the members of his administration set back the clock on civil rights and, after the momentous attacks on the twin towers of the World Trade Center and the Pentagon, on civil liberties as well.

Although he came into power with seemingly little interest in foreign affairs, after "9/11," he became preoccupied with them—and with asserting America's role on the world stage. His first term was dominated by military actions in Afghanistan and Iraq, and with "homeland security," prompted by the desire to stave off future attacks on the country, particularly by Islamic terrorists. One result of this was a growing fear in the ranks of American Muslims—many of Arab background, many others African American converts—that they would become the scapegoats seen as responsible for many of the country's problems.

In November 2004, after a protracted and, in many ways, very ugly campaign for the presidency, the conservative George W. Bush won a second term over the liberal senator from Massachusetts, John F. Kerry. Despite growing disillusionment with foreign adventures and many domestic matters, especially in the "blue" (heavily Democrat) states of the Northeast and the West Coast, the Republicans prevailed, not only keeping the presidency but strengthening their positions in both houses of Congress.

In his very brief, twenty-two-minute inaugural address in January 2005, the president not only mentioned the word "freedom" more than two dozen times, but he boldly stated that "our country must abandon all the habits of racism, because we cannot carry the message of freedom and the baggage of bigotry at the same time." His forceful words seemed to jibe with his personal proclivity toward color-blindness in appointments. His cabinet and senior staff were the most "multicultural" to that point in the nation's history. In addition to those of East Asian, South Asian, Hispanic, and African origins, Bush also appointed more women than any of his predecessors. But the jury remained out on how his rhetoric and actions in the White House would translate into greater opportunities for those with whom the likes of Condoleezza Rice, Alberto Gonzales, Elaine Chao, and Norman Mineta are identified.

It did not take long for a dramatic indication that such appointments were welcome but were hardly sufficient to effectively address the persisting dilemma linked to slavery's legacy and the plight of African Americans. No better example is to be found than in perceptions of the federal government's response to hurricane Katrina that hit Louisiana, Alabama, and Mississippi in early September 2005. A disproportionate percentage of those who suffered most from devastation and displacement were black and poor. Their plight dramatically increased long-held suspicions of ordinary African Americans about presidential empathy and the true commitments of the Bush administration. This was most clearly evident in the results of a nationwide *USA Today*/Gallop Poll conducted a week after the calamity. In answer to the question "Do you think President Bush cares about black people?" 67 percent of whites said "Yes," compared to only 21 percent of blacks. These differences offered a stark reminder that racism, and the pervasive poverty that is often linked to it, remained one of the most divisive social issues in the United States. It pointedly underscored the belief of many people that we are a nation still divided, separate, and unequal. Then came the election of Barack Obama in 2008 and his reelection four years later.

In many ways Obama's victory was the result of four decades of efforts on behalf of private parties, political organizations, and congressional actions, not least the Voting Rights Act of 1965, to assure fairer treatment. Ironically, in the spring of 2013, by a 5–4 decision, the Supreme Court struck down a major component of that 1965 bill that had required all states with a historic record of discrimination against African Americans to obtain federal approval of any change in their election laws. Conservatives argued that, because so many more blacks were now voting without impediments, there was no longer a need for what they contended had been a violation of states' rights even when implemented. Those in dissent worried that the decision would now lead to new ways of controlling the votes of significant blocs of people in many states and municipalities, not least by gerrymandering districts to assure white domination.

The politics of race is still a significant issue; and, of late, there has been a resurgence of concern about "newcomers" to our shores.

In the last decade dramatic demographic shifts have meant that, very soon, the majority of Americans will be those long seen as "minorities," with Latinos the fastest growing population group in the nation. So important is this shift that even those long resistant to immigration reform and, especially, to regularizing the status of undocumented migrants, have begun to get on the bandwagon in hopes of capturing some of the votes of the newly enfranchised segment of the electorate.

The situation remains volatile, especially in the face of the lingering results of conquest, capture, exploitation, exclusion, segregation, and other hardships endured by some of the oldest minorities in the country—native people and African Americans.

The two steps forward, one step back course of race relations over the past fifty years was clearly stated by Senator Bernie Sanders of Vermont on the fiftieth anniversary of the March on Washington: "There has been some real progress in breaking down barriers of discrimination and segregation, including the election and re-election of an African-American president. On the other hand, in terms of unemployment, low wages and more wealth disparity, we are worse off than we were in 1963."

While many significant changes in social policy and definitive gains on the "race relations front" have occurred since the early 1960s, not least a decided broadening of the tolerance limits for enhancing then accepting diversity in the populations—and enforcing laws related to it—much of what was said about the dynamic character of American society and about ways of studying it then still seems appropriate. In the first edition, I sketched out the ways sociologists looked at what was then called "intergroup relations," at America's ethnic history, at some of the principal arguments put forth to handle the flow of newcomers, at prejudice and discrimination, and at minority responses—and at the persistence of the "they vs. we" dichotomy.

The preparation of each subsequent edition has involved reassessment, revision, and, often, the introduction of new ideas and new information on such matters as "Black Consciousness" and its significance for African Americans and other nonwhite minorities; the challenge of minority assertiveness and its effect on the "resurgence of ethnicity" among other groups; debates over intelligence testing and affirmative action policies, political correctness, and multiculturalism. The sixth edition involved a major overhaul of the text, including an expansion of the historical sections and those dealing with contemporary issues—such as "political correctness." This one did, too.

Much of this seventh edition of *They and We* follows the outline and the arguments of the preceding ones. But, in addition to new discussions of such concepts as "immigrants" and "refugees," an update of statistics cited and further interpretation of what they mean, and the introduction of fresh ideas and recent findings by social scientists and historians, what is most different here is the attention paid to several recent phenomena: the rise of anti-Americanism abroad and the stark reality for many of being placed in the role of stereotyped "minorities" on the world stage; the rebirth of nativism in this country as growing fear of what foreigners might bring with them—from secreted weapons to ideas and ideologies that run counter to those of the mainstream—that seems to shape both foreign and domestic policy; the rapidly changing demography (an overall doubling in the number of foreign-born in the past decade and the influx of dramatically increasing numbers of both legal and undocumented aliens in certain areas that, to some, give legitimacy as well as license to the expression of such fears); the surge in the growth of Hispanic communities assuring that within a few years they will not only be the largest single group in the society but, along with other ethnic minorities, will become the statistical majority of people in the United States; the continuation of two parallel phenomena, the increasing "ethnicization" of African Americans and the "racialization" of Latinos; and, despite the election and reelection of the first African American to be president of the United States, the persisting difficulties of many African Americans to attain full equality, especially at a time when many so labeled feel, once again, that, as happened in the past, they are being pushed aside or leapt over by yet another cohort of relative newcomers, immigrant groups in a number of spheres.

One additional feature is a new, final chapter that takes the reader beyond our shores to examine the growing tensions among ethnic and religious groups in other lands.

As explained in the preface to the original edition, while organized efforts to bring about a reduction in racial and ethnic tension represent an important part of contemporary life, and the tactics and strategies employed are a matter of great concern to many social scientists, including the author, they can only be introduced within the compass of this small book. It is hoped, however, that what is presented here will help to replace some of the popular misconceptions of the problems discussed and will thus serve as a basis for understanding, the first step toward change.

As I have six times before, I welcome the chance to thank many teachers, colleagues, students, and friends who have taught me, encouraged me, and offered assistance, advice, and criticism. Here I especially want to acknowledge Charles D. Lieber, an editors' editor who commissioned me to write a small book on American minorities for a Random House series way back in 1960 (that became *They and We*), and, later, as president of Atherton books, published my two-volume collection, *Americans from Africa*; the late Charles Hunt Page who, as a consulting editor at Random House, taught me much about writing and editing and remained a trusted adviser and close friend until his death in 1992; and Ely Chinoy, a superb social scientist, sensitive critic, and wonderful colleague at Smith College, whose untimely death forty years ago I still mourn.

I also offer my appreciation for the support and guidance of Ted Caris, Arthur Strimling, David Bartlett, Philip Metcalf, Phillip A. Butcher, Peggy C. Rehberger, Jill Gordon, and Kathy Blake, editors at Random House and at McGraw-Hill, who each played a part in the publication of one or more of the first five editions of *They and We*. To that list, I add special thanks to Dean Birkenkamp and his wonderful staff at Paradigm Publishers who published the sixth edition and are now bringing out this seventh—and fiftieth anniversary—edition.

Finally, I am pleased to note that every edition of this book has been dedicated to my Dutch wife, Hedy. From the start, it benefited from her insights gained from a childhood during the period when she, like Anne Frank, was a hidden child in Amsterdam, and her lifelong attempt—as both student and teacher—to combat the scourge of hatred and the consequences of discrimination.

Our daughter Lies and son Dan literally grew up with *They and We* and its underlying message. And now, as I write this (re)dedication, I hope that our now-adult grandsons, Jordan and Robert, will flourish in a country in which the dream of Martin Luther King Jr. will finally be realized—that there will be a day when all people will be judged by the content of their character and not the color of their skin, and that all those "theys" will become part of an all-encompassing "we."

Peter I. Rose

Part I

Contexts and Concepts

Race, Ethnicity, and the Sociological Perspective

Reaping the Whirlwind

As a native of the area, I have been appalled by the wanton riots, the pillaging and the total disregard for law and order exercised by some members of the community the past few days. As a lifelong advocate of integration, I am deeply troubled, for I see in the streets of the city the acceleration of the "boomerang effect" that responsible civil rights leaders have so assiduously tried to avoid. But, as a social scientist, I am not at all surprised by what is happening. There have been changes, but in too many instances they have been token measures, which have done little to alleviate the basic malaise.

For years there have been warnings of the consequences of continued denial and exclusion, of the real possibility of violent upheaval, of dislocation and civil strife. And now the predictions are the frightening facts of daily life.

No one wins in these skirmishes. The police may succeed in maintaining or restoring order, but only at the expense of greater alienation and repeated charges of brutality (many real, many fabricated). The white community may say that this merely proves that Negroes are unfit for entry into their *sanctum sanctorum,* but they do so only by failing to recognize that the hatred and deprivation which pervade the ghettos is not mainly the Blacks' problem but their own. The rioters may thrill at the power they wield as they run amok through the streets striking their blows for freedom as they give "whitey" his comeuppance, but even the satisfaction gained is short-lived and, too frequently, off target.[1]

The quoted paragraphs, only slightly emended, are excerpted from a letter to the editor published by the author in the *New York Times* fifty years ago—on July 27,

1964, to be precise. They referred to what had just occurred in my hometown of Rochester, New York, in the area but a block from where my mother was raised and where her mother still lived. Many who lived through the events of the 1960s or read the numerous reports by the National Advisory Commission on Civil Disorders (also known as the Kerner Commission)[2] and others who studied similar events and their causes, then saw the same things happen again and again, had a sinking sense of déjà vu. We had been there before.

Political activists of the period when Rochester, Newark, Harlem, Detroit, Watts, and downtown sections of many other cities were burning—and the first edition of this book was published—used to sing an antiwar song in which each stanza ended with the refrain, "When will they ever learn? When will they ever learn?" Some are still asking the same question.

While, as noted in the preface to this book, there has been considerable progress in the legal position of minorities in this country, there is still a long, long way to go to realize Martin Luther King Jr.'s dream of true freedom and justice for all.

Few matters of contemporary life are more in need of continuous investigation and assessment than the tensions and cleavages that still exist between racial and ethnic groupings in this country and in many others. One need look no further than the pages of a daily newspaper or a television screen to see evidence of this fact. The conflicts reported from distant places describe national rivalries, regional disputes, tribal warfare, sectarian hatreds, and campaigns of "ethnic cleansing." Political sociologist and US senator Daniel Patrick Moynihan once described this as a kind of "global pandemonium";[3] the sociologist Robin M. Williams Jr. referred to them as "the wars within."[4]

It is especially noteworthy in countries long under the yoke of the Soviet Union, where the fall of communism often proved less an occasion for true democratic reform and more a time of return to bitter group-based politics and overt discrimination. At the time, Isaiah Berlin wisely noted, "Nationalism is not resurgent. It never died. Neither did racism. They are the most powerful movements in the world today."[5]

These movements are still evident on every continent and subcontinent. Many are based on demands for self-rule from long-suppressed groups and marked by resistance of those in power to relinquish it. Most recently such strains against autocratic rule by those seeking autonomy have been notable not only in the former "Soviet bloc," the lands of Eastern and Central Europe, but throughout the Middle East (one thinks of the independence movement of Kurds in Turkey and Iraq, the continuing struggles for dominance between Shiite and Sunni Muslims in Iraq and Syria), Africa (where the recent conflict in the Darfur region of the Sudan and the civil war in South Sudan are only the most publicized of many), Central and South America (where native peoples struggle for recognition), and various parts of South, East, and Southeast Asia (as between Buddhists and Hindus in Sri Lanka, and ethnic Chinese and Malays in Malaysia). They are even to be found in Australia and New Zealand, where indigenous peoples, Aborigines and Maori, respectively, are increasingly active in asserting their rights.

And in Canada and here in the United States, surely two of the most multiethnic nations in the world, the persistence of both "nationalism" and racism are clearly evident. In Canada, a society that, like Australia, has institutionalized the idea of "multiculturalism" as national policy and has often been characterized as a mosaic of distinct and separate peoples,[6] the strain best known is the continuing struggle by some in the French community determined to make the Province of Quebec a separate country, but it is also evident in mounting resistance to nonwhite migrants across the entire country, from the Maritimes to British Columbia.

Although conflicts between those of different color, group membership, religious affiliation, gender, and political orientation are global phenomena—a topic that we will return to in the final chapter—this book is mainly about *the house we live in.* In looking at ourselves, the intention is to provide a framework with which to examine the character of a society built almost entirely by outsiders, voluntary migrants and those forced to come; a society in which diversity—whether celebrated or not—was endemic from the first confrontations native tribes had with one another and then with those who came from abroad.

From long before it became an independent nation, what we call America has been a multiethnic society and one that seems always to have been struggling to define itself in terms of this basic fact of social life. Throughout US history political leaders and policy advisers have tacked back and forth between an isolationist stance and a more welcoming and tolerant one.

The former position is often expressed by the use of the word "American" as synonymous with the descendants of those who came on the *Mayflower* or the "Founding Fathers," folks who deemed themselves the progenitors and guardians of the core culture as well as the turf itself. Their greatest fear seems to be con-tamination by alien ideas brought in by those of different backgrounds. Its most recent expression is to be found in the writings of the political scientist Samuel P. Huntington, whose latest book poses the question "Who are we?" then answers it by claiming the "we" to be white, Anglo-Protestants of English background—like himself![7]

The latter, a far less monocultural position, is reflected in three things: an ideo-logical commitment to the spirit of asylum and openness ("a home for all God's children"), a belief that there is "strength in diversity," and a far more pragmatic attitude relating to the opportunities afforded by welcoming those eager to come to the land of milk and honey thought to exist behind our "Golden Door." What-ever the motivation of those who came (and continue to come), the results have been significant, not only for non-"Anglo-Saxon" European immigrants and their descendants, but also for others, most notably the growing number of Latino and Asian newcomers whose ranks have swelled in the past five decades through the liberalization of restrictive immigration policies.

It is important to pause to take note of the fact that those concerned with inter-group tensions often tend to overlook successes in the move toward true integration. There have been many, and not just for immigrants. America's oldest minorities, native peoples and the descendants of African slaves, have made considerable gains in the struggle for full participation, particularly through the results of the civil rights movements that removed many legal barriers. But, even in acknowledging the accomplishments that have been made (often, it must be noted, because of the vigorous protests of those who demanded access to the opportunity structures enjoyed by those in the dominant groups), serious problems remain. As sociologists Douglas Massey and Nancy A. Denton clearly indicate in their detailed analyses of race relations in the United States, many fail to acknowledge what ought to be obvious to even casual observers, the persistence of segregation in many areas of American life.[8] Despite a number of dramatic improvements on a variety of fronts, our society remains a divided nation in which separation and inequality persist in too many sectors of the polity and the society.[9]

Although examples of the overt manifestations of intolerance in this country, as in so many others, are readily observed, the forces that create, maintain, perpetuate, or alleviate intergroup tensions are highly complex.

To understand such challenges, it is helpful to have a sense of the historical context in which group relations are shaped and to be able to define, discuss, and debate the meaning of such ideas as democracy, meritocracy, and the civic culture; such concepts as prejudice, discrimination, institutional racism, and group rights; such processes as assimilation, amalgamation, and accommodation; and such slogans and expressions as "Freedom Now," "Black Power," and "Why can't they be like us?" within a framework of sociological inquiry.

Why Sociological Inquiry?

Sociologists are primarily investigators of group life and intergroup interaction; they are social scientists concerned with the study of social relationships and varied patterns of social behavior. Sociologists share with other scientists the fundamental view that only through the orderly accumulation of empirical evidence and rigorous analysis can the realities of the physical and social world be revealed. The commitment is to the investigation, description, and analysis of what is, to social realities, not to what ought to be. Yet, in seeking to uncover the complexities of social life, for many there is the ever-present conviction that we may benefit from greater knowledge of the human condition. As Auguste Comte, the founder of sociology, put it, *Savoir pour prévoir et prévoir pour pouvoir.* From knowledge comes foresight, from foresight, power, the ability to influence others.[10]

Many sociologists have long striven to engage in value-free social science. Increasingly, however, more and more recognize the difficulties of maintaining strict neutrality in the face of behavior felt to be detrimental to the functioning of society or injurious to its members. In examining such phenomena as crime and delinquency, political upheaval, family disorganization, or racial and ethnic relations, they often walk a tightrope. They recognize that it is a difficult but necessary task to maintain the principle of scientific rigor.

They know it is difficult because they want to study such aspects of social life precisely because they are considered problems. But even for those—perhaps, especially for those—particularly sensitive to injustice, it is necessary to try to maintain objectivity in the collection of data and its assessment because, as Robert M. MacIver once observed, "A moral judgment—no matter how much we may agree with it, cannot be a substitute for the proper study of causes."[11] (Put differently, we must avoid the tendency to think, "My mind is made up; don't confuse me with the facts!")

Coming to Terms

Because it is necessary to have a common vocabulary to address such matters, it is essential to begin with the definition and explication of several key sociological concepts. We start with *differentiation*.

> Boys will be boys....
> Some people are born to lead, others to follow.
> The "white man's burden" is a heavy one.
> A woman's place is in the home.

In all societies individuals are differentiated by biologically and socially defined criteria. Everywhere people are ranked in hierarchical fashion, as superior or inferior, according to those attributes that are considered important. Even in the simplest, most isolated societies, where subsistence is apt to be the primary concern, distinctions are made on the basis of age, gender, and kinship ties. More advanced societies, in addition to those methods of ranking, are usually divided into distinct social strata. Those higher on the scale have access to greater opportunities for wealth, prestige, and social control.

The discrepancies between those in superior and subordinate positions are generally quite evident. There is an obvious disparity in the lifestyles and material possessions of landlords and peasants, bosses and workers. No less significant is the differential access to political and economic power for those on top and those below. Such distinctions often account for intense feelings of intraclass identification and interclass rivalry. The rich and powerful seek to maintain their positions; those below try to raise themselves in the status hierarchy or, in some instances, to turn the entire system upside down.

Opportunities for improving one's position largely depend upon the socially defined nature of social stratification. Where a rigid caste system exists, there is little hope for individual advancement for status is fixed by birth and marriage is endogamous (within the caste group).

In societies with feudal social structures, placement is determined largely by heredity. The estate system, as it is also called, sometimes does provide limited channels for mobility and individuals are sometimes able to change their estate by royal decree, by marrying someone of higher status, by entering the clergy or military service, or by becoming artisans or tradesmen. Such a system has been most prevalent in agricultural societies, where status is directly related to the ownership and use of land.

In societies with communist governments, heredity is largely replaced by party position as a basis for status. One thinks of the post–World War II changes in China, beginning with the civil war, the ousting of the "nationalist party" (the Kuomintang), the development of the system of state socialism, and the subsequent "Cultural Revolution," all ostensibly designed to rid the society of its feudal character.

In industrial societies, where land tenure is relatively unimportant, wealth and income become the relevant measures of social position. In some such societies an "open class system" is said to prevail. Ideally, every individual should be able to gain recognition based on personal ability and performance, regardless of birth or previous condition of inequality. Although greater opportunities do exist for movement up and down the ladder of social mobility within the open class system, there is no society where individual merit is the sole criterion for determining status.

In the United States several already noted factors have long served to inhibit full realization of the traditional ideal of equal opportunity; not the least of these is membership in a particular group or cohort. Foreign-born persons, females, members of certain religious groups, individuals with suspect political affiliations, and, especially, those with dark skin have long been handicapped in their attempts to advance strictly on the basis of personal ability. Many members of such groups have been categorically denied the right to fulfill their own potentialities in the "pursuit of happiness."

What the Swiss sociologist Kurt Mayer said about this society sixty years ago still pertains: "If the absence of estate-like characteristics makes the American class system unique, it is likewise true that the intrusion of racial caste-like features is almost without parallel in modern Western experience."[12]

Mayer's statement is well understood when put into historic context, something that the political scientist Lawrence H. Fuchs did quite succinctly:

> The myths that account for the origins of nations are usually tribal—based on genealogy or blood—as when God told Abraham to create a new nation, or when a favorite descendant of the Sun Goddess created the Japanese islands and became the first emperor, ancestor of all subsequent emperors. Such myths, which revolve around the dominant role of a favored or chosen people, have often provided a rationalization for the exploitation and oppression of subordinate groups in multiethnic societies. The founding myth of the American republic was not tribal but ideological, and became the basis of a sense of shared identity among peoples of diverse national backgrounds. But if the American founding myth was not tribal, it was implicitly racial. The new nation's spokesmen, when they explained that the United States was created by God as an asylum for liberty, opportunity and award for achievement, understood the myth as an ideal meant, especially, perhaps exclusively, for white men.[13]

It would be obvious, even to a Martian visiting the United States for the first time, that a critical aspect of placement in the status hierarchy of American society is keyed to color—and to gender as well. The Martian sociologist, perhaps struck by the fact that the principal leader was a dark-skinned man, still would note that most of the leadership positions and much of the power is held by white males, and wealthy ones at that. In fact, if the visitor looked at recent history he or she would note some very positive moves toward greater inclusion of many previously marginalized groups. This would include various minorities, women, gays, and lesbians.

But another revelation—the increasing gap between rich and poor—would loom very large in the assessment. As *New York Times* columnist Chrystia Freeland wrote in March 2013, a recent study by five economists found a great paradox: "political inclusion of groups that were once beyond the pale is steadily increasing. But at the same time, the economic divide between the top and the bottom is becoming both wider and deeper."[14] And it should be noted that in this country while most poor people are white, it is still the fact that most blacks are poor.

Race and Culture

The words "culture" and "race" are widely misused and often misunderstood. Culture refers to the way people live; the rules they set for themselves; the general ideas around which they organize their lives; the things they feel are good or bad, right or wrong, pleasurable or painful. Cultural norms or standards for behavior are learned from those around us—relatives, teachers, friends, and, in recent times, from what is generically called "the media."

We often speak of "Western culture" as the principal source of the American heritage. This characterization, although hardly telling the whole story, is quite accurate because, despite many modifications, our social system is largely a product of European values and attitudes. Ideas from across the North Atlantic were replanted in the New World, providing a sort of seed corn for many of the assumptions that shaped the social contexts in which we are now living, especially those relating to race and race differences.

From ancient times to the present, people in various parts of the world have made distinctions between one's group and others. In the European minds that shaped much of the thinking and many of the practices in this country, the tendency has long been to divide the human species in terms of "racial" classifications, visually distinct, color-keyed categories, once reduced to five simple if simplistic divisions: "white," "black," "red," "brown," and "yellow." David Hollinger recently has referred to the latter phenomenon as our "ethno-racial pentagon."[15]

Although today it is difficult to find those who belong to any "pure" race, and many would like to discontinue using the word *race* altogether, many pundits, politicians, and ordinary people still find it useful to place humans into separate racial pigeonholes. Political, economic, and psychological considerations almost invariably combine to provide the motivation for doing this.

When it seems that everything else has been grouped and packaged according to appearance or some other means of making distinctions, it is not illogical that many want to categorize people according to gross similarities. Moreover, it ought not be surprising that such external criteria as skin color; head form; facial features (like broad or narrow noses); stature; and color, texture, and distribution of body hair are used as criteria for such taxonomies. Indeed, although the use of the concept of race is one of the most discussed and debated issues, especially today,[16] some anthropologists, even adding the caveat about the rarity of pure groupings, still would be comfortable defining a race as "a statistical aggregate of persons who share a composite of genetically transmissible physical traits."[17] For the layperson, such conclusions make considerable sense. Why, then, all the fuss about making "racial" distinctions?

Surely, even today, using well-known composite images, it is not difficult for observers to pick out an "Asian," "Caucasian," or "Black" person on a crowded street in almost any American city. To do this they simply look at those they observe, mentally "measuring" them against a set of criteria associated with each category. A person with brownish or yellowish skin, straight black hair, almond-shaped eyes, and a nose that seemed to lack a pronounced bridge would most likely be considered Asian. A person with whitish, pinkish, or ruddy skin; blond, brunette, or red and wavy or straight hair; blue or green eyes; and a straight, hooked, or pug nose would fall in the category "White." A person with dark brown skin, kinky or tightly spiraled black hair, brown eyes, a rather broad nose, and thick lips undoubtedly would be considered "Black."

Of course, it is harder to categorize someone who has a straight, high-bridged nose, dark wavy hair, and a dark brown complexion. Yet most Americans, regardless of background, would probably say such an individual "must be black." Why? Because in this society, like many others, racial designations are not merely simple ways of classifying people according to their biological makeup. Instead, "race" is used for locating or placing people according to *culturally defined social positions*.[18] It is, in the words of Richard Delgado and Jean Stefancic, "not something that is objective, inherent, or fixed.... [Races] are categories that society invents, manipulates, or retires when convenient." They continue:

> People with common origins share certain physical traits, of course, such as skin color, physique and hair texture. But these constitute only an extremely small portion of their genetic endowment, are dwarfed by that which we have in common, and have little or nothing to do with distinctly human, higher-order traits, such as personality, intelligence, and moral behavior. That society frequently chooses to ignore these scientific facts, creates races, and endows them with pseudo-permanent characteristics....[19]

The sociologist Rubén G. Rumbaut has suggested that race is merely "a pigment of the imagination."[20] His half-joking comment is quite accurate. But beneath the humor is an important lesson: race, as it is commonly used in our society, is a prime example of how concepts are socially constructed and then defined. Even those such as geneticist Neil Risch, whose recent research notes a strong connection between self-identified race and genetically defined categories, say that "while being genetically differentiable, [members of so-called racial groups] also differ for a large variety of environmental factors—socioeconomic, cultural, behavioral and so on."[21] Without putting it in so many words, Risch joins Rumbaut in implying a distinction between race and racism. The latter concept refers to those who assume that there is a connection between looks and outlooks, between one's genetic makeup and the way one thinks and acts. And, going further, implicit in the idea of racism is the assumption of group-based superiority and inferiority. This is most clearly manifest in the ways those said to belong in a particular pigeonhole are perceived and treated.

As the English sociologist Paul Gilroy has stated, despite "the founding absurdity of 'race' as a principle of power, differentiation, and classification, [it] must now remain persistently, obstinately, in view."[22] As any number of critics of old race theories contend, it may not be real but it is the omnipresent phantom that haunts all aspects of life in the United States. Consider the case of those of "biracial" parentage.

Our history is filled with instances of "race mixing." Most Mexican Americans are descendants of European Spaniards and indigenous "Indians"; Puerto Ricans, like Dominicans, are the offspring of white and black as well as "Indian" ancestors; and many American people called "black" are actually very light skinned. In fact, to find pristine Negroid types is very difficult in this country (as compared with almost any place in sub-Saharan Africa). Even so, until 1960, the United States Census Bureau gave instructions to its enumerators to include the following criteria for designating Negroes: "In addition to persons of Negro and mixed Negro and white descent, this category includes persons of mixed American Indian and Negro descent, unless the Indian ancestry very definitely predominates or unless the individual is regarded as an Indian in the community."[23] Many nonwhite Americans long have been aware of the fact that racial labels mean something special. In the words of the old sardonic reproach,

> If you're white, you're right.
> If you're brown, hang around.
> But if you're black, brother,
> Get back, get back, get back.

If no cultural value were placed upon ancestry—whether "pure" or "mixed"—it would matter very little what one was called or under which rubric one was placed. But in a race-conscious society like the United States, those who are "colored" (as opposed to "white") have generally been put in inferior positions and treated accordingly. In almost every American town there has long been a close connection between the tasks people perform, the place in which they live, and the color of their skin. Menial work has been disproportionately the province of "colored" citizens, the shabbier neighborhoods their principal domain. White people have tended to have a greater percentage of better and more varied jobs and, in many instances, finer homes in better neighborhoods.

The sociological importance of such a correlation lies in the fact that it is culturally, not genetically, determined. There is nothing in their nature that predisposes nonwhites to lives of inferior status—or whites to rule. There is much, however, in the social image of the nature of those so designated, which largely determines their places in the social hierarchy, limits access to opportunities, and predetermines that they will be handicapped in efforts to obtain education and jobs—key factors in climbing the socioeconomic ladder.

Even today, when political correctness dictates watching much more carefully what people say about others, some still harbor old if modified views such as that expressed in the doggerel "If you're white, you're right." The black journalist Rend Smith recently gave a contemporary example of such thinking:

When white people trumpet their ability to see past color, they tend to cite the admiration they hold for black politicians, athletes, actors and musicians, people whose good looks, charm and lack of physical proximity make them easy to feel good about. The rest of the black population can represent a kind of aggregate stranger danger.[24]

Defining Situations

When men define situations as real they are real in their consequences.[25]
—*William I. Thomas*

These words, written very early in the twentieth century, remain among the most quoted in the field of sociology. In jargon-free, straightforward language, the single sentence underscores the principle of the social construction of reality. We have already seen evidence of William I. Thomas's principle about definitions of situations in regard to how individuals and groups are placed and regarded in status hierarchies based on class and "race."

Such placement is often internalized. When given inferior positions in the social order, individuals often reflect in their attitudes and behavior the status imposed upon them.[26] The Japanese writer Shingoro Takaishi, discussing the traditionally subordinate status of Japanese women, illustrates this quite clearly: "The education of our women was neglected, and her intelligence became more and more narrow owing to there being little or no chance for her to see things in the outer world. The next thing, which was bound to happen, was man's contempt and disdain for her narrow-mindedness and stupidity."[27]

In similar fashion, in the United States members of certain designated groups (like women in Japan) considered by many to have lower potentiality than others often have been given low-status, poorly paying jobs, and denied equal opportunities for achievement. Excluded and often embittered, lacking in advantages, and limited in their access to employment and schooling, they may in fact reflect in their behavior and attitudes the stereotypes held by those in dominant positions. This is a classic example of what Robert K. Merton called "a self-fulfilling prophecy."[28]

Migrating Populations

In the following chapters it will be noted that all Americans came from somewhere else, and this includes those we often think of as indigenous, those who call themselves Native Americans. In fact, our entire society has been a creation of migrants. The motivations of migrants, however, have been (and continue to be) as varied as their origins and, as we hone the conceptual tools for analyzing relations between and among America's people, it is important to make some distinctions that are useful not only in demographic analyses but also in understanding political tensions and persisting social issues.

The first distinction that deserves brief consideration is that between those peoples who go to new places voluntarily and those who are forced to do so. In the first instance, incentives for leaving home and moving to other territories include everything from those of nomadic hunters and gatherers who have little choice but to keep moving as they forage for food, to pilgrims searching for nirvana and religious zealots seeking converts, to adventurers and explorers looking for new worlds to conquer, to settlers and those called immigrants, to labor migrants. The political scientist Samuel Huntington makes a distinction between two of the three largest types of voluntary migrants: the settlers and the immigrants.

"Settlers," he suggests, "leave an existing society, usually in a group, in order to create a new community. They are imbued with a sense of collective purpose.... Immigrants, in contrast, do not create a new society."[29] Here Huntington is both correct and quite wrong. Motivations may vary—and there are differences between settlers and immigrants, but, as we shall see in the next three chapters, there is little question that many in the latter category do, indeed, create new societies and, when very different immigrants enter the same foreign territory at roughly the same time, as has happened in several periods of American history, they can dramatically transform what has already existed. This reality is often troublesome to those who wish to preserve what they see as the collective consciousness of those who claim preeminence by having been among the first settlers.[30]

Members of each of these rather disparate groupings have one thing in common: they are attracted by hope of achieving something beneficial for themselves. The force is magnetic. Poor folks who cope with the scourges of poverty and are looking for ways of improving their lives and those of their families would rarely leave home if there were no thought of advantages provided at the end of their journeys.

Although most voluntary migrations are quite benign in the intentions of the migrants, with few thoughts of hurting others, sometimes the motives are more Machiavellian: setting out to "convert the heathens," to conquer new territories, to colonize, or to capture slaves to bring back to the homeland.

Involuntary migrations are quite different. They are carried out by people forced to flee and those who are quite literally carried away. In the first case there are those who represent the obverse of all of the people mentioned above. They are rarely pulled in. Instead they are those who have been expelled or are driven out by those who target them as threats to the society, subversives, enemies of the state. Victims of persecution often seek asylum or refuge in other places. Such dispossessed and often displaced persons are known as refugees rather than immigrants.[31]

The second case of involuntary migration, although not based on centrifugal or "push" factors, is both poignant and pernicious. The classic example is African slavery. It seems almost obscene to call those brought to the New World against their will "migrants" of any sort, yet they were. And like all migrants—voluntary and involuntary—the slaves from Africa brought with them all sorts of cultural baggage, values and beliefs and traditions, the characteristics we now associate with culture and call "ethnic."

Ethnic Groups

"Man [meaning humankind] is separated from man, not only by real or assumed physiological traits, but by differences of group traditions, national or regional or religious, that may or may not be associated with biological distinctions."[32] Groups whose members share a unique social and cultural heritage passed on from one generation to the next are known as ethnic groups. Ethnic groups are frequently identified by distinctive patterns of family life, language, recreation, religion, and other customs that cause them to be differentiated from others.[33] They often live, by choice or because of the requirements of others, in their own enclaves, ghettos, or neighborhoods. Above all else, members of such groups feel a consciousness of kind[34] and an interdependence of fate with those who share their identity.[35] Members of different ethnic groups may look very much alike (think of the Catholics and Protestants in Northern Ireland or the Hindus and Muslims in India) but have very different views of the world and of their roles in it.

In the United States, members of most ethnic groups or their ancestors have come from a common homeland, as in the case of Italian, Irish, and Mexican Americans—and the descendants of the early European settlers. In this sense, it is fair to speak of "Yankees and other ethnics," for those early colonists who settled from Massachusetts Bay to Virginia had all the traits we just defined as ethnic. But it must also be recognized that those in power often try to impose their ways on others, as has frequently happened in our history as a nation.

Whether power holders and rule setters or minorities, when feeling beleaguered by those who share neither their looks nor outlooks, members of ethnic groups tend to assert their special-ness through rhetoric and policies that heavily stress in-group/out-group distinctions.

Not surprisingly, such groups were long referred to as "nationalities." Some ethnic group members, however, like Jews or Gypsies (called *Roma* or *Sinta* in Europe); Basques who live in both Spain and France; Kurds in Iraq, Turkey, and Syria; and many others that are joined by common traditions and experiences that cut across the political boundaries of modern nation-states, are frequently known as "peoples." And some who may come from different countries and even different continents but are treated as a singular entity may begin to see themselves as others see them, as possessing a collective, unifying identity. This has certainly been the case for Americans who came from various parts of Africa and whose ancestors may have belonged to different and rival tribal entities.

In a country made up of many cultural groups like our own, the intensity of ethnic identity or ethnicity is apt to be determined by the attitude of the dominant members of society toward the "strangers" in their midst. This attitude, in turn, often depends on how closely the "newcomer group" approximates the characteristics of those in the cultural mainstream. Acceptance may loosen the bonds of ethnic identity, as in the case of Scottish and German immigrants to America; deep-rooted notions of the biological inferiority of certain groups—and reactions to such assumptions manifest in norms of conduct sometimes referred to as institutional racism—regardless of how closely they seem to reflect dominant group values, may serve as a barrier to acceptance; rejection and subordination may strengthen bonds to those most like themselves,[36] as among Mexican Americans or African Americans today.

Many sociologists have studied the relationship between membership in an ethnic group and social acceptance. They concur that "when the combined cultural and biological traits [of the ethnic group] are highly divergent from those of the host society the subordination of the group will be very great, their subsystem strong, the period of assimilation long, and the processes slow and usually painful."[37] (It should be noted that this widely expressed view is based on the assumption that "assimilation" is the goal of most minority peoples. Of late, many serious questions have been raised about the ideology that underlies what the critics would see as a classic case of liberal dogma.[38])

The Significance of Gender

Racism and sexism: these two terms refer, respectively, to categorical discrimination against members of a particular "racial" category or against women based on assumptions of inferiority, and frequently resound with a kind of connectedness, as Swedish social scientist Gunnar Myrdal noted many years ago.[39] Both practices reflect ideological stances relating to notions of superiority by those in positions of power and influence, generally meaning white people and males.

For centuries people have presented arguments, some already introduced, explaining or justifying the treatment of those of different colors. The same has been true for women, also often relegated to second-class or lower status,[40] as reflected in the writings of many authors of the Western world's literary "classics." It is even more evident in practices that have kept women marginal in male-dominated societies.

Unlike racial groups, whose labels are so often socially defined ("a drop of negro blood"), physiological and physiognomic differences between men and women are quite unambiguous. These differences are biological. And these determine much of gender identity. But there are also assumptions that have more to do with nurture than nature in the "assignment" of roles men and women are expected to play.

In most societies women have long been seen as belonging to "the weaker sex." In many places ruled by colonial powers—or in cultures that are legatees of European conquest and influence, like the United States—women of color are, or have been put, "in double jeopardy."[41] They carry a double burden.[42]

Explaining this phenomenon, Deborah King, writing on the dual and systematic discriminations of racism and sexism, has noted that "black women have long recognized the special circumstances of our lives in the United States: the commonalities we share with all women as well as the bonds that connect us to the men of our race. We have also realized that the interactive oppressions that circumscribe our lives provide a distinctive context for black womanhood. For us, the notion of double jeopardy is not a new one."[43] As Mary Church Terrell, the first president of the National Association of Colored Women, said in 1904, those for whom she spoke were handicapped "not only because they are women, but because they are colored women."[44]

Add the dimension of "class," and one readily notes that many poor nonwhite women suffer a form of "triple jeopardy." One commentator, a black delegate to a convention of the National Organization for Women, also spoke of the relationship in very explicit terms: "Minority women share with all women the experience of sexism as a barrier to their full rights of citizenship ... the institutionalized bias based on race, language, culture and/or ethnic origin in governance of territories or localities has led to the additional oppression and exclusion of minority women and to the conditions of poverty from which they disproportionately suffer."[45]

"The effect of race, class and gender does 'add up'—both over time and in intensity of impact, but," sociologists Margaret Andersen and Patricia Hill Collins caution, "seeing race, class and gender only in additive terms misses the social structural connections between them and the particular ways that different configurations of race, class, and gender affect group experience."[46] These words offer a clue to the fact that there are and have long been strains in the movements to challenge racism and sexism in America, with not a few "women of color" arguing that they have little to gain from joining the feminist cause because racism is, or ought be, the most important priority.[47] Some go further and say that strengthening the position of the males, especially in a society that tries to emasculate them or keep them in childlike dependency, is a principal goal. Evidence of this continuing conundrum is to be found in the latest statistics on the educational successes and failures of African American women and men.

According to a report released by the American Council on Education early in 2005, the number of African American, Hispanic, Asian American, and Native American students enrolled in college doubled in the decade from 1990 to 2000. It would double again in the next decade. But this good news is offset by some other facts. For African Americans the gender gap widened considerably—and it was not females who were found to be falling further and further behind, but males in terms of percentages of high school graduates (43 percent for males as opposed to 56 percent for females) and college enrollment. Twice as many African American women attended college in the period than African American men, and college graduation rates showed the same discrepancy. Many explanations have been offered, with most pointing to such matters as inappropriate role models for young black males, broken homes, and bad school experiences where many are shunted off to special education, reinforcing the view that they are unfit for mainstream opportunities.[48]

It should be quite clear to the reader that race, class, and gender are at once independent and interdependent variables relating to social differentiation and its institutionalization. Like definitions of race and class, sex roles, although partly related to biology, are most often culturally defined. Here, however, issues are made somewhat more complex owing to physiological factors, many of which, whatever their true distinctiveness, play into the hands of those who define status. The expectations of what men and women can and ought to do in different societies are strongly influenced by cultural factors. This point is made abundantly clear by Donna Gabaccia in her book *From the Other Side: Women, Gender and Immigrant Life in the U.S.*[49]

In a middle section, called "Foreign and Female," Gabaccia notes, "Demographically and culturally, women immigrants closely resembled men of their own backgrounds ... [at] work, at home and in their communities, however, their lives diverged from the men's: regardless of their exact origin, women's and men's responsibilities were more often complementary than shared."[50] These roles, which often are found to be significantly out of balance, with women still being subordinated despite the fact that they may be the primary caregivers, stabilizers, and agents of acculturation, are often "ethnically specific." Thus women in some societies may be far more involved in entrepreneurial activities than those in neighboring ones. And both expected and accepted roles are often carried into new situations.

Minorities

In 1932, Donald Young, writing about group relations in the United States, stated, "There is, unfortunately, no word in the English language which can ... be applied to all these groups which are distinguished by biological features, alike national traits, or a combination of both."[51] He proposed *minority*, a term that had been used in a related but different context. Earlier, "minority group" had been applied to subsegments of European societies inhabited by conquered persons or those incorporated by annexation to another national group. Many persons of different ethnic backgrounds who lived under Soviet rule in the former USSR represent such minorities.

Since Young's adoption, sociologists have used the term *minority* to refer to those groups whose members share certain racial or ethnic similarities that are considered to be different from or inferior to the traits of the dominant group and who are thereby "singled out for differential and unequal treatment."[52] In recent years the term has come to be applied in a related but more restricted sense. Since its implementation during the early years of the Nixon presidency, the US government and its various agencies have taken to labeling as minorities only those in specified categories—African Americans, Asian Americans, Hispanic Americans, and Native Americans. (In Canada such groupings are more graphically known as "visible minorities.") In this book, although I will discuss the reasoning behind such arbitrary designations and their implications for "affirmative action" policies, the term will be used in the less limited manner, as Donald Young intended.

Thirty-five years ago, Graham Kinloch suggested that the mere existence of racial and ethnic minority groups raises a number of issues relating to their relationship to those in the dominant society in terms of social organization, patterns and mechanisms of social control, basic cultural values, levels of societal development, and indices of social change.[53] Of course, racial and ethnic groups are not the only ones "singled out for differential and unequal treatment."

Of late, many people have been categorized in similar fashion—women, children, the aged, the poor, the disabled, homosexuals, and various other groups labeled by some as social deviants, sometimes called "behavioral minorities."[54] Although fully cognizant of the problems encountered by those groups and the many similarities relating to their treatment—including the phenomena of being variously stigmatized, criticized, ostracized, and discriminated against in different ways—attention here will still be focused primarily on those originally considered by Donald Young, the members of racial and ethnic bodies.

Statistical underrepresentation does not, in itself, explain why a racial or ethnic group is considered a minority in the sociological sense. It is not even a necessary condition. Until the dramatic changes that recently took place in the Republic of South Africa, the black "minority" far outnumbered the white rulers. Prior to independence in Algeria the community of colonists was very small compared with the native "minority" group. For much of the nineteenth and twentieth centuries a relatively small number of Europeans dominated "minority" peoples in the East Indies (now Indonesia), the islands of the West Indies, most of Africa, and the entire Indian subcontinent. In many towns in the southern states of this country black people constituted the largest ethnic element in the population but remained a sociological minority. Within a few decades those traditionally placed under the rubric of "nonwhite ethnic minorities" in the United States will form a statistical majority of citizens. Yet is seems safe to predict that they may long retain their "minority" status.

Careful observers of the changing scene on the world stage note that neither dominant nor subordinate status is fixed or immutable. Not only is it possible that a majority group in one place may be what some call "a strategic elite" in another (one thinks of Chinese on the mainland and in Malaysia), but a subordinate group in one country may be dominant in another. The position of Jews in Russia compared to those in Israel; French Canadians living in New England versus those in the Province of Quebec; and "ethnic" Chinese in Jamaica, the Philippines, and Vietnam compared to those in Taiwan or Singapore are cases in point.

Still, today, in most Western societies the power-holding group is made up of persons having white skin and professing a belief in Christianity. In the United States the dominant group long consisted largely of white individuals of North European background who belonged to one of the Protestant denominations (people sometimes referred to as WASPs—white, Anglo-Saxon Protestants). Those who bear the title were for most of the seventeenth, eighteenth, nineteenth, and twentieth centuries the determining element in public policy. In language, customs, and moral codes, these descendants of early settlers set many of the standards for American behavior.

A Culture of Inequality

Although the issues that concern us are hardly limited to our shores, there is still good reason for choosing the United States as the focal point for a study of racial and ethnic relations. Few nations can match the heterogeneous quality of American society. No other modern society can claim a history characterized so markedly by the importation of foreign ways and ideologies. All Americans originally came from somewhere else. In this sense ours is literally a nation of immigrants.

The history of this country bears witness to the fact that the absorption and accommodation of many racial and ethnic groups have been an essential element in developing an elastic, ever-expanding culture.[55] Ralph Linton once described the extent of "outside" influence when he wrote, "Our solid American citizen ... reads the news of the day, imprinted in characters invented by the ancient Semites upon a material invented in China by a process invented in Germany ... and as he absorbs the accounts of foreign troubles he will, if he is a good conservative citizen, thank a Hebrew deity in an Indo-European language that he is 100 percent American."[56]

In a recent social history of multicultural America, *A Different Mirror,* Ronald Takaki elaborated on the point, emphasizing the contributions not only of those who came but also of those already here:

> The signs of America's ethnic diversity can be discerned across the continent—Ellis Island, Angel Island, Chinatown, Harlem, South Boston, the Lower East Side, places with Spanish names like Los Angeles and San Antonio or Indian names like Massachusetts and Iowa.
>
> Much of what is familiar in America's cultural landscape actually has non-Yankee ethnic origins. An early Chinese immigrant named Ah Bing developed the Bing cherry. American Indians were cultivating corn, tomatoes, and tobacco long before the arrival of Columbus.... The "Forty-Niners" of the Gold Rush learned mining techniques from the Mexicans; American cowboys acquired herding skills from Mexican *vaqueros* and adopted their range terms—such as lariat from *la reata,* lasso from *lazo,* and stampede from *estampida.* Songs like "God Bless America," "Easter Parade," and "White Christmas" were written by a Russian Jewish immigrant named Israel Baline, more popularly known as Irving Berlin.[57]

The influence of many peoples in creating one nation is an idea that has gained considerable currency in recent years. Even today, that idea is still hard for some to accept.

As already noted, America has not been—nor is it now—immune from group hatred and discrimination. Throughout its history there have been those who have persisted in denying their fellow citizens the right to full participation in American life, who wished to maintain a society where the "right" skin color or religious preference or cultural heritage was considered to be an essential requisite to acceptance on an equal basis.

Gunnar Myrdal, who studied race relations in the 1940s, observed that the United States as a nation possessed a wide gulf between the democratic ideal of brotherhood and the overt manifestations of intergroup conflict.[58] What he called "the American dilemma" remains evident, but the problems that beset minorities in this country are far more complex than the simple discrepancy between the national ethos and individual behavior. As Robert K. Merton suggested, the failure to recognize the intricacies of these problems tends "to simplify the relations between creed and conduct as to be seriously misleading both for social policy and for social science."[59]

Between the prescription set forth in the Preamble to the Constitution and its first ten amendments and people's actual conduct, there exists a wide range of standards for behavior, which vary markedly from group to group, from place to place, and from time to time. The formal and informal policies of a region, state, and local community; the social, economic, religious, and political groups to which one belongs; the attitudes of parents, teachers, and peers; and the demands of particular intergroup and interpersonal situations all greatly influence the way individuals act toward others. Some of these complexities are analyzed in the following chapters.

Notes

1. Peter I. Rose, "Letter to Editor," *New York Times* (July 27, 1964), p. 30.

2. *The Report of the National Advisory Commission on Civil Disorders* (Washington, DC: US Government Printing Office, 1968).

3. See Daniel Patrick Moynihan, *Pandemonium: Ethnicity in International Politics* (New York: Oxford University Press, 1993).

4. See Robin M. Williams Jr., *The Wars Within: Peoples and States in Conflict* (Ithaca, NY: Cornell University Press, 2004).

5. As quoted in Nathan Gardels, "Two Concepts of Nationalism: An Interview with Isaiah Berlin," *New York Review of Books* (November 21, 1991), pp. 19–23.

6. John Porter, *The Vertical Mosaic: An Analysis of Social Class and Power in Canada* (Toronto: University of Toronto Press, 1965).

7. See, for example, Samuel P. Huntington, *Who Are We? The Challenge to America's National Identity* (New York: Simon and Schuster, 2004).

8. See Douglas S. Massey and Nancy A. Denton, *American Apartheid: Segregation and the Making of the Underclass* (Cambridge, MA: Harvard University Press, 1993).

9. Andrew Hacker, *Two Nations: Black and White, Separate, Hostile, Unequal* (New York: Scribner's, 1992).

10. Auguste Comte, *The Positive Philosophy,* Vol. I, pp. 22–21 (1896 edition), as quoted in Lewis Coser, *Masters of Sociological Thought* (New York: Harcourt Brace Jovanovich, Inc., 1971), p. 4.

11. Robert M. MacIver, *Social Causation* (Boston: Ginn, 1942), p. 148.

12. Kurt B. Mayer, *Class and Society,* rev. ed. (New York: Random House, 1955), p. 30.

13. Lawrence H. Fuchs, "The Reactions of Black Americans to Immigration," in Virginia Yans-McLaughlin (ed.), *Immigration Reconsidered* (New York: Oxford University Press, 1991), p. 293.

14. Chrystia Freeland, "Paychecks Tell a Tale of Unfairness," *New York Times* (March 21, 2013).

15. David Hollinger, *Postethnic America: Beyond Multiculturalism* (New York: Basic Books, 1995).

16. See David L. Wheeler, "A Growing Number of Scientists Reject the Concept of Race," *Chronicle of Higher Education* (February 17, 1995), pp. 8–9, 15.

17. See, for example, Douglas G. Haring, "Racial Differences and Human Resemblances," in M. L. Barron (ed.), *American Minorities* (New York: Knopf, 1957), pp. 33–39.

18. For some further views on the use of the term "race" see Ashley Montague, "The Concept of Race," *American Anthropologist,* 64 (October 1962), pp. 919–928; Juan Comas, "Scientific Racism Again?" *Current Anthropology,* 2 (October 1961), pp. 303–340; Manning Nash, "Race and the Ideology of Race," *Current Anthropology,* 3 (June 1962), p. 285; and Marvin Harris, "Race," in the *International Encyclopedia of the Social Sciences* (New York: Macmillan, 1968), Vol. XIII, p. 263.

19. Richard Delgado and Jean Stefancic, *Critical Race Theory: An Introduction* (New York: New York University, 2005), pp. 7–8.

20. Rumbaut has discussed this in many places, most recently in his essay "The Melting and the Pot: Assimilation and Variety in American Life," in Peter Kivisto (ed.), *Incorporating Diversity* (Boulder, CO: Paradigm Publishers, 2005), pp. 154–173.

21. See, for example, the results of recent research by Neil Risch and a team from the Stanford Medical School as reported in the *American Journal of Human Genetics.* See also

Jessica Zhang, "New Study Links Race and DNA Material," *Stanford Daily* (February 4, 2005), pp. 1–2.

22. Paul Gilroy, *Against Race Imaging: Political Culture Beyond the Color Line* (Cambridge, MA: Belknap Press of Harvard University Press, 2000), p. 42.

23. US Census Bureau, 1960 Census of Population, Supplementary Reports, PC (S1)-10, Washington, DC, September 7, 1962, p. 2.

24. Rend Smith, "Diary of a Creep," *New York Times* (January 9, 2013).

25. See William I. Thomas, "The Behavior Pattern and the Situation," Publication of the American Sociological Society (Papers and Procedures), 1927, pp. 1–13.

26. See Robert K. Merton, "The Self-Fulfilling Prophecy," *Antioch Review,* 8 (Summer 1948), pp. 192–210. Merton says, "The public definitions of a situation (prophecies and predictions) become an integral part of the situation and thus affect subsequent developments."

27. The original source of this quotation appears in the Introduction to Kaibara Ekken, *Greater Learning for Women,* and appears in David and Vera Mace, *Marriage East and West* (New York: Doubleday, 1960), p. 78.

28. The effect of this situation on the development of anti-black sentiments is, in part, the basis of Norman Podhoretz's controversial essay, "My Negro Problem—And Ours," *Commentary,* 35 (February 1963), pp. 93–101. Also see "Letters from Readers," *Commentary,* 35 (April 1963), pp. 338–347.

29. Samuel P. Huntington. *Who Are We?,* p. 39.

30. See Peter I. Rose, "The Persistence of (an) Ethnicity," in Kate Delaney and Ruud Janssens (eds.), *Over (T)Here: Essays in Honor of Rob Kroes* (Amsterdam: VU University Press, 2005), pp. 37–48.

31. Peter I. Rose, Introduction to the section "Forced Out," in Peter I. Rose (ed.), *The Dispossessed: An Anatomy of Exile* (Amherst and Boston: University of Massachusetts Press, 2005), pp. 1–5.

32. Robert M. MacIver and Charles H. Page, *Society: An Introductory Analysis* (New York: Rinehart, 1949), p. 386. See also Robin M. Williams Jr., *The Reduction of Intergroup Tensions* (New York: The Social Science Research Council, 1947), p. 42.

33. Max Weber, *Economy and Society,* Guenther Roth and Claus Wittich (eds.) (New York: Bedminster Press, 1968), pp. 387–398. For discussions of Weber's views of ethnicity, see Howard M. Bahr, Bruce A. Chadwick, and Joseph H. Stauss, *American Ethnicity* (Lexington, MA: D.C. Heath, 1979), pp. 4–6. See also Pat Shipman, *The Evolution of Racism: Human Differences and the Uses and Abuses of Science* (New York: Simon and Schuster, 1994).

34. On consciousness of kind, see Andrew M. Greeley, *Why Can't They Be Like Us?* (New York: Dutton, 1971), pp. 120–121.

35. On independence of fate, see Kurt Lewin, *Resolving Social Conflicts* (New York: Harper, 1948), chaps. 10–12.

36. See, for example, J. Milton Yinger, "Social Forces Involved in Group Identification and Withdrawal," *Daedalus,* 90 (Spring 1961), pp. 247–262; and Charles F. Marden and Gladys Meyer, *Minorities in American Society,* 2nd ed. (New York: American Book Company, 1962), p. 26.

37. Lloyd Warner and Leo Srole, *The Social System of American Ethnic Groups* (New Haven, CT: Yale University Press, 1954), p. 286.

38. See L. Paul Metzger, "American Sociology and Black Assimilation: Conflicting Perspectives," *American Journal of Sociology,* 76 (January 1971), pp. 627–647.

39. Gunnar Myrdal, *An American Dilemma* (New York: Harper, 1944), pp. 1073–1078.

40. See Helen Hacker, "Women as a Minority Group," *Social Forces,* 30 (1951), pp. 60–69.

41. Margaret Andersen and Patricia Hill Collins, "Preface" to *Race, Class and Gender: An Anthology,* 2nd ed. (Belmont: Wadsworth Publishing Company, 1995), pp. xi–xii.

42. See Yanick St. Jean and Joe R. Feagin, *Double Burden: Black Women and Everyday Racism* (Armonk, NY: M. E. Sharpe, 1998).

43. Deborah K. King, "Multiple Jeopardy, Multiple Consciousness: The Context of Black Feminist Ideology," in Beverly Guy-Sheftall (ed.), *Words of Fire* (New York: The New Press, 1995), p. 294.

44. Mary Church Terrell, "The Progress of Colored Women," *Voice of the Negro,* 1:7 (July 1904), p. 292.

45. The commentator was Jane Addams. Her remarks are quoted in Vincent Parrillo, *Strangers to These Shores,* 4th ed. (New York: Macmillan, 1994), p. 506.

46. Andersen and Collins, op. cit,, p. xii.

47. See the writings of bell hooks, especially *Ain't I a Woman: Black Women and Feminism* (Boston: South End Press, 1981).

48. A summary of the American Council of Education's report appeared under the heading "Black Men Fall Behind," *USA Today* (February 16, 2005), p. 10A.

49. See Donna Gabaccia, *From the Other Side: Women, Gender, and Immigrant Life in the U.S., 1820–1990* (Bloomington: University of Indiana Press, 1995).

50. Ibid., p. xiii.

51. Donald Young, *American Minority Peoples* (New York: Harper, 1932), p. xiii.

52. Louis Wirth, "The Problems of Minority Groups," in Ralph Linton (ed.), *The Science of Man in the World Crisis* (New York: Columbia University Press, 1945), pp. 3–7. MacIver and Page state, "even when mere recognition of difference is all that marks the relationship between groups—an inevitable situation in complex society—there is a necessary antithesis between the 'they' and the 'we,' between in-group and out-group." See MacIver and Page, op. cit., p. 387.

53. Graham C. Kinloch, *The Sociology of Minority Groups* (Englewood Cliffs, NJ: Prentice Hall, 1979), pp. 11–13.

54. For a more detailed discussion see Kinloch, op. cit., esp. pp. 33–46.

55. See, for example, Oscar Handlin, "Historical Perspectives on the American Ethnic Group," *Daedalus,* 90 (Spring 1961), pp. 220–232. See also Maxine Seller, *To Seek America* (Englewood, NJ: Jerome S. Ozer, 1977), pp. 1–13.

56. Ralph Linton, *The Study of Man* (New York: Appleton-Century-Crofts, 1936), pp. 326–327.

57. Ronald Takaki, *A Different Mirror: A History of Multicultural America* (Boston: Little, Brown and Company, 1993), pp. 15–16.

58. Gunnar Myrdal, *An American Dilemma,* op. cit., especially chapter 1.

59. Robert K. Merton, "Discrimination and the American Creed," in Robert M. MacIver (ed.), *Discrimination and National Welfare* (New York: Harper, 1949), p. 99. See also Ernest Q. Campbell, "Moral Discomfort and Racial Segregation—An Examination of the Myrdal Hypothesis," *Social Forces,* 39 (March 1961), pp. 228–234; Nahum Z. Medalia, "Assumptions on Race Relations: A Conceptual Commentary," *Social Forces,* 40 (March 1962), pp. 223–227. See also Andrew Hacker, *The Two Nations,* op. cit.

Part II

Encounters

Natives, Settlers, and Slaves

Origins

In his famous poem "Song of Myself," Walt Whitman described the United States as a place populated by those "of every hue and caste."[1] Although a rather exaggerated characterization of this country in the nineteenth century, the portrait is much more accurate today. More than any other country, including other "immigrant societies," the United States is home to one of the greatest cross sections of humankind ever assembled under a common flag.

Although a detailed description of the origins of the incredibly heterogeneous American people is not an aim of this volume,[2] a brief review of American racial and ethnic history and highlights of changes that have occurred since the days of the first settlement provide a baseline for understanding the contemporary scene. Here we begin the story by considering three major cohorts: the natives; the North European conquerors, colonists, and settlers; and the African slaves.

The First Americans

It is often said about this country that "everyone came from somewhere else." The statement usually means everybody but the indigenous people. But according to many archaeologists, they, too, should be included in the generalization. The ancestors of those often referred to today as "Native Americans" were once strangers themselves, migrants who crossed over from Asia and began to disperse in a southward and southeastward direction more than 20,000 years ago. For many centuries they were the sole inhabitants of the land taken over and, in time, overrun by Europeans.

It is estimated that in the days before the conquests began 1,500,000 people already occupied the territory now comprising the United States and Canada and that as many as thirty to forty million people were living in the Western Hemisphere.[3] Hundreds of different tribal groups speaking many different tongues inhabited the forests, plains, deserts, and mountain ranges of the Americas. A wide range of culture patterns marked their differing social structures, and their political organizations were as varied as those of modern industrial societies.[4] Many, especially in Meso-America and in what later became known as Latin America, built and participated in complex if autocratic civilizations, with politics and art forms that matched those of ancient Greece. Some of these still existed when Spanish conquerors destroyed them in their quest for treasure and their zeal to convert them to Christianity. In North America there were also highly developed societies, rich in cosmologies, art, architecture, and agricultural practices. Some, like the Mayans, Toltecs, and Aztecs of Mexico were also highly authoritarian. Others, such as those federated in the Iroquois Nation of the Northeast, were far more democratic.

There never was a characteristic or single "Indian" culture of the kind frequently fictionalized by novelists and writers of Hollywood screenplays.

The vast majority of Native Americans did, however, share in common the fact that the conquerors—who often treated them as one people (claimed by many to have been misnamed "Indians" by Christopher Columbus, who thought he was somewhere else)—markedly influenced their customary ways. Many tribes were annihilated by genocidal policies. (Lord Jeffrey Amherst, who helped to settle the Pioneer Valley of western Massachusetts, is reported to have distributed smallpox-laden blankets to the local natives in order, in his words, "to extirpate this execrable race.")

Many who did not suffer such blatant attempts to exterminate them were fated to die a slower death, a death of the spirit and the culture. They were made to suffer the humiliation of being dispossessed from their traditional areas of domain. In fact, from almost the first excursions to the New World, the natives were exploited and mistreated by whites who laid claim to their lands for their kings and countrymen, extorted the riches that lay above and beneath the soil, tried to convert them to Christianity and—through bargain, barter, and brutal force—succeeded in taking over the vast territories that had been their homes for millennia.

In the early days of colonial rule, each group of settlers dealt with the Indians in its own way. Some tried to make treaties, others established trade relationships, and still others fought to maintain their holdings in Indian Territory. In 1754 a general policy was established by the British Crown that took decision and jurisdiction away from local communities and from the various colonial administrations. The tribes were recognized as "independent nations under the protection of the Crown; Indian lands were inalienable except through voluntary surrender to the Crown; any attempt by an individual or group, subject to the Crown, or by a foreign state, to buy or seize lands from Indians, was illegal."[5]

Attempts to implement this new policy met with strong resistance from many settlers. Some writers, reviewing the situation, have suggested that this conflict indirectly contributed to the American Revolution.[6]

As the frontier moved westward and homesteaders hungered for land for cultivation and grazing, the new American government vacillated between attempts at bilateral negotiations with the members of the various Indian nations and outright massacre or removal. What could not be accomplished by treaty—such as the Congressional Indian Removal Act of 1830, which specified that consent of the natives or their leaders was required by those to be moved to new territories—was accomplished by military force. In the first half of the nineteenth century, thousands of Indians from eastern states were transported, often under brutal conditions, to the territories of the West. It is estimated that one-third of the Cherokees, who in 1838 were driven from their homes in North Carolina and Georgia, died en route to Oklahoma. Their route is still referred to as the "Trail of Tears."

Then came the California gold rush, described by Pierre van den Berghe as "the final phase of the territorial expansion of the United States by a process of land encroachment and frontier wars between white settlers and a small number of Indian groups. It took several more decades to beat the last remnants of the indigenous population into total submission and to reduce the last Indian lands to the status of human zoos for the amusement of tourists and the delights of anthropologists."[7] Van den Berghe's bitter reflection suggests that few were any longer interested in the fate of the original Americans, save for their own selfish motives. This is an exaggeration—but only a slight one.

After the Civil War, attempts were made to resolve the "Indian problem" by means of government reservations established for the alleged purpose of assimilating the now subdued and severely depressed Indians. In 1871, Congress ruled that henceforth no tribe would be recognized as an independent power. Treaties were abrogated and the native peoples became wards of the federal government.

Federal agents were to help the tribes adjust to reservation life and to farming. Yet, as should have been foreseen, adjustment proved difficult since both land ownership and agriculture were foreign ideas to a number of native peoples. Moreover, the programs to educate them in efficient land utilization were woefully inadequate. The provisions of the General Allotment Act of 1887 (also known as the Dawes Act) gave every male Indian the right to a tract of land (40 to 160 acres) to be kept in possession and not sold for twenty-five years. Because the property was to be divided equally among his heirs upon the death of the landholder, however, each succeeding generation necessarily would have less and less land to till. This situation provoked the comment, "Indians sometimes live a long time, and when Old Charlie Yellowtail dies at the age of 99, the number of heirs may be something little less than astronomical. Forty acres of land divided among, say 120 heirs, gives each just about enough room to pitch a tepee."[8]

The story of Wounded Knee was but one episode in a series of tragedies that ultimately spelled the complete subjugation and humiliation of proud Indian nations, in this case the Sioux of the Dakotas. Plainsmen and hunters, the Sioux had been steadily pushed onto reservations by government troops. In 1890, rumors of uprisings brought the wrath of the cavalry. Black Elk, an eyewitness, described it as follows:

Men and women and children were heaped and scattered all over the flat at the bottom of the little hill where the soldiers had their wagon-guns, and westward up the dry

gulch all the way to the high-ridge, the dead women and children and babies were
scattered.... It was a good winter day when all this happened. The sun was shining.
But after the soldiers marched away from their dirty work, a heavy snow began to
fall.... There was a big blizzard, and it grew very cold. The snow drifted deep in
the crooked gulch, and it was one long grave of butchered women and children and
babies, who had never done any harm and were only trying to run away.[9]

They couldn't, nor could many others. Reservation life created many problems
of adaptation—and sheer survival—for the captive residents. Moreover, their
removal from the mainstream of life had other consequences. For those in areas
where the competition of truly emancipated native peoples would have constituted
an economic threat (as in the northern plains states, the Pacific Northwest, or the
desert areas of New Mexico and Arizona), reservations provided places for finally
putting to rest any claims on the land. For missionaries and anthropologists they
provided a locus for proselytizing and for research. For many other Americans the
reservations began to be seen as living museums where part of our rich heritage
was to be preserved in perpetuity.

Few non-Indians were aware of the true conditions of life in these places of
perpetual internment, nor did they fathom the extent to which even the idea of
preserving of traditional ways was undermined by paradoxical "assimilationist"
policies that demanded the denigration of traditional ways and the adopting of new
ones with no promise of where those who would undergo such resocialization might
enjoy life in the new American mode. The tragic-farcical character of the whole
charade was made clearly evident as more and more West Coast filmmakers and
East Coast commentators romanticized the life of the Indian. No longer seen solely
as objects of derogation, the "red men" came to be viewed as faithful companions
(as in the case of Tonto, the Lone Ranger's loyal assistant), or as heroic, if still
primitive, people, living reminders of a glorious past. Early in the twentieth century,
the "proud and resourceful" Indians were represented in names of children's camp
units: Senecas, Cayugas, Mohawks, Oneidas, and Onondagas. They also became
favored symbols and mascots of many college teams like the "Dartmouth Indians,"
often represented in crude caricatures of tomahawk waving, big-nosed, war-painted
wild men. (They remain so even in this twenty-first-century time of "politically
correct" expression. The continuation of the tradition is most evident in the realm
of professional sports. One need only think of the Washington "Redskins," Atlanta
"Braves," Kansas City "Chiefs," and Cleveland "Indians.")

It wasn't until June 2, 1924, that the long-demeaned and then (sometimes)
idealized original residents of the nation were even recognized as United States
citizens. Four years later the Institute for Government Research published a report
on "The Problems of Indian Administration," pointing out the dismal failure of
assimilationist policy and setting forth bold recommendations. At last somebody
seemed to be caring.

When John Collier became Commissioner of Indian Affairs in 1933, a new program was instituted to permit indigenous people to retain their traditions without
the overwhelming imposition of "white" ways. The Indian Reorganization Act of

1934 also permitted Indians to sell their land to tribal members, establish tribal councils to manage local affairs, and incorporate into self-governing units. Since then progress has been very uneven. Here and there fallow lands have been irrigated and erosion halted. In some places education has been improved, especially with the long-overdue closing of the assimilationist boarding schools. Birth rates increased dramatically and death rates declined as health and welfare problems began being dealt with more effectively through such government agencies as the Public Health Service, which took over medical services from the Bureau of Indian Affairs in 1955.[10] Yet the same Bureau of Indian Affairs (a branch of the Department of the Interior, which also supervises national parks and wilderness areas) still maintains administrative control over most Native Americans, now numbering well over several million, the largest majority of whom live on reservations, two-thirds of them concentrated in the states of Oklahoma, Arizona, New Mexico, and the Dakotas.

The government's policies continued to vacillate significantly after the Reorganization Act more or less reversed the orientation of the Dawes Act. Although the general thrust has been toward greater self-determination for many, this has been a mixed blessing. For example, in the 1950s, attempts were made to terminate all special arrangements and obligations. If implemented, such plans would have meant the severing of all ties to the federal government and the loss of lands as well. They were never put into effect. However, a more positive approach was institutionalized in the Self-Determination and Educational Assistance Act of 1975, the terms of which gave tribal leaders the rights to allocate federal funds to serve the special needs of their peoples.[11] Even with this new and seemingly enlightened policy, there were difficulties—difficulties in communication between local agents and the bureaucrats in Washington, between younger and older Indian spokespersons, between traditional leaders and more radical ones, often including those involved in pan-Indian activities such as those of AIM, the American Indian Movement.

Over the years many young Indians thought it best to leave the reservations. The first major effort came during World War II, when many served in the armed forces, including a number of Navajo "code talkers" in the Marines who used their native language to baffle the Japanese. (Native Americans continue to have a high percentage of members in the military to this day.)

Some of those who left the reservations over the years were among the best trained and the most success-oriented. They took their skills and talents with them, leaving a vacuum behind. But most of those who left were poor. Like other impoverished peoples, they frequently sought opportunities in urban centers. Yet in spite of the fact that some were integrated into the general community or found employment in specialized trades (for example, the high-steel workers among the Mohawks of New York State), most of those who relinquished their status as wards of the government suffered the plight of other "colored" minorities. Figures are difficult to obtain, but estimates suggest that in the early years of the twenty-first century three-fourths of those who identify themselves as Native Americans are living in cities rather than on reservations. Most urban Indians are concentrated in metropolitan areas on the West Coast, in the Southwest, and in the Midwest. There are, however, as many as 15,000 in New York City, mostly East Coast natives but many from the West—"Hopi from Arizona, Navajo from New Mexico, Creek from Oklahoma, Blackfoot from Montana, and others."[12] Discriminatory practices in all of these places continue to limit severely opportunities for advancement and achievement.

For most of those who remain on the reservations life continues to be harsh. In spite of further improvements that have taken place since World War II, the first Americans—and this includes those long known as Eskimos, the Inuit people, and the Aleuts, native people of Alaska—remain members of a depressed minority situated in the bottom tenth of the economic hierarchy.

The 1970 Census of Population showed that the average Indian had but five years of schooling, that the family income was only $1,500 per year, and that the rate of unemployment was a miserable 45 percent. Some young Native Americans did not wait to see the 1970 census figures. They knew what was happening and many decided to fight. Following, and in many ways attempting to emulate, black militants, representatives of different tribal groups formed "Red Power" organizations as both cultural centers and bases for challenging the system that in their view did little of a positive nature and much that was destructive to Indian peoples.

In some areas the loose confederation of militants gained notoriety and limited success. Perhaps the most dramatic cases were the invasion and occupation of the abandoned island of Alcatraz and its empty prison buildings in 1970, the takeover of the Bureau itself in Washington in 1972, the two-month siege of Wounded Knee in 1973, and the bloody skirmish at the Red Lake Reservation in Minnesota in 1979 in which two Chippewa were killed in a confrontation with federal authorities. Other attempts to dramatize their cause, to bring all native peoples together, or to effect change have been less successful. One of the many reasons for this record is the important fact that Pan-Indianism was a rather new idea. Many Native Americans did not see themselves as brothers and sisters to members of distant (or sometimes even proximate) tribes. They were Navajo or Seminole or Cherokee or Sioux, not "Indians," often having very different notions of what they wanted and where they wanted to go. Still, there was a growing belief that all were owed reparations—of land, money, and respect. And for good reason. The 1980 census showed that the problems of unemployment, poor health, exceedingly high instances of alcoholism, and a birth rate that is double the national average were still major problems—and despite evidence of pockets of improvement, the census of 1990 showed little aggregate change, especially for those who continued to live on government reservations.[13]

Specific gains have been made, however. Over the past three decades a number of suits were filed to regain large tracts of land, especially in New England, in western and midwestern states, and in Alaska. In several celebrated cases in the late 1980s and early 1990s, 150-year-old treaties about fishing rights were recognized. In perhaps the best known one, sixteen recognized tribes in the state of Washington were, on the basis of previous agreements, finally assured the legal right to harvest shellfish from private beaches, state parks, and even in places where commercial oystermen have their beds. Others, by virtue of their special status, have been exempted from certain taxes and zoning regulations allowing them to further expand giant enterprises on their own lands. Two dramatic examples are in Mississippi and Connecticut. In the first case, members of the Choctaw tribe became primary employers with five car parts factories and other businesses. The second is in Ledyard, Connecticut, where casino gambling has made a number of the once-poor Mashantucket Pequot natives exceedingly wealthy. (Native American groups have established over 300 casinos in twenty-six states in addition to Connecticut.) Although these are clearly important economic breakthroughs, in many instances, settlements "out of court" have ended in "buying off" the Native American plaintiffs. Such a practice is an old story, going back to the time of the first encounters with Europeans.[14]

According to the census of 2010, nearly 2,500,000 people claimed tribal membership. In addition, half a million self-identified American Indians or Native Alaskans did not specify a particular tribe. But, of the others, the two tribes with the largest membership were the Cherokee and Navajo, each with more than 265,000 members. The Chippewa, Sioux, and an assortment of cross-border (Canadian or Mexican) groups numbered over 100,000. Information gathered since the 2000 census has shown a rather bifurcated pattern.

Although many of the descendants of America's first peoples are still plagued by poverty, some have gained considerable ground on the economic front. Between 1990 and 2010, the average income of Native Americans increased by 30 percent. Moreover, the number of American Indian– and Native Alaskan–owned firms, which had increased 84 percent between the years 1992 and 1997, continued to rise; the businesses were concentrated in four states, California, Texas, Oklahoma, and Florida, the home to three in ten Native Americans. Of industries classified by the researchers, most involve service of some sort.[15]

Despite these clearly positive signs, Native Americans still have a long way to go to achieve parity with their fellow citizens. In a projection reported early in 2005, economists estimated that the per capita income of America's native population would not reach that of other Americans for at least five decades! More recent predictions make similar claims.

But, perhaps, greater public awareness of the continued struggles of the natives first encountered by European explorers and adventurers in the fifteenth century will serve to accelerate the move toward equality. A major step in that direction occurred in September 2004, when the National Indian Museum, supported by Congress and organized by tribal consultants, historians, and anthropologists, was opened.

This newest part of the Smithsonian Institution welcomed thousands of representatives of tribes from their homes on reservations, in small towns and big cities. They poured into the capital to take part in opening ceremonies and associated festivities. Many proudly wore the symbols of their cultures and their tribes. As important in terms of serving as a stimulant to change was the interest other Americans seemed to take in this extraordinary event. One hopes that the curiosity of the onlookers and the euphoria of the participants widely felt on several fall days in Washington, DC, are auguries of better days for the native peoples of the United States.

Conquerors and Colonists

For many years historians debated the question of who first "discovered" America. Some claimed Vikings, led by Leif Ericson, first set foot on these shores around AD 1000. Most long favored the view that it was Christopher Columbus, the Genoese sea captain whose several voyages to the Americas were financed by King Ferdinand and Queen Isabella of Spain. To some observers the whole matter is not much more than a game of ethnic one-upmanship. (Rumor has it that one prominent Italian American jurist once sought to raise money to hire his own historian to discredit "Norsephiles" at Yale University who claimed to have discovered an old Viking chart of the eastern coast, the "Vinland Map.") The debate is also purely academic, for, whichever Europeans—or Africans, for some contend that transatlantic voyages brought people from Africa to North America long before they were forced to come—first set foot in America, they were clearly not the original "discoverers." Yet it must be said that the shaping of what is today known as "American culture" began with the landings of Columbus. The contact he and other explorers had with the native population was crucial to the shaping of the destiny of the entire Western Hemisphere.

In an article published in the *American Journal of Sociology* in 1921, Arthur Meier Schlesinger Sr. argued that "the ratio between man and land became changed for the whole civilized world, and there opened up before humanity unsuspected opportunities for development and progress.... The event itself stands forth as one of the tremendous facts of history. So far as the human mind can foresee, nothing of a similar nature can ever happen again."[16]

Recent discussions about Columbus's "discovery," now more correctly called "the encounter," have appropriately begun to focus less on who came and more on what happened, on the nature of the interaction between the newcomers and the natives and the legacy that was left by those who overpowered and overran the "New World," establishing new orders and laying foundations for not one but a chain of nations of immigrants from what would become Canada to Tierra del Fuego, the most southerly part of South America.

Columbus was followed by many more explorers and conquerors, then by colonists and settlers. The latter groups not only established control but also imposed a culture, a way of life.

The first outsiders to lay claim to substantial portions of American soil were the Spanish conquistadores who penetrated the southwestern sector of what was to become part of the United States and established settlements on the Florida peninsula. Unlike the British who were to follow, the Spaniards, many of whom were single men, mingled extensively with the native populations. Their cadres—and their priests—left an indelible impression upon the art and building design (especially that known as "mission style") of the southwestern and Floridian culture. Many of their direct descendants, the Hispanics of mixed Spanish and Indian ancestry, are still to be found in the Southwest, especially in New Mexico. But, most noteworthy of all are those who would later cross into the United States from what was once the Spanish land of Mexico, now constituting one of the largest ethnic groups in the United States.

Had the Catholic Spaniards remained in power, intergroup problems, attitudes toward minority populations, and patterns of discriminations would undoubtedly have assumed characteristics different from those that now exist. But this was not their destiny.

After the defeat of the Spanish Armada in 1588, rival nations began to establish and develop territories in the Western Hemisphere. Under the auspices of the West India Company, the Dutch established trading posts throughout much of the eastern part of the Western Hemisphere—South and North America—on the coast of Brazil, on the islands of Aruba, Bonaire, and Curacao in the Antilles, and at the estuary of the Hudson River (New York was originally called Nieuw Amsterdam) and northward along its banks. Holland's control over these territories was short-lived, but the Dutch legacy lingers on, especially in the folklore and architecture of many parts of New York State and in the names of many famous families—Roosevelt, Van der Heuvel, Rensselaer, and Vliet. The Dutch also left the English with a nickname, "Yankees," an anglicized version of "Jan Kees," the label given in Holland to the sort of person we might call a bumpkin. According to some historians, it was said to be used in mocking reference to the unsophisticated English farmers the wealthy Dutch met in and around Nieuw Amsterdam and in the Hudson Valley. But, in fact, the English would have the last word on this. Although over the next two centuries small groups of Dutch immigrants would make their way to North America, with the exception of a number of words that enriched the vocabulary of English speakers—particularly those interested in seafaring—such as "schooner," "sloop," and "spinnaker," Dutch influence waned considerably by the middle of the seventeenth century.[17]

In 1654, Holland lost her foothold in Brazil and, only a decade later, New Netherlands and Delaware, a Swedish territory that had been surrendered to the Dutch in 1655, became British possessions.

France, too, had colonial ambitions in America and sent explorers and missionaries to stake out new lands. Eastern Canada and the huge Louisiana Territory came under French domination. Bitter warfare brought an end to French rule over Canada; the Louisiana Purchase during the administration of Thomas Jefferson (1803) ended French control over the Mississippi Valley and the Northwest Territories. Yet French nationalism persists in the Canadian province of Quebec, where the majority of citizens are Roman Catholic, speak the French language, retain many French customs, and continue to debate the issue of secession and the establishment of a separate French-speaking nation.

In the United States today, thousands of French Canadians, descendants of poor, Catholic migrants—similar in many ways to the Mexican migrants of today—settled in New England, especially in Maine, Massachusetts, and New Hampshire, and many of their transplanted relatives, variously called Acadians or Cajuns, still live in Louisiana. There the imprint of France is seen in architecture and festivals such as the famed carnival, Mardi Gras. Moreover, the contribution of French intellectuals, including descendants of the Huguenots, is still apparent.

But it was England, "Perfidious Albion," that became the supreme colonial power in North America. And, both symbolically and literally, it was Albion's offspring that gave birth to the new nation.[18] From the early seventeenth century, for the first time large numbers of common folk crossed the Atlantic to settle here. Unlike the earlier explorers from Spain and France, the English came in family groups, often with others from their hometowns. In not a few cases entire communities moved from the British Isles to America.

The British colonists consisted of soldiers and sailors, tradesmen and fortune seekers, civil administrators, political refugees, religious dissenters, rugged individualists, and dedicated communitarians. The English settlers had their own ways of living: their own norms and values, their own culture—and subcultures, too. They shared a history, a language, a legal tradition, and a general sense of what it meant to be British, but they also differed from each other, sometimes in quite profound ways. The pious Puritans who sought "the city on the hill," a new Jerusalem on New England's rocky shores, were not the same as Virginia's far more cosmopolitan cavaliers, nor were they very much like Pennsylvania's Quakers or those who settled in the hills of Appalachia. Despite their differences of class background, religious belief, and political orientation, what they shared gave them unique opportunities, near exclusive power, and a common identity. The combination of their British heritage and growing "Americanness" created the first new North American "ethnic group." Though in recent decades that expression seems to have become almost synonymous with "minority," there is little question but that they qualify for such a sobriquet. Indeed, in the seventeenth and eighteenth centuries and well into the nineteenth, this country might have been described, only half facetiously, as "a nation of Yankees and other ethnics.[19]

The establishment of British America was a struggle from its inception. The death toll—from the hardships endured en route, from diseases that plagued the settlers after arrival, from conflicts with the native population—was exceedingly high. And for those who survived these hazards there were other problems. Religious prejudices were transplanted from the mother country to New England and the mid-Atlantic colonies. Colonists often were set against one another in their desire to maintain their particular brand of Christianity. Fighting the invisible ogres of blasphemy, heresy, and sin, colonists perpetrated persecutions as acts of faith, the victims often being members of minority sects—Quakers, Unitarians, Roman Catholics, and others.[20]

In addition to the former residents of England who constituted the largest portion of settlers, there were the Presbyterians from North Ireland, the Scotch Irish, and German refugees from the ravages of the Thirty Years' War. Small groups of Frenchmen, Welshmen, Irish Catholics, and Jews of Spanish and Portuguese descent, known as Sephardim, were also numbered among the early colonists. Together, they laid the cornerstone of modern American society. Although not all of identical cultural backgrounds, they did share many ideas and practices and in their Declaration of Independence and subsequent struggles to establish a new, independent nation, they became the white, predominantly Anglo-Saxon, and predominantly Protestant majority. (This is clearly evident in Table 2.1, which breaks down the colonial population of the United States in the earliest days of nationhood.) It would be almost two centuries before they would acquire the acronym WASPs, but the image it conjures today was well established by the time of the American Revolution.

Table 2.1 Approximate Colonial Population in 1776

Ethnic Group	New England	%	Middle	%	Southern	%	Total	%
English	461,400	70.5	369,700	40.6	382,400	37.4	1,213,500	46.9
Scots	26,100	4.0	60,700	6.7	71,400	7.0	158,200	6.1
Scots-Irish	18,100	2.8	59,200	6.5	39,200	3.8	116,500	4.5
Irish	9,800	1.5	31,100	3.4	30,500	3.0	71,400	2.8
German	2,400	0.4	138,700	15.2	36,100	3.5	177,200	6.8
Dutch	1,600	0.2	57,700	6.3	2,100	0.2	61,400	2.4
French	5,200	0.8	17,000	1.9	11,100	1.1	33,300	1.3
Swedish	—	—	12,100	1.3	2,500	0.2	14,600	0.6
Unassigned	110,700	16.9	24,900	2.7	6,400	0.6	142,000	5.5
African	14,800	2.3	113,200	12.4	401,100	39.2	529,100	20.5
Indigenous[a]	4,000	0.6	26,000	2.9	40,000	3.9	70,000	2.7
Total	654,100	25.3	910,300	35.2	1,022,800	39.5	2,587,200	100.0

[a]Data for indigenous tribes include only those living east of the Mississippi. Some anthropologists and historians give higher estimates.

Source: Figures result from a compilation and extrapolation of data from the US Census Bureau, *Colonial and Pre-Federal Statistics,* Series Z 1–132 as presented by Vincent Parrillo in *Sociological Forum,* December 1994, p. 530.

Americans from Africa

The first people of African descent to come to America arrived in 1619. Brought originally to Virginia and later to other colonies, they were, like many whites, indentured servants. Servitude was not uncommon in the middle colonies and these black-skinned newcomers did not occupy a unique status. Some gained their freedom after serving their masters for a specified period of time; others became free through conversion to Christianity. Most remained as "unfree" men and women, but even they were not considered to be slaves. In fact, neither Virginia nor any of the other colonies of British America had yet recognized the institution of chattel slavery.

By the 1660s the conditions of the involuntary migrants from Africa began to deteriorate. The expansion of agriculture and the growing demand for a large and cheap labor force brought slavery to American shores. More and more Africans, wrenched from their native villages and sold into bondage by Spaniards and Englishmen, by Muslim and Christian outsiders, and, sometimes, by fellow Africans, were taken to coastal ports to be transported under the most brutal conditions imaginable to the islands of the Caribbean and to the port cities of the East Coast of America. Many died of disease, hunger, and melancholia en route; many—some say the lucky ones—by throwing themselves overboard or by inviting execution by proving too intractable. Once in the New World, the survivors were sold at auction. One such slave, Olaudah Equiano, told his own story in a journal published in the 1770s. There he related how he had been captured and put aboard a slave ship; witnessed and experienced brutal treatment; was taken to Barbados, put on the auction block, and sold.

After a few days we were sold in the usual way, which is this: A signal is given, such as the beating of a drum. Buyers rush into the yard where the slaves are kept. They choose the group they like best. The general noise, and the eagerness of the buyers, increases the fears of the Africans. They regard the buyers as the people who have come to destroy them.

With no feeling at all, people separate relations and friends. Most of them never see each other again. In the ship that brought me over, there were several brothers. In the sale, they were sold to different buyers. They cried when they were parted.[21]

Stories such as Equiano's have become better known in recent years through various popular accountings; repeated showing of a television series based on Alex Haley's *Roots*, a historical novel published in the late 1970s;[22] and a number of much more recent and widely discussed studies of slavery.[23]

By the middle of the eighteenth century the practice of slavery was legalized in every English colony in America. With the emergence of the United States as an independent nation, the issue became the subject of congressional and local debate. The northern states began fairly early to abolish the practice by law, beginning with Pennsylvania where the Assembly, under the prodding of Thomas Paine, passed the first act for the emancipation of Negro slaves on March 1, 1780. Other states followed suit.

In the South, however, the system was maintained intact. The "peculiar institution" had become a mainstay of the economic structure, and what some have called a "slavocracy" characterized a large section of the country dominated by dependence on plantation labor.[24]

There had been a brief period in the second half of the eighteenth century when declining profits in tobacco (the principal cash crop) seemed to portend a change in the social arrangements, but the invention of the cotton gin in 1793 and the rapid development of the British textile industry not only forestalled the anticipated change but made the southern planters even more intransigent.

The conditions under which the slaves lived and worked varied considerably, not only from one region to another (the upper South as compared with the Piedmont or the Mississippi Delta), but also dependent upon the size and character of the plantations themselves. Moreover, even within slave communities there was stratification, a hierarchy of status determined by the masters but affecting relations with everyone, including fellow slaves. Everyday life under slavery was tempered by reactions to harsh circumstances and molded by necessity. This was true of everything from religious practices to relations between family members.[25]

Social activities were narrowly circumscribed. Freedom in all phases of life was highly limited. Yet, as in any local community (even prison camps), a way of life and complex social organization did emerge, which, significantly, included rules of behavior and patterns of adaptation to cope with the oppressive system. Although there were revolts, they were hardly common. It was difficult to attack the system directly. It was simply too dangerous.

For a number of years a debate has been waged over the question of how the slaves actually fared and how they survived. Some argue, for example, that even with the now widely conceded recognition that there was some sort of "slave culture," blacks still internalized the low status in which they were held and came to see themselves as inferior to whites. Others have said they never fully succumbed. That debate continues.[26]

What is undisputed is the fact that by the 1830s slavery was beginning to come under severe attack. Many southerners, in order to justify their continued subjugation of the Africans, invoked the doctrine of racial superiority. Earlier, few had argued that the Negro slaves were biologically inferior and a menace to white society, but they did so now. Moreover, they underscored the idea that, as "property," the slave had no rights that whites were bound to respect. Even the Supreme Court was to support this argument when it upheld the finding of a lower court in the famous *Dred Scott* decision of 1857.

Dred Scott, a slave, having been taken into a territory that prohibited slavery, considered himself a free man under the rules of the Missouri Compromise. The Court claimed that the compromise was unconstitutional since "Congress has no right to enact a law which deprived persons of their property in the territories of the United States." Even so, there was great agitation to rid the nation of the institution of slavery and a powerful movement for abolition emerged in the North led by such white spokesmen as John Brown and such free blacks as Frederick Douglass.

Ultimately the slavery issue was to be resolved in the midst of the bloody Civil War. Although President Lincoln insisted in the beginning that the war had nothing to do with slavery as such (indeed, early in the war Union soldiers returned slaves to their masters under flags of truce), the matter became one of central concern. In terribly oversimplified terms, the South fought to defend its way of life, which depended significantly on the slave system; the North fought to keep the Union whole. In a short time the emancipation of slaves was regarded as necessary, first politically and then morally, to achieve the northern objective.

On January 1, 1863, by Executive Order, the president issued the Emancipation Proclamation. All slaves in the United States (referring to the rebellious Confederacy as well as the rest of the Union) were declared free—though not yet equal. Equality was to come with the Thirteenth Amendment to the Constitution. By the summer of 1863 the Union Army sought "Negro" recruits to fight for their country, and it is estimated that close to 200,000 eventually donned uniforms, half of them to see action on the battlefield.

At the end of the war Black Codes were proposed. These were laws that would give freed blacks legal rights to marry and bear witness in courts of law but would not extend to such things as the ownership of land or work in particular trades. In the end, little came of these seriously limited but, given the times, progressive measures. The codes were never put into effect. Others were.

During the postwar era known as "Reconstruction" African Americans gained equal status in law and, in many places, they did so in fact. But these gains were repeatedly overturned. Congress passed a civil rights bill in 1866, but it was vetoed by Lincoln's successor, President Andrew Johnson. In 1868, a million blacks were enfranchised. Yet the surge toward equal rights in the decade after the war began to fade and radical reconstruction policies, maintained in large part by federal forces, proved to be but a temporary interlude between slavery and segregation.

In a repeat of earlier reverses, although the Sumner Act of 1875 secured equal rights in public transportation, in hotels, and in theaters and other places of amusement, it was to be declared unconstitutional by an eight-to-one decision of the Supreme Court in 1883. Soon what many diehard southerners saw as their redemption, the reinstitution of white power over African Americans, was fully under way.

The era of what we know today as "segregation" had already officially begun with the Hayes-Tilden Compromise of 1876. Hayes, an Ohio Republican, won the presidency in an Electoral College victory over the popularly elected New York Democrat. This event, and the deal that brought it about, was to be a major turning point. Local autonomy was returned to the states of the South, the Freedmen's Bureaus that had been set up to help freed slaves adjust to the new conditions were closed, and federal troops were withdrawn. In their wake many northern businessmen called "carpetbaggers" (a reference to the valises they carried) left, too. With what many southern whites called "redemption" came the chipping away of the newly won rights of blacks.

By the 1890s, "Jim Crow" statutes divided southern society into a two-caste system with whites occupying positions of power and blacks reduced to second-class citizenship. Newly imposed laws prohibited the mixing of the races and barred "colored people" from virtually all white institutions.[27]

The states with the heaviest concentrations of former slaves ignored or circumvented the Fourteenth Amendment (giving citizenship to former slaves and free Negroes) and the Fifteenth (specifying that the right to vote could not be denied because of race). Most people in the North seemed no longer to be interested in rallying to the cause of freedom. Moreover, the system of segregation, which had emerged after 1876, was legally sanctified in the famous *Plessy v. Ferguson* decision of the US Supreme Court, which, in 1896, proclaimed the principle of "separate but equal" to be the law of the land.

At the time of the Plessy case, nine out of ten African Americans lived in the South, 80 percent in rural areas. Although segregation existed in many states outside the old Confederacy, it was there that they suffered the most.

In the last decade of the nineteenth century, many southern blacks moved north, "north to freedom." There they often found themselves in competition with other newcomers, people who were very different from the white folks they knew back home. (Conflicts with those who came to the Eastern Seaboard at the turn of the century will be discussed in a succeeding section, but it should be noted that, with the curtailing of European immigration during and after World War I, many blacks accelerated their northward migration.[28]) Between 1910 and 1920 a half million moved to northern cities where they settled in tenement districts forming black islands in a sea dominated by people more foreign and yet, in some ways, less alien and less alienated than they. And they stayed. The city became their new home and, for far too many, the ghetto became their jail.

Although the opportunity to escape southern conditions led to the ever-growing trek northward, blacks experienced residential, social, and economic discrimination wherever they went. In addition, they faced the competition of European immigrants streaming into the cities of the Eastern Seaboard and some farther inland. In many cases the poor immigrants, once established, would "leapfrog" over the African Americans and begin moving up the ladder of social mobility while leaving the blacks behind. (This pattern would be repeated in the last third of the twentieth century as others, mainly from Asia and Latin America, would move in, up, and over many in the black communities.[29]) Moreover, with World War I veterans returning and with nativist sentiment running at an all-time high, the new migrants frequently found themselves isolated, alone, and under attack whenever they dared to cross the color line. It was during this era that race rioting became a new feature of urban life. Thirty-three major interracial disturbances occurred between 1915 and 1949—eighteen of these between 1915 and 1919. With the exception of the Detroit riot of 1943, the urban "burnings" of the 1960s, and the conflagration that occurred in South Central Los Angeles in the early 1990s, none of the more recent riots have been as fierce as those of the earlier period. The bloodiest of these were in East St. Louis and in Chicago, both cities in the northern state of Illinois.

The competition between whites—WASPs and those who came later—who sought to maintain their superordinate positions and African Americans who were hungry for work, housing, and respect continued. By and large, the blacks made very slow progress. And even this progress—especially stimulated by the emergence of prideful new political and cultural movements in the 1920s (the era of the Harlem Renaissance)—was slowed, then stopped altogether, by the Great Depression of the following decade. And, as might be expected, competition for increasingly scarce jobs served to intensify the prejudices of competitors. By 1940 a two-to-one black-to-white unemployment ratio emerged—and it persists to this very day. Aside from a growing cohort of college-educated African Americans who hold executive, administrative, or managerial jobs in almost the same ratio as whites, for the vast majority of those employed, a significant black/white income gap remains quite noticeable.[30]

During Franklin Roosevelt's "New Deal" some changes began to bring the African Americans closer to full equality before the law. Various groups, within and outside the black community, tried and sometimes succeeded in gaining fairer treatment for America's largest racial minority. World War II accelerated the move.

Northward movement increased again and so too did the trek to the West where the defense industry served as the magnet. President Roosevelt's Executive Order 8802 sought to assure fair employment practices. By 1940 one in four African Americans lived in the North or West and, with the nation on wartime footing, many found employment in factories earning higher wages than they had ever known and at least a million African Americans entered the armed forces. But even during the war they found themselves in segregated units of the army and navy.

The military was not ordered integrated until 1948 (President Truman's Executive Order 9981), three years after the end of World War II. The order was not finally implemented until 1952 when, during the height of the Korean War, President Eisenhower made the changes in traditional policy.

In the early days of the postwar period, African Americans in the North and in the South did gain new status in law, though relatively few advantages in fact. They shared in the economic boom of the era, but although the absolute gains they made were sometimes considerable, the gap between the racial categories "Black" and "White" remained as wide as ever. Many thought that the independence movements in Africa might lead to the final and irrevocable emancipation of black Americans. The African situation did not have that effect, but it served to provide a new reference to people who knew little of their origins or their heritage. Most important of all was the Supreme Court decision handed down a half century ago, on May 17, 1954, which unanimously struck down the constitutionality of the separate but equal doctrine and opened the door to widespread desegregation. Unfortunately, this decision proved difficult to enforce and prompted a variety of legal subterfuges that sought to reverse or at least to forestall a 1955 directive to move toward desegregation "with all deliberate speed."

The apparent failure of the people to honor the Court's decision, coupled with the seemingly unfulfilled promises in which African Americans had rejoiced, accelerated a movement that had been growing from the turn of the century: the movement for civil rights. That movement and the changes that took place during the 1960s and 1970s are the subjects of Chapter Nine. Several points concerning this period should be made here, however, before moving on to the histories of other American minority groups.

First, in the decade between 1954 and 1963 the principal thrust for desegregation and, in many cases, integration came from a coalition of black and white reformers, most of whom tried to persuade their fellow citizens to honor the nation's highest ideals. Many became disillusioned; many lost faith in interracial organizations; many said that cooperation was a mask for white co-optation. Yet most of those who marched and picketed and boycotted and rode the "freedom buses" during those years saw integration as the primary goal.

The integration phase reached its height with the grand march on Washington in August of 1963 when 250,000 black and white Americans joined hands to sing "We Shall Overcome" and Reverend Martin Luther King Jr. spoke of his dream of a society in which people would be known and judged by the content of their character instead of the color of their skin.[31]

Within a year King's dream seemed shattered or, at least, compromised. What happened is a complicated story, better saved for a later chapter. But it is important to note that whatever progress had been made up to that centennial celebration of the Emancipation Proclamation and even in the years immediately following was in many ways much less the result of goodwill than of hard work and political pressure.

By the second half of the 1960s "integration" as a dominating orientation was largely replaced by a new, more strident, and far more racially conscious ideology: Black Power. New and young leaders began to tire of promises of things to come. They felt that the civil rights movement was failing to reach those who needed help most, especially those in the northern ghettos. Although acknowledging certain successes—the Civil Rights Acts of 1964, 1965, and 1968, for example—many of these leaders felt that the victories were, in reality, rather hollow. They had been won at too great a cost and the net result, it was often argued, was that white guilt had been assuaged but too few blacks had really been helped.

Whatever the reality, and doubtless there was more than a kernel of truth in their portrayal, the new leaders shifted the focus and concentrated on the issue of "getting it together," that is, the coalescence of community among black people throughout the nation. In many ways the wildest dreams of Stokely Carmichael and H. Rap Brown and other new-breed leaders were to be realized.[32] At least some of them.

Within a few years African Americans began to walk taller and to express publicly the rage boiling up inside. Within a few years "Black Power" had become a household slogan. Within a few years, universities and other particularly vulnerable institutions conceded that they had been guilty of racism or, at least, had failed to cast a wide enough net. These institutions began actively to recruit black students who, in turn, demanded and often won special programs in Afro-American Studies. But during those same years the average wages of black unskilled laborers fell further behind their white counterparts, the average reading level of African American children fell further behind that of white children, and the average contribution of white supporters of black liberation movements (no small factor) fell dramatically.

The period of the mid and late 1970s was one of both consolidation and hesitation. There was consolidation on the part of certain segments of the black community, particularly those in the growing middle class. However, in making considerable progress, as sociologist William Julius Wilson pointed out, they made even more apparent the widening gap in Black America.[33] The hesitation came from various sources: a government rededicated to moving toward desegregation but beset by contradictory directives emanating from its own various agencies; a wary white community, especially in working-class areas, concerned about the consequences of school busing and forced integration; confused African Americans—and other minorities—uncertain as to whether it was better to continue pressing for "class action," that is, categorical treatment via affirmative action programs, or to work toward more strictly meritocratic principles. The situation was not helped by vacillations in official policy, cutbacks in support for reform programs and urban rehabilitation, or court rulings regarding such celebrated cases as that of Allen Bakke, the white California medical school applicant who claimed he was reportedly denied admittance to a state institution solely on the basis of "reverse discrimination." Bakke's claim was eventually supported by the Supreme Court, which still urged that some affirmative action measures be employed. That decision, to be discussed in detail later, was symbolic of the confusion that existed at the end of the decade. It was variously interpreted as a victory for egalitarians and as a cop-out for others.

Before leaving the subject of the African American experience, at least leaving it to be examined further in subsequent chapters, it is essential to note an important caveat: not all blacks in this country are (or were) involuntary migrants. As Roy S. Bryce-Laporte puts it, although "voluntary immigration has been a principal mode of peopling this hemisphere and has become a prominent aspect of its ideology and self-image—and projection to the world ... as a term and concept, it has rarely been associated with people of African descent."[34] Although doubtless due to the "uniqueness, magnitude, and meaning of the African slave trade and American slavery itself," the experience of black people in this country would be incomplete without consideration of a voluntary movement that has been going on for centuries. There were free blacks at the time of the Revolution and in the War of 1812 and throughout the remainder of the nineteenth century. Beginning early in the twentieth, increasing numbers of West Indians began migrating to the United States, the largest percentage to New York City. By 1930 more than half the West Indians in the country lived in New York and one-fourth of Harlem's population was from the Caribbean. The movement of Caribbean migrants and Latin American migrants with roots in Africa continued well into the postwar years, averaging some 100,000 new entrants per annum.[35] Exemption of those from former British colonies from the restrictions on Western Hemisphere migration specified in the McCarran-Walter Act passed in 1952 and a subsequent cutoff of access of "Commonwealth Immigrants" to Britain in 1962 pulled, then pushed more West Indians to these shores. According to demographer Elizabeth Bogen, the number of Jamaican immigrants in New York City increased almost ninefold between 1960 and 1980, from 11,000 to 93,000. Immigration from Trinidad and Tobago increased sevenfold, from 5,500 to 40,000. An even more dramatic rise in the presence of a Caribbean group occurred in the case of the Dominicans. According to the census, there were 9,000 Dominicans in New York in 1960; by 1980 there were 121,000. Today the latter number has increased fourfold.[36] Many came and more were to come—and become more visible—through the liberalization of restrictions as set forth in the Immigration Reform Act of 1965 (to be discussed in succeeding chapters).

Red, White, and Black

Although much is made of the "discoverers" of America and the Founding Fathers, the tricolored heading symbolically characterizes the actual mixture of peoples who populated what was to become the new nation, a nation in which the white Europeans established total control and cultural domination. It wasn't until the middle of the Civil War that the African slaves gained their freedom and their citizenship; it wasn't until the decade after World War I that Native Americans gained theirs. In the years between the emancipation of the slaves and the mid-1920s, the land of the Indians—and North Europeans and Africans—was to become a haven for millions of others who participated in the Great Atlantic Migration. Their experiences, in many ways, were to be recapitulated by Asian and Latino migrants who came to America in the next large wave of migration, one that began in 1965 and is continuing to this day.

Notes

1. Walt Whitman, "Song of Myself," in James E. Miller (ed.), *Complete Poetry and Selected Prose* (Boston: Houghton Mifflin, 1959), p. 36.

2. There are many general texts that describe the history of and reaction to America's minorities. Among the most useful are Roger Daniels, *Coming to America* (New York: HarperCollins, 1990); Leonard Dinnerstein and David Reamers, *Ethnic Americans* (New

York: Harper and Row, 1975); Lawrence H. Fuchs, *The American Kaleidoscope: Race, Ethnicity and the Civic Culture* (Middletown, CT: Wesleyan University Press, 1990); Oscar Handlin, *The Uprooted* (Boston: Little, Brown, 1951); Marcus Lee Hansen, *The Atlantic Migration 1607–1860* (New York: Harper Torchbook, 1961); Marcus Lee Hansen, *The Immigrant in American History* (Cambridge: Harvard University Press, 1940); John Higham, *Strangers in the Land: Patterns of American Nativism, 1860–1925* (New Brunswick, NJ: Rutgers University Press, 1955); Desmond King, *The Liberty of Strangers: Making the American Nation* (New York: Oxford University Press, 2005); and Ronald Takaki, *A Different Mirror* (Boston: Little, Brown, 1993). See also David Reimers, *Still the Golden Door: The Third World Comes to America* (New York: Columbia University Press, 1985); Richard A. Schermerhorn, *These Our People: Minorities in American Culture* (Boston: D. C. Heath, 1949); and Maxine Seller, *To Seek America* (Englewood, NJ: Jerome Ozer, 1977).

3. John Collier, "The United States Indian," in J. B. Gittler (ed.), *Understanding Minority Groups* (New York: Wiley, 1956), pp. 34–36. See also Frank Lorimer, "Observations on the Trends of Indian Populations in the United States," in Oliver La Farge (ed.), *The Changing Indian* (Norman: University of Oklahoma Press, 1942). Lorimer cites estimates of the number in the Western Hemisphere at the time of the first white settlement as between 8 and 13 million.

4. See, for example, Ruth Benedict, *Patterns of Culture* (Boston: Houghton Mifflin, 1934); Paul Radin, *The Story of the American Indian* (New York: Liveright, 1944); and Peter Farb, *Man's Rise to Civilization* (New York: Dutton, 1968).

5. John Collier, *Indians of the Americas* (New York: Mentor Books, 1947), pp. 116–117.

6. Marden and Meyer, op. cit., pp. 361–362.

7. Pierre van den Berghe, *Race and Racism* (New York: Wiley, 1967), p. 86.

8. Alden Stevens, "Whither the American Indian?" in Milton L. Barron (ed.), *American Minorities* (New York: Knopf, 1958), p. 148.

9. John Neihardt (ed.), *Black Elk Speaks* (Lincoln: University of Nebraska Press, 1961), p. 258.

10. Marden and Meyer, op. cit., pp. 362–371. See also William and Sophie Brophy, *The Indian: America's Unfinished Business* (Norman: University of Oklahoma Press, 1966) and the much more recent assessment, Stephen Cornell, *The Return of the Native: American Indian Political Resurgence* (New York: Oxford University Press, 1988).

11. For fuller discussion see Joseph Hraba, *American Ethnicity* (Itasca, IL: F. E. Peacock, 1979), esp. pp. 229–236.

12. Patrick Huyghe and David Konigsberg, "Bury My Heart at New York City," *New York* (February 19, 1979), p. 54.

13. *Native American Population, 2010* (Washington, DC: US Bureau of the Census, 2010).

14. One of the most interesting assessments of the story of Connecticut Native Americans and the development of big-time gambling and its benefits and pitfalls is to be found in a new novel by Robert H. Steele, *The Curse* (Amherst, MA: Levellers Press, 2012).

15. US Bureau of the Census, Census Brief, "American Indian and Alaska Native–Owned Businesses: 1997" (Washington: US Department of Congress, October 2001), pp. 1–2.

16. Arthur M. Schlesinger Sr., "The Significance of Immigration in American History," *American Journal of Sociology* (July 1921), p. 71.

17. See Rob Kroes, *The Persistence of Ethnicity: Dutch Calvinists in Amsterdam, Montana* (Champaign: University of Illinois Press, 1992).

18. See David Hackett Fischer, *Albion's Seed* (New York: Oxford University Press, 1989). See also S. Dale McLemore, "The Rise of Anglo-American Society," in *Racial and Ethnic Relations in America,* 4th Ed. (Boston: Allyn and Bacon, 1994), pp. 41–64.

19. Peter I. Rose, "The Persistence of (an) Ethnicity: Nativism Revisited," in Kate Delaney and Ruud Janssens (eds.), *Over (T)Here: Transatlantic Essays in Honor of Rob Kroes* (Amsterdam, the Netherlands: VU Press, 2005).

20. See Arnold and Caroline Rose, *America Divided* (New York: Knopf, 1953), pp. 28–31.

21. "The Interesting Narrative of the Life of Olaudah Equiano, or Gustavas Vassa, the African," as cited in Peter I. Rose (ed.), *Many Peoples, One Nation* (New York: Random House, 1973), p. 77.

22. See Alex Haley, *Roots* (New York: Dell, 1979).

23. Among some of the most important recent studies are George M. Fredrickson, *The Arrogance of Race* (Middletown: Wesleyan University Press, 1988); David Brion Davis, *Challenging the Boundaries of Slavery* (Cambridge: Harvard University Press, 2004); and Ira Berlin, *Generations of Captivity: A History of African-American Slaves* (Cambridge, MA: Belknap Press of Harvard University Press, 2004).

24. See Kenneth M. Stampp, *The Peculiar Institution* (New York: Vintage Books, 1956).

25. See, for example, Herbert Gutman, *The Black Family in Slavery and Freedom, 1750–1925* (New York: Random House, 1976).

26. There is considerable controversy over these issues. See Stanley Elkins, *Slavery* (Chicago: University of Chicago Press, 1959); and Ann J. Lane, *The Debate over Slavery: Stanley Elkins and His Critics* (Urbana: University of Illinois Press, 1971). See also Peter I. Rose (ed.), *Slavery and Its Aftermath* (Vol. I of *Americans from Africa*) (New York: Atherton Press, 1970), esp. pp. 103–194.

27. See C. Vann Woodward, *The Strange Career of Jim Crow* (New York: Oxford University Press, 1957), p. 8.

28. See Douglas S. Massey and Nancy A. Denton, *American Apartheid: Segregation and the Making of the Underclass* (Cambridge: Harvard University Press, 1993), esp. chap. 2, "The Construction of the Ghetto," pp. 2–59.

29. See Peter I. Rose, "The Persistence of (an) Ethnicity: Nativism Revisited," in Kate Delaney and Ruud Janssens (eds.), *Over (T)Here: Transatlantic Essays in Honor of Rob Kroes* (Amsterdam, the Netherlands: VU Press, 2005), pp. 37–48.

30. Steven A. Holmes, "Income Gap Persists for Blacks and Whites," *New York Times* (February 23, 1995), p. A21.

31. Martin Luther King Jr., "I Have a Dream," SCLC Newsletter (September 12, 1963).

32. See Peter I. Rose (ed.), *Old Memories, New Moods* (Vol. II of *Americans from Africa*) (New York: Atherton Press, 1970), esp. pp. 237–320.

33. See William J. Wilson, *The Declining Significance of Race* (Chicago: University of Chicago Press, 1978).

34. See Roy S. Bryce-Laporte, "Voluntary Immigration and Continuing Encounters Between Blacks: The Post-Quincentary Challenge," in Peter I. Rose (ed.), *Interminority Affairs in the U.S.: The Challenge of Pluralism. The Annals of the American Academy of Political and Social Science,* 580 (November 1994), pp. 28–41.

35. See Suzanne Model, "Caribbean Immigrants: A Black Success Story?" *International Migration Review,* 25, pp. 248–276.

36. Elizabeth Bogen, *Immigration in New York* (New York: Praeger, 1987), p. 23.

Atlantic Migrations

Unto a Good Land

From its very beginnings the United States was a magnet for the rich and poor of Europe. It was a land that, by the middle of the nineteenth century, had become, in Walt Whitman's immortal words, "Stuff'd with the stuff that is coarse and stuff'd with the stuff that is fine."[1]

Colonial America was made up of distinct and distinctive populations—the natives, settlers, and slaves—all mentioned in the last chapter. But with the establishment of the world's first modern democracy and its appeal to many across the sea, the early national period (from the time of the establishment of the new nation until the Civil War) was to see an unpredicted and surely unprecedented rise in the medley of people who came on ever larger sailing vessels, many designed as transport ships. The vast majority of the newcomers were from northern Europe and the British Isles, especially Ireland. In the second half of the nineteenth century and the first part of the twentieth century millions more were to come as steamships plied the North Atlantic laden with human freight, the majority coming from Southern, Central, and Eastern Europe. Decennial censuses clearly reflected these demographic changes.

The first census to include the "nationalities" of Americans was that of 1820 when all those who had entered the United States along the Eastern Seaboard and the Gulf Coast were listed by country of origin. According to the findings of the early enumerators there were 9,638,000 Americans, 20 percent of whom were "Negroes" and the rest mainly persons of Anglo-Saxon stock. Between 1820 and 2000 over seventy million immigrants had come to the United States, the overwhelming majority from across the Atlantic. (While most Americans still have roots in

Europe, Canada, and various parts of Africa, in recent decades an increasing number have come—or their parents have come—from Mexico and other Latin American countries or from Asia and, as an aggregate, those groups will soon represent a new majority. Their experiences are discussed in the next chapter.)

Despite the poetic ring to the expression of Whitman's "nation of nations" imagery and to the motto "*E pluribus unum*" ("Out of many, one"), historians of the various waves of migration have noted that not all or even most of the immigrants were welcomed with equanimity.[2] The reception was very uneven. Once in this country, newcomers found themselves ranked and treated according to a congeries of criteria that determined their collective as well as individual places in the hierarchy of acceptability and acceptance. Time of arrival, region of origin, cultural attributes, religious preferences, and physical appearance were among the factors that determined how they were greeted and how they were treated.[3]

During the pre–Civil War era over 3,500,000 Europeans arrived in America. Although quite a number came from Scandinavia, the two largest groups of émigrés were from German-speaking areas and from Ireland. Mixed motives prompted different groups of Germans to leave for the New World. For the Irish, migration had one overriding motivation: poverty. Harsh economic, political, and social conditions led many Irish citizens to seek new lives in America. Between 1847 and 1854 approximately 1,200,000 men, women, and children left the "Emerald Isle" for this country. By the end of the Civil War period the Irish constituted 7 percent of the white population.

The Irish

As many writers have pointed out, the Irish Catholics were in the vanguard of the new period of immigration. Forced off the land by the combined forces of British exploitation and repeated crop failures caused by devastating potato blights, they were at once pushed by the disasters that befell their homeland and pulled by the promise of new opportunities for a better life in America—in many ways they were both economic migrants and political refugees. Despite the fact that the majority came from the rural counties of the country, most settled in the growing cities along the Eastern Seaboard. As President Kennedy described them, "in speech and dress they seemed foreign; they were poor and unskilled; and they were arriving in overwhelming numbers. The Irish are perhaps the only people in our history with the distinction of having a political party, the Know-Nothings, formed against them in 1849."[4]

The Know-Nothings, whose main objective was to put an end to Irish immigration, were extremists. Yet, they reflected the thoughts of many Protestants in the cities to which the Irish were coming, especially Puritan Boston. Many Bostonians saw the newcomers as disgruntled paupers and superstitious Papists, dirty, ignorant, heavy drinkers whose real allegiance would always be to the hierarchy of their church and to the pope in Rome. They doubted the Irish had the capacity for functioning in, or contributing to, the democratic state. But even among those most hostile to their presence, some did see them as an exploitable labor force. The

Irish may have been the first group of many for whom the sarcastic expression "We can't live with them and we can't live without them" was all too apt.

In addition to that dubious distinction, they were unique in another respect: a disproportionate number of early Irish Catholic immigrants were unattached females.[5] It was one of the few cases where single women emigrated in large numbers. By contrast, later history is filled with stories of large influxes of male workers who came from China, Russia, Italy, Mexico, and the Caribbean to find jobs either as migrant workers or latter-day settlers hoping to establish themselves in the United States and then bring their families to join them.

From desperately poor homes in a society in which marriage was frequently postponed until the men were well established, many young women set off from Ireland on their own. Domestic service was, for them, a source of protection and employment. It "provided them with a roof over their head and a degree of personal security until they were able to forge a more desirable set of circumstances."[6] Working in the homes of middle- and upper-class Americans had an unanticipated result. It provided the Irish maids with models of "proper decorum," a fact that was to make them valuable agents of acculturation within the growing Irish enclaves.

Of course, women were not the only migrants from Ireland. Millions of men came too. Without the "cap-and-apron" niche the women were ready, willing, and able to fill, the Irish males suffered severe discrimination in the new land and often could find employment only in the lowest-paying and most physically demanding jobs: as ditch diggers, longshoremen, or workers in the canal beds and on the railroads.

It was the Irish "tarriers" working on the railroad that provided the context for the folk ballad that began

> Every mornin' at seven o'clock
> There's twenty tarriers, a drillin' on the rock.
> The boss comes along and says keep still,
> And bear down heavy on the cast iron drill,
> And drill ye tarriers, drill.

Yet, despite their own heritage of exploitation by English heavy-handed landowners back home, and the fact that they were subjected to considerable intolerance based upon certain presumptions about their Catholicism and their alleged "racial" proclivities for drinking and fighting, once in this country few Irish immigrants saw a connection between their plight as a put-upon "under class" and that of American blacks. In fact, many Irish newcomers opposed abolitionist activities and frequently sided with some of the most reactionary forces in the North during the Civil War period.[7] Some argue that the Irish proletariat did so because they feared the potential competition of blacks and Chinese railroad workers, as would other European immigrants in the not-too-distant future. Others claim anti-black sentiment was more a form of displaced aggression, blaming blacks for what they could not blame on white Protestant bosses and landlords.[8]

In time, the Irish adapted to American ways, and other immigrant groups became even more visible targets for the animus of the nativists. Yet in 1891, fifty years after the first large waves came to this country, Henry Cabot Lodge, United States senator and scion of an old Boston family, called the Irish immigrants "undesirable ... hard drinking, idle, quarrelsome and disorderly."[9] But as Martin F. Nolan recently noted, even in Boston, where upper-class old family members or "Brahmins" like the Lodges had held sway for more than a century, the Irish soon began to challenge their authority. Sixty years after Lodge's nasty remarks, John Fitzgerald Kennedy, the grandson of one of the first Irish politicians to gain power in Massachusetts, defeated Lodge's grandson Henry Cabot Lodge Jr. for the US senate. In 1962, with his brother elected president of the United States, Edward Kennedy beat Lodge's great-grandson, George Cabot Lodge, for the same seat.

Although these are particularly dramatic examples, there is little question but that what Nolan called "populist" politics among the Irish served to create dramatic changes on the local as well as the national stage, signaling one of the best examples of the rising power of ethnic-based interest-group politicization.[10] Many Irish entered politics, establishing effective "machines" largely based on ethnic affinity to press their own causes and promote their own candidates. Many more would find their niche in public service, especially in the police forces of New York, which used to be *the* Irish city, and in Boston, which became and for a century remained the political stronghold of the Irish clans so sharply portrayed in the novels of Edwin O'Connor, especially *The Last Hurrah* (1956).

The Irish also were to dominate the hierarchy of the Catholic Church in America. Even today, when Catholic dioceses are undergoing considerable scrutiny from within, the percentage of Irish American compared to Italian American, German American, or Hispanic bishops and archbishops (to say nothing of parish priests) far exceeds their proportion in the Catholic segment of the population. For decades, for many Irish Americans, parish and precinct were frequently one and the same, and priests frequently spoke out on non-ecclesiastical but politically charged subjects. A remnant of this is still seen in attempts to influence fellow Catholics regarding birth control, abortion, attempts to relax rules regarding the role of women in the Church, same-sex marriages, and other matters anathema to Catholics.

A contemporary irony is the fact that a number of the "sending nations" of Europe, the places from which the largest groups of new Americans had emigrated, have become seen as new lands of opportunity for immigrants. Ireland is one of these. In a perverse way, history seems to be repeating itself. As just noted, when the waves of poor migrants from the Emerald Isle came to the United States they often were greeted with hostility and described as undesirable by many Americans; today Ireland is one of the nations with the strongest anti-immigrant sentiments in all of Europe.

The Germans

Many German-speaking people came to America, too. They came from southern German lands and from northern ones. They also came from parts of the Austro-Hungarian Empire. Most immigrated for economic reasons, though some came, in the late 1840s and the late 1930s, seeking refuge. Far more apt to have come in family groups than the Irish, many Germans who migrated before the Civil War quickly moved out from the port cities of the East, dispersing themselves widely across the land and entering myriad occupations. Some, especially the Amish, settled in Pennsylvania. Others became homesteaders in the Midwest and others settled in such cities as Baltimore, Buffalo, St. Louis, Minneapolis, and Milwaukee. In these cities German Americans began various businesses, including such to-be-famous breweries as Anheuser-Busch, the makers of Budweiser, and Schlitz, "The beer that made Milwaukee famous."

Large numbers of Germans—Protestants as well as Catholics—came to this country early in the nineteenth century, in its middle years (especially as political refugees after the failures of reform in 1848), and well into the early twentieth century. In time they would become the largest immigrant cohort in America, followed by those of Irish, English, and African descent. That rank order still held in 2000, when those of Mexican background were about to break the long-established mold. Yet, unlike those of Irish or African—or Mexican—background, few people today think of Americans from German lands as members of a distinct or particularly distinctive group. Why not?

For one thing, the Germans did not arrive in a single wave that lasted but a decade or two like so many others. For another, they shared many of the values and cultural traits of the older American groups and Scandinavians among whom they often settled. Although they retained some of their own cultural baggage, they also shared it (the Sunday picnic, the kindergarten, New Year's parties, and the frankfurter or "hot dog"). Moreover, adaptation seemed relatively easy for them, perhaps because they were themselves a rather heterogeneous cohort. This made stereotyping and pigeonholing far more difficult. The Milwaukee brewers were a far cry from the St. Louis intellectuals such as the illustrious Carl Schurz, historian and newspaper publisher, who became an adviser to presidents (beginning with Lincoln), ambassador to Spain, US senator, and secretary of the interior. And both were quite different from the stalwart and religious farmers known as the "Pennsylvania Dutch" (the term a corruption of the German word *Deutsch*).

During World War I, German Americans did undergo a difficult period when their original "Fatherland" became their new country's enemy. Some suffered from discrimination by fellow Americans encouraged by people in strategic private and public sectors. Even President Woodrow Wilson, who had long advocated the avoidance of involvement in foreign wars, changed his policy early in his second term. He not only urged Congress to declare war on Germany after threats by that country against American interests and shipping, but also soon became a leading advocate to squelch any opposition to his new policies and to strike out against possible subversion by immigrants and those of German extraction.

To avoid identification and ostracism, some Germans anglicized their names: Schmidt became Smith; Eisenhauer, Eisenhower. And, at the same time, other Americans, disdaining anything that sounded German, made some changes of their own as when "sauerkraut" became "liberty cabbage."

A similar attitude did not emerge during the years after Adolf Hitler took power, even when some German Americans, sympathetic to the aims of Nazism, joined pro-Hitler organizations known as Bunds.[11] Only a few German Americans were singled out and incarcerated as threats to security. Unlike their Japanese American counterparts (to be discussed in the following chapter), they never experienced any large-scale roundups from any centers of population, or internment of whole communities of German Americans in special camps.

To be sure, the overwhelming majority of Americans of German origin supported and defended the United States and applauded its victory over the forces of the Third Reich in 1945. (In recent years, although there has been a resurgence of Nazi-like activity, complete with Nazi regalia, paraphernalia, and symbols, including the swastika and iron cross, there is little evidence that German Americans have been particularly prominent in such programs or supportive of them.)

The Tired and Poor

In 1855 the Castle Garden immigration depot was opened in New York. The depot was put to the test in the years following the Civil War (a war in which many immigrants fought side by side with citizens). After the war immigration began to flow more freely; the flow became a stream, and the stream, a torrent. By the middle of the 1880s hundreds of ships were steaming toward the Eastern Seaboard carrying human cargo. They epitomized what historians would refer to as the third significant wave of immigration. The first was that of the colonists and settlers that occurred before the Revolution; the second wave took place during the first half of the nineteenth century. (Note: After a hiatus of four decades, between 1924 and 1965, a fourth wave would bring millions more to the United States, mostly from Asia and Latin America.)

Between 1880 and 1914 about 7,500,000 Southern, Eastern, and Central Europeans—Italians, Hungarians, Bohemians, Slovaks, Czechs, Russians, and Poles—immigrated to the United States. Here they established or joined specific "nationality" communities and helped to create and maintain what some saw as spiritual and cultural homes away from home. Some such enclaves were named by outsiders: "Little Italy" or "Russian Town" or "The Ghetto";[12] others were known by their locales: "The Lower East Side [of Manhattan]," "Hester Street," "Greenwich Village." For many of the immigrants, it was sometimes the case that their new enclaves were not so much places on the map as places in the mind. "Polonia," for example, the name given by Polish immigrants to their "place" in America, was one such borderless land.[13] During the period of what came to be known as "The Great Atlantic Migration," four million Italians, mainly from southern Italy and Sicily, came to this country. The Italians, like many of those from Eastern Europe, came from farming areas but they did not see themselves as farmers in the conventional sense of the term. They were farm laborers called *contadini*. According to various estimates well over 90 percent of the Italian immigrants settled in cities where they engaged in occupations ranging from pick-and-shovel work in the building trades to shoemaking and barbering.[14]

Unlike so many European immigrants who came with their family members or with the intention of settling down in this country, many of the Italian "breadwinners" ventured to America seeking work to earn money to send home and to support themselves and their families when they returned to Italy. Many came and went back, then came again. In the end, many of these so-called "birds of passage" decided to stay and brought their families to this country.

In the overcrowded tenements of already worn-out slums, they bedded down, sought work, dreamed of success—or of home—and rubbed elbows with others who were equally poor, bewildered, and bedraggled. The novelist Pietro DiDonato describes the conditions in a vivid passage from his classic work, *Christ in Concrete* (1939):

> The tenement was a twelve-family house. There were two families on each floor with the flats running in boxcar fashion from front to rear and with one toilet between them. Each flat had its distinctive powerful odor. There was the particular individual bouquet that aroused a repulsion followed by sympathetic human kinship; the great organ of Tenement fuguing forth its rhapsody with pounding identification to each sense.... Missus Donovan, an honest Catholic woman, was old, cataplasmic, and sat for hours in the closet-small hallway toilet breathing in private heavy content, or at the front-room window munching her toothless gums.... The large Farabutti family in one of the upper flats had an oily pleasing aroma—the Maestro carrying with him a mixture of barbershop and strong di Nobili tobacco—and the children savoring of the big potato-fried-egg sandwiches which they chewed while shouting at cat-stick. The Hoopers had a colorless moldy emanation that hung and clung anemically but drily definite. The gaunt woman on the top floor who wore the gaudy old-fashioned dresses and brought men home with her talcumed herself stark flat white and left an insistent trail of old bathrooms littered with cheap perfumes. The top floor right— Lobans'—gave off a pasty freshness as though the bowels were excreting through the pores. Their breaths were revolting, and everyone in the family had snarling lips ready to let go profanities.[15]

Along with the Italians, many other immigrants from southern, central, and eastern Europe arrived and settled. Together they represented some of the most impoverished peoples on the continent of Europe. Most had come as labor migrants to work in the expanding industries of this country, and many, especially those from southern Italy and Sicily, had every intention of going home. They were known as "birds of passage," a reference to their movements back and forth across the Atlantic. (Today in Europe such economic sojourners who move from one country to another initially intending to return home are known as "guest workers.")

During this same period, many others came to American shores with no intention of returning to the lands in which they had felt stifled by social systems that thwarted any thoughts of or opportunities for mobility or where they had been oppressed and persecuted. It was such voluntary émigrés and involuntary exiles about whom Emma Lazarus wrote in her famous poem about the symbolism exuded by the Statue of Liberty (which Lazarus herself called the "Mother of Exile"):

> Give me your tired, your poor,
> Your huddled masses yearning to breathe free,
> The wretched refuse of your teeming shore,

Send these, the homeless, tempest-tost, to me:
I lift my lamp beside the golden door.[16]

The new arrivals, who had often traveled to America in "steerage," in the bow-
els of the ships, were put ashore at nearby Ellis Island, the reception facility that
replaced Castle Garden in 1892 as the principal portal of entry. Very few of these
immigrants were the adventurers, explorers, traders, or conquerors of an earlier
era. Yet they, too, were pioneers. As Max Lerner once put it, "the experience of the
immigrants recapitulated the early American pioneer hardships, in many ways on
harder terms, since the difficulties they encountered were those of a jungle society
rather than a jungle wilderness."[17] Oscar Handlin called them "the uprooted."[18]

Because of their limited resources, few ventured far beyond the ports of debarkation
or the inland cities along the main railroad lines. The members of each immigrant
group tended to gather together and ethnic islands became a natural feature of the urban
topography. Somewhat like the local communities of medieval Jews, these modern
"ghettos" emerged in the older sections of the cities. Within their enclaves many tried
their hand as entrepreneurs, selling dry goods and foodstuffs from pushcarts and tiny
shops. Many more found employment as laborers outside the neighborhoods, working
in heavy industry, in the building trades, or in the expanding garment trades. Jobs
were obtained through labor contractors, old country family and village connections,
employment agencies, or through newly found friends and neighbors.

The tasks the men and women performed were arduous, the hours long, the
conditions frequently intolerable, and the paychecks often inadequate to provide
for growing families. For the first generation there was little time for recreation.
What little leisure they had was spent within the confines of neighborhoods where
attempts often were made to keep Old World traditions alive. Such practices had
both positive and negative consequences. On the one hand they provided a familiarity and some security, lifeboats in a stormy, uncharted sea. On the other, they were
also viewed as overly protective environments, especially for young people eager
to adapt to more "modern" ways and to move out into the bigger world.

It was in the neighborhoods where sex-role differentiation and conflict over it was
most marked. Although many immigrant women worked—some, like the Irish, as
domestics, but many more in mills and factories—their home and community lives
were often circumscribed by traditional attitudes that continued to define males as
the heads of households, principal breadwinners, and decision makers. Exposure
to the wider culture and the necessity of earning money to contribute to family
coffers led to many problems, especially generational ones. Among the greatest
challenges that women faced were those related to socializing, schooling, and career
choice. (Even the thought of women having a vocation aside from homemaking
and, perhaps, doing piecework for garment manufacturers to augment income or
working in a family enterprise such as a restaurant or shop was anathema to many.)
The more patriarchal the environment, the greater the conflicts.[19]

Not all of the conflicts were related to gender. One of the biggest hurdles to
overcome was learning a new language. Yet for many of those who came to America
as poor peasants or farm laborers, opportunities were still greater than what most

had known at home and, overcoming barriers of language and hostility, many took advantage of them.

As individuals improved their economic and social positions, they often moved "uptown," leaving their older neighborhoods to later arrivers. In the metropolitan centers of the North, the pattern, often called "urban succession," was often repeated. The areas of original settlement became the new communities of the latest arrivers: the Irish might be replaced by Germans, then by Jews, Italians, or Slavs, blacks from the South, and Puerto Ricans—and, more recently, Asians and Latinos. A simple exercise in urban ethnography would demonstrate this quite graphically. One can easily note the changes such as, for example, finding old churches that became synagogues and later became churches once again or, of late, mosques.

In the process, the European immigrants and their children began to move from the margins of society toward and, sometimes, into its mainstream. Initially immigrants—and ones who tended to maintain their strongest loyalties to specific places, like southern Italy or Sicily—facing the generalized labels of those in the wider society (as, say, "Italians") often began to see themselves as "ethnics" or hyphenated Americans (such as Italian-Americans) and to identify themselves as part of the white majority. This phenomenon is the subject of a fascinating study by Mathew Frye Jacobson called *Whiteness of a Different Color.*[20]

Jacobson points out that it was often the case that their new reference group—white, Anglo-Saxon, and Protestant (WASP)—was not all that welcoming to Italians and Jews and others who were most involved in the process of being "whitened." Indeed, the fact that they were still often thought of as strangers and dangerous threats to American culture would lead to a resurgence of efforts to restrict their co-nationalists and co-religionists from continuing unrestricted entry into the United States.

The Move Toward Restriction

Many of the children of European immigrants who were born abroad but were to come of age in America found themselves torn between the customs of their parents and the world into which they sought admission. The sociologist Rubén G. Rumbaut aptly labeled these newcomers members not of the "first generation" (that was the proper label for their parents) or the "second" of their American-born siblings, but the "one and a half generation."[21] It was they who were often the most torn between the Old World and the New. They were the ones who experienced the results of the interaction of different sets of rules, roles, and defined relationships—a generation often challenged by conflicting value systems. As they learned the norms of American life and tried to adhere to them, and as their American-born brothers and sisters worked hard to eschew traces of their "immigrant origins" in an effort to be included as full participants in *their* society, they frequently evoked the antagonism, even the wrath, not only of the old Protestant Establishment but of the members of other groups who had already "arrived"—sometimes but a few years before.

It was an old story. Fear of the stranger had greeted their parents; now hostility toward those eager to compete added fuel to the smoldering embers of anti-foreign prejudice. In many places restrictive practices became commonplace, and increasing numbers of jobs, schools, fraternities, restaurants, and social clubs became forbidden territory. The signposts were clear: "No Irish Need Apply." "Restricted Clientele." "No Jews Allowed." "Americans Only." The last expression refers not to all Americans, but to those who fancy themselves as the only *real* Americans, usually those who claim that special status by virtue of the fact that they or their ancestors had gotten here first. Many were legatees of those who opposed the arrival of the Irish in the decades just before the Civil War—triggering the establishment of organizations such as the Know-Nothings—and the movement of the Chinese in the immediate postbellum era. The growing animus of those viewed as "foreigners" began to refocus on those who were part of the Great Atlantic Migration, those later called "white ethnics."

The first restrictive legislation directed against European immigrants was passed in 1891. The language of the Immigration Act seemed indiscriminately to link the mentally incompetent with the indigent. An excerpt clearly illustrates the point:

> All idiots, insane persons, paupers or persons likely to become a public charge, persons suffering from a loathsome or a dangerous contagious disease, persons who have been convicted of a felony or other infamous crime or misdemeanor involving moral turpitude, polygamists, and also any person whose ticket or passage is paid for with the money of another or who is assisted by others to come, unless it is affirmatively and satisfactorily shown on special inquiry that such person does not belong to one of the foregoing excluded classes, or to the class of contract laborers excluded by the act of February twenty-sixth, eighteen hundred and eighty-five, but this section shall not be held to exclude persons living in the United States from sending for a relative or a friend who is not of the excluded classes under such regulations as the Secretary of the Treasury may prescribe....[22]

In 1894 the Immigration Restriction League began. It was to be the strongest force against unrestricted acceptance of immigrants for the next quarter of a century and was largely responsible for congressional action in 1917 that added further limits to earlier legislation by stating that every immigrant had to demonstrate an ability to read. As Joseph Hraba and others have pointed out, such a literacy test was clearly an attempt to cut down the flow of Slavic and Italian immigrants.[23]

Following World War I, mounting isolationism and anti-foreign feelings reached their zenith. The main questions with reference to immigration were starkly posed by the immigrant—and immigration advocate—Mary Antin in her 1914 book *They Who Knock at Our Gates*: "First, A question of principle: Have we any right to regulate immigration? Second, A question of fact: What is the nature of our present immigration? Third: A question of interpretation: Is immigration good for us?"[24]

In 1921 and, again, in 1924 further restrictive legislation was passed, sharply curtailing the immigration of "undesirable" national groups and setting forth rigid quotas favoring North Europeans and all but excluding others. In 1921 the Immigration Quota Act, signed by President Harding, provided that the annual number of aliens permitted to enter the United States from any nation was not to exceed three percent of the total number of foreign-born members of that particular nationality residing in this country in 1910. The Johnson Act of 1924 (sometimes known as the National Origins Act) limited immigration even more severely. The formula provided for the admission of 150,000 persons each year, with national quotas fixed at 2 percent of the total of foreign-born members of any given nationality group residing in the United States in 1890. These enactments served to close the "Golden Door."[25]

The Immigration and Nationality Act of 1952 (also known as the McCarran-Walter Act) recodified the national immigration laws, slightly improved the opportunities for some, such as those from Asian countries, but, in general, reduced the flow and increased the categories of restriction. Reflecting concerns about "communist subversives" at the height of the Cold War, the bill required very careful screening of "security risks."

The following year President Truman, over whose veto the McCarran-Walter Act had been passed, was able to enact the Refugee Relief Act of 1953, admitting slightly more than 200,000 refugees over the quota limits in a three-year period. Most of the newcomers were expellees and escapees from communist-controlled Eastern Europe. Not long after, 32,000 Hungarian refugees were permitted to enter the United States as "parolees." (Parolees were those given temporary visas but who were later able to apply for permanent residence. In succeeding years parolee status was used to give asylum to other refugees, especially Cubans, Soviet Jews, and various people from Southeast Asia after the fall of Saigon in 1975.)

When still a United States senator, John F. Kennedy initiated new legislation that was to significantly alter general immigration policies in the United States. He did not live to see it pass, but in 1965 his successor in the presidency, Lyndon B. Johnson, signed a bill that allowed people to apply for immigration to the United States not on the basis of strict national ratios but on hemispheric quotas. The government said it would now accept up to 170,000 people from Europe and an equal number from Asia up to a maximum of 20,000 individuals from any single country (regardless of how many had come from that place in the past) and as many as 120,000 from this hemisphere without any national limitation. There was one caveat in all instances: preferences were to be given to relatives of citizens, resident aliens, and those with special skills and talents. Moreover, special provisions were included to continue to consider the admission of certain people seeking political refuge in the United States. (A decade later the Indochina Immigration and Resettlement Act of 1975 was passed to further assist "sponsored" refugees. In many ways, the 1975 Act was a forerunner of the Refugee Act of 1980, the most comprehensive piece of refugee legislation in US history. It finally brought US refugee policy in line with the United Nations' protocol addressing the needs of those seeking asylum who had "a well-founded fear of persecution.)[26]

A policy as flexible as this might have saved thousands upon thousands of victims of Nazism in the years before and during World War II, but, for a variety of reasons, few exceptions were then permitted. Until the postwar period, the general sentiment that prompted the restrictive legislation of the 1920s remained reflected in the laws of the land. Certain peoples were favored; certain others were considered undesirable and severely limited in their opportunities to enter the country.

The Jews

Although some 200,000 Jewish, mostly German and Austrian, refugees, including a number of scientists, professionals, artists, and intellectuals, managed to acquire visas to enter the United States, the vast majority of ordinary European Jews in flight from Germany and Nazi-occupied lands in the 1930s and 1940s were barred from entry by restrictive immigration laws. The administration and, in particular, its State Department, was reluctant to change the rules even during that period of racial oppression in the Third Reich. (Here one finds an excellent example of what was referred to in Chapter One as "race" being a socially defined concept. The Nazis defined Jews, an ethnoreligious group, as a race, "an inferior race.")

There is considerable evidence that many attempts to relax the quotas by issuing more visas to allow Jewish refugees were met with firm resistance.[27] To many of those who have studied the era, one indirect result of the policies of the Roosevelt administration of "abandoning the Jews" was that hundreds of thousands of those trapped in Europe and who might have been saved would perish in the Holocaust.

Those few who did make it would join the ranks of what was already a well-established Jewish community whose members had come to America prior to the imposition of the "quota acts" discussed above, some many years before it was even proposed. The largest cohort had come from Eastern Europe after 1880. But these were hardly the first Jews to enter the country.

As early as 1654, twenty-three Jewish refugees from Brazil settled in Nieuw Amsterdam, the Dutch settlement later to be known as New York. By the time of the Revolution almost three thousand Jews—mainly of Spanish and Portuguese descent (called Sephardim)—were living in the Seaboard colonies.

The first Jewish settlers, generally traders and merchants, found little opposition to their presence in most of the cities and towns where they worked and lived. There were scattered instances of discrimination in the areas of Dutch control and some Jews suffered religious persecution in certain English colonies, where they were sometimes forbidden to hold public office or to bear arms. More often, these barriers were absent, ignored, or offset by the fact that many Protestants looked with favor upon the "Israelites" in their midst.

By 1700, freedom of worship was widely recognized and in 1740, when the Jews of British America were granted full citizenship, they achieved a degree of freedom probably unmatched anywhere in the world.

The Sephardim were joined by Ashkenasic Jews (whose origins were in German-speaking lands and Eastern Europe). Throughout the nineteenth century the number of Jews emigrating from Germany rose steadily. It is estimated that the American Jewish population was 15,000 in 1840, 50,000 in 1850, 150,000 in 1860, and 250,000 in 1880. By 1925 it was to exceed three million.

Quite a number of the German Jews left the Seaboard cities soon after their arrival and moved to smaller communities to the south and west. In many instances they went as peddlers and stayed to build many of the large retail emporia now found scattered in towns and cities across the nation. Although the Jews often had to live down the "curse of Shylock"—the images and portraits of Jewish merchants as being dishonest—blatant bigotry was rarely found. Like their more cosmopolitan countrymen from the upper strata of German Jewish society, most had little difficulty in establishing themselves economically, in forming religious congregations, and in adapting themselves to local patterns. It was not until the 1880s, when waves of East European immigrants began moving toward the United States, that anti-Jewish discrimination gained a significant foothold in this country.

At the time Jews in Poland, Russia, Romania, and other East European lands, squeezed between a growing middle class and recently emancipated serfs, found themselves increasingly threatened by forces beyond their control. Their villages became vulnerable to pogroms (anti-Jewish attacks often sanctioned by local authorities) and many decided to leave. For most, America was the place of hope, "the *guldene Medina*" [the golden city].

Many who came in the large wave of European Jewish immigrants were economically impoverished and traditional in their religious beliefs. Most settled in the largest cities, where they could find work (especially in the expanding clothing industry) and where they could continue their religious practices. Like other ethnically distinct groups, they, too, began to develop their own communities.

The conspicuousness of their dress, uniqueness of their customs, strangeness of their everyday language (Yiddish), and religious practices all combined to reinforce the images of Jews as a clannish and mysterious people. Yet, because the Jewish immigrants possessed several cultural traits that enhanced their adjustment and rapid mobility in American society, they belied some assumptions and reinforced others.

Years of relegation to marginal occupational roles, the fact that most were already bilingual (speaking Yiddish as well as Russian or Polish or German) in their home countries (making it somewhat easier to learn yet another language), traditions that placed high value on education and the learned professions, and emphasis on familial responsibility all served to aid many Jews in their struggle to find acceptance and, in time, prosperity in competitive America. But the very fact that a substantial number of Jews began to surpass others in the rapidity of their ascent increased animosity and fanned the embers of anti-Semitism (an old phenomenon distinct from more general anti-foreign attitudes).

Because some Jews were successful financially, they were referred to as "crass capitalists" (combining traditional ideas about "money changers" with more modern images). Because some Jews were deeply engaged in radical politics and labor organizations, others tried to paint them "red." And some, like the members of the Ku Klux Klan and even as notable and powerful a figure as Henry Ford, ignoring the ridiculous contradictions in their allegations, called the Jews *both* "parvenu" and "pinko."

The search for scapegoats during the Great Depression often found the Jews ready targets for the bitter frustrations felt by many Americans. (As mentioned previously, the rise of Nazism evoked some sympathy here as well, and several new "hate" organizations sprang up to defame the Jews.)

Postwar revelations of the horrors practiced by the Nazi regime greatly served to reduce anti-Jewish sentiments. In the two decades following World War II virulent anti-Semitism showed a marked decline, although restricted neighborhoods and social discrimination continued to exist in many of our cities and suburbs. Still, an epidemic of swastika daubing in 1960, temple bombings in 1962, the rise of George Lincoln Rockwell's American Nazi party (later called the American National White Workers' Socialist party) and other neo-Nazi organizations, the emergence of certain reactionary patriotic movements of the radical right in the early 1960s, and the occurrence of "black anti-Semitism" and Third World anti-Zionism on the part of the radical left in the late 1960s indicated the continued existence of anti-Semitic feelings in certain segments of the population. Some thought it a portent of more serious difficulties. Yet, by the late 1960s, it seemed reasonable to say this:

> American Jews, delighted at Israeli victory in the Six-Day War, have evinced much less enthusiasm for their own country's protracted conflict in Southeast Asia and its stalemated war against poverty at home. Other groups in American life share the sense of frustration. In the search for scapegoats that may soon ensue, Jews may find themselves most vulnerable to attack from right, left, and below. By seeking reform and compromise on most issues instead of radical change they may come increasingly to appear too white for the black militants, too red for the white conservatives, and too yellow for their own children.
>
> Jews are not unaware of such possibilities. They know that latent anti-Semitism can be revived in America as it has been in the past. But they do not seem worried. They feel they can ride out the coming storms. Like their forebears who came to settle on the Lower East Side, the majority of Jews still believe in America and in the American people.[28]

The predictions were, in fact, quite accurate. Certain black leaders did begin to separate themselves from too strong identification with Jews. Some Jews, with memories of how "numerus clausus" or quotas had been used to deprive them of admission to universities and limit access to certain professions still fresh in their minds, feared that "targets and goals" set to percentages in the population, regardless of the good intentions of the advocates of equal opportunity, would greatly reduce hard-won opportunities for achievement based on merit. Objecting to this particular aspect of policies to insure entry of African Americans did not mean that Jews who held such views had rejected the abiding objective of the civil rights campaigns. They still remained, in the aggregate, the most liberal of all minorities in support of blacks. They remain so today.

At the same time that African Americans were raising doubts about the steadfastness of Jewish support, others echoed their own concerns about Jewish liberals. And some Jewish children (like many non-Jewish youngsters) did seek to distance themselves—physically and socially—from parents they thought were too bourgeois.

The Yom Kippur War of 1973 exacerbated the situation as increasing numbers of non-Jews blamed Israelis and, indirectly, all Jews, for the oil crisis that occurred in conjunction with it. In the following seven-year period popular support for Israel

among non-Jewish Americans waned considerably as sympathy for the Palestinian refugees and their cause gained favor in various circles, including a number of
church groups once publicly pro-Israel.

By 1980, many Jews and blacks seemed to recognize the need to re-form old
coalitions, many white conservatives began to have second (or third) thoughts
about Israel (seeing it once again as a bastion of democracy and military power
in a turbulent Middle East), and many young Jews were found in the vanguard of
new religious movements, some of which also involved resurging ethnic pride.
Still, tensions continued. Some of these were all too familiar reminders of earlier
periods. Jewish institutions—synagogues, community centers, even graveyards—
once again became targets for anti-Semites; attacks on identifiable Jews, especially
those who were Orthodox and dressed in the traditional manner, increased; and on
many campuses, rallies on behalf of supporters of Palestinians sometimes turned
their anger on Jewish counterdemonstrators. Ironically, the plight of the Palestinians
also led to significant soul searching—and action—within the general American
Jewish community.

For years, the majority of American Jews had given unqualified support to
Israeli policies. Although most applauded the accord with Egypt engineered by
President Jimmy Carter, they remained wary of the intentions of those in other
Arab states and of the Palestinian Liberation Organization, which had vowed to
recapture what was claimed as Arab land. Yet the hard measures used to suppress
the uprising of the Palestinians living within the occupied West Bank and in the
Gaza Strip in the late 1980s raised troubling questions for increasing numbers of
American Jews about both the morality and efficacy of Israeli actions. By the end
of the decade, many broke ranks with those who continued to support the Israeli
hard-liners, favoring a policy that would give genuine autonomy to the Palestinians.
A breakthrough of sorts came in the early years of the presidency of Bill Clinton
when his high office was used to forge the first of several agreements between the
Israeli government of Yitzhak Rabin and the Palestine Liberation Organization, led
by Yassar Arafat. Rabin's involvement in fostering a detente with the Palestinians
led to his assassination in November 1995 by a Jewish fanatic seeking to torpedo
the peace process.

The succeeding two decades were marked with increasingly violent conflict and
repeated failure as moderate Israelis and Palestinians and their allies in the United
States, Britain, and continental Europe all tried to bring about some resolution to
the vexing problems of trying to ensure national integrity and security for both
peoples. That struggle continues. Many hope that it finally will be resolved by a
"two-state solution," but in the wake of Arab uprisings in neighboring countries,
concern about Iranian nuclear capabilities, and sharpening divisions within both the
Palestinian and Israeli communities, an imminent breakthrough seems most unlikely.

The Muslims

Although there has been an American presence of the followers of the Koran for
many decades, native-born Americans of the Muslim faith, as well as immigrants,

have gained considerable attention in recent years. The Israeli-Palestinian conflict in the Middle East was, perhaps, the catalyst for Muslims to become objects of curiosity and concern, especially when ideas of the Palestinian side were well articulated by such prominent spokespersons as Edward Said. But it was not the most significant. Rather, public consciousness of a large Muslim presence in the United States began with the first Iraq War during the administration of President George Herbert Walker Bush in the 1990s and reached a fever pitch in the aftermath of the attacks on the twin trade towers in New York City in 2001. At the time, his son George W. was president.

Americans who were willing to listen would learn that, as there are Jews of varied national backgrounds, occupations, and political persuasions, there also are Muslims who are of different origins, engaged in a wide array of professions, and holding both political and religious beliefs that range from very liberal to very conservative.

Although most, like the majority of Palestinians, Egyptians, Syrians, Iraqis, and Saudis, are Arabs, the followers of Muhammad are found in many parts of the world. They are the dominant group in such non-Arab states as Bosnia, Turkey, Iran, Pakistan, Malaysia, and Indonesia and a prominent minority in India. Followers of the Islamic faith are a major presence in many parts of Africa.

In this country, where some, mostly African Americans, are fairly recent converts to the Temple of Islam, most Muslims are immigrants or the children of immigrants. And yet, despite significant differences, a spirit of shared religious identity that crosses bounds of political ideology, race, and ethnicity unites them. Their unity was long reflected in the words of the Syrian American poet, Kahlil Gibran.

> Light of day and peace of the night ...
> Remember, my brother,
> That the coin which you drop into
> The withered hand stretching toward
> You is the only golden chain that
> Binds your rich heart to the
> Loving heart of God.[29]

Gibran, who was raised in a Maronite Catholic family, was among the first to give voice to people like himself—and his Muslim grandparents. They came from Syria or from the Syrian province of the Ottoman Empire known as Lebanon. Between 1920 and World War II, approximately 100,000 Syrian migrants had come to the United States. Most were Christians, with only a small number (between 5 and 10 percent) being Muslim.[30] Few were Arab nationalists, an attitude far more apt to characterize the large numbers of Muslim Arabs who migrated to the United States more recently. By the mid-1980s the number of all who identified themselves as Muslims had reached four million.[31] (Today this number has increased by 25 percent.[32]) Included are people from the Middle East and North Africa (who comprised over half of those in the cohort) and from Asia (slightly more than a third). Others came from sub-Saharan Africa and Eastern Europe. The overall figure also includes African American converts.

Yvonne Yazbeck Haddad, a specialist in the study of Muslims in America, attributes the enormous growth in the percentages of foreign-born Muslims to changes in American society, changes in immigration laws, and the changing demands of the labor market. They are concentrated in three states: California, New York, and Illinois. Haddad and Adair T. Lummis argue that although most have been integrated economically, and frequently become citizens, they have remained a targeted minority, not least because of the stereotypes many hold of Arabs as well as of Muslims.[33] They attribute these to distorted media images of Islam, the lack of substantial political influence, and a general prejudice against Arabs too often seen as "lustful, greedy bungling polygamists."[34] One result, it is argued, is that Muslims in America have to rely on the goodwill of others for their survival.

Summarizing the writings of several commentators, some time ago Stephanie Van Buren suggested that the color-coded racism that pervades American society helped Muslim Americans transcend differences in national identity, form interdependent bonds through common faith on the one hand and defense against categorical discrimination, in this country and elsewhere, on the other. Following the views of Haddad and Lummis, she notes that "it may [be] only incidental that the majority of Muslims in the world are located in 'Third World' nations that have been victimized by western imperialism, ... [which] may serve to form a common bond, or brotherhood, among yellow and brown people."[35] Van Buren was prescient.

In the wake of the terrorist attacks on New York City and the Pentagon, then in Madrid and London, and with the strife in Afghanistan and the upheaval and polarization that followed the "Arab Spring" in 2011, many American Muslims felt increasingly beleaguered. They were and remain especially fearful that new rules relating to the screening of migrants, surveillance of communal institutions, and general distrust of those who share their faith may portend both a rise in hostility against them and a hardening of ideological battle lines and fundamentalist beliefs within their ranks. The concerns are hardly groundless. Several thousand Muslim migrants have been deported since September 11, 2001, and many others continue to worry that they are under an increasing threat of expulsion in attempts "to protect the homeland."

In the wake of serious setbacks in America's actions in Iraq in the preemptive war launched in 2003, increasing numbers of Muslims began to feel they and those with whom they are identified were becoming the latest victims of many Americans in need of targets for their frustrations over failures to win their own seemingly crusade-like campaigns for the minds and souls of people in such places as Afghanistan and Iraq, an equivalent of the Cold War demons, the "atheistic communists." These anxieties are not without reason. In recent years there has been increasing surveillance of Muslim communities and community centers, especially mosques, in the United States. Civil rights lawyers have decried such dragnet-like activities. When discovered, the defense is usually that these actions are to protect all Americans, Muslim and non-Muslim, from radical elements bent on destroying the country. Such thinking was reinforced in the wake of the bombings by two immigrant brothers at the end of the Boston Marathon in the spring of 2013.

It is not surprising that, given such concerns, a new word was added to the lexicon of categorical xenophobia (fear of the stranger): *Islamophobia*. Like anti-Semitism, Islamophobia thrives on stereotypes of people who "are not like us," who are perceived as a threat, and who serve the need for convenient scapegoats to blame when things go awry.

Notes

1. Walt Whitman, "Song of Myself," in James E. Miller (ed.), *Complete Poetry and Selected Prose* (Boston: Houghton Mifflin, 1959).

2. See Ellis Cose, *A Nation of Immigrants: Prejudice, Politics and the Populating of America* (New York: Morrow, 1992); Roger Daniel, *Coming to America* (New York: Harper, 1990); Lawrence H. Fuchs, *The American Kaleidoscope: Race, Ethnicity and the Civic Culture* (Middletown, CT: Wesleyan University Press, 1990); and Walter Nugent, *Crossings: The Great TransAtlantic Migrations, 1870–1941* (Bloomington: Indiana University Press, 1992).

3. See Ronald Takaki, *Iron Cages: Race and Culture in 19th-Century America* (New York: Knopf, 1979).

4. John F. Kennedy, *A Nation of Immigrants,* rev. ed. (New York: Harper and Row, 1964), p. 18.

5. See, for example, Hasia R. Diner, *Erin's Daughters in America* (Baltimore: Johns Hopkins University Press, 1983) and Kathryn Kish Sklar and Thomas Dublin, *Women and Power in American History* (Englewood Cliffs, NJ: Prentice Hall, 1991).

6. Stephen Steinberg, *The Ethnic Myth: Race, Ethnicity and Class in America,* rev. ed. (New York: Beacon Press, 1989), p. 160.

7. See, for example, John B. Duff, *The Irish in the United States* (Belmont, CA: Wadsworth, 1971), pp. 31–36; also see Oscar Handlin, *Boston's Immigrants 1790–1880* (Cambridge, MA: Belknap Press of Harvard University Press, 1987).

8. See Tyler Anbinder, *Nativism and Slavery: The Northern Know Nothings and the Politics of the 1850s* (New York: Oxford University Press, 1992).

9. As quoted in Martin F. Nolan, "In Politics, the Populists vs. the Elitists," *New York Times* (July 25, 2004), DR 5.

10. Nolan, loc. cit.

11. For a recent novel that discusses the appeal for some German Americans and others of the Nazi movement, see Philip Roth, *The Plot Against America* (New York: Houghton Mifflin, 2004).

12. See, for example, Hutchins Hapgood, *The Spirit of the Ghetto: Studies of the Jewish Quarter of New York* (New York: Funk and Wagnalls Company, 1902).

13. Helen Znaniecki Lopata, *Polish Americans* (Englewood Cliffs, NJ: Prentice Hall, 1976), pp. 12–32.

14. Joseph Lopreato, *Italian Americans* (New York: Random House, 1970), pp. 36–44.

15. Pietro DiDonato, *Christ in Concrete* (Indianapolis: Bobbs-Merrill, 1937), pp. 137–138.

16. Emma Lazarus, "The New Colossus," *Poems* (Boston: Houghton Mifflin, 1889), pp. 202–203.

17. Max Lerner, *America as a Civilization* (New York: Simon and Schuster, 1958), p. 88.

18. Handlin, op. cit.

19. For a comprehensive overview of these issues, see Donna Gabaccia, *From the Other Side: Women, Gender and Immigrant Life in the U.S.: 1820–1990* (Bloomington: Indiana University Press, 1994).

20. Mathew Frye Jacobson, *Whiteness of a Different Color: European Immigrants and the Alchemy of Race* (Cambridge: Harvard University Press, 1998).

21. Rumbaut discusses this in many of his writings, most recently in Rubén D. Rumbaut and Rubén G. Rumbaut, "Self and Circumstance," in Peter I. Rose (ed.), *The Dispossessed: An Anatomy of Exile* (Amherst: University of Massachusetts Press, 2005), p. 332; and Rubén G. Rumbaut, "Ages, Life Stages, and Generational Cohorts: Decomposing the Immigrant First and Second Generations in the United States," in Alejandro Portes and Josh DeWind (eds.), *Rethinking Migration: New Theoretical and Empirical Perspectives* (New York: Berghahn Books, 2007), pp. 342–353.

22. As cited in Hraba, op. cit., pp. 16–17.

23. Ibid., p. 17.

24. See Mary Antin, *They Who Knock at Our Gates* (Boston and New York: Houghton Mifflin, 1914).

25. See, for example, William S. Bernard, *American Immigration Policy—A Reappraisal* (New York: Harper and Row, 1950), pp. 23–24. Also see Benjamin M. Ziegler (ed.), *Immigration: An American Dilemma* (Boston: D. C. Heath, 1953).

26. Gail Paradise Kelly, *From Vietnam to America* (Boulder, CO: Westview Press, 1979). See also Norman and Naomi Zucker, *The Guarded Gate* (New York: Harcourt Brace Jovanovich, 1987).

27. See Richard Breitman and Alan M. Kraut, *American Refugee Policy and European Jewry, 1933–1945* (Bloomington and Indianapolis: University of Indiana Press, 1987); David S. Wyman, *Paper Walls: America and the Refugee Crisis, 1938–1941* (Amherst: University of Massachusetts Press, 1968); and David S. Wyman, *The Abandonment of the Jews: America and the Holocaust, 1941–1945* (New York: Pantheon, 1984).

28. Peter I. Rose, "The Ghetto and Beyond," in Peter I. Rose (ed.), *The Ghetto and Beyond* (New York: Random House, 1969), p. 17.

29. Gregory Ofralea and Sharif Elumusa (eds.), *Grape Leaves: A Century of Arab American Poetry* (Salt Lake City: University of Utah Press, 1988), pp. 31–34.

30. Alexia Naff, *Becoming American: The Early Arab Immigrant Experience* (Carbondale: Southern Illinois University Press, 1985), pp. 2–3.

31. See Carol Stone, "Estimate of Muslims Living in America," in Yvonne Y. Haddad (ed.), *The Muslims of America* (New York: Oxford University Press, 1991), pp. 25–36.

32. See Pew Research, Religion and Public Life Project, www.religions.pewforum.org /reports (January 11, 2014).

33. Yvonne Haddad, *The Muslims of America,* op. cit, p. 4.

34. Yvonne Haddad and Adair Lummis, *Islamic Values in the United States: A Comparative Study* (New York: Oxford University Press, 1987), p. 165.

35. Stephanie Van Buren, "American Muslims: Islamic 'Ethnics' as Models for Pluralism," unpublished report, Smith College, Northampton, MA, May 1995, p. 12.

Chapter 4

From Other Lands

Newer Waves of Immigrants

It is obvious today that not all Americans are of European or African or Middle Eastern "stock." In the last third of the twentieth century and the first years of the present one, this country became more of a "nation of nations" than even the poet Walt Whitman could have imagined. America's "nonwhite" and "nonblack" citizens represent a diversity of background and appearance, culture, and character that has greatly enriched the United States. But this very diversity has also played into the long-held views of those wary of people who are quite unlike themselves, who, in Ronald Takaki's graphic phrase, have come to America "from different shores."[1] Although the majority of those who crossed the Pacific and the Rio Grande are relative newcomers, many of those with whom they are most identified have been in the country a very long time.

Pacific Migrations

The Lower East Side of New York, where Russian Jewish immigrants first congregated, was sometimes referred to as an "Oriental Enclave," for, to some people, the Jews were not Europeans but "Orientals" or, compounding the pejorative tag, "swarthy Orientals." They were also called "Street Arabs." In the years to come many observers would notice that members of each cohort—Jews, Arabs, and Americans from Asia—appeared to have certain common traits, not least rather similar attitudes toward family, work, and education. But the true Orientals (or Asians, as they much prefer to be called) who came to America in the nineteenth century also were very different from the Jews and other transatlantic immigrants. They had physical characteristics that set them apart and made them special targets for those who feared "the Yellow Peril."

The Chinese

The first Chinese came to America during Gold Rush days. In the years following the Civil War their migration increased sharply and by 1880 there were about 320,000 Chinese people living in America, mainly on the West Coast. Most had come from a single province in Southeast China where economic conditions forced many men to leave home as contract laborers or "coolies" to work in this country as miners or track layers on the railroads during the early days of westward expansion. Many intended to return to China to attain new status based on the wages of their toil. As a result of this hope and because of strong allegiance to their emperor and strong filial ties, few made much effort to adapt to Western institutions. Some did return, but most stayed in the United States, to be increasingly perceived as an alien element. Many Chinese suffered from ostracism, exploitation, and extreme violence. There were outright murders in Los Angeles in 1871 and a massacre of twenty-nine persons took place in Rock Springs, Wyoming, in 1885.[2]

When the railroads were finished and the mines were shut down, many Chinese moved back to the West Coast cities where, desperate for ways of earning a living, they were forced into occupations that had nothing especially "oriental" about them—running hand laundries, curio shops, and restaurants—and a few remained in outdoor labor. Moreover, since "merchants" had higher status in the eyes of immigration officials than "workers," many called themselves merchants, thus giving an exaggerated statistical sense of the size of a growing Chinese American middle class.

Immigration officials were an important factor in the lives of the Chinese. California, the state with the largest Chinese population, had long looked with disfavor upon these (and, it turned out, other) people from Asia. They repeatedly passed discriminatory legislation to curtail the activities of Chinese residents.

In 1882 the Chinese had the dubious distinction of becoming the first nationality group singled out by the federal government for separate treatment, when the Chinese Exclusion Act was passed. It was renewed in 1892, and in 1902 all Chinese immigration was made illegal. The ban was not lifted until 1943 when China was our military ally and then only a crack: 105 persons were to be admitted each year. The Immigration Reform Act of 1965, explained in Chapter Three, changed things considerably and hundreds of thousands of Chinese (and other East Asians) were able to come to America.

The early restriction against immigration did not reduce anti-Chinese sentiments. "Chinatowns," inhabited mainly by single men, were considered by many Americans to be centers of licentiousness, narcotic addiction, corruption, and mystery. Traditional ties and loyalties, clan connections, and "company" allegiances, gave these areas local community control years before that phrase was to become a part of everyday language. Ever-present suspicions increased the pressure for in-group solidarity in Chinese neighborhoods. But, as in the case of so many immigrant groups who had come to America, on their turf and in their own way, economic and welfare and educational institutions were established in Chinatowns in a number of cities, as were places of recreation and amusement. Today, many new Chinese immigrants from the mainland, from Taiwan, and from places where they were already a minority population, such as Vietnam and Laos, still find solace in these neighborhoods and many, especially those who are foreign-born, want to maintain—and are maintaining—many traditions.

But the "one and a half generation" and even more American-born Chinese (or "ABCs" as they are popularly called) are more oriented to mainstream American life and culture. It is noteworthy that many third-generation Chinese Americans (the grandchildren of the original immigrants) seem to give support to a much-debated hypothesis that sociologists and historians have long called "Hansen's Law." The idea, first expressed by Marcus Lee Hansen in 1938 (in regard to Swedes) is simply stated: "What the son wishes to forget, the grandson wishes to remember."[3]

These days Chinese Americans suffer much less discrimination than in earlier years; still, Chinatowns remain—especially in San Francisco, Los Angeles, Chicago, and New York—and so do many problems. Most of these have to do with internal conflicts in the communities, as between citizens and recent immigrants from China, between the Chinatown-based "downtown Chinese" and the "uptown Chinese" who have moved out of the enclave, and between the generations. Also, as might be expected, for a time, the shift of American foreign policy toward Beijing and ultimate recognition of the People's Republic of China (PRC) as the sole legitimate government after almost a quarter of a century of support for Nationalistic China and the Chiang Kai-shek regime confused and angered many Chinese Americans who felt a sense of kinship with the old nationalists who had relocated in Taiwan after the communist revolution of the late 1940s. That change—and the more recent changes in the People's Republic itself, especially its rapid economic growth—has also delighted many Chinese Americans who see China the place, not the political entity, as their rich cultural homeland.

Whatever sentiments the Chinese Americans held regarding this country's entente with Beijing, the opening of the People's Republic in the 1980s served to interest millions of other Americans in Chinese culture and society. If anything, America entered the 1990s in a positive mood toward China, a sentiment that continued well into the following decade. Now, in the second decade of the twenty-first century, the biggest fear is not of an ideological sweep by communism emanating from the PRC but economic domination of much of Asia and, eventually, many other parts of the world.

The Japanese

The Japanese were a half step behind the Chinese at each phase of their early settlement on the US mainland. The first Japanese settlers came to Pacific shores in 1869, twenty-one years after the first Chinese landed on the American mainland. The large migration took place a decade after the Chinese Exclusion Act had been invoked. The latter point is important, for it shows that although the two groups were frequently lumped together, significant distinctions were also made between them.

Save for the few members of the Wakamatsu Colony of pioneers who came here in the late 1860s under very special circumstances, no Japanese migrated to this country until 1885; until then almost no one could leave Japan. With a shift in the policy of the new regime of Emperor Meiji, however, many left their native land to find work in what was then the American territory of Hawaii and in the United States itself. When they arrived on continental shores some sought work in the cities, but it was hard to obtain and so they turned to mining and logging and, particularly, to farm labor. The latter proved to be advantageous to employers and newcomers alike—for a large number of immigrants had worked the soil before and took pride in what they could do with it. But they proved too good for some Californians to tolerate.

As they saved and began to buy land for their own farms or, as in the case of quite a few members of the second generation, left their jobs as laborers or domestics and sought to enter competitive vocations, they began to feel the brunt of anti-Japanese racism used as "a mask for privilege," to use Carey McWilliams's graphic phrase. The Japanese and Korean Exclusion League was formed to protest against "unfair competition."

Immigration was greatly reduced in 1907 as a result of President Theodore Roosevelt's "Gentlemen's Agreement" with the Japanese government, designed to stop the issuance of passports to potential farm workers. Others, including some merchants and many students, continued to come, as did the storied "picture brides," women selected for marriage on the basis of photographs sent by marriage brokers from Japan. But this was not enough to satisfy the Californian nativists. They sought, and their legislature passed their own Alien Land Law in 1913; it prevented the Japanese—"aliens ineligible for citizenship"—from purchasing their own farms.

Owing to World War I and the need for produce, the threat of denial—and/or removal—was stayed. In fact, immigration restrictions were lifted and about 75,000 Japanese entered the country as farm workers. Harry Kitano, a student of the period, noted "farm income reached a peak in 1920 when the Japanese in California produced land crops valued at sixty-seven million dollars."[4] Kitano also pointed out that "after the [first world] war, the release of war workers from city factories, the return of soldiers, and the 'increasing danger' from a rising nationalistic Japan reignited agitation against the Japanese. Although they had developed much of the marginal land of California, they were accused of having secured the richest and most desirable farmland."[5] The land law was soon amended and ultimately served to curtail sharply Japanese agricultural activities—though it did not stop them entirely.

The Japanese reaction to discrimination against them was quite different from that of many other ethnic groups, including the Chinese. Although they, too, often lived in enclaves and helped one another in every way possible, for the most part they fought the idea of "ghetto existence." Although feeling pressure from the *Issei* (first generation), the *Nisei* (second generation) were more inclined to live and work beyond the confines of the "Little Tokyos" or "Japan towns" of Seattle, San Francisco, and Los Angeles.

The attack on Pearl Harbor on December 7, 1941, changed everything. Almost the entire Japanese American population—citizens and aliens alike—was removed by military decree from the cities of the West Coast and placed in "security" camps in the desert, the Rocky Mountains, and as far away as Arkansas. Japanese Americans living in other parts of the country were carefully watched, but were not interned. This unprecedented action of the Roosevelt administration was prompted by fear of disloyalty from the Japanese American minority at a time of considerable tension over the actions of the armed forces of imperial Japan and a fear of subversion by those who might harbor loyalty to the emperor. Even then there was considerable evidence that the hysteria played on seeds of suspicion long sown by those for whom the Japanese were perceived as a significant economic threat.

Eventually the order was rescinded, and a year after the evacuation, the 110,000 Japanese internees began to resettle. Many established new homes in the Midwest, some in the mountain states and in the East, and others finally returned to the West Coast.

It is estimated that the Japanese Americans suffered a financial loss of over $350 million through the forced evacuation. Although Congress appropriated some money for restitution to these displaced persons, few were able to recoup their losses, many could not offer sufficient proof of their claims, and no government, of course, could compensate them for the disruption of their lives.[6]

More often than not, Japanese Americans had to begin again in different occupations from those they had engaged in prior to the war. Without sufficient funds only a small number could return to their prewar activities. Nonetheless, in the main, the status of Japanese Americans improved dramatically after 1945.

Being more widely dispersed throughout the country, by the 1960s they began to occupy a minority group position somewhat analogous to that of the highly mobile American Jews.[7] It is noteworthy that it was the Japanese, not the Jews, whom sociologist William Petersen singled out as America's "model minority" in his 1971 book *Japanese Americans: Oppression and Success.*[8] His label became a controversial one for all Americans from Asia—and many resented the "outsider's" seemingly congratulatory definer. Even while admitting it has more than a kernel of truth, especially when applied to Japanese Americans (as originally intended), "model minority" is a phrase that still evokes considerable controversy.

The Koreans

Another rapidly growing community under the rubric of Asian Americans is Korean. The major force of their resettlement in the United States has occurred since 1965.

Long subjected to the same restrictions as the Japanese (whose government controlled Korea throughout most of the first half of the twentieth century), the small numbers of Koreans who came in the early years of the last century were, like the Japanese, mostly farm laborers. A second wave appeared in the mid- to late 1950s, the vast majority Korean wives of American servicemen who had fought in the Korean War. Since passage of the Immigration Reform Act of 1965, a third and much larger influx of Koreans, many of them practitioners of one of the Protestant denominations, has come to the United States as regular immigrants. (The 1970 census indicated that there were over 200,000 Koreans in this country; by 1980 there were nearly twice that number; by 1990 it had quadrupled, and the trend, although no longer exponential, continues to show rapid increases in the first two decades of the new century.)

Often highly educated and armed with bachelor's and even higher degrees but having difficulty with the language and other cultural barriers, many members of the first generation of immigrants reluctantly left professions for which they had been trained and carved their own economic enterprises in this society. Most prominent were the groceries that began to abound in many of our major cities. In many ways the preponderance of Koreans in this single industry recapitulated an old immigrant pattern of establishing small businesses and providing work for family members and other compatriots. Examples include Irish in the priesthood and in urban politics; Jews in the needle trades; Italian barbers, cobblers, and construction workers; Chinese hand launderers; Greek restaurateurs; and Japanese gardeners.

Like other enterprising immigrant entrepreneurs, those who see them as chauvinistic and clannish have sometimes resented the Korean greengrocers. They have also been seen as threats to established shopkeepers and, particularly, as many of the Koreans' customers are blacks and Latinos, as exploiters of other minorities. One dramatic recreation of the latter tension is masterfully portrayed in director Spike Lee's 1989 film, *Do the Right Thing.* The setting is Brooklyn, New York, but it could as easily have been Los Angeles.

Because of their strong commitment to family and education, over a decade ago it had been predicted that few children of Korean grocers would remain in the produce business. The assumption is corroborated by the high and climbing rates of enrollments of Korean American youngsters in American colleges and universities and by the numbers already becoming well established in white-collar jobs, especially in new industries, such as computers, as well as in the more traditional professions.

Other Asians

Aside from the Chinese, Japanese, and Koreans who, in large measure, share common origins and certain values relating to familial ties and responsibilities, and the fundamentals of a common written language based in part on Chinese pictograms, there are three other major immigrant groups in the United States also called "Asian" and are so designated in many census statistics. The first are those from one nation, the Philippines, a large, multi-islanded country whose people share a common nationality but are of quite diverse racial, cultural, and religious backgrounds.[9] The second, known in the aggregate as South Asians, are an equally diverse aggregate of Hindu, Muslim, and Buddhist people from the Indian subcontinent and the countries of India, Pakistan, Bangladesh, and Sri Lanka. The third cohort is "Indochinese."

The two largest entities—South Asian and Filipino—have very little in common save for the fact that a disproportionate number of foreign doctors and nurses working in American hospitals come from India and from the Philippines.

South Asians

The Filipinos have a long history of residence in the United States, dating back almost 250 years, to 1763 in New Orleans. The South Asians are, by contrast, recent arrivals. Until 1980, the Census Bureau did not account for the latter group at all, although there have been small numbers of Indians in this country since early in the twentieth century. Most of those in that early group came from the Punjab region to California, where they worked as farm laborers. Despite their long period of residence and their contributions to the local economy, it wasn't until 1946 that they were allowed to own land, become citizens, or request permission to bring in their relatives. And, even then, although their numbers increased considerably, opportunities for immigration from South Asia didn't really open up until the Immigration Reform Bill of 1965 was passed. After that, large numbers applied for and received permission to enter the United States as resident aliens and to work toward citizenship.

Many of those who are of Indian origin in the country today came (or their parents came) directly from the subcontinent. Others migrated from East Africa, the West Indies, especially Trinidad and Tobago, Guyana, and the United Kingdom, where their families had lived, sometimes for several years, often for several generations. Their ranks included both Hindus and Muslims.

Although they represent a wide spectrum of ethnic, religious, and linguistic groups, the most recently arrived South Asians constitute a uniquely high-status group of immigrants. According to several reliable sources, more than 90 percent are either "professional/technical workers" or the "spouses and children of professional/technical workers" when they arrive. Those who are less well trained or have difficulty finding professional jobs have been quite enterprising. Like the Koreans, they have established their own economic niches and become quite successful entrepreneurs, especially in the newsstands, gas stations, and convenience shops they have purchased and operate in large cities and small towns across the country.

One of the most interesting sociological aspects of the South Asians' odyssey in American society is the way they have seen themselves in relation to other minorities, immigrant and native-born.

For many years, prominent Indian and other South Asian spokespersons claimed that their official racial designation should be "Caucasian." The federal judiciary—and the Census Bureau—thought otherwise and repeatedly denied their claim to "whiteness." Maxine Fisher, one of the first scholars to study Indians in the United States, reported that, even though they were finally permitted to be classified as they had long wished, some members of the same communities soon desired to change back to a non-Caucasian designation. She cited "the economic benefits to be derived from being considered nonwhite" as a possible reason for this.[10] Despite the objections of many, there have been continuing efforts to use the category "Asian American" to lump such diverse parties as those of Indian and Filipino background and others from countries in Southeast Asia, as well as "Pacific Islanders" (with roots in Polynesia, Micronesia, Melanesia), along with those of Chinese, Japanese, and Korean origins under one broad rubric, "Asian." This, it was claimed, was not only for statistical purposes but in order to achieve the benefits of newly established affirmative action programs. Those Indians and others who feel they benefit from this hardly cultural but strictly geographic designation may owe a debt of gratitude to a little-known Filipino writer, Lemuel Ignacio.

The Filipinos

In his book *Asian Americans and Pacific Islanders: Is There Such an Ethnic Group?*, first published in 1976, Ignacio argued for a common label that simultaneously would counteract and emulate the successful movement of Black Power brokers. He wanted his people to get their fair share of government funding. Because Filipinos are, like South Asians, a highly diverse, multilingual, multiethnic community, he argued they ought to come together, allying themselves with others who shared their fate if not their history.[11] Shortly after the publication of Ignacio's treatise, Maxine Fisher noted that it was clearly evident that "Asian American ethnicity—and even Filipino ethnicity to a lesser extent—are artifacts which he helped to create."[12]

Ignacio sought to fashion a powerful third bloc, "Asians," that could make its own claims for special consideration for "group rights" in competition with African Americans and those with roots in Central and South America. In many ways, he was to prove successful. The ostensible rationale for linking these seemingly odd bedfellows was that all had originally come to the United States from the East; all had suffered from some form of racial discrimination.

That such a move should originate with a spokesman from the Filipino American community is not surprising. For—of all the large, trans-Pacific groups that have come here—the Filipinos, or "Pinoys," as they often call themselves,[13] are at once the most marginal and the most "American" of all "Asian" subgroups.

The Philippine archipelago, situated in a strategic area of the South Pacific, was long a colony of Spain from whose King Philip it derived its Western sounding name. Spanish conquerors, administrators, priests, and businessmen left a profound imprint on the culture, religion, and character of the predominantly Malayan population by the time they were finally expelled at the end of the nineteenth century, at the end of the Spanish-American War. In 1902, after but several years of independence, American forces overthrew the nationalists, took possession of the islands, and reorganized the society, its laws, and, in many ways, its mores. After several hundred years of Spanish rule and then several decades of American influence, the people of the Philippines were subjected to yet another takeover when the Japanese conquered the country in the early days of World War II.

In 1944 American forces, who had been forced to leave the embattled country, were eventually to avenge their defeat at Bataan and return. Two years later, the Philippines became one of the many oxymoronically named "independent dependencies" of the victorious allies.

To some, the modern Philippines is a case study in cultural amalgamation. To others, it is a highly volatile, fragmented, and schizophrenic society that, like Puerto Rico, isn't quite sure what it is or what it wants to be. No better example of its own confusion is to be found than in the practice of many Filipino patriots who, citing the absence of an "F" sound in the principal native language, Tagalog, disdain its use in the spelling of their official name. They say they are "Pilipino" not "Filipino." Ironically, the same local boosters still render gender distinctions in the traditional Spanish manner ("Pilipino" for male, "Pilipina" for female) while requiring everyone in the nation to learn English! To confound matters further, once they get to the United States, they are sometimes classified as "Hispanics" owing to the preponderance of Spanish surnames.

The fact is that, since the first "Manila men" jumped ship in Louisiana in the eighteenth century, Filipinos have been difficult to pigeonhole. They have never quite fit in to standard schemes and have frequently followed their own paths toward integration. They are from the East and they may be "Asians," but except for the many people of Chinese background who live as minorities in the Philippines, they are surely not "Orientals." They often have Spanish names and some Filipinos of the old, partially European elite can still speak Spanish. Nonetheless, the Filipinos are not "Hispanics" or "Latinos" (at least in terms of the current usage of those terms).

With regard to their migration to this country, it is to be noted that by 1930 there were over 45,000 Filipinos on American soil, many of them agricultural laborers working in the then-territory of Hawaii. After the war increasing numbers came to the United States. Among their ranks were veterans who had fought in American uniforms or served as mess stewards aboard US ships and the Filipino brides of American servicemen. Two decades later, this postwar group would be followed by large numbers of countrymen and women who benefited from the changes in immigration legislation.

Many of the newcomers were far better educated than their predecessors. The immigrants included many nurses, physicians, lawyers, engineers, and teachers who came to benefit from job opportunities. Most recent immigrants come knowing English, already trained in needed skills, and sharing many of the same attitudes about making it in the United States that other trans-Pacific migrants possess. Far from all who wish to come to the United States have been able to do so for even the relaxed immigration laws have set limits to annual flows. And one of the biggest backlogs of petitioners consists of lists of those seeking entry from the Philippines.

The Indochinese

The war in Vietnam and its complicated aftermath brought a new lot of Asian people to America, those from the southeastern part of the continent. Although some were from Thailand, mostly the spouses of American soldiers who spent time in their country on leave from the battlefronts, most were from Vietnam, Laos, or Cambodia, the three countries of what, for a time, was French Indochina.

The first Indochinese refugees to come were government officials and military leaders who were airlifted out of Vietnam after the fall of Saigon in April 1975. Aided by public and private agencies, they were moved to Pacific island bases, then moved to camps in various parts of the United States, and then helped to resettle in many cities, where they often began to form new ethnic communities.

In the late 1970s the world was alarmed by reports of "boat people" who had escaped from Vietnam but were having difficulty finding places of asylum on the shores of neighboring countries. An international agreement set up an elaborate system by which the new refugees could find temporary havens in camps established under the authority of the United Nations High Commissioner for Refugees (UNHCR) in Thailand, Malaysia, Singapore, Indonesia, Hong Kong, Macao, and the Philippines. There, in what were called the "countries of first asylum," they were cared for and interviewed by American immigration authorities and their counterparts from other Western nations for possible movement to their homelands. Acceptance guaranteed what was called "third country resettlement." The vast majority of Vietnamese and Laotians who applied to come to the United States were eventually accepted and brought to this country.

Cambodians were not as fortunate. Victims not only of the international war but also of the terrible reign of Pol Pot and his Khmer Rouge, which took power in 1975, many had escaped into Thailand. There, additional border camps, operated by the UNHCR, were also set up. However, unlike most of the other camps, these were essentially holding centers. In general, only those who had fought with the Lon Nol forces allied with the United States and South Vietnam during the war, a relatively small percentage of those seeking resettlement in the United States, were considered and found eligible.

Under new regulations, the Vietnamese and other Indochinese refugees—and refugees from other lands at the time, including Cubans and Soviet Jews and Pentecostalists—entered the country with refugee status but the right to stay and apply for citizenship at the end of the prescribed period. In the process, their official status shifted from "refugee" to "immigrant," and, as they became acculturated, like other newcomers who often started their new lives in America within the confines of "nationality-based" enclaves, they quickly moved to the next stage, from immigrants to ethnics.

Today there are nearly one million Vietnamese and Laotian Americans and around 150,000 persons of Cambodian background in the United States.

In the earliest days of their resettlement, not a few Americans had resented the presence of the refugees. Among those concerned were some African Americans and other nonwhites who argued that the public seemed more concerned with the refugees' plight than with their own continuing needs.[14] Yet in the aggregate most Vietnamese, Laotians, and Cambodians found acceptance in the United States and made their marks, excelling in a variety of spheres. (These issues are discussed more fully in Chapter Nine.)

Among those who entered the United States from the three countries of Indochina were several groups who were minorities in the lands from which they fled. The most prominent of these are the so-called "ethnic Chinese." Others include tribal people from the highlands of Laos, especially the Hmong. Rejected and exploited in their own society, the Hmong were active allies of US forces during the war.

Statistics gathered by the US Immigration and Naturalization Service and the US Census Bureau indicate that in the past three decades there has been a reverse migration of a small but steadily rising number of individuals who have decided to return to their native lands across the Pacific.[15] Most prominent are highly trained specialists in computers and other high-tech fields who are going back to participate in the economic booms in China and in the "mini-dragon" states—Taiwan, Singapore,

Hong Kong, and South Korea. In addition, a number of Vietnamese, Laotian, and Cambodian former refugees have returned home to help rebuild their native lands.

Latinos

In this country Spanish speakers from former colonies, sometimes referred to as Hispanics but also called Latinos (the term most prefer), are in fact a multigroup cohort. In 2003 they became the nation's largest minority, outnumbering African Americans.

Those now grouped under the broad rubric "Hispanic" include descendants of very early settlers living in areas taken over from Mexico after the Treaty of Guadalupe Hidalgo at the end of the Mexican American War, recent immigrants from Mexico and other Latin American countries, Cubans (who constitute the largest ethnic group in Miami), Dominicans (the fastest-growing foreign-born population in New York City[16]), and Puerto Ricans, who have been citizens since 1917.

Before being included as a separate census category, most people from any of the backgrounds just listed were more or less forced to identify themselves to enumerators as "White," "Black," "Asian," "Native American," or "Some Other Race"; although 48 percent chose to place themselves under the first rubric, 42 percent checked the last one. As Carlos Chardon, chairman of the Census Bureau's Hispanic advisory committee, explained in a *New York Times* interview in October of 2004, "We don't fit into the categories that the Anglos want us to fit in."[17] Many opted for a new category: "Latino."

Associate director for the decennial census Preston Jay Waite countered that "if somebody writes down that their race is Latino, that doesn't give us any information about which of the race categories they're in. We're making up the race for 15 million people. We would prefer not to do it. It doesn't seem wise to me that we would put at risk the racial statistics of the nation in order to answer an interesting sociological question."[18] Waite seemed to fail to understand that the "interesting sociological question" about such a clear example of addressing race as a social construction is at the very core of the concern of those who prefer not to call themselves by one of the fixed categories. As noted previously, many Puerto Ricans, Dominicans, and Cubans are of mixed African, Indian, and Spanish heritage, and most Mexicans are of Indian and Spanish background. Moreover, if asked, many will explain that they come from societies that are "racially continuous" rather than "racially dichotomous" like the United States. Still, what some have called a process of "racialization" did occur; part of this was institutionalized in the development of "affirmative action categories" developed not only for census purposes but also to identify minorities who were still enduring various forms of categorical discrimination.

The Mexicans

The ancestors of a large sector of the Mexican American population can hardly be called migrants, at least in the modern sense. They are among the oldest Americans, perhaps second only to the native "Indian" peoples of what became the United States. Their history of living on that land dates back to the days of the Spanish conquest. Some such old-timers are often called *Hispanos.* The Southwest has been their traditional home for over four centuries. Many became Americans by default when New Mexico, California, and other southwestern territories were ceded to the United States. Prior to their annexation, the social patterns of Mexican society prevailed in these territories, and the life ways of some of the descendants of those who lived there still sometimes mirror those of people south of the Rio Grande.

Shortly after the turn of the twentieth century, increasing numbers of laborers from Mexico crossed the border to work in the United States. Restrictions on overseas immigration during World War I gave impetus to this migration and almost a million Mexicans entered the country between 1910 and 1930. Most found employment doing "stoop labor" on huge farms and ranches in the southwestern states—Texas, Arizona, and California; some became migratory workers moving northward and eastward with the seasons. Over half of these newcomers took up residence in the United States, with increasing numbers gravitating to urban areas; eager to improve their lot and to earn enough money to send remittances back home, they seemed to recapitulate patterns of earlier immigrants from predominantly Catholic, peasant-like societies such as Ireland, Italy, Poland, and French Canada.

In time, especially in the years following World War II, many Mexican Americans would achieve middle-class status, a success story that is largely ignored by those more comfortable with traditional images of Mexican Americans.[19] Still, many others found their paths to mobility blocked by a variety of social barriers reinforced by a particular but convenient (at least for growers) form of racism that contended that Mexicans were only suited for farm labor. This widespread attitude served to keep many influential people in the Southwest from making the necessary changes in the educational system and in social welfare to assist the Mexican Americans in the *barrios* (or Mexican American enclaves) of El Paso and San Antonio, in Trinidad, Colorado, in Tucson, Arizona, and in Los Angeles and San Diego, as well as farm workers in the labor camps and the rural settlements that still pock the fertile valleys of California.

In such places (and similar ones throughout the Southwest) in the past, in addition to legally admitted immigrants, there were two other widely recognized types of migrants from Mexico: "wetbacks," so named for having crossed the Rio Grande illegally in search of employment; and *braceros,* those with permits to work as contract laborers under strict restriction. At its height in 1960, 427,000 entered as "guest workers." Few were admitted under the special provisions of the Mexican Laborer Acts after 1965 and none by 1970. In recent years there has been much discussion of reinstating some type of contract-labor scheme to bring in needed workers on a temporary basis.

Although the *bracero* program was sharply curtailed, then phased out, many Mexicans continued to try to enter the United States to find work. Despite much greater surveillance of the border areas than ever before, so-called "undocumented aliens" continued to pour into the country for another decade. Their crossing, which continues today, although at a slower place, is often facilitated by the assistance of "coyotes," men and women who make their living as smugglers of human beings. Even when captured and deported, it is not uncommon for those desperate to get to this country to try again.

Because they were often willing to work for lower wages or contracted in large groups for agricultural and industrial employment—the reason growers found them so attractive—American low-wage workers saw them as an economic threat. Some "Anglos" (as white people in the area are known), steeped in anti-Mexican sentiment, tried to exploit this resentment. To counteract this, several prominent farm worker leaders sought to join with them to fight for union representation and collective bargaining in the vineyards, lettuce fields, and orange groves where they toil. And not only did a growing sense of cohesiveness begin to assert itself among the disparate members of *La Raza* (their own term meaning "The Race"), but a demand for both political power and recognition of cultural pride began to be voiced by an increasing segment of this minority of as many as eight million people.

"Chicano" (meaning "little Mexican") used to be a term of derogation, but for many so labeled in the 1960s it became a term of pride and solidarity and remained so for several decades. As one well-known Mexican American has said, "Call us whatever you like, we know what we are and are proud of it."[20]

Increasingly, the voices of Mexican Americans—Cesar Chavez in California, Corky Gonzalez in Colorado, Reyes Tijerina in New Mexico, and a variety of new leaders in Texas—were raised, and many, Anglos and Mexican Americans, started to listen closely. They saw changes that altered both the public stereotypes ("Frito Bandito") and the substance of life for Mexican Americans. In the late 1970s one factor, perhaps more than any other, boosted the self-esteem of Mexican Americans, as well as their brothers, sisters, and cousins south of the border. This was the discovery of enormous reserves of fossil fuels in Mexico, a deposit reportedly as large as that in Saudi Arabia. For the first time, the giant to the north was put on the defensive, and Mexicans possessed an important bargaining chip as they negotiated various matters of significance to them, not least immigration policies.[21]

Like other people so often categorized as "nonwhite" minorities, Mexican Americans are seeking a legitimate and equal place in a pluralistic America. The overwhelming majority is determined to be recognized for something far more important than the ubiquitous taco stands that dot the byways of the Southwest.

Today, Mexican Americans are the fastest growing "nationality" group in the United States and this fact has raised concerns in many quarters, not least in the ranks of those who still cling to the notion that they, descendants of the early Anglo-Americans, have certain entitlements that others are determined to take away from them. There was a time when it was the "unassimilable" Irish, then the Chinese of the "Yellow Peril," then the Jews who were seen as the principal subversives. Today, to some, it is the "brown wave of Mexicans" coming across the border that is said to be poised, not only to undercut the farm labor market but to destroy American civilization itself.

In a chapter in his book *Who Are We?*, published in the early days of the twenty-first century, political scientist Samuel Huntington minced few words in creating, or contributing to the creation of, a self-fulfilling prophecy. He wrote that "the most powerful stimulus to white nativism is likely to be the threat to language, culture, and power that whites see coming from the expanding demographic, social, economic, and political roles of Hispanics [meaning, in this instance, Mexicans] in American society."[22] We will return to this argument in Chapter Seven. For now, it is sufficient to indicate that of all the immigrant groups still trying to establish themselves in the United States, the Mexicans have become a prominent lightning rod relating to the true meaning of integration.

Before temporarily leaving the latest principal subjects in the continuing debates about immigration and its reform, mention need be made of the tens of thousands of Central and South Americans other than Mexicans who cross the Rio Grande to enter the United States. Many of them, like a number of Mexican border-crossers, have no papers. They, too, are often known as "the undocumented." Like the Mexicans, most of them are economic migrants eager for employment and opportunities for a better life, although for many years some entered this country illegally hoping to find a safe haven from political persecution.

Unlike the refugees from Indochina, Cuba, and the Soviet Union, the agents of the Naturalization and Immigration Service (INS) frequently viewed such Central American asylum-seekers with suspicion. There are many explanations for this. One of the most plausible is that, despite changes in American immigration laws that no longer defined refugees as "individuals fleeing communism" (as they did from 1952 to 1980), the fact remains that our government officials continued to favor those fleeing left-wing regimes (like those in Vietnam or Cuba) over those leaving countries the United States supported (such as El Salvador).

The Puerto Ricans

Often grouped with Mexican Americans and others called "Latinos," including those from South America and such island nations in the Caribbean as the Dominican Republic, are the Puerto Ricans. Although they too are of mixed racial origins and are Spanish-speaking, they are a distinct—and distinctive—people. They are neither refugees nor immigrants.

Puerto Rico has been an American possession since the end of the Spanish-American War. By their own choice the inhabitants of the island became United States citizens in 1917. (Until recently, few Americans knew this, or much else about these fellow citizens. In fact, until the mid-1950s many mapmakers misspelled the name of their home island, calling it "Porto Rico.")

Migration from the island to the mainland began early in the twentieth century and continues today. Although movement back and forth has fluctuated with economic conditions in the states, since World War II, Puerto Rican migration, with a prime objective of staying in the United States, has risen sharply, in large part because of increasing job opportunities, the appeal of the popular culture of large cities, and dramatically improved transportation facilities, which have dramatically closed the distance.

As in earlier days, New York is still the principal gateway for new arrivals, and as in the past, many who first arrive in New York remain there. Puerto Ricans—like their predecessors from Southern and Eastern Europe and southern blacks whose migration to New York has paralleled their own—have found employment in the garment industry and as service workers in the great commercial and tourist center.

Although Puerto Ricans are to be found in all parts of the country—including Alaska and Hawaii—over three-fourths of their total number live in New York, and many others in nearby areas.[23] Like other newcomers to the city, when they first came, the Puerto Ricans found themselves relegated to the worst and most overpriced neighborhoods. Their children attended crowded schools; they often held the lowest-status jobs; they frequently suffered "winter temperatures and more chilling social contacts."[24] Unfortunately, despite the fact that in many ways they have come better prepared for life in the United States than many other ethnic minorities, many have long had difficulty climbing the ladder.[25]

Census Bureau data has long provided graphic evidence of the difficulties Puerto Ricans have had in making it on the mainland, despite the fact that they are far more likely to have come from urban areas and have a much higher proportion of skilled and semiskilled workers than the native population. Furthermore, in contradiction to the assertion that "primarily Puerto Rico's unemployed come to New York," it has been found that the migrants were more regularly employed than the rest of the population back home and received a slightly higher income than the Puerto Rican average. They continue to come not to seek work, but to seek better work. Finding it for many is still a problem and nearly a third of Puerto Rican families continue to live below the poverty level.[26]

There is little question that Puerto Ricans have faced considerable racial discrimination in the United States. Some specialists feel it has been especially hard for members of this particular cohort to cope with the "racially dichotomous" (white versus nonwhite) character of mainland thinking, a rather sharp contrast to the "racially continuous" (from white to black) situation on their home island. In fact, Puerto Ricans were the first major group to migrate to the urban centers of the United States that brought with them a tradition of widespread racial mixing. Although it is true that lighter-skinned Puerto Ricans generally have higher status in San Juan than New York, there are many exceptions. Indeed, it is said "on the mainland, the color of a person determines what class he will belong to; in Puerto Rico, the class a person belongs to determines his color." Another popular expression for the same phenomenon is that "money whitens!"

The Cubans

The Spanish-American War began in February 1898 with the sinking of the American ship known as the *Maine* in Havana Harbor. The war ended less than a year later with the signing of the Treaty of Paris. As a result, Spain lost its far-flung empire that stretched from the Philippines and Guam in the Pacific to the nearby Caribbean islands of Puerto Rico and Cuba.

Until the Cuban Revolution in 1959, in addition to those historical facts, most Americans knew Cuba only as a series of snapshot images: Teddy Roosevelt and his Rough Riders charging up San Juan Hill; stories by Ernest Hemingway and

Graham Greene; glossy pictures of bars and beaches in Old Havana; and as the locale of a one-night fling by Sky Masterson and his Salvation Army girlfriend in the 1955 musical *Guys and Dolls.*

At that time there were relatively few Cubans in the United States. Of those who were here, mostly in southern Florida, some were in business, some were students, and most were laborers. With the fall of the dictator Fulgencio Batista, and the coming to power of Fidel Castro, hundreds of thousands of Cubans sought and gained admittance to this country as exiles from the new, communist regime.

Between 1959 and 1970 some 700,000 refugees entered the United States, most arriving and staying in the Miami area.[27] Although some were exceedingly wealthy, the majority was of modest means and had to start their lives anew. That these political refugees were successful accounted for the favorable press they began to receive across the country and the reception extended by a government that often seemed blind to the suffering of others, such as thousands of Haitians, who took great risks to cross open water to get into the country.

In south Florida, however, things were different. Other asylum seekers envied the Cubans—and their tight-knit community organization—and they were frequently resented even more by the old minorities, especially African Americans, who claimed the Cubans were elbowing their way into the system and taking jobs away from members of their community. As the Cubans began to move into the political arena, the tensions rose even higher.

In 1980, a second large wave (approximately 150,000) of Cuban exiles made the ninety-mile trip to the Florida coast. These "boat people" were quite different from those in the "first wave." They were generally poorer and less well educated. And many more were black.

Among the boat people were a large subgroup who, unlike those who fled from Cuba, had been given permission by Fidel Castro to go. They sailed from the port of Mariel. It was rumored that Castro saw his chance to rid the country of numbers of criminals and mentally retarded persons and, indeed, some such people were among the *Marielitos.* Wary of this ploy, American officials allowed them to be "saved at sea" and brought to the beach but they were not given the same refugee status as their countrymen. They were subject to deportation or detention whenever they violated a law, no matter how petty. It took twenty-five years to regularize their status and to remove the blot on the reputation of the vast majority of those who came from Mariel. In January 2005, the Supreme Court handed down the ruling that the open-ended detention policy was illegal and, as writer Mirta Ojita reported, "The highest court in the land they have chosen as their own has validated the status not only of those convicted of crimes but of all Cubans who in 1980 set sail for the United States.[28]

In the late 1980s, thousands of political refugees from Guatemala, El Salvador, and Nicaragua entered the country illegally, mainly through Mexico. Although the authorities were highly selective in their willingness to consider such undocumented aliens as refugees—being somewhat more kindly disposed to those fleeing Nicaragua, a Marxist state, than El Salvador, an ally of the United States and heavily supported by American aid—they finally did allow large numbers to stay in the country, at least temporarily. In January 1989, a large contingent of Nicaraguans moved from the border areas in Texas to Miami and Dade County, Florida, where they were assisted by various social service and employment agencies, many of them run by sympathetic Cuban Americans. The presence of these Central American anticommunists, the political allies of the Cuban expatriates, greatly exacerbated an already strained relationship between the city's black and Hispanic populations and resulted in several days of violent confrontation.

In recent decades, Cuban and other refugees and immigrants from Latin America have succeeded in making Miami one of the principal bilingual, bicultural cities in the United States, often, it is argued, especially by African Americans, at their expense. That reality, coupled with fears expressed by so-called Anglos about the "Mexican invasion" in the Southwest and, especially, in California, is already the subject of much debate about the future of American society, the rights of groups and individuals, and the long dominant "majority culture." These disputes have been occurring simultaneously with the growing chasm between two cultural camps, overly simplified in the election season of 2004 as "red" (mainly conservative, fundamentalist, and Republican) and "blue" (liberal, permissive, and Democratic), each vying for support from certain new American groups. A principal prize for both sides was seen—and will be seen—as the support of Hispanic Americans. The Democrats won the allegiance of the majority that year and in every election since. In fact, some attribute Barack Obama's reelection as president in 2012 to the bloc voting of so many Latinos.

Summing Up

The number of foreign-born people in the United States is currently at an all-time high—just shy of forty million in a population of nearly 320 million—although their overall representation is smaller than it was in the years of peak immigration in the late nineteenth and early twentieth centuries.

According to a report of the Pew Research Hispanic Trends Project published in January 2013, by 2011, 29 percent of this overall group was born in Mexico, with another 20 percent from countries of Central America, the Caribbean, and South America. This matches the findings of the United States Census Bureau. Of others born abroad, 25 percent were from Asia, 3.7 percent from the Middle East, and the rest from Canada (2 percent), Africa (2 percent), or Europe (with no more than 1 percent from any single country, including Germany, England, Ireland, or Italy, for decades the principal sources of immigration to the United States). The largest concentrations of the latest newcomers are to be found in four states: California, New York, Texas, and Florida.[29]

Between 2002 and 2012, while the percentage of immigrants from Asian countries remained relatively constant (around 25 percent), the percentage of Latinos continued to climb. As noted in a May 8, 2013, report from the Congressional Budget Office to the chairman of the House Committee on the Budget, Latino immigrants overall are a younger cohort than native-born people—three-quarters are of working age, between twenty-five and sixty-four, compared to only half of the native-born population.

The report noted that educational attainment is somewhat less, on average, among foreign-born than among native-born people, but it varies considerably depending on immigrants' country of origin. In 2010, 27 percent of all foreign-born people in the United States between the ages of twenty-five and sixty-four had not completed high school, compared to 7 percent of the native-born population. However, 55 percent of immigrants from Asia had at least a bachelor's degree, as did 51 percent of those from Europe and Canada, in contrast to just 33 percent of the native-born population.[30]

The jury is still out as to whether these new Americans will overcome their handicaps and recapitulate the successful mobility of earlier groups, including those severely impoverished, but there are many signs that, eager to fulfill their own American Dreams, they, too, will make it in this country.

Of course, "Latinos" who left Cuba as refugees, Dominicans, various Central and South Americans, and the largest group—Mexicans—are not all the same. What is interesting and important to note is that, by far the largest cohort of Latinos or Hispanics, those from Mexico, show an American odyssey very similar to that of the Poles, Italians, Greeks, and Slavs who came to the United States in the Great Atlantic Migration and the Irish who started coming even earlier. Most of those folks were also poor, Catholic, had limited educational attainment, and were looking for economic opportunities said to abound in the United States. In those days such European migrants were often tarred with the brush of religious intolerance. And many of the most active anti-immigrant organizations stressed their members' "white, Protestant" character. Except for concern about Muslims after 9/11, religion per se is no longer a principal basis for animosity or anti-immigrant rhetoric; rather it is the specter of the economic and cultural threat to all "good" Americans (now including Catholics and Jews as well as Protestants). Yet there is ample evidence to show that, even faster than the Poles, Italians, Greeks, and Slavs, in spite of the fears of the latter-day Know-Nothings in a number of southern and southwestern states, the majority of Mexican migrants are rapidly learning and functioning in English and acculturating at a very rapid rate.[31]

Many of those who voluntarily migrated to America in the nineteenth and twentieth centuries left their countries of origin seeking freedom and a new life in the New World. Some came to make their fortunes; some came to escape religious persecution or political tyranny; the majority came for economic reasons. For most, immigration was the beginning of a new and exciting adventure, but for others the journey to America was a bitter and harrowing experience as it still remains for some.

In the brief sketches of America's principal immigrant groups presented in this chapter and the previous one, the reception of newcomers by those already in the United States is only occasionally touched upon. But in Chapter Five a discussion of various proposals for coping with "strangers" in the land, an interpretation of these, an examination of the patterns of ethnic separation that emerged, and a statistical breakdown of America's racial, religious, and ethnic composition are considered.

Notes

1. See Ronald Takaki (ed.), *From Different Shores* (New York: Oxford University Press, 1987).

2. See, for example, Rose Hum Lee, *The Chinese in the United States of America* (New York: Oxford University Press, 1960); Francis L. K. Hsu, *Challenge of the American Dream: The Chinese in the U.S.* (Belmont, CA: Wadsworth, 1971); and Stanford M. Lyman, *Chinese-Americans* (New York: Random House, 1973).

3. Marcus Lee Hansen, *The Problem of the Third Generation Immigrant* (Rock Island, IL: The Augustana Historical Society, 1938). Many studies have suggested that the hypothesis is hardly generalizable to all or even most immigrant populations. See, for example, Peter Kivisto and Dag Blanck (eds.), *American Immigrants and Their Generations* (Urbana: University of Illinois Press, 1990).

4. Harry H. L. Kitano, *Japanese Americans* (Englewood Cliffs, NJ: Prentice Hall, 1969), p. 17.

5. Ibid. See also William Petersen, *Japanese Americans: Oppression and Success* (New York: Random House, 1971).

6. Leonard Bloom and Ruth Riemer, *Removal and Return* (Berkeley: University of California Press, 1949), pp. 202–204. See also Maisie and Richard Conrad, *Executive Order 9066: The Internment of 110,000 Japanese-Americans* (Sacramento: California Historical Society, 1976).

7. Stanford M. Lyman, "Japanese-American Generation Gap," *Society,* 10 (January–February 1973), pp. 55–63.

8. See Petersen, *Japanese Americans.*

9. The discussion of South Asians and Filipinos that follows is an updated and amended section—"The Other Asians"—of a longer essay by the author. See Peter I. Rose, "Asian Americans: From Pariahs to Paragons," in Nathan Glazer (ed.), *Clamor at the Gates* (San Francisco: Institute for Contemporary Studies, 1989), pp. 196–203.

10. Maxine Fisher, *The Indians of New York City: A Study of Immigrants from India* (Columbia, MO: South Asia Books, 1980).

11. Lemuel Ignacio, *Asian Americans and Pacific Islanders: Is There Such an Ethnic Group?* (San Jose: Philipino Development Associates, Inc., 1976).

12. Fisher, op. cit., pp. 136–137.

13. See Antonio J. A. Pido, *The Pilipinos in America* (New York: Center for Migration Studies, 1985), p. 87.

14. See Jeremy Hein, *From Vietnam, Laos, and Cambodia: A Refugee Experience in the United States* (New York: Twayne, 1995).

15. For a brief summary, see Ashley Dunn, "Skilled Asians Leaving U.S. for High-Tech Jobs at Home," *New York Times* (February 21, 1995), pp. 1, B5.

16. "Record Immigration Is Changing the Face of New York's Neighborhoods," *New York Times* (January 24, 2005), p. A16.

17. Rachel L. Swarns, "Hispanics Debate Census Plan to Change Racial Grouping," *New York Times* (October 24, 2004), pp. 1, 16.

18. Ibid., p. 16.

19. See Lionel Sosa, *The Americano Dream* (New York: Plume, 1998).

20. See Ilan Stavans, *The Hispanic Condition: Reflections on Culture and Identity in America* (New York: HarperCollins, 1995).

21. See John H. Burma (ed.), *Mexican-Americans in the United States* (New York: Schenkman, 1970); Ellwyn Stoddard, *Mexican-Americans* (New York: Random House,

1973); Joan Moore, *Mexican Americans,* 2nd ed. (Englewood Cliffs, NJ: Prentice Hall, 1976); and such recent studies as Peter Skerry, *Mexican Americans: The Ambivalent Minority* (Cambridge: Harvard University Press, 1993) and Marcelo M. Suarez-Orozco (ed.), *Crossings: Mexican Immigration in Interdisciplinary Perspectives* (Cambridge: Harvard University Press, 1998).

22. As quoted in Peter I. Rose, "Damned Yankees?" *Congress Monthly* (September/October 2004), p. 13.

23. Joseph P. Fitzpatrick, *The Puerto Rican New Yorkers,* 2nd ed. (Englewood Cliffs, NJ: Prentice Hall, 1987), p. 15.

24. Clarence Senior, *Strangers—Then Neighbors* (New York: Freedom Books, 1961), p. 25.

25. See also Elena Padilla, *Up from Puerto Rico* (New York: Columbia University Press, 1958); Christopher Rand, *The Puerto-Ricans* (New York: Oxford University Press, 1958); and Patricia Cayo Sexton, *Spanish Harlem* (New York: Harper, 1965); Maria Pérez y Gonzalez, *Puerto Ricans in the United States* (Westport, CT: Greenwood Press, 2000).

26. See report by Edward C. Burks, "Affluence Eludes Blacks, Puerto-Ricans," *New York Times* (August 17, 1972), p. 33.

27. Vincent N. Parrillo, *Strangers to These Shores* (Boston: Houghton Mifflin, 1980), p. 417.

28. See Alejandro Portes and Robert L. Bach, *Latin Journey: Cuban and Mexican Immigrants in the United States* (Berkeley: University of California Press, 1985).

29. Summary reports are available online from the US Census Bureau (www.uscensus .gov) and the Pew Research Center's Population Reports (www.pewresarch.org).

30. Letter from Douglas Elmendorf, director, Congressional Budget Office, US Congress, to Honorable Paul Ryan, chair, Committee on the Budget, US House of Representatives, Washington, DC, May 8, 2013.

31. See, for example, recent reports of the Public Policy Institute of California, available at www.ppic.org/main/publication_show.asp?i=817.

Chapter 5

The Dilemmas of Diversity

Coming Full Circle

Sometime in the 1970s—the decade during which we celebrated the bicentennial of the United States—a significant part of the American saga seemed to come full circle. An attempt was made by a dozen Mohawks to establish a beachhead on Ellis Island, the place where thousands upon thousands of European immigrants had first touched American shores. The motorboat failed and the plot to take over the island on the East Coast as others had seized the island of Alcatraz in San Francisco Bay was foiled.

When someone suggested that "the Indians were stupid for attempting the occupation of the island," a member of the raiding party retorted, "We're stupid? It was your ancestors who landed on these shores, thought they were somewhere else, and called *us* Indians. Indians live on the other side of the world!"

That bit of repartee is more profound than it seems on the surface. In a few words it expresses the frustration of many American minority group members who feel they have long been looked down upon by the early settlers and their descendants.

Ko Lum Bo

But suppose, as George Stewart once suggested, that the English and other North Europeans had not settled our eastern and southern shores first. Suppose that the approach had been from the west and that Asians, rather than Europeans, had landed and established political and cultural hegemony over the new territories. Stewart put it this way:

> During one of the vigorous and expansive periods of the Chinese Empire, one of their navigators (who might have been named Ko Lum Bo) conceived the idea of sailing eastward from China and thus arriving at Ireland, which was known to be the farthest outpost of Europe. The Chinese wished to reach Ireland it may be believed, because they had heard tales that those barbarous islanders made a certain drink called Wis Ki.
>
> Ko Lum Bo made his voyage, and discovered a country that he supposed to be part of Ireland, although he was disappointed in not finding any Wis Ki being manufactured by the natives.
>
> During the course of the next two centuries the Chinese colonized this country, eventually discovering it to be not Ireland, but a wholly new continent. Nevertheless they continued to call the natives Irish, or sometimes Red Irish.
>
> The Chinese colonists introduced their own well-established ways of life. They continued to speak Chinese, and to practice their own religion. Being accustomed to eat rice, they still ate it, as far as possible. Vast areas of the country were terraced and irrigated as rice paddies. The colonists continued to use their comfortable flowing garments, and pagodas dotted the landscape. In short, the civilization was Asiatic and not European.[1]

Dropping Stewart's delightful and pointed bit of social science fiction, we hardly have to remind ourselves that it was Christopher Columbus and other European explorers who first laid claim to the New World, bringing with them their ideas and values and rules from Spain and France and, especially, England to this continent. The English and other North Europeans who had the greatest impact on what would become the original states of the union came on their wooden barks carrying along much of their own cultural baggage, which, from the start, they thought superior to that of the natives. Manners of speaking and dressing, organizing communities, regulating commerce, teaching, and preaching were transplanted across the Atlantic. Of course, the New World (and, especially, the hinterlands of North America) was of a scale that was hard to comprehend.

As the new society developed, adjustments were constantly necessary. Innovations were commonplace. Even so, many aspects of the colonists' cultures were retained. And so, like the Chinese who never came (at least not in the manner imagined), the English and others who did developed modified versions of their old societies. And all who were here (meaning the diverse tribes of indigenous Americans) or were to come (including thousands of slaves and millions of immigrants), discussed in the preceding two chapters, were to be affected by the laws and life ways of the Anglo-American "Establishment."

In Search of a Dream

For more than four centuries America has served as a magnet—first for the rich and venturesome and later for the "tired and poor and tempest-tost."[2] As has been noted in previous chapters, the majority of immigrants—English, Irish, German, Scandinavian, Italian, Jewish, and Slav and, more recently, Latino and Asian—came of their own free will, ready and willing to share in the wealth and bounty of America.

Many were disillusioned; many suffered from discrimination by those who had so recently been newcomers themselves; many found it difficult to reconcile their Old World ways with those of the new.

Some expressed their frustration by profaning "The Discoverer" himself. In 1892, when the majority was enthusiastically celebrating 400 years since Columbus's "discovery," there were those who saw him and his exploits in very different terms—and said so. "A curse on Columbus," they said in Yiddish and Russian and Polish. Even in the language of his putative *paisani* it was sometimes said, "*Maladitu lamerica e chi la spirminta*"—"Curses on America ... and the man who thought it up."[3]

Those who recited such maledictions were hardly, like the critics of today, damning Columbus for his paving the way to conquests of new lands, the annihilation of hundreds of thousands of natives, and the subsequent "hegemonistic Eurocentricity" that would dominate the culture for centuries to come. They swore at the Genoese mercenary for less lofty reasons. In mock sorrow they deplored the fact that he ever found the place that was, to them, no shining medina where the streets were paved with gold, but instead urban jungles and, beyond them, a rugged, untamed, uncivilized wilderness. Their sarcastic epithets were spewed out in frustration rather than as true critiques.

In spite of the difficulties and disappointments—and there were many—and despite the divisions and conflicts between the various waves of newcomers and their "hosts," *for those who were white,* almost all things were to prove possible. The early dreams did become realities. As Raymond Aron, the French sociologist, accurately observed,

> As far as I am concerned, the greatest achievement of American society is to have drawn millions of people from the lower classes of Europe and made them into good American citizens. That is an extraordinary performance, an unprecedented marvel of acculturation.
>
> But you didn't do it without paying a heavy price. Poverty in America is aggravated by ethnic heterogeneity, by the unfinished acculturation of certain fragments of the American population. You have a permanently unintegrated fringe, consisting chiefly of Blacks and Puerto Ricans. You did very well in assimilating national minorities, but not nearly as well with racial minorities.[4]

There are various explanations of these facts of American life. One that is the simplest is quite persuasive. Those who proposed programs for the best way of integrating disparate peoples into a single nation did so generally without regard to color and yet rarely were "colored people" ever seriously considered on a par with white immigrants. The theorists and policy makers dealt with those they saw as "national" minorities, not racial ones—at least not until recently.

Ideas about Integration

The nature of adjustment of increasing numbers of immigrants to life in America has been of concern to both scholars and politicians since the early days of the colonial period. In the deliberations and debates over the problem of integrating ethnically heterogeneous peoples into a unified, English-speaking national group, various courses of action with explicit goals in mind have been promulgated. Three of the most discussed theories of adjustment have been popularly referred to as "Anglo conformity" (a term coined by George Stewart and Mildred Cole), "the melting pot," and "cultural pluralism."[5] In sociological terms, these social processes are *assimilation, amalgamation,* and *accommodation,* respectively.

Assimilation

During the eighteenth century the majority of those who had come to America— white, Anglo-Saxon, and mainly Protestant—participated in the establishment of what some have described as a truly new nation. The United States itself was conceived in the spirit of liberty and dedicated to the belief "that all men are cre- ated equal ... endowed by their Creator with certain inalienable Rights." However, the authors of these phrases shared the belief of many others that American social norms and values of the future lay within the framework of traditionally British social, religious, and cultural institutions; and, although America was sometimes envisaged as an asylum for Europe's refugees, some of the leading figures of the day had strong reservations about what the effects of unrestricted immigration might be. In *The Federalist Papers,* John Jay argued that the Americans were "a united people, a people descended from the same ancestors, speaking the same language, professing the same religion, attached to the same principles of govern- ment, very similar in their manners and customs."[6] As for those who didn't quite fit the profile, George Washington expressed the following view: "My opinion, with respect to immigration, is that except of useful mechanics and some particular descriptions of men or professions, there is no need of encouragement, while the policy or advantage of its taking place in a body (I mean the settling of them in a body) may be much questioned; for, by so doing, they retain the language, habits and principles (good or bad) which they bring with them."[7]

Most of those who thought an open-door policy should prevail emphatically maintained that the immigrants "should discard their foreign mantles" (an expres- sion referring to European attitudes and mannerisms) and quickly adapt themselves to *American* ways. John Adams made this position quite clear when he wrote, "They come to a life of independence, but to a life of labor—and, if they cannot accommodate themselves to the character, moral, political, and physical, of this country with all its compensating balances of good and evil, the Atlantic is always open to them to return to the land of their nativity and their fathers.... They must cast off the European skin, never to resume it."[8]

If the Founding Fathers had their ideas about the best course of national inte- gration, so, too, did many of the newcomers.[9] The immigrants often envisioned America as a vast land affording unlimited economic and social opportunities in an atmosphere free from harassment and interference. By the mid-nineteenth cen- tury many came to this country with clear intentions of maintaining their separate cultural identities. The Germans, for example, who settled in Wisconsin, Missouri, and Texas, succeeded in establishing a number of settlements where the German language was the vernacular and where German nationalism persisted, even though they had to modify many behavior patterns to adjust to the new frontier they faced.

According to historian Frederick Jackson Turner, assimilation itself was enhanced by the opportunities that abounded on the frontier. Writing especially about the settlement and acculturation of German immigrants, Turner stated,

> Our early history is the study of European germs developing in an American environment. Too exclusive attention has been paid by institutional students to the Germanic origins, too little to the American factors. The frontier is the line of most rapid and effective Americanization. The wilderness masters the colonist. It finds him a European in dress, industries, tools, modes of travel, and thought. It takes him from the railroad car and puts him in the birch canoe. It strips off the garments of civilization and arrays him in the hunting shirt and the moccasin. It puts him in the log cabin of the Cherokee and Iroquois and runs an Indian palisade around him. Before long he has gone to planting Indian corn and plowing with a sharp stick; he shouts the war cry and takes the scalp in orthodox fashion. In short, at the frontier the environment is at first too strong for the man. He must accept the conditions which it furnishes, or perish, and so he fits himself into the Indian clearings and follows the Indian trails. Little by little he transforms the wilderness but the outcome is not the old Europe, not simply the development of Germanic germs, any more than the first phenomenon was a case of reversion to the Germanic mark. The fact is that here is a new product that is American.[10]

Turner continued, making a second point: the farther west people traveled, the greater the influence of the frontier and the less the counter pulls of the Old Country. "Thus," he wrote, "the advance of the frontier has meant a steady movement away from the influence of Europe, a steady growth of independence on American lines."[11]

For many years westerners, especially Californians, made a corroborating point, claiming what is now popularly called "ethnicity" is much more an "Eastern" phenomenon than a "Western" one. Referring mainly to those of European origins, they would say that if you ask a New Yorker or Philadelphian or even a Chicagoan where he or she comes from, the answer would likely be "Ireland," "Russia," "Italy," "Poland," or perhaps, "England." But if you ask a person from Los Angeles or San Jose the same question, the reply is more apt to be "Kansas," "Oklahoma," or "back East." In recent decades, there has been a notable inversion of this tendency. Many second and third generation Americans with roots in Asia whose parents or grandparents first settled in Hawaii or on the West Coast and then moved east identify themselves as being Hawaiian or Californian though many whites persist in seeing them as foreigners.[12]

Still, on either coast and in many cities in between, even casual probing reveals the existence and persistence of strong cultural ties and the maintenance of many ethnic communities and neighborhoods. Such enclaves have long existed. They were evident even on the frontier itself. One thinks of those of the Scandinavians, rugged farmers and fishers idealized in Willa Cather's *O Pioneers,* Ole Rolvaag's *Giants in the Earth,* and in Vilhelm Moberg's trilogy *The Emigrants, Unto a Good*

Land, and *The Last Letter Home.* Although some settled in the Delaware Basin, most did not dally long on the East Coast but moved on to the prairies and woodlands of the northern Midwest, areas that became strongholds of Swedish and Norwegian culture and religion.[13] Their trek to the wilderness, first by wagon train, later by rail, was a lesson in adaptation but also a study in resistance to change as well. They attacked the frontier and shaped it; perhaps, some might say, more than it shaped them—reversing the variables in the Turner hypothesis. Isolation from the dominant drift of American social patterns permitted the widespread and long-lived retention of their "foreign" life ways, many of which continue to this day.

As indicated in Chapter Three, the Irish—and most of the other immigrants who came later—tended to concentrate in urban areas where it was more difficult to maintain a separate existence. Yet, the presence of these new immigrants in the same communities as the older Americans brought about a reevaluation of sentiments about assimilation. The newcomers, whose backgrounds differed even more radically than those of the Germans or Scandinavians from those of the early settlers, were often viewed as constituting a substantial threat to the established majority. Time and again, that Establishment asked, "Could *these* aliens ever become real Americans?"

Labor unrest and agitation attributed largely to the "foreign elements" in the population, the specter of Catholicism in Protestant America, and the growth of overcrowded urban slums inhabited by groups of oddly dressed people who seemed to speak in various forms of gibberish revived and reinforced anti-foreign attitudes. As a result of those developments, new movements arose to keep the United States "American."

First there was the anti-Irish Know-Nothing party of the pre–Civil War period. In the 1890s the American Protective Association was created to "save the country from the papacy." Later, anti-Semitic organizations arose, including the Ku Klux Klan (which was also violently anti-Negro) and other hate groups mirroring earlier nativist sentiment and the pronouncements of such prominent Americans as the novelist Kenneth Roberts, the industrialist Henry Ford, the aviator Charles Lindbergh, and the "radio priest" Father Charles Coughlin.[14]

Again, we should remember that it was in 1882 that the first restrictive legislation was passed to limit the flow of immigrants (in this case, Chinese laborers) to the United States. In the years that followed, increasing numbers of European nationals established ethnic communities where many Old World customs were perpetuated, and resentment grew against them as well. New organizations, such as the Immigration Restriction League, were established to "reform" immigration policies. Such groups and their growing cadres of allies were eventually successful in realizing their goals of sharply curtailing the influx of outsiders. But in the four decades between the beginning of the Great Atlantic Migration and the closing of the gates for all but a tiny number of would-be Americans by further restrictive legislation—the "Quote Acts" of 1921 and 1924—many felt something had to be done to come to address the more immediate problem of dealing with immigrants who were arriving at the rate of a million a year and whose political strength alone was very great. A new kind of assimilationist policy emerged to enforce more directly the adoption of American ways. This was the Americanization Movement, which, through propaganda and education, sought to break down the immigrants' ties to the past.

Here is how Henry Pratt Fairchild described the situation in 1926:

> It was perhaps in keeping with the interest and faith in education, which has been called the outstanding feature of the American nationality, that the task of Americanization should have presented itself to the pioneers in the movement primarily as an educational matter. Recognizing that the process of assimilation consists in the elimination of unlikeness, it was natural that in considering the unlikeness of the foreigner they should have been impressed with the difference in what he knew. It was perfectly clear that one of the great barriers that separated the native from the foreigner was the fact that the native knew certain things that the foreigner did not know. Prominent among these were the English language and United States civics and history. The first and most obvious step in Americanization, therefore, seemed to be to teach these things to the foreigner.
>
> Thereupon there was launched upon the country one of the most remarkable campaigns of intensive specialized education that the world has ever known. Every conceivable educational device was utilized. The land was flooded with lessons, lectures, and literature. Night schools and shop classes were organized. Rallies, pageants, and conferences were held. A special magazine was established and issued for a few numbers. An elaborate training course for workers among immigrants was planned and offered for adoption among colleges and universities. As the movement grew, and the needs of the immigrant woman as well as the immigrant man were recognized, classes were set up in millinery, dressmaking, diet, and the American care of babies. To these enterprises time, money, and personal service were contributed by men and women, professionals and volunteers, with a devotion and enthusiasm which could be enlisted only by loyalty to the nation in a time of stress and danger. Coming at any other time, when we were not accustomed to displays of self-sacrifice and public spirit, the Americanization movement would have been a striking exhibition of the operation of altruistic sentiments.[15]

Fairchild went on to describe the failure of the movement, which, in his eyes, was never clearly understood for it confused means with ends and its advocates never really appreciated the difficulties of altering character along with language instruction and history lessons. There was more to divesting oneself of "alien" ways than the protagonists, many of them vehemently xenophobic, could understand or effectively deal with.

Many advocates of such Americanization were not anti-foreign but were troubled by what they saw as the slowness of assimilation and the growing potential for conflicts, especially during the World War I period. They felt the need for a device to unite the people. Yet, whether anti-foreign or assimilationist, there was often the common view that every effort should be made to get newcomers to rid themselves of their old ways. The sentiment was summarized by one American who expressed the views of many nativists. "I am sure foreign people make a mistake in keeping customs of their own land alive and featured in this country. If this country meets their expectations they should forget the folklore of Europe, St. Patrick's Day

Parades, German Days, and get behind American things. If they can't do this they should be returned to the land they love. This country is supposed to be the world's melting pot. If they won't melt, they should not belong."[16]

This is, to be sure, a rather odd rendering of the melting pot expression, which, as shall be explained, referred to combining with rather than accepting the ways of others. But it is typical of the sentiment of those who saw their country being threatened and changed by outsiders. Similar expressions have been heard in recent years.[17]

Amalgamation

Although the idea of assimilation—or "Anglo conformity"—was prevalent through much of our history, there have been other views about the best way to achieve an integrated society. Some hoped to develop a society where the best traditions of the various nations would be blended into a dynamic unity. This conception of amalgamation was already established in the years immediately following the American Revolution and is clearly illustrated in comments of the French-born, naturalized American J. Hector St. John de Crévecoeur. In his 1782 *Letters from an American Farmer,* he described the new American as he saw him:

> He is either a European or the descendant of a European; hence, that strange mixture of blood, which you will find in no other country.... He is an American, who, leaving behind him all his ancient prejudices and manners, receives new ones from the new mode of life he has embraced, the new government he obeys, and the new rank he holds.... Here individuals of all nations are melted into a new race of men, whose labours and posterity will one day cause great changes in the world. Americans are the western pilgrims, who are carrying along with them the great mass of arts, sciences, vigor, and industry, which began long since in the east. They will finish the circle.[18]

The English writer Israel Zangwill expanded on Crévecoeur's idea to include persons from every corner of the globe. In a preface to his play, "The Melting Pot," dedicated to President Theodore Roosevelt, a vehement opponent of hyphenation, Zangwill wrote, "In respectful recognition of his strenuous struggle against the forces that threaten to shipwreck the great republic which carries mankind and its fortunes ... ," and then portrayed America as "God's Crucible":

> There she lies, the great melting pot—listen! Can't you hear the roaring and the bubbling? There gapes her mouth—the harbor where a thousand mammoth feeders come from the ends of the world to pour in their human freight. Ah, what a stirring and a seething—Celt and Latin, Slav and Teuton, Greek and Syrian, Black and yellow—... Jew and Gentile....[19]

The politician William Jennings Bryan echoed the sentiments of Zangwill. "Great has been the Greek, the Latin, the Slav, the Celt, the Teuton, and the Saxon; but greater than any of these is the American, who combines the virtues of them all."[20]

Summarizing the views of various writers many years later, sociologists Donald Light and Suzanne Keller indicated that both assimilation and amalgamation are more likely to be possible when "(1) the immigrants' appearance and customs resemble those of the dominant group, (2) they arrive in small numbers, (3) they are too far from their homeland to return for visits, and (4) they possess skills that the dominant group admire and need."[21]

The problem of immigrant adjustment often has been presented as an either/or proposition. The assimilationists argue that newcomers must become apostates from their old and established ways, "get behind American things," and reconcile themselves to the new and strange way of life of the host society. Those supporting the melting pot view feel that people should merge themselves through cultural fusion.

The first position presumes that by forcibly assimilating immigrants to a single, already established pattern, in time they would benefit from a way of life superior to that which they brought to America. But many newcomers, however eager they were to become Americans, were understandably reluctant to abandon their familiar ways, and many resisted the more draconic aspects of the Americanization campaign.

The melting pot philosophy, although far more democratic in intent, came to be seen by many keen observers as unrealistic. People were not about to simply mix together in the great crucible to form one new American type, the result of a blend of the cultural ingredients of Europe, Africa, and Asia. Recognition of these facts of social life encouraged the emergence of the idea of cultural pluralism.

Accommodation

As the sociologist Milton Gordon once suggested, "Cultural pluralism was a fact in American society before it became a theory—a theory with explicit relevance for the nation as a whole.[22] This theory developed into an image of the United States as a country enhanced by its diversity. Against the ideas of both absorption and fusion, advocates of pluralism saw America as "a multiplicity in a unity."[23] Jane Addams, John Dewey, and Randolph Bourne were among those who spoke out against the policy of "Americanization" and the destruction of traditional cultural values of immigrants. But no one more eloquently presented the case for cultural pluralism than the philosopher Horace Kallen. He likened the new society to a symphony orchestra:

> As in an orchestra, every type of instrument has its special timbre and tonality, found in its substances and form; as every type has its appropriate theme and melody in the whole symphony, so in society each ethnic group is the natural instrument, its spirit and culture are its theme and melody, and the harmony and dissonances and discords of them all make the symphony of civilization, with this difference: a musical symphony is written before it is played; in the symphony of civilization the playing is the writing, so that there is nothing so fixed and inevitable about its progressions as in music, so that within the limits set by nature they may vary at will, and the range and variety of the harmonies may become wider and richer and more beautiful.[24]

Advocates of cultural pluralism based their case on the assumption that there is strength in variety, that the nation as a whole benefits from the contributions of

different groups. Cultural pluralism involves giving and taking and, most importantly, the sharing of and mutual respect for other ideas, customs, and values. In
such terms America could be seen as a mosaic of ethnic groups, each retaining
many of its unique qualities while contributing to the overall pattern. Some were
later to want to replace the metaphor of a melting pot with that of a "salad bowl,"
where the various ingredients were still quite distinctive.

Kallen's pluralism was especially appealing to the immigrants from Eastern
and Southern Europe. At the time, others, including those in the small Asian communities and the growing Latino ones, seem to have paid it little mind. The same
was true of the far larger black community. For good reason. It was heavily biased,
"encapsulated," as historian John Higham put it, "in white ethnocentrism."[25]

Although generally sympathetic and frequently in league with supporters of
better treatment to those still called Negroes, few of the pluralists had had much
to say about the contribution of those from Africa, or, for that matter, from Asia or
Latin America, to the society they liked to characterize as "The New America." As
Bob Suzuki and Nicholas Appleton pointed out, when first proposed, "Pluralism
in the United States was concerned with liberty and equality [of European immi-
grants] and not with promoting the historic identities of non-English subcultures."[26]
The latter was not to come until the last decades of the twentieth century, when
"multiculturalism" became an alternate shibboleth, a slogan most enthusiastically
endorsed by nonwhite Americans and looked upon with considerable suspicion
by many others.

We now know that the acculturation and acceptance of the "national minorities"
to which Raymond Aron referred did occur, but not overnight. It was a slow and
uneven process, taking place mainly in the four decades between the mid-1920s
and the mid-1960s, a time when immigration from outside was almost at a standstill
and debates shifted from the rights of foreigners to the rights of Americans; a time
when the society underwent a series of dramatic political and economic reversals
as well: boom, bust, war, peace, prosperity, and the wrenching conflicts in Vietnam
and the streets of America. Affecting the speed of the integration were a number
of cultural, social, and situational factors, many related to these ups and downs.

Despite periodic resurgences of old prejudices and the implementation of new
ways of blocking entry to neighborhoods, jobs, and social institutions, and a number
of serious interethnic conflicts,[27] the majority of white ethnics did begin to move
from the margins into the mainstream. Especially after World War II, often abetted
by such entitlements for schooling and housing as the G.I. Bill for armed service
veterans, the *arrivistes* faced a world of expanding opportunities and took advantage
of them. Although some were left behind, increasing numbers moved to new homes
in new neighborhoods where they were to enjoy life as proud, patriotic Americans,
often defining themselves more in class terms rather than strictly ethnic ones.

One result of their "making it" was the loosening of many bonds to old communities. But, in most cases, the ties were rarely severed completely. Even in what
some saw as a twilight of [white] ethnicity,"[28] there was almost always a glow of
nostalgia and the retention of symbolic ties.[29] Perhaps a new, more accurate metaphor would be that of a "lumpy stew," which, like the salad idea, still has clearly

distinctive parts—in this instance, some sort of anthropomorphized chunks of meat, potatoes, carrots, and so forth—but also is held together by an ever thickening glutinous binder of common values and beliefs.

In the early part of the century, most of those who spoke for cultural pluralism emphasized the fact that ethnic groups ("nationalities," as they were often called) should have the right to remain separated, and Kallen, in an oft-quoted sentence, suggested that individuals who were born into such groups were inextricably bound to them. He said that "Men may change their clothes, their politics, their wives, their religions, their philosophies, to a greater or lesser extent, [but] they cannot change their grandfathers."[30]

Despite a considerable degree of adaptation to dominant patterns of life and the invention of new forms based on the fusion of ideas and practices, America remains in many ways what it has always been, a structurally pluralistic country, a nation of ethnic blocs whose members are joined by the labels they inherited; by the ties of kinship, social organization, and economic interest; and by the prides and prejudices of others. (Other variables—religion, class, region, and politics—are important too and need to be factored in along with ethnicity.)

Those "outsiders" who tend to be found enjoying the highest degrees of social integration are likely to be members of the academic community, or artists, writers, journalists, and entertainers and many of those in the professions and, increasingly, in business organizations. But although these are no longer strictly exceptional cases, what Gordon observed some fifty years ago, those contexts in which persons from different ethnic backgrounds interact in primary group relations with considerable frequency and with relative comfort and ease, although more common today, are still fairly rare.[31] For many Americans, perhaps the majority, closest social relations occur within what Gordon called the *ethclass,* defined as "that subsociety created by the interaction of the vertical stratification of ethnicity with the horizontal stratification of social class."[32] In simple terms this means, for example, that by and large, upper-class white, Anglo-Saxon Protestants (WASPs) still tend to associate at an intimate level with those who share their ethnicity and their social class position; and middle-class Jews, middle-class Italian Americans, working-class Polish Americans, poor whites, and poor blacks tend to socialize most often with people like themselves.[33] While Gordon's formulation makes a good deal of sense, data we have on patterns of interaction with those who are different indicate that they are often affected by educational and economic mobility as well as residual prejudices. Therefore, it might be better to modify Gordon's gridlike model, with the horizontal lines of social class staying the same but the vertical lines of ethnicity almost converging at the top, teepee-style. Thus, the most culturally specific traits remain far more salient than those in the lower levels of the socioeconomic hierarchies, while greater behavioral assimilation characterizes those who are able to move up the ladder. There is no question that those who start the climb with outlooks and behavioral patterns most like those of the members of the dominant group have an easier time adapting to their ways. For others, "moving up" often means consciously shedding traits, such as foreign accents or regional dialects, or even changing names to make themselves more acceptable in higher circles. This is an old pattern in the United States but one that still persists, as evidenced by the extent to which the second generations of new immigrants, like old ones, are often willing to eschew tradition to enhance mobility.

While there are parallels in nonwhite communities, especially African American ones, the stigma of color still serves as a handicap to jobs and opportunities that determine who gets to climb the ladder.

White Ethnics and Others

In the many discussions and debates about assimilation, amalgamation, and, especially, pluralism in American life, all sorts of racial, religious, and nationality groups are included in both the explanations of what has happened and in blueprints for the future. Yet proponents of each view often tended to deny or to overlook fundamental differences among and between "voluntary" immigrants, those who belong to the native populations whose lands were overrun, and, especially, the Africans who were forced to come and who now comprise close to 15 percent of the population.[34]

Many have argued—and, perhaps, wanted to believe—that blacks would take their place in the manner of the other "newcomers." Although it is patently naïve to refer to people whose ancestors came when only indigenous people and Pilgrims and other early European settlers populated the land as "newcomers," it is true that their urban experience is relatively recent and that the northward trek, made by so many African American men and women over the past hundred years, does represent an important migration.[35] There are many parallels. But even in such terms the analogy does not hold completely.

During the late nineteenth and early twentieth centuries, hope, a belief in the American Dream, and definite opportunities were important incentives for poor people from many lands. Overcoming various obstacles, many Irish, Italians, Polish Catholics, and East European Jews managed to make it, and in time found successful accommodation in the new environment. These "national minorities," as Aron had referred to them, did succeed in becoming "ordinary Americans," and, whatever others thought, saw themselves as such. As A. M. Rosenthal put it,

> Wherever our parents came from, whatever language we spoke at home, we reached for a common, overriding identity. Those born abroad, or to immigrants, understood that in part it was an identity given to us by the country. We took it with pleasure. When we sang "land where our fathers died" we knew it was not our fathers we were singing of but it was sure our country. Our teachers knew that. Everybody knew that.[36]

Well, not everybody. The descendants of the involuntary migrants from Africa who, in many ways, had long been quite ordinary Americans in manners and mores and religious practices were not so lucky. They remained marginalized. This reality has continued to affect not only relationships between black and white people—including the white ethnics—but also those many African Americans have had with people in other groups, including those who are frequently categorized as racial minorities themselves, like Japanese, Chinese, Koreans, Filipinos, Indians, Vietnamese, Cubans, Mexicans, and many others.

The fact of the matter is that opportunities for Europe's immigrants—even the desperately poor—were always far greater than those afforded nonwhite people and, especially, African Americans. Economist John Kenneth Galbraith is reported once to have quipped, "If you have to be poor, at least have the good sense to be born at a time when everybody is poor."[37] It should be noted that not only did black people enter the urban economy at the "wrong time" according to the Galbraith dictum but that, unlike the members of most other American minority groups, they did not have the same choices to inspire them nor did they have the same sorts of communal resources to fall back upon (as did many of the European immigrants).

"The Immigrant Advantage"

Despite periodic and sometimes prolonged episodes of strong anti-immigrant sentiments, immigrants—and not only those from Europe—did quite well in finding their places in this society. Sometimes it happened in the course of a single generation; more often it took two.

Today, there is considerable evidence that the largest group of recent immigrants, those from Mexico, have many traits that are similar to the eastern and southern Europeans who came 100 years ago and within two generations became a part of the mainstream. They, too, were mostly Catholic, poor laborers with little or no knowledge of the English language and often with little prior exposure to different cultures or different religions prior to their emigration. In many ways the Mexican immigrants' stories are quite similar to those of people who came in the years 1880–1920.

Mexicans, like many other Latinos, also tend to come from communities where there are strong supportive social and religious networks. A recent book by the journalist Claudia Kolker offers both anecdotal and hard evidence of what she calls a persisting "immigrant advantage." While the expression seems almost hyperbolic, Kolker points to several reasons that explain the seeming paradox of success in the face of tremendous barriers; namely, help, happiness, and hope.[38]

The help to which the author refers is not government assistance, but communal support, both familial- and community-based associations where immigrants assist others of their ilk to overcome hurdles, including economic ones. The happiness comes in large part from the strength of family relationships, many multi-generational. And both of those factors play a huge part in keeping kith and kin from despairing of their chances for social mobility. In addition to these three factors, there is one other that is crucial: *realism.*

Many voluntary immigrants, knowing that times will be difficult (although not always realizing how very hard they might be) generally have the fortitude of those called survivors. Motivated by the belief that their children's lives will be better than their own, they often become stalwart exemplars of fortitude. Taken together these four factors are essential ingredients in the social capital that is so important for success in American society. And it should not be surprising that recent immigrants and their children often try harder and work harder than many other Americans who have lived in the United States for generations.

Kolker notes something quite striking: Latino immigrants, even the poorest, tend to be healthier and live longer than non-native-born blacks or true native Americans. She also notes that data indicates that "West Indians, South Asians, East Asians and recently arrived Africans have the same edge."[39]

Maintaining pride in their own cultures and being attracted by the core spirit of the American Dream has made it possible for many *to realize aspects of all three approaches to integration.* There has been some assimilation, considerable amalgamation, and persisting accommodation. Those of immigrant background have long known they must learn the language and observe the laws of their new nation. And they have (and still do). Rubbing elbows with others and, just as important in recent decades, being exposed to a media that speaks to the spirit of the melting pot ideology have given many a fulsome sense of their contribution to a certain kind of plural society. At the same time, they are able—and even encouraged—to take pride in where they came from as well as in their new home.

Unique Americans

African Americans have had experiences quite different from any group of voluntary migrants, and this includes many non-Europeans whose people suffered considerable discrimination themselves over the years.

To say they are different opens a Pandora's box packed with practical, political, emotional, and theoretical implications. The long-held argument that African Americans could resolve their dilemma in the manner of other cases of "immigrant adjustment" assumed that their dilemma was the same. It isn't—and it never was.

Forty years ago sociologist Robert Blauner, one of the early opponents of the "Negro-as-Immigrant" school, wrote that

> The entrance of the European into the American order involved a degree of choice and self-direction that was for the most part denied people of color. Voluntary immigration made it more likely that individual Europeans and entire ethnic groups would identify with America and see the host culture as a positive opportunity rather than an alien and dominating value system. It is my assessment that this element of choice, though it can be overestimated and romanticized, must have been crucial in influencing the different careers and perspectives of [the] immigrants and colonized in America, because choice is a necessary condition for commitment to any group, from social club to national society.
>
> Sociologists interpreting race relations in the United States have rarely faced the full implications of these differences. The *immigrant model* became the main focus of analysis, and the experiences of all groups were viewed through its lens. It suited the cultural mythology to see everyone in America as an original immigrant, a later immigrant, a quasi-immigrant or a potential immigrant. Though the Black situation

long posed problems for this framework, recent developments have made it possible for scholars and ordinary citizens alike to force Afro-American realities into this comfortable schema. Migration from rural South to urban North became an analog of European immigration, Blacks became the latest newcomers to the cities, facing parallel problems of assimilation. In the no-nonsense language of Irving Kristol, "The Negro Today Is Like the Immigrant of Yesterday."[40]

But the fact is that the black-American experience is unique—it has no real parallel. Paradoxically, *African Americans may well be at once the least foreign and the most alienated of all our citizens*: least foreign because, ironically, having been cut off from their native roots, with notable exceptions, their principal guides were the slave masters and their agents; most alienated because of their special history, which began in subjugation, continued in segregation, and persists in many places to this day under the legacy of both.

This is not to say that no "Africanisms" survived. Of course they did. And with each passing year we are learning more and more of the linkages in "art, act, and artifact" as anthropologists and folklorists and historians make inroads into recapturing the murky, often suppressed, past. (In recent years, some African Americans have abandoned Christianity and accepted the polytheism of the traditional Yoruba religion; some have become Muslims; and many have maintained their connection to Christian churches while integrating some syncretistic practices and celebrations, such as the recently invented holiday of Kwanzaa.) Still, despite the revelations of rich cultural legacies deeply rooted in story and song and other expressions, the principal socialization experiences of most Africans whose ancestors were brought to America, for good or ill, included indoctrination into accepting the importance of many of the same norms, values, goals, and aspirations as those of the dominant group and the region where they found themselves. Many of what are often referred to as cultural traits were similar too.

Putting aside the somewhat different backgrounds and experiences of the many immigrants from Africa, the West Indies, and Latin America who were to enter the United States during the middle and late years of the last century, what most of those who were to become known as African Americans said and what they ate, what they believed, and, in some ways, the way they worshiped, were heavily "American," much of it southern in shape and form and expression. And so with their names. In these names one finds the true paradox of being both a part of and apart from this society.

Names are labels by which others know you. Most black people's names in the United States are those of whites, frequently those of those who held their ancestors in bondage. Because of this it is little wonder that one of the symbolic gestures in the search to assert both selfhood and peoplehood by young African Americans in the turbulent 1960s and 1970s was to cast off their "slave names" and to adopt African ones and, for some who converted to Islam, Islamic ones, or simply to call themselves "X."

For most of our history, African Americans, named Smith and Jones and Brown and Washington, also quested after the American Dream and sought to take their place with whites. In the terminology of integration processes: they were mainly assimilationists. Yet, for many, the venture proved quixotic. Some succeeded, however, and became African American equivalents of the white *nouveaux riches,* with all the material trappings to indicate having arrived. Other successful African Americans shunned such lifestyles but sought other benefits in the dominant society, especially through higher education and work in the professions. But even these "mainstreamers" often found that barriers remained; their rejection often heightened smoldering bitterness and exacerbated doubts about the rightness of seeking to integrate in the first place.[41]

The bourgeois blacks sometimes proved more akin to the Arabs in French Algeria than the Italians or Jews or Irish Americans with whom they were so often compared. As Raymond Aron points out, "The French never established an integrated society in Algeria. Ironically, the young Algerians who came closest to being French, by education and training, were usually the most hostile. But this is understandable, because they were the most sensitive to their rejection by the French ruling class."[42]

Persistent relegation to inferior status and the internalization of values regarded as most typically American (such as the idea of individual achievement through hard work) also led to a different sort of response on the part of many blacks compared to members of most other American ethnic groups. Some began to argue that the more they learned about the wider society and its members' unwillingness to honor its own lofty ideals, the less they should encourage their "brothers" and "sisters" to accept its basic tenets. Since whites appeared eager to maintain their position of dominance, some African Americans began saying that integration (again, read: assimilation) was, in fact, highly dysfunctional for them—just as it was for the indigenous people of Algeria.

These observations are not to suggest that all social scientists or policy makers who saw African Americans as the latest immigrants were or are white supremacists. But they may have been quite naïve in thinking that merely desegregating schools, opening neighborhoods, and saying, in effect, "You're as good as I am" would solve the problem. Assimilation may have been the goal at one time but it has been severely challenged (see Chapter Nine).

Many observers simply failed to comprehend the uniqueness of the African Americans' experiences and offered what in an earlier reference to immigrants was called an either/or response. In the context of the 1960s the argument often went like this: if black people are not to be segregated, they must be integrated. But "integration," as used in such a context, turned out to be little more than a liberalized and modernized version of "Anglo conformity." Ironically, the cultural pluralism that many wanted for others (and sometimes for themselves) was rarely even considered as a model for blacks, the people who by all counts would benefit most by accepting their uniqueness.

Until recently many liberal integrationists in the universities, in the government, and even in the civil rights movement itself saw but one side of the problem. They recognized but failed to understand the subculture that had grown out of reactions to barriers erected by whites during and after slavery. To those who wanted a fairer deal at the hands of the society, they were invariably told, "Throw off your unacceptable ways and become like me." James Farmer, the founder of the Congress of Racial Equality (CORE), once put this point of view in very clear perspective. Writing on this type of integration, he said,

> We [blacks] learned that America simply couldn't be color-blind, it would have to become color-blind and it would only become color-blind when we gave up our color. The white man, who presumably has no color, would have to give up only his prejudices. We would have to give up our identities. Thus, we would usher in the Great Day with an act of complete self-denial and self-abasement. We would achieve equality by conceding racism's charge: that our skins were afflicted; that our history is one long humiliation; that we are empty of distinctive traditions and any legitimate source of pride. . . .[43]

This interpretation was very difficult for many white Americans to accept for they saw little advantage in encouraging blacks to retain behavior patterns that they frequently defined as unproductive or dysfunctional deviations from those considered "standards." Robert Blauner called this stance a part of the "dogma of liberal social science," which reflects in large measure general liberal sentiments.

The argument—or "dogma"—is evident in many places and sources. It was first most clearly articulated in the monumental study *An American Dilemma,* in which Gunnar Myrdal and his colleagues asserted that "the Negro is an exaggerated American" and that his principal values are "pathological elaborations" of those commonly shared.[44] Historian Kenneth Stampp referred to those who were "white men with black skins."[45] Nathan Glazer and Daniel Patrick Moynihan, in the first edition of *Beyond the Melting Pot,* a study of New York City's ethnic groups, asserted, "the Negro is only an American and nothing else. He has no values and culture to guard and protect."[46] (Glazer and Moynihan were to modify this position in a later edition.[47])

These ideas were put forth by others, too, many of them relying in no small measure on the work of E. Franklin Frazier, one of America's best-known black sociologists. For example, here is what Frazier wrote in his 1957 revision of *The Negro in the United States*:

> Although the Negro is distinguished from other minorities by his physical characteristics, unlike other racial or cultural minorities the Negro is not distinguished by culture from the dominant group. Having completely lost his ancestral culture, he speaks the same language, practices the same religion, and accepts the same values and political ideals as the dominant group. Consequently, when one speaks of Negro culture in the United States, one can only refer to the folk culture of the rural southern Negro or the traditional forms of behavior and values which have grown out of the Negro's social and mental isolation. . . .[48]

Frazier went on to say, "Since the institutions, the social stratification, and the culture of the Negro minority are essentially the same as those of the larger community, it is not strange that the Negro minority belongs among assimilationist rather than the pluralist, secessionist, or militant minorities."[49] Yet, even at the time

he was writing, others within the black community and outside it were already raising questions about his analysis. Within a few decades, African Americans would
prove to be as vigorous in the support of pluralism as any members of white ethnic
groups, including white southerners, the latter often described by sociologist Lewis
M. Killian as an ethnic group and quasi-minority themselves.[50]

Frazier, along with many commentators on "The Black Experience," assumed
that to have a culture, a unique culture, one must possess a distinctive language, a
unique religion, and a national homeland. In his critique, Robert Blauner suggested
that although such a view may be appropriate for what anthropologists would call a
holistic culture, complete with the institutions of an integrated social system, African
Americans did not possess this kind of culture. Rather, they developed their own
ways of life and sensitivities, often combinations of African remnants and southern
Protestant characteristics developed through encounters with racist America.

African American writers such as Zora Neale Hurston, Countee Cullen, Langston
Hughes, Richard Wright, LeRoi Jones, and Ralph Ellison—and, more recently,
Cornel West, bell hooks, Ellis Cose, Toni Morrison, Shelby Steele, Henry Louis
Gates Jr., and Derek Bell—in quite different ways have each portrayed the extent
to which African Americans have had to respond to the "either/or" interpretation.
For example, in his brilliant novel *Invisible Man,* Ellison wrote,

> I am an invisible man. No, I am not a spook like those who haunted Edgar Allan Poe;
> nor am I one of your Hollywood ectoplasms. I am a man of substance, of flesh and
> bone, fiber and liquids, and I might even be said to possess a mind. I am invisible,
> understand, simply because people refuse to see me. Like the bodiless heads you see
> sometimes in circus sideshows, it is as though I have been surrounded by mirrors
> of hard distorting glass. When they approach me they see only my surroundings,
> themselves, or figments of their imagination—indeed, everything and anything except
> me. Nor is my invisibility exactly a matter of biochemical accident to my epidermis.
> That invisibility to which I refer occurs because of a peculiar disposition of the eyes
> of those with whom I come into contact. A matter of construction of their inner eyes,
> those eyes with which they look through their physical eyes upon reality.[51]

In contrast to most whites, most African Americans have long found themselves
in a perpetual state of cultural schizophrenia. They have had to deal with what
W. E. B. Du Bois called a sense of "twoness." "One ever feels his twoness," he
wrote, "an American, a Negro; two souls, two thoughts, two unreconciled strivings;
two warring ideals in one dark body."[52]

Vernon Dixon once argued, "the application of the 'either/or' conceptual approach to race relations produces racial harmony [only] when the blacks and whites
embody total sameness."[53] And this is an impossibility. Therefore, Dixon proposed
a new and different approach, called by the rather cumbersome term "di-unitalism,"
in which one simultaneously recognizes the similarities and differences between
blacks and whites. Above all, the analyst (and, presumably, the policy maker) would
have to learn to understand the ambiguity that marks the social position and often
helps shape the personalities of African Americans.[54]

The Motif of Diversity

Increasing numbers of African Americans claimed that they ought not to be defined simply by their color but that they too were members of an ethnic group. Such an assertion had an interesting side effect. It strengthened the general ideology of pluralism and fed the politics of identity.

Responding to the demands of Black Power advocates, and, as importantly, using their tactics of raising group consciousness, many white, Asian, and Latino "ethnics" sought to rediscover their own roots and assert their strength as united forces. Although this phenomenon is further discussed in Chapter Nine, for now it is to be noted that, in principle at least, the doctrine of cultural pluralism—and several variations on it—has come to pervade the conventional wisdom concerning intergroup relations in the United States.

Beginning in the 1970s, the "nation of nations" idea was extolled by public officials, educators, and religious leaders. School children were told that every group member has the right voluntarily—not by will of the majority—to retain (or to give up) his or her separate identity, and that although people should be judged as individuals, one must recognize the significance of membership in an ethnic, racial, or religious group. Some went further, asserting that groups—at least "minorities"—themselves have rights.

The phrase "affirmative action" was one of the first new expressions that signaled the official recognition of such group-based policy. From its inception as a means of addressing certain grievances such recognition stirred considerable debate among many thoughtful and troubled Americans, especially at the end of the twentieth century. It continues to be a source of controversy.

Behavioral Assimilation and Social Separation

In the United States many people of varied backgrounds have turned the traits of minorities into all-American phenomena.[55] Well-known examples include such linguistic adaptations as "moccasin," "faux pas," "kibbitz," and "Gesundheit"; and such ethnic dishes as pizza, bagels, "Danish" pastry (known in Denmark as *Wiener Brot* or Vienna bread), and "sacramental" wine; as well as such social activities as Latin American dances, "soul" music, the games of mah-jongg and chess; and the sports of judo, lacrosse, soccer, and jai alai.

Generally, however, the cultural patterns of the dominant groups have been impressed upon and adopted by members of racial and ethnic minorities. They have accepted as their own, patterns of living, dress, and speech—much in the way that Washington, Jay, and John Adams had hoped would be the case. Constantly exposed to the dominating modes of life of the majority group, it is not surprising that minority group members accommodate themselves to expected behavior patterns. Milton Gordon calls this "behavioral assimilation."

Yet, it must be stressed that taking over dominant group behavior patterns does not necessarily lead to a substantial amount of social interaction on a close, personal basis between members of the established majority and minority group members. Instead, behavioral assimilation is limited to such general norms as a common respect for law and order, acceptance of modes of employer-employee relationships, conformity to styles and fashion touted by the mass media, and widespread use of the symbols of success as nurtured by advertisers. It is less apt to be found in intimate personal relations.

The more personal the nature of a potential situation for social interaction, the greater are the barriers to primary and intimate intergroup participation. Here, once again, Gordon's notion of the *ethclass* is important. Since, as he points out, most close social interaction takes place where social class and ethnicity intersect, it is not surprising that movement in either direction—vertically (up and down the social ladder) and horizontally (from one ethnic category to another)—may present difficulties. Some of the problems are related to normative patterns of what is appropriate behavior with whom; some are related to manners of dress, speech, and other attributes that are class-bound and, often, culturally specific. Of course it is always possible to change one's apparel, learn new ways of speaking, and take on the characteristics of the trendsetters or upper classes. Such adaptation is not unlike the "Anglo-conformity" referred to earlier as a form of behavioral assimilation. But it is not the whole story.

Being able to dress, talk, and act like those in the dominant group does not necessarily carry over into social interaction. Social distances are frequently maintained even as cultural barriers fall. Despite the outward manifestations of acceptance and a high degree of behavioral assimilation, various minorities have been—and are—excluded from social cliques, informal groups, and even such communal activities as religious services and leisure time pursuits. In the not so distant past, Jewish-Gentile relations in a number of American cities were quite clearly circumscribed. There was very limited informal social mixing between Jews and Christians.[56] Even among Christians themselves for a long time there were similar patterns of separation between Protestants and Catholics.[57] Although neither situation characterizes most relations between Jews and Christians (at least white Christians) or Protestants and Catholics (at least white ones) today, such "interpersonal distancing" is still evident in terms of white and nonwhite interaction, particularly at the most intimate of levels.

It is evident that the structural definitions of social situations as formal or informal, secondary or primary, are relevant cues to the levels at which behavioral assimilation breaks down and social separation is required and maintained. It should be noted, once again, that the actual levels of acceptance or tolerance vary markedly; that the behavior of those in "dominant groups" is far from uniform; and that within all minorities differential modes of reaction to rejection and discrimination prevail.

Of course, not all members of minority groups wish to have close relationships with others who differ from them culturally. The desire to maintain social distance is most clearly evident among members of certain religious groups—such as Mennonites, Islamic fundamentalists, and Hasidic Jews—who, in order to retain their systems of belief intact without threat of exposure to, or enticement from, the members of other faiths, avoid almost all intergroup activities. Similarly, certain cultural traditions may be thought to be threatened by the overpowering influence of a cordial host society. Solomon Poll's description of the Hasidim of Williamsburg, Brooklyn, provides an illustration of social separation: "Resistance to Americanization is such that although there is no physical wall to isolate them, a strong "sociological wall" separates this group from activities that might encroach on its cultural stability. All the institutions, including the economic activities of the group, are such that they are conducive to a Hasidic 'way of life.'"[58] Yet, such intensive resistance to general Americanization and to opportunities to develop and maintain relationships on the basis of personal considerations rather than ethnic status is not the prevailing mode. In fact, most members of minority groups welcome opportunities for greater acceptance in the wider society. Those holding such views still include many African Americans, despite the growing pride in self and community referred to previously. Many would be pleased not to always be judged as ambassadors or exemplars of whatever group they happened to belong to.

Studies of social distance long have shown that such individual recognition is more possible in certain realms of social life than in others. Even within these spheres, minority groups and their members are ranked according to various criteria of acceptability. As suggested earlier, notable cases include those in the academic world, the arts, entertainment, sports, the "demi-world," and the underworld.

Nevertheless, away from the academy, the ballpark, the arena, or the theater, where people are patrons or spectators or engage in a certain amount of risk-taking, many are unable to be exempted and unable to bridge the status gap. They turn instead to traditional occupations, select friends from within their own groups, withdraw into the minority community, and resign themselves to lives in which their status as members of minority groups becomes of utmost importance, whether they wish it or not. And where the gap between the dominant and minority group is great, social inbreeding within the minority community heightens group cohesion and simultaneously reinforces the image of clannishness. There are variations, but the general and pervasive pattern is one of behavioral assimilation and social separation, or what Milton Gordon calls "structural pluralism."

America's People Today

The United States remains a nation of identifiable and often separable racial, religious, and ethnic groupings. Some of this is closely correlated with nations of origin, which in themselves indicate a great deal about the composition of the polity and recent dramatic demographic shifts. For example, until 1960 the vast majority of immigrants to the United States listed a European nation as their country of origin. Since then, Mexico has been number one. According to the most recent decennial census, the top ten countries of origin are all in Latin America or Asia, with Mexico followed by China, India, the Philippines, Vietnam, El Salvador, Cuba, Korea, the Dominican Republic, and Guatemala. (Canada and the United Kingdom were eleventh and twelfth on the list.)[59]

Information regarding the racial and religious composition and, as noted at the end of the last chapter, the national origin of the population is also readily available in the periodic reports of the US Census Bureau and other sources. This kind of information, however, should be understood in the context of the methods used to gather information. Equally important is to note that definitions of "race" (consider the changing demands of South Asians and the reactions of Hispanics to the assignment of "racial" categories), "creed," and "ethnicity" each present different problems for both data gatherers and analysts.

Racial designation, for example, has long been assessed on the basis of information that "cannot be hidden from the enumerator, about which [he] can make assumptions without serious error, and about which people will be willing to furnish information."[60] Until 1960 this meant that the census-taker was the ultimate judge of a given respondent's "race" and, as a result, statistics often reflect their biases rather than the preferred identities of respondents. (Since 1960 self-classification has been the method of defining both race and ethnic affiliation, probably resulting in greater accuracy than in earlier censuses.)

"Racial" Groups in the United States

The extent to which the social definition of "race" (referred to in Chapter One) has long affected the ultimate percentages given for the population is indicated in the description of the category of "Negroes" or "blacks." For many decades the US Census Bureau claimed that besides persons of mixed Negro and white descent, the category includes those of mixed American Indian and Negro descent, "unless the Indian ancestry very definitely predominates or unless the individual is regarded as an Indian in the community."[61] To the present day, although "white" and "black" (however loosely the terms may be defined) are set aside as separate and distinct groupings, others are categorized by a combination of color and/or place of ancestral origin. In the 2010 census, included among the "Other Races" options were American Indians, Japanese, Chinese, and Filipinos; under the heading "All Others" were grouped Aleut, Asian Indian, Eskimo or Inuit, Hawaiian, Korean, Indonesian, Polynesian, and "other races not shown separately."[62]

Census Bureau studies show that, compared with the last decennial enumeration, there has been a sharp increase in the proportional representation of those who identified themselves as Hispanics, and projections to the year 2020 indicate an even steeper climb in the statistics of this multigroup cohort.[63] At the time of the last decennial census, five of every ten African Americans in the country were found to be residing in the South. (In recent years, the number moving to the South surpassed the number of blacks moving out of the South.) Even more dramatic has been the increase of African Americans in the overall percentage of city residents. An increase in the percentage of whites moving from these same inner-city areas to the suburbs has also been noted, thereby increasing the ratio of blacks to whites rather markedly, especially in certain centers. In addition to Washington, DC, a city that was 71 percent black by 1970,[64] Newark, Gary, Atlanta, Cleveland, and Detroit all had African American majorities by the end of that decade and the trend has continued well into the new century.

In contrast to the situation of blacks, members of other nonwhite groups are most heavily concentrated west of the Mississippi; seven of every ten members of this category—the majority Latino or Asian—live in the western states, eight of ten in the coastal area. The only states with a substantial proportion of residents who are neither black nor white are Alaska (20 percent—mainly Aleuts, Eskimos, and Indians) and Hawaii (67 percent—mainly Japanese and Chinese).

Religious Groups in the United States

In American society the freedom to worship in one's own way—or not to worship at all—is a fundamental guarantee of the Bill of Rights. There is a proliferation of religious organizations, ranging in structure from the highly bureaucratized Roman Catholic Church to transitory and loosely organized storefront Protestant churches. Some religious groups are basically fundamentalist; others are more liberal in their interpretations of sacred writings and theology.

Despite this diversity in organization and religious perspective (and despite the proclivity of some Americans to search for new avenues to express religious feelings, as in the appeal of Hare Krishna, Zen Buddhism, Scientology, and the aforementioned Yoruba religion, none of which follow orthodox Western religious traditions), Americans have long been a church-going people and still score higher on measures of "religiosity" than any other industrialized nation in the world.

Long ago, sociologists of religion suggested that, although the old "melting pot" idea was not ever going to accurately characterize American society, the notion of a "triple melting pot" might. They meant that Americans could increasingly be seen and, presumably see themselves, as Protestant or Catholic or Jewish, rather than as members of particular nationality groups, such as Irish Catholic.[65] Many accepted the idea, observing a tendency of third- and fourth-generation "ethnics" to act more and more like members of the social classes in which they find themselves or toward which they aspire although still retaining nominal affiliations with the churches in which they were raised. However, the trend suggested by Ruby Jo Kennedy and Herberg might have been prematurely predicted. First of all, as Gerhard Lenski pointed out in *The Religious Factor,* a report on a study of Detroit conducted as far back as the 1950s, there were at least four groups: Catholics, Jews, white Protestants, and black Protestants.[66] Lenski's work was followed by a series of studies by Andrew Greeley, which suggested that Catholics were not so ready to slough off their ethnic identities and cease being Irish Catholics, Polish Catholics, or Italian Catholics,[67] though many began to do so with increasing frequency in the latter part of the twentieth century and the beginning of the twenty-first when "intermarriage" of partners from different religious traditions became more and more common.

To complicate matters, the commitment of many Americans to the basic tenets of their faiths became more and more vague starting in the 1960s, a period of considerable upheaval in this country and abroad. In the early 1960s religious principles underscored many of the activities of activists who challenged the status quo, especially in the area of civil rights. Most of the leaders came from clerical backgrounds, and many of their organizations were explicitly identified with religious bodies such as the Southern Christian Leadership Conference. Yet, the rising tide of Black Consciousness led simultaneously to a sense of failure on the part of many traditional religious liberals and a resurgence of ideas of separatism. The "roots phenomenon," as we shall see, slowed the trend toward integration in certain circles while bringing about a revival of ethnic pride, including a pride in older traditions and beliefs.

Late in that same decade a second disillusionment, this one over the failure to effect marked changes in the general social system, resulted in a new quest, a quest for meaning. Many young people left the radical political movement for new religious organizations, including the "Campus Crusade for Christ," the Unified Christian Church ("Moonies"), "Jews for Jesus," and similar bodies. Within the traditional churches a new spiritualism was also evident, and new practices involving much more active participation of congregants (as in "charismatic Christianity") attracted many who came to observe and stayed on to enjoy the warmth that they felt now pervaded the sanctuaries.

The next three decades were marked by a steady increase in church participation as well as membership and, by the millennium, more Americans belonged to religious organizations than ever before. But, to many observers, it was the attack on the United States by Islamic terrorists in September 2001 that opened a new chapter in an age old struggle between the forces of good and the forces of evil. Often couched in religious rhetoric, it was "a twenty-first-century crusade" with each side calling the other "infidel." The vast majority of Americans backed President George W. Bush in his military campaign against the Taliban in Afghanistan and, at least in the beginning, also supported his preemptive strike against Iraq. Although, in the latter case, the rationale was to rid the country of weapons of mass destruction, it soon turned into what many saw as a holy war.

During that same period, it became more and more common to hear open discussion of faith, particularly of Christian faith, in public forums across the country. Members of groups that collectively were labeled as the "religious right" fired up renewed debates—not the least of which were over the teaching of creationism or "intelligent design" as a counter to evolutionary theory, urging a return to prayer in school, advocating the promotion of faith-based initiatives and government grants to religious institutions, opposing initiatives to remove the words "under God"—introduced during the Eisenhower administration—from the Pledge of Allegiance, supporting the public display of clearly religious objects and iconic symbols like the Ten Commandments—and moved with increasing boldness into the political arena itself.

Candidates for local and state offices wore their religious preferences on their sleeves, urging fellow believers to join them in battling the sinners who opposed them. This was most dramatically evident in the second campaign of the "born again" George W. Bush. Many pundits argued that "value issues," often stated in religious terms, were a determining factor in his second presidential-election victory.

At the same time this sort of evangelical fervor was sweeping the country, particularly in those states that were solidly Republican, a growing sex scandal was challenging the power of priests and bishops in the Roman Catholic Church. Although some left the church for other denominations, many more stayed the course though not without embarrassment or self-criticism.

Will Herberg once suggested that ours is a nation ever caught in a paradox of "pervasive secularism and mounting religiosity."[68] This had become more evident in recent years as greater and greater expressions of profanity, unabashed sexuality, and violent action were expressed in theaters and on television. Many Americans were shocked and many fundamentalists saw these trends as the work of the devil incarnate, often conflated into a single boogie man—the liberal, free-thinking, cosmopolitan atheist—who was seeking to corrupt God-fearing, law-abiding Americans.

In fact, although those who rejected the rigidity of the religiously conservative and so-called "true believers" were often liberal, freethinking, and cosmopolitan, only a few of them were atheists. Most Americans continued to belong to religious organizations and to proclaim some sort of faith.

According to surveys conducted by sociologists at the Graduate Center of the City University of New York in 2001, nearly 210,000,000 American adults claimed identification with some religious body. The largest single group was then and remains Roman Catholic, with nearly 160,000,000 members. Next is a broad array of people in various Protestant denominations, beginning with fifty million Baptists, fourteen million Methodists, and an equal number who simply called themselves "Christians." In addition there are nearly ten million Lutherans, 5,500,000 Presbyterians, and 4,500,000 "Protestants," who also didn't specify a denomination but, given shifts in self-identification, may be more liberal members of that group that now say they are "Christians." There are some four million Pentecostalists, 3,500,000 Episcopalians, and nearly three million Mormons. And these are just the largest groups. There are many other Christian groupings, as well as a far smaller number of minority religions and sects; Jews comprise close to 2 percent of the population and Muslims, Buddhists, Hindus, and even Spiritualists, Wiccans, Druids, and others collectively account for less than 1 percent.

Ethnic Groups in the United States

The distinctions between the major religious denominations in America are fairly well defined, and membership statistics are not difficult to obtain. Racial breakdowns, although open to many questions about the precise definitions of particular racial aggregates (which are usually quite arbitrary) are likewise available, but accurate data on ethnic group membership and identification are far more elusive. As noted in Chapter One, ethnic divisions include various kinds of groupings: people with common national backgrounds, those whose racial designation places them in a special category with which they are identified by others—and often then identify themselves, and those whose group identity may transcend both racial and national boundaries. The complexity of the problem of ethnic classification is illustrated by such facts as the following: Jews are both a religious and cultural minority; the descendants of Irish, Italian, and Polish immigrants are predominantly Roman

Catholic, but they also are members of particular nationality groups—and they are white; Puerto Ricans, mainly Catholic, sometimes considered to be black, bring distinctive cultural and linguistic patterns from Puerto Rico to the mainland; African Americans are often lumped together with other black Americans, especially those from the West Indies. Many such people may share common appearances (especially in terms of social definitions of race) but have decidedly different cultural backgrounds—and, in turn, are often disturbed by being called "African American" themselves. (This is also true of some recent immigrants from Africa, especially from Ethiopia, Nigeria, or Ghana, and refugees from Somalia, who have been known to distinguish themselves from the majority of "blacks" in this country by saying they are "African African-Americans.")

Enclaves of ethnic groups are most prominent today among people recently arrived from Puerto Rico and the Dominican Republic, China and South Korea, Cuba and Haiti, Vietnam and Cambodia, India and Pakistan, Somalia and Ethiopia, and Mexico, a pattern that recapitulates what existed a century ago when the newcomers were mostly from Europe. And even for those of European background, many third- and fourth-generation Americans continue to retain a strong sense of identification with the country from which grandparents or great-grandparents migrated. Survey researchers find that most people, despite a growing trend toward intermarriage and the increasing numbers of people who identify themselves as "biracial," often still make a single selection when asked to indicate with which of the larger known ethnic groups in the community they identify themselves.

Notes

1. George Stewart, *American Ways of Life* (Garden City, NY: Doubleday, 1954), pp. 11–12.

2. From the poem, "The New Colossus," by Emma Lazarus, inscribed at the base of the Statue of Liberty, 1892.

3. As quoted in Jerre Mangione and Ben Morreale, *La Storia: Five Centuries of the Italian American Experience* (New York: HarperCollins, 1992), p. xiii.

4. As quoted in Milton Vorst, "Talk with a Reasonable Man," *New York Times Magazine* (April 19, 1970), p. 96. See also Candace Nelson and Marta Tienda, "The Structuring of the Hispanic Ethnicity," in Richard D. Alba (ed.), *Ethnicity and Race in the USA* (New York: Routledge, 1988), pp. 49–74.

5. See, for example, Milton M. Gordon, "Assimilation in America: Theory and Reality," *Daedalus,* 90 (Spring 1961), pp. 263–285.

6. As quoted in Richard Shenkman, *Legends, Lies and Cherished Myths of American History* (New York: Harper and Row, 1989), p. 108.

7. W. C. Ford (collector and ed.), *The Writings of George Washington* (New York: Putnam, 1889), Vol. XII, p. 489. This quotation is discussed in greater detail by Milton M. Gordon, op. cit., pp. 266–267.

8. This letter was published in *Nile's Weekly Register,* 18 (1820), pp. 157–158. See the discussion in Marcus L. Hansen, *The Atlantic Migration, 1607–1860* (Cambridge: Harvard University Press, 1940), pp. 96–97.

9. See Nathan Glazer, "Ethnic Groups in America: From National Culture to Ideology," in M. Berger, T. Abel, and C. H. Page (eds.), *Freedom and Control in Modern Society* (Princeton, NJ: Van Nostrand, 1954), p. 163.

10. Frederick Jackson Turner, *The Frontier in American History* (New York: Henry Holt, 1920), pp. 3–4.

11. Ibid.

12. See Ronald Takaki, *Strangers from a Different Shore* (Boston: Little, Brown, 1989), p. 3.

13. See Dorothy Burton Skordal, *The Divided Heart: Scandinavian Experience Through Literary Sources* (Oslo: Universitetsforlaget, 1974).

14. For a detailed discussion of nativism, see S. M. Lipset and Earl Raab, *The Politics of Unreason* (New York: Harper and Row, 1970).

15. Henry Pratt Fairchild, *The Melting Pot Mistake* (Boston: Little, Brown, 1926), pp. 158–159.

16. This is the comment of a lifelong resident of a small town in upstate New York. See Peter I. Rose, "Small-Town Jews and Their Neighbours in the United States," *Jewish Journal of Sociology* (England), 3 (December 1961), p. 187.

17. See Peter Brimelow, *Alien Nation: Common Sense about American Immigration* (New York: Random House, 1995). See also Samuel P. Huntington, *Who Are We? The Challenges to America's National Identity* (New York: Simon and Schuster, 2004).

18. J. Hector St. John de Crévecoeur, *Letters from an American Farmer* (New York: Albert and Charles Boni, 1925), pp. 54–55; originally published in London, 1782. For a critical commentary, see Marcus Cunliffe, "Crévecoeur Revisited," *Journal of American Studies,* 9 (August 1975), pp. 129–144.

19. Israel Zangwill, *The Melting Pot* (New York: The Jewish Publication Society of America, 1909), pp. 198–199.

20. As quoted in Robert E. Park and Ernest W. Burgess, *Introduction to the Science of Sociology* (Chicago: University of Chicago Press, 1924), p. 734.

21. Donald Light Jr. and Suzanne Keller, *Sociology* (New York: Knopf, 1975), p. 241. See also W. Lloyd Warner and Leo Srole, *The Social Systems of American Ethnic Groups* (New Haven: Yale University Press, 1945); and Ronald J. Silver, "Structure and Values in the Explanation of Acculturation Rates," *British Journal of Sociology,* 126 (March 1965), pp. 68–79.

22. Gordon, op. cit., pp. 274–275.

23. Horace M. Kallen, "Democracy versus the Melting-Pot," *The Nation,* 100 (February 18, 1915), pp. 190–194, and (February 25, 1915), pp. 217–220; see also Horace M. Kallen, *Cultural Pluralism and the American Idea* (Philadelphia: University of Pennsylvania Press, 1956).

24. Kallen, "Democracy versus the Melting-Pot" (February 25, 1915), p. 220.

25. John Higham, *Send These to Me* (New York: Atheneum, 1975), p. 208.

26. Nicholas Appleton, *Cultural Pluralism in Education* (New York: Longman, 1993), p. 3.

27. See, for example, Ronald H. Bayor, *Neighbors in Conflict: The Irish, Germans, Jews, and Italians of New York City, 1929–1941* (Baltimore, MD: Johns Hopkins University Press, 1978).

28. See Richard D. Alba, *Italian Americans: Into the Twilight of Ethnicity* (Englewood Cliffs, NJ: Prentice Hall, 1985).

29. Herbert M. Gans, "Symbolic Ethnicity: The Future of Ethnic Groups and Cultures in America," *Ethnic and Racial Studies,* 2:1 (January 1979). See also Stephen Steinberg, *The Ethnic Myth,* rev. ed. (Boston: Beacon Press, 1989), esp. pp. 44–74 passim.

30. Kallen, op. cit.

31. Gordon, op. cit., pp. 279–285. See also Gordon, "Social Structure and Group Relations," in Berger, Abel, and Page, *Freedom and Control in Modern Society,* pp. 141–157.

32. Milton M. Gordon, *Assimilation in American Life* (New York: Oxford University Press, 1964), pp. 51ff.

33. For a novelist's view of the "ethclass" phenomenon, see Tom Wolfe, *Bonfire of the Vanities* (New York: Farrar, Straus and Giroux, 1988). Also see the author's review of *Bonfire of the Vanities,* Peter I. Rose, "The Real McCoy?," *Congress Monthly,* 55:4 (May/June 1988), pp. 20–22.

34. See L. Paul Metzger, "American Sociology and Black Assimilation: Connecting Perspectives," *American Journal of Sociology,* 76 (1971), pp. 627–647. See also Harry H. Bash, *Sociology, Race, and Ethnicity* (New York: Gordon and Breach, 1979); and Stanford M. Lyman, *The Black American in Sociological Thought* (New York: Capricorn Books, 1972).

35. See the latest in a series of studies of the migration, Nicholas Lemann, *The Promised Land: The Great Black Migration and How It Changed America* (New York: Knopf, 1991).

36. A. M. Rosenthal, "The Lucky Americans," *New York Times* (December 8, 1992).

37. As quoted in Charles Silberman, *Crisis in Black and White* (New York: Random House, 1964), p. 41. See also James Weldon Johnson, *Black Manhattan* (New York: Knopf, 1930); Claude McKay, *Harlem: Negro Metropolis* (New York: Dutton, 1940); and Oscar Handlin, *The Newcomers* (Cambridge: Harvard University Press, 1959).

38. Claudia Kolker, *The Immigrant Advantage: What We Can Learn from Newcomers to America about Health, Happiness and Hope* (New York: The Free Press, 2011).

39. Ibid., p. 11. Italics in original.

40. Robert Blauner, *Racial Oppression in America* (New York: Harper & Row, 1972), pp. 56–57. Irving Kristol's article, referred to by Blauner, and several others dealing with the question of "The Negro as Immigrant" appear in Peter I. Rose (ed.), *Nation of Nations* (New York: Random House, 1972), pp. 197–279 passim.

41. See Ellis Cose, *The Rage of a Privileged Class* (New York: HarperCollins, 1993).

42. As quoted in Milton Vorst, op. cit., pp. 96–97.

43. James Farmer, *Freedom—When?* (New York: Random House, 1965), p. 87.

44. Myrdal, *American Dilemma.*

45. Kenneth Stampp, *The Peculiar Institution* (New York: Vintage Books, 1956).

46. Nathan Glazer and Daniel Patrick Moynihan, *Beyond the Melting Pot* (Cambridge: MIT Press, 1963), p. 53.

47. See 1971 edition.

48. E. Franklin Frazier, *The Negro in the United States* (New York: Macmillan, 1957), p. 680.

49. Ibid., p. 16.

50. See Lewis M. Killian, *White Southerners* (New York: Random House, 1970).

51. Ralph Ellison, *Invisible Man* (New York: Random House, 1947), p. 3.

52. W. E. B. Du Bois, *The Souls of Black Folk,* 1903 (as published in New York: Fawcett Publications, Premier Americana Editions, 1961), pp. 15–16.

53. See Vernon J. Dixon, "Two Approaches to Black-White Relations," in Vernon J. Dixon and Badi Foster (eds.), *Beyond Black or White* (Boston: Little, Brown, 1971), pp. 22–66ff.

54. The sort of position articulated by Dixon is much more fully developed in Cornel West, *Race Matters* (New York: Beacon Press, 1993).

55. Gordon, "Assimilation in America," pp. 279–285. See also Gordon, "Social Structure in Group Relations," *Freedom and Control in Modern Society,* op. cit., pp. 141–157.

56. John P. Dean, "Patterns of Socialization and Association between Jews and Non-Jews," *Jewish Social Studies,* 17 (July 1955), pp. 249–251. Dean's hypothesis was substantiated in the author's study of isolated Jews. The majority of Jews interviewed indicated that they enjoyed a degree of close interfaith socializing in their very small city, which was unparalleled in the urban community; see Rose, "Small-Town Jews," p. 182.

57. Andrew Greeley, *Why Can't They Be Like Us?* (New York: Dutton, 1971).

58. Solomon Poll, *The Hasidic Community of Williamsburg* (New York: Free Press, 1962), p. 3.

59. See Steven A. Camarota, *Immigration in the United States, 2010: A Profile of America's Foreign Born* (Washington, DC: Center for Immigration Studies, 2012).

60. Donald Bogue, *The Population of the United States* (New York: Free Press, 1959), p. 122.

61. US Census Bureau, *1960 Census of Population Supplementary Reports,* PC (S1)-10, Washington, DC, p. 2.

62. US Census Bureau, QuickFacts, www.census.gov/qfd, July 2012.

63. US Census Bureau, "Resident Population by Race, Hispanic Origin, and Single Years of Age," *Statistical Abstract of the United States,* 2013, Table 14, p. 16.

64. US Census Bureau, "Resident Population by Region, Race, and Hispanic Origin 2010," *Statistical Abstract of the United States,* 2013.

65. See Ruby Jo Kennedy, "Single or Triple Melting Pot? Intermarriage Trends in New Haven, 1870–1940," *American Journal of Sociology,* 58 (January 1952), pp. 56–59.

66. Gerhard Lenski, *The Religious Factor* (New York: Doubleday, 1961); see also Gerhard Lenski, "The Religious Factor in Detroit, Revisited," *American Sociological Review* (February 1971), p. 50.

67. Andrew Greeley (ed.), *Ethnicity in the United States: A Preliminary Reconnaissance* (New York: Wiley, 1974).

68. Will Herberg, *Protestant-Catholic-Jew* (New York: Doubleday, 1955), p. 14.

Part III

Attitudes, Actions, and Minority Reactions

Chapter 6

The Nature of Prejudice

On Being Culture Bound

> All good people agree,
> And all good people say,
> All nice people like Us, are We
> And everyone else is They.[1]

In a few short lines, Rudyard Kipling captured the essence of what sociologists and anthropologists call *ethnocentric* thinking.

Members of almost all societies tend to believe that "All nice people like Us, are We." They find comfort in the familiar and often denigrate or distrust others. Of course, with training and experience in other climes, they may learn to transcend their provincialism, placing themselves in others' shoes. Or, as Kipling also noted,

> If you cross over the sea,
> Instead of over the way,
> You may end by (think of it!) looking on We
> As only a sort of They.[2]

In a real sense, a main lesson of the sociology of racial and ethnic relations is to begin to "cross over the sea," to learn to understand why other people think and act as they do and to be able to empathize with their perspectives even if one still does not accept them. But this is no easy task. Many barriers—political, economic, social, and personal—stand in the way of such international (and intergroup) understanding. According to William Graham Sumner (who coined the word), "*ethnocentrism* leads a people to exaggerate and intensify everything in their own folkways which is peculiar and which differentiates them from others."[3] Intensive indoctrination to particular points of view and notions of what is right and wrong and good and bad has a long-lasting effect.

Sometimes the teaching is very explicit regarding the superior quality of one's own culture; sometimes it is subtler. Consider the following poem written by Robert Louis Stevenson and, for years, taught to many English and American children.

> Little Indian, Sioux or Crow,
> Little frosty Eskimo,
> Little Turk or Japanee,
> O! Don't you wish that you were me?
> You have seen the scarlet trees
> And the lions over seas;
> You have eaten ostrich eggs,
> And turned the turtles off their legs.
>
> Such a life is very fine,
> But it's not so nice as mine:
> You must often, as you trod,
> Have wearied, not to be abroad.
>
> You have curious things to eat,
> I am fed on proper meat;
> You must dwell beyond the foam
> But I am safe to live at home.
>
> Little Indian, Sioux or Crow,
> Little frosty Eskimo,
> Little Turk or Japanee,
> O! Don't you wish that you were me?[4]

Raised on such literary fare, it should not be surprising that children develop negative ideas about the ways of others. Despite greater sensitivity to such explicitly racist language, many young people in this society still make clear distinctions between those like themselves and others. Even the curious often find it hard to understand how those in other lands can worship ancestors, engage in polygamy, or practice infanticide; or why many Muslim women wear body-covering burkas while many native women from the island of Bali to the Darien Gap of Panama go bare-breasted. They may be surprised to learn that many nations emerging from colonial status favored various forms of one-party rule over our democratic political system.

Sometimes ethnocentrism appears in unlikely places, such as in writings by those long viewed as experts on the comparative study of culture. Consider the following remarks of the famous anthropologist Margaret Mead in a book on American character published in 1942, during the darkest days of World War II: "If I were writing about the way in which the Germans or the Japanese, the Burmese or the Javanese would have to act if they were to win the war, I would not need to use so many moral terms. For none of these peoples think of life in as habitually moral terms as do Americans."[5]

American ethnocentricity, although manifest in general attitudes toward others, is, of course, tempered somewhat by the very heterogeneity of the population that we have been examining. Thus, although there are broad standards expressed in the ways most Americans set goals for their children, organize their political lives, and think about this society in contrast to others, living in our racial and ethnic mosaic makes us more inclined to think in terms of layers or circles of familiarity. Blacks from Chicago feel and think very "American" when they are in Lagos or Nairobi, as do ethnic Chinese from Houston when visiting relatives in Shanghai or Beijing. But when they get home, they may quickly revert to feeling *African* American or *Chinese* American, respectively.

Ethnocentrism is found in political as well as in ethnic contexts. Much of the discussion of patriotism and loyalty is couched in language that reflects rather narrow, culture-bound thinking. At various periods in our history this phenomenon has been particularly marked. The nativistic movements of the pre–Civil War period, the anti-foreign organizations during the time of greatest immigration, and the McCarthyism of the early 1950s are three dramatic examples. During the McCarthy era there was a widespread attempt to impose the notion that, in addition to card-carrying communists, anyone who had ever joined a Marxist study group, supported the Loyalists in the Spanish Civil War, or belonged to any one of a number of liberal organizations was "un-American." It is clear that not only those "over the sea" are viewed (and view others) ethnocentrically. These distinctions between "they" and "we" exist within societies—including our own—as well.

In the majority of industrial societies most individuals belong to a wide array of social groups that differentiate them from others—familial, religious, occupational, recreational, and by gender, too. Individuals are frequently caught in a web of conflicting allegiances. A hierarchical ranking of groups as referents for behavior often surmounts this situation. In most places the family is the primary reference group. As we have seen in the United States, ethnic or racial identity and religious affiliation are also relevant referents. Members of other ethnic, racial, and religious groups are often judged on the basis of how closely they conform to the standards of the group passing judgment.

For years sociological surveys indicated that in American society many whites holding Christian beliefs and constituting both the statistical majority and the dominant group rank minorities along a continuum of social acceptability. They rate members of minority groups in descending order in terms of how closely the latter approximate their image of "real Americans." Although over the years Americans generally have considered those of English or Canadian ancestry to be the most acceptable of fellows, good neighbors, social equals, and desirable marriage partners, relatively few feel the same way about those who rank low in scales of social distance.

There is an interesting correlate to this finding. Investigators consistently have found that minority group members themselves frequently accept the dominant group's ranking system—with one exception: each tends to put his or her own group at the top of the scale.[6]

Ranking is one characteristic of ethnocentric thinking; generalizing is another. The more another group differs from one's own, the more one is likely to generalize about its social characteristics and to hold oversimplified attitudes toward its members. When asked to describe our close friends, we are able to cite their idiosyncratic traits: we may distinguish among subtle differences of physiognomy, demeanor, intelligence, and interests. It becomes increasingly difficult to make the same careful evaluation of casual neighbors. It is almost impossible when we think of people we do not know firsthand. The general tendency is to assign strangers to available group categories, which often include gross traits: "passionate" Latinos, "melancholy" Irish, "penny-pinching" Scots, "clannish" Chinese are some examples. These are *stereotypes,* a term with origins in ancient Greece, later used to describe a metal printing plate.

In a thoughtful essay, Judith Andre considers the conceptual and normative aspects of stereotyping, and stresses that the practice is more often applied to those thought to deviate from the characteristics of the dominant group.[7] Thus, she writes, "There are relatively few stereotypes about white men; white men are, in this culture, unreflectively taken to be the standard human being from whom women and other races deviate." Andre goes on to suggest, "What stereotypes there are concern not men as such, but men in relation to women."[8] Jeanne Bloch, a psychologist, has reported that sex differences among girls and boys are often related to the pressures and expectations of those most responsible for their socialization, parents and teachers—and, of late, advertising and television. Specific areas she noted based on a study that lasted more than ten years were that boys tend to be more aggressive, engage in more outdoor activities, tend to be risk takers, and have higher opinions of themselves than do girls. Girls are more fearful and anxious, more obedient to authority, and have greater concern for others' welfare.[9] She also indicates that "males tend to set higher goals and be more confident, blaming failure on external factors, whereas females blame themselves."[10] Such behavior is largely a reflection of the paths people are encouraged, allowed, or permitted to follow, and those they are prohibited from taking.

If, as noted in Chapter One, "self-fulfilling prophecies" are predictions made to come true, "self-fulfilling stereotypes" are assumptions that are often made to come true by the actions of those who seek or are forced to live up to (or down to) the expectations of others. Numerous studies of race and gender give ample evidence that minorities such as African Americans and women internalize the views others have of them, including lower esteem, and low rank, and often act accordingly.[11]

Ranking others according to one's own standards and categorizing them into generalized stereotypes together serve to widen the gap between "they" and "we." Sigmund Freud once wrote, "in the undisguised antipathies and aversions which people feel toward strangers with whom they have to do we may recognize the expression of self-love—of narcissism."[12] In sociological terms, *a function of ethnocentric thinking is the enhancement of group cohesion.* There is a close relationship between a high degree of ethnocentrism on the part of one group and an increase of antipathy toward others. This relationship tends to hold for ethnocentrism of both dominant and minority groups.[13]

Many writers see such antipathetic attitudes as bases for *group prejudice.* For example, "It is this very group consciousness, or ethnocentrism, which lays the foundation of group prejudice. If there were no strong feelings for one's own group, there would not be strong consciousness of other groups. Awareness of one's own group as an in-group and of the others as out-groups is fundamental in group relationships."[14]

Defining Prejudice

Prejudice—literally, prejudgment—may be defined as "a system of negative beliefs, feelings, and action-orientations regarding a group of people."[15] While prejudgments can be positive as well as negative, because of the detrimental psychic and social consequences that often result from hostile attitudes, sociologists usually concern themselves with and accentuate the negative.

The definition of group prejudice stated above incorporates the three major dimensions of all attitude systems: the *cognitive* (beliefs), the *affective* (feelings), and the *conative* (predispositions to act in particular ways, or policy orientations).[16]

The cognitive component pertains to the "intellectual" side of prejudice, for it involves knowledge, however faulty. This is expressed in stereotypical conceptions and misconceptions of various social groups by others, for example: whites who think that African Americans are shiftless, lazy, and untrustworthy, but wonderfully musical; Gentiles who imagine that Jews are avaricious, brash, and smart, but "too intelligent for their own good"; Englishmen who think of the Irish as argumentative, heavy drinkers; Irishmen who imagine Englishmen to be stuffy bores; and men of all ethnic backgrounds who think women are "the weaker sex."

Cognition refers to "cranial" reactions, that is, pictures in the mind's eye. Although the ethnocentric individual frequently generalizes about groups he knows little or nothing about, the prejudiced person generalizes about groups he thinks he knows well.

The second dimension, called "affective," refers to the way one feels about what is perceived. The emotions evoked are "visceral" in that they are often manifested in gut feelings of revulsion, fear, hate, or indignation, as illustrated by the following expressions:

"It makes me mad just thinking about my kid going to school with all those workaholic Asians. He'll never be able to keep up."

"Don't you just hate the way the Mexicans are moving in? I simply can't stand them."

"I know it's wrong, but I really shiver at the thought of rooming with a Muslim student next year."

Often emotions aroused in the prejudiced person are based upon presumptions about certain people, and thinking about or confronting members of particular groups frequently elicits thoughts about how to act.

Group prejudices involve both thoughts and feelings about people. "However false as to fact, prejudice has a certain logic, a logic not of reason but of the emotions.... Prejudice is more than false belief; it is a structure of false belief *with a purpose,* however unconscious."[17] This is why prejudice as an attitude represents

a predisposition to act (the conative dimension) in a particular way toward a social group. It is a state of readiness for action but not in itself overt behavior or
discrimination.

Prejudice and Discrimination

Discrimination may be defined as the differential treatment of individuals belonging
to particular groups or social categories.[18] Although frequently they are opposite
sides of the same coin, prejudice and discrimination, as both analytical and concrete
concepts, should not be confused. The difference between prejudice as an attitude
and discrimination as overt behavior was summed up by an English judge in his
comments to nine youths convicted of race rioting in the Notting Hill section of
London: "Everyone, irrespective of the color of his skin, is entitled to walk through
our streets in peace with their heads held erect and free from fear.... These courts
will uphold (these rights) . . . *think what you like.... But once you translate your
dark thoughts into savage acts, the law will punish you, and protect your victim.*"[19]

American civil rights workers have long recognized the significance of the
distinction. The late Dr. Martin Luther King Jr., in his first address to the Atlanta,
Georgia, Junior Chamber of Commerce, put it bluntly: "The law may not make a
man love me, but it can restrain him from lynching me, and I think that's pretty
important."[20]

The prejudiced person may not actually behave outwardly the way he or she
thinks or says he or she will act. Attitudes do not always lead to hostile or aggressive actions. Furthermore, many individuals discriminate against others without
harboring particularly negative feelings toward the groups to which they belong.
In one of several books on intergroup relations published in the mid-1950s, Dean
and Rosen reported, "Conformity with the practices of segregation and discrimination is often quite unrelated to the intensity of prejudice in the individuals who
conform."[21] Others have continued to corroborate the generalization, adding the
following corollary: social contact itself and the conventions characteristic of the
particular circumstances in which contact takes place often help to determine how
an individual will act at a given time. Sometimes people may even behave toward
others in direct opposition to their own predispositions. The situation itself frequently provides the cues for "appropriate" behavior. For example, for years many
liberals conformed to practices of segregation when vacationing in the South, and
southerners who held moderate views about the desegregation issue often remained
silent on the matter in their home communities.

Merton's Typology

Nearly sixty-five years ago, comparing the presence or absence of prejudicial attitudes on the part of individuals with their willingness or reluctance to engage
in discriminatory activity, Robert K. Merton described the relationship between

prejudice and discrimination. The typology he devised is still useful. It includes four types of persons and their characteristic response patterns.[22]

The Unprejudiced Nondiscriminators

These "all-weather liberals," as Merton called them, sincerely believe in the American creed of freedom and equality for all, and practice it to the fullest extent. They are the vigorous champions of the underdog, take the Golden Rule literally, and cherish American egalitarian values. It would appear that liberal individuals such as these would be most able to influence others in the realm of intergroup hostility and discrimination. Yet, as Merton indicates, their effectiveness is limited by certain "fallacies."

First there is the "fallacy of group soliloquies." Liberals tend to expend their energies in seeking out one another and talking chiefly to others who share their point of view. The feeling of agreement that logically ensues by interacting mainly with those who agree leads to the second fallacy, that of "unanimity." Through discussions with like-minded individuals the liberal may feel that many more people agree with his attitudes regarding ethnic relations than do in fact. Finally, there is the "fallacy of privatized solutions," depicted by Merton as follows: "The ethnic liberal, precisely because he is at one with the American creed, may rest content with his own individual behavior and thus see no need to do anything about the problem at large. Since his own spiritual house is in order, he is not motivated by guilt or shame to work on a collective problem."[23]

The problem of the unprejudiced nondiscriminator is not one of ambivalence between attitude and action—as in the case of the two types described below—but rather it is a lack of awareness of the enormity of the problem and a clear-cut approach to those who are not so liberally inclined.

Unprejudiced Discriminators

The many homeowners throughout the urban North and Midwest long denied having any personal feelings against black people, but steadfastly tried to keep them out of their neighborhoods for fear of what others would say and do. This illustrates the case of the unprejudiced discriminator, who is, at best, a "fair-weather liberal." More pragmatic than "all-weather liberals," they discriminate when such behavior is called for, seems to be appropriate, or is in their own self-interest. Expediency is the motto; "Don't rock the boat" the guiding principle.[24] Merton suggests that the "fair-weather liberal" is frequently the victim of guilt because of the discrepancy between conduct and personal beliefs and is thus especially vulnerable to the persuasion of those more willing to press for civil and human rights and more amenable to making changes when authorities impose them.

Prejudiced Nondiscriminators

This third type might be called "timid bigots." Like so many of those who have half-facetiously been called "the gentle people of prejudice," they are not activists. They feel definite hostility toward or dislike many groups and subscribe to conventional stereotypes of their negative attributes. Yet, like "fair-weather liberals," they too react to circumstances. If the situation—as defined by law or custom—precludes open discrimination, they conform. They serve African American and other minority group customers, sit next to them on buses or trains, and send their children to school with them. Feeling they are forced to "grin and bear it," they often take the position that they are merely cogs in a big machine. "What can I do," they say, "fight the system, fight city hall?"

Although both the "fair-weather liberal" and the "fair-weather illiberal" share the theme of expedience, Merton states,

> Superficial similarity in behavior of the two in the same situation should not be permitted to cloak a basic difference in the meaning of this outwardly similar behavior, a difference which is as important for social policy as it is for social science. Whereas the timid bigot is under strain when he conforms to the creed, the timid liberal is under strain when he deviates.... He does not accept the moral legitimacy of the creed; he conforms because he must, and will cease to conform when the pressure is removed.[25]

Prejudiced Discriminators

These are the people who embody the commonly held assumption that prejudice and discrimination are mutually dependent. Such "active bigots" neither believe in the American creed nor act in accordance with its precepts. Like the "all-weather liberal," the prejudiced discriminator conforms to a set of standards; but in this case "his ideals proclaim the right, even the duty, of discrimination."[26] He or she does not hesitate to express the basic attitude—"all whites are superior to colored people"—or to convert it into overt behavior. He or she is willing to defy law, if necessary, to protect beliefs and vested interests.

In recent years in this country we have witnessed a resurgence of organized "resistance" movements, some taking the form of citizen's militias, made up of those who would readily fit under Merton's rubric "Prejudiced Discriminators."

Each of these categories is, of course, an ideal type, a model against which reality is to be measured. Although it is rare that one finds a single individual who is all saint or all sinner, "fair-weather liberals" and "timid bigots" do exist. Several caveats should be borne in mind: although many people prejudiced against one minority, say Italians, often tend to dislike others, such as Jews and blacks,[27] prejudice toward one minority does not necessarily mean prejudice toward all. Those who are anti-black are not, ipso facto, anti-Semites—or vice versa.[28]

Nor do dominant groups have a monopoly on prejudice. Many minority group members subscribe to images of other minorities that coincide with those held by members of the dominant groups. Examples include the anti-Semitism of some blacks as well as anti-black sentiments expressed by some Jews, both of which came to light during the crisis over the community control of schools in New York City in 1968–1969,[29] during the presidential primaries of 1988 when Jesse Jackson was a Democrat contender, and in continuing debates about support for Israel.[30]

Furthermore, for many racial, religious, and ethnic minorities the dominant group represents "the enemy camp."[31] Brewton Berry and Henry L. Tischler indicate that such hostility is often a direct product of socialization. They cite a story told by editor of the *Carolina Israelite,* Harry Golden, to illustrate the point—focusing on how prejudice is learned.

> My first impression of Christianity came in the home, of course. My parents brought with them the burden of the Middle Ages from the blood-soaked continent of Europe. They had come from the villages of Eastern Europe where Christians were feared with legitimate reason.
>
> When occasionally a Jewish drunk was seen in our neighborhood, our parents would say, "He's behaving like a Gentile."
>
> For in truth, our parents had often witnessed the Polish, Romanian, Hungarian, and Russian peasants gather around a barrel of whiskey on Saturday night, drink themselves into oblivion, "and beat their wives." Once in a while the rumor would spread through the tenements that a fellow had struck his wife, and on all sides we heard the inevitable, "Just like a Gentile."
>
> Oddly enough, too, our parents had us convinced that the Gentiles were noisy, boisterous, and loud—unlike the Jews.... If we raised our voices, we were told, "Jewish boys don't shout." And this admonition covered every activity in and out of the home: "Jewish boys don't fight." "Jewish boys don't get dirty." "Jewish boys study hard."[32]

What Causes Prejudice?

There are many explanations for the causes of prejudice and the sources of discrimination.[33] Until the first quarter of the twentieth century, most theories focused primarily on physical traits and group differences. Some writers attempted to prove that certain groups are innately superior to others; others speculated that there is an instinctive aversion of people to the unfamiliar that accounts for antipathy toward aliens and strangers.

Biology and Behavior

In spite of the influence of Voltaire, Rousseau, and others who argued that there is a universal oneness in human nature, the eighteenth and nineteenth centuries saw the birth of a doctrinaire theory of group prejudice. Taxonomical classifications of human "races" paved the way for elaborate schemes that "proved" that some varieties of humankind were superior to others and that, inevitably, sought to justify the maltreatment of nonwhite people by Europeans.[34]

For example, the eighteenth-century scientist Carl von Linne (also known as Carolus Linnaeus) divided *Homo sapiens* into four racial groupings, each of which was purported to instill a distinctive "mentality" in its members. The African (*Afer niger*) was said to be slow and negligent, cunning and capricious. The American Indian (*Americanus rufus*) was described as tenacious, free, and easily contented.

The Asiatic (*Asiaticus luridus*) was viewed as a haughty, stern, and opinionated fellow. The European (*Europaeus albus*) was envisaged as possessing the traits of liveliness and creativity and was considered to be superior to the other racial types. Whereas Linnaeus based his typology on color—black, red, yellow, white—and region, others (such as J. F. Blumenbach, Anders Retzius, Samuel G. Morton, and Josiah C. Nott) divided human beings into categories according to other physical attributes, and each series of measurements led to a different kind of classification of "races."

These classifications, devised by Europeans or white Americans, for the most part seemed to come to the same conclusion: "Nonwhites are innately inferior." The equation of somatic differences with culture traits gave birth to the theory of racial superiority or racism. Throughout the Western world it was asserted that colored people were degenerate, simple-minded, untamed, uncivilized. Such thinking was used by several writers to justify the slave system in the United States and to sanction exploitation by American, British, and other colonialists, many of whom viewed conquest and subjugation as the "white man's burden." Darwin's theory of evolution and the possibility of "separate creation" gave added legitimacy to the doctrine. The superordinate status of whites was taken to be evidence that the fittest survive and that the aggressive, not the meek, inherit the earth.

Since its inception, the dogma of racism has persisted in various forms. Nietzsche, Gobineau, H. S. Chamberlain, and Adolf Hitler, among others, argued that certain "racial" groups possess the traits of leadership, greatness, and nobility, and others are born to follow, to serve, or to be exterminated as useless parasites.

Early in the twentieth century many social scientists rejected the doctrine of racial superiority and the supposition that racial origins determine culture patterns. Yet, some held to the view that people instinctively dislike the strange and different. They saw *xenophobia* (the fear of foreigners) as an inborn trait passed from one generation to the next. This was an element in the social thought of the early American sociologist F. H. Giddings, who argued that people identified with the members of their own social groups and excluded outsiders, owing to a "consciousness of kind." It was "natural" he claimed, for people to like what they know and to fear the unknown. Sociologists E. B. Reuter and C. W. Hart, in one of the early introductory textbooks in sociology, stated that prejudice was to be attributed to "the universal fear of things new and strange."[35] For a time even Robert E. Park, the scholar who was to become one of the major guiding forces behind the empirical study of intergroup relations, subscribed to the view. In 1924 Park wrote, "It is evident that there is in race prejudice as distinguished from class and caste prejudice, an *instinctive* factor based on the fear of the unfamiliar and uncomprehended."[36]

The I.Q. Controversy

Those who assume biological superiority (and inferiority) and innate or natural group aversion imply that there is something inherent in racial and ethnic bodies largely determining the thoughts, abilities, and group-focused loves and hates of their members. To most modern social scientists such a view is unacceptable. Looks may be transmitted through the genes, but not outlooks. The perspectives people have are thought to be the result of nurture, not nature. Even within similarly social-ized groups, idiosyncratic differences are very great. Some people are strong and others are weak; some are intelligent and some are feeble-minded. But the strong and the intelligent are to be found in all racial and cultural groups. The manner in which given individuals are able to optimize whatever innate potentialities they may possess is dependent, in part at least, upon the opportunities afforded in the social milieu into which they are born and in which they are raised. Indeed, according to the members of the American Anthropological Association, "all races possess the ability needed to participate fully in the democratic way of life and in modern technological civilization."[37]

With the development of systematic methods of investigation and a scientific orientation toward social life itself, the ideas that certain groups are born to lead and others to follow, that xenophobia is rooted in the genes, have been found to be theoretically and empirically untenable. However, this conclusion does not mean that research on the relationship between racial background and behavior has ceased. On the contrary, it has taken new forms—often variations on old themes that seek by use of such culturally biased instruments as intelligence tests to demonstrate persisting differences between blacks and whites.

Intelligence testing began in the 1890s and was used extensively in the early decades of the last century. The most famous measures were the Stanford-Binet and the Yerkes Alpha and Beta tests used to assess American soldiers in World War I. Other psychologists, including Carl C. Brigham, who already assumed blacks to be inferior in intelligence, took data from Army tests claiming that native-born, white Americans "proved" more intelligent than new immigrants. Brigham was one of several behavioral scientists whose contentions about the deleterious effects of al-lowing newcomers to enter the United States lent considerable academic legitimacy to the restrictive immigration legislation of the 1920s discussed in Chapter Three.

Although later research clearly contradicted Brigham's claim regarding the dif-ferential scores of "natives" and immigrants (and their children), the black-white dichotomy still remained evident. Perhaps the best examples of such reasoning were to be found in the work of Audrey Sheuey, a Columbia University–trained psychologist and author of *The Testing of Negro Intelligence,* published in the late 1950s,[38] and in the debates over the work of Harvard University psychologist Arthur Jensen, published a decade later.[39] After an extensive review of the literature in which I.Q. test scores of white and African American subjects were compared, Sheuey concluded that the data clearly belie the claim that there are no native differences. The biggest problem was the leap she made between the finding that blacks scored proportionately lower and the argument that this was attributable to innate intellectual inferiority.

In perhaps the most pointed gibe at Sheuey's work (and the work of others who made similar claims), Adrian Dove, a social worker from the Watts section of Los Angeles, clearly illustrated that, at the time she did her research, the vast majority of white people would flunk his black-oriented "Dove Counterbalance Intelligence Test," but most African Americans would do quite well. The test consisted of thirty multiple-choice questions, including the following:

Which word is out of place here? (a) splib, (b) blood, (c) gray, (d) spook, (e) Black.

A "handkerchief head" is a(n) (a) cool cat, (b) porter, (c) "Uncle Tom," (d) hoddi, (e) preacher.

"Hully Gully" came from (a) "East Oakland," (b) Fillmore, (c) Watts, (d) Harlem, (e) Motor City.[40]

Not all critics of the Sheuey argument used humor to counter it. Systematic research indicated the persisting cultural biases of the traditional tests.[41] Sometime after the debates over Sheuey's book had simmered down, psychologist Arthur Jensen gained widespread attention for an article, "How Much Can We Boost I.Q. and Scholastic Achievement?," published in the *Harvard Educational Review* in the winter of 1969 in which, on the basis of his research, he stated that it is "a not unreasonable hypothesis that genetic factors are strongly implicated in averaged Negro-white intelligence difference." This hypothesis was based on findings that alleged to show that (1) compensatory education programs designed to improve intellectual performance of those euphemistically called "culturally disadvantaged" failed to raise I.Q. scores; (2) children with low I.Q.s tend to be handicapped genetically as well as culturally (or environmentally); (3) the genetic proclivity for certain types of performances is an important factor not merely in determining potential differences in intelligence ratings from the same group but also differences between groups; and (4) one should recognize and compensate for the fact that rote learning seems easier for some than abstract learning.[42] Aware that he might raise, once again, the specter of "scientific racism," Jensen nevertheless felt that a number of important questions about the relationship between nature and nurture needed consideration, especially by people who were concerned with the attainment of improved education for all children.

Reactions, especially to the shakiness of some of Jensen's assertions, as expected, were harsh—in some cases quite extreme. "Jensenism" became a word that was linked to "imperialism" and "fascism" and "genocide" by militant critics. Even those who attended the annual business meetings of the American Anthropological Association found themselves asked to vote on the censure of the *Harvard Educational Review* for publishing Jensen—and they proceeded to do so without protest. (The protest came later, and it was not only from reactionary quarters.)[43]

As Christopher Jencks, an authority on educational research, noted in a lengthy review of Jensen and his critics,

> Were there a dispassionate observer, who could look at these arguments without political or personal bias, I think he would conclude that neither Jensen nor his critics have offered a persuasive explanation of IQ differences between African Americans and whites. He would probably also conclude that neither geneticists nor social scientists know enough about the determinants of IQ scores to design a study which would fully resolve our present confusion. Nonetheless, Jensen's decision to reopen this ancient controversy without first gathering more evidence strikes me as a serious political blunder.[44]

An even more thorough assessment of Jensen's work was made by political scientist Philip Green, who, in three lengthy articles published in *Dissent*, challenged what he called "the fallacy of heritability."[45] In a few pointed paragraphs, Green suggested two ways of defining heritability. First he offered the "standard" definition: "The heritability of a trait refers to the extent to which variations in measurement from the average value of the trait may be traceable to genetic variation in the measured population."[46] Noting that the key word is "population," Green pointed out that this has generally meant "specific breeding and rearing populations"—at least according to most geneticists—but he suggested, "the heritability of a trait can equally be conceived of as nothing more than a function of the extent to which salient features of the environments the observed population lives in are themselves alike or unlike."[47] In his essays, Green proceeded to elaborate on this contention that, after a review of the literature, he found "not a single aspect of the history of inherited deficiency is ascribable to genetics: it is all a product of social conditions and thus potentially susceptible to social amelioration."[48]

In the late 1980s and the early 1990s, a number of articles and new books reopened and reexamined the issue of cognitive stratification. Some, like Mark Snyderman and Stanley Rothman's *The I.Q. Controversy,* focused mainly on the media reactions to a matter that was linked to all sorts of other public policy issues, not least to growing disenchantment with social programs that favored certain groups and the ominous threat of polarization in American society.[49] Some were attempts to review the literature and offer sober assessments, which recognized the difficulties of sorting out truly independent variables. But, according to the biologist Stephen Jay Gould, the books that received the most attention, having zeroed in, once again, on the genetic, "race-based" character of intelligence, held "no new arguments or compelling data but cashed in on the depressing temper of our time—a historical moment of unprecedented ungenerosity, when a mood for slashing social programs can be powerfully abetted by an argument that beneficiaries cannot be helped, owing to inborn cognitive limits expressed as low I.Q. scores."[50] By far the most comprehensive and controversial was *The Bell Curve,* by Richard J. Herrnstein and Charles Murray.[51]

In their book, Herrnstein and Murray offer a contemporary argument for what has been called "Social Darwinism," the idea that the smartest survive, coupled with a categorical imperative, that the reason that whites and Asians do better than blacks is that there is a "racial" basis to intelligence. This is not the only one they make. In fact, Murray now claims it is not even the central issue, but there is no doubt about the message and the ammunition it provides for those wont to believe that I.Q. tests are fair measures, that they are (or can be made) culture-free and unbiased, and that, given the fact that those belonging to certain cohorts score lower in the aggregate than others, they must be less intelligent, requiring different means of assistance (or treatment) than that now provided. Despite the dubiousness of the tests used to determine intelligence, the failure to address social structural inequities, limits placed on those who are stigmatized, or other mitigating circumstances, *The Bell Curve*'s "scientific approach" has been used as a weapon in recent battles about race and social policy. Although Charles Murray repeatedly denies that this was their intention, no such disclaimer has come from Seymour Itzkoff, author of *The Decline of Intelligence in America,*[52] a volume even more blatant in its acceptance of Social Darwinism, which spells out policy positions akin to those of early eugenicists (such as curtailing immigration), than that of Herrnstein and Murray.

Whatever else, the renewed debates—known by some as "The Bell Curve Wars"[53]—forced the examination of a number of important assumptions, not the least being those related to the persistent blurring of the study of race per se (and of race differences) and the study of prejudice and discrimination and their effects. The significance of the distinction becomes clearly apparent when one moves away from the emotionally charged realm of "intelligence" and "performance" to that of health and illness.

It has long been asserted by some that racial purity is a virtue and that, by sticking to one's own race, many problems can be avoided. Perhaps, as some African Americans now argue (and as many whites have long contended) there is a psychological truth embedded in the assumption but not necessarily a physiological one. Recent medical research has shown several important negative results of endogamy (marriage to a member of one's own group, especially an ethnic or racial one) in the so-called "race-based" diseases, such as sickle-cell anemia, thalassemia, and Tay-Sachs disease, which are prevalent among African Americans, Mediterranean peoples, and Ashkenazic Jews, respectively.

The suggestion here is that, as the famous geneticist Theodore Dobzhansky has noted, "Faced with a revival of 'scientific' racism, one is tempted to treat the matter with the silent scorn it so richly deserves. . . . [Yet] it may perhaps be useful to add a warning against exaggerations which some writers bent on combating racism are unwittingly making."[54] In one sense, making official statements such as the unanimous declaration of the American Anthropological Association cited above denies to the discreditors the notion that those categorized as members of a given racial group (such as the far-from-"pure"-American African Americans) are innately inferior, but in another sense it begs several questions that remain scientifically legitimate.[55] The study of race and the ideology of racism must be dealt with as separate phenomena.

Social Structure and Individual Personality

Concern about racism is clearly at the center of most current discussions of prejudice in American society. But various students of the subject tend to concentrate their attention on just one or another aspect of the overall problem. Some focus on the social system and its various parts (organizations, classes, and institutions), its rules or norms, and its purported values. Society itself is often the principal unit of analysis. Others eschew so grand a scope of study, preferring to concentrate on individual behavior and personality. George A. Kourvetaris has called these polar approaches "macroscopic" and "microscopic."[56] As a number of social scientists have indicated, there are "levels" in between. In their well-known multi-edition text, *Racial and Cultural Minorities,* George Simpson and J. Milton Yinger made the point that "to say simply that there is an 'instinct' or natural tendency toward prejudice, or that there is an inevitable 'dislike of the unlike,' or that so-called prejudice against minority groups is a natural reaction to their factual inferiority—explanations that abound in the literature—is to fail to bring the study of prejudice into the framework of contemporary theory of human behavior."[57] They suggest posing a set of questions:

> Do groups differ in the direction and amount of prejudice that they exhibit? If so, why?
> Is there change, through time and space in the groups, and kinds of groups toward which prejudice is directed?
> What is the process by which an individual acquires prejudice?
> What forces, in the lives of individuals and of groups, operate to sustain, and to reduce prejudice?[58]

Simpson and Yinger then attempted to answer the questions they posed by looking from the micro (or the individual) level, focusing on personal needs, to the macro level, examining the structure of society—power arrangements and economic, political, religious, and other structural variables. In between they considered culture and cultural values and norms and the way in which these are transmitted.[59] This latter category is about socialization, a most significant factor in the writing of Gordon W. Allport, author of *The Nature of Prejudice*.[60]

Allport, too, described levels in discussing his diagram reproduced in Figure 6.1.[61] The approaches mentioned by Allport include examining the rationalized

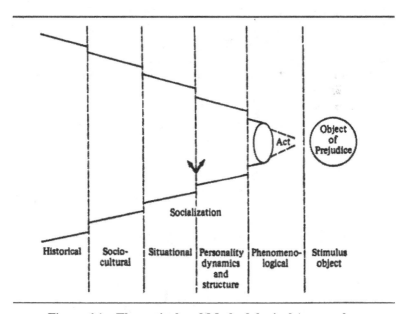

**Figure 6.1   Theoretical and Methodological Approaches
to the Study of the Causes of Prejudice**

Source: G. W. Allport, "Prejudice: A Problem in Psychological and Social Causation," *Journal of Social Issues,* Supplement Series, No. 4 (1950).

self-interests of upper classes in various societies; studying traditions that lead to conflict, upward mobility, and the challenge of certain elements in society; and looking at population density and various types of contact, all of which occur when social change is intensive, as in the case of rapid urbanization. But, said Allport, in addition to these approaches, comprehensive analysis must consider social climates, the settings of social interaction where rules are interpreted and acted upon. Moreover, Allport recognized the importance of the characteristics placed upon groups who are often the very objects of discrimination itself. (For example, in medieval Europe, many Jews, denied the right to own land or to work in any occupations other than those involving high risk such as petty finance, became moneylenders and tax collectors, thereby fulfilling the prophecy that Jews are money brokers.) In the last instance we almost come full circle for, according to Allport, the minority group member is the stimulus object, the object of prejudice, and the target of discrimination. (Here is the classic case of scapegoating to rationalize the self-interest mentioned above.)[62]

In the sections to follow, we look at some of these areas of concern with special attention to economic and class factors, culture and personality, and the socialization process itself.

Economic Causes

Marx's followers and a good many other social scientists view prejudice primarily in terms of the strained relationship between the exploited and the exploiter. Carey McWilliams, for example, argued that anti-Semitism has traditionally been "a mask for privilege" and is based on the efforts of those in economically advantageous positions to exclude rising groups.[63] Long ago Oliver Cox and others hypothesized that the whole system of race relations and segregated patterns, especially in the United States, is directly related to the maintenance of a cheap labor supply.[64] In not very different terms many contemporary analysts of American racial patterns argue that they are a form of domestic colonialism based on a continuing policy of exploitation of poor people, especially minorities.[65]

According to William J. Wilson, the "Colonial Model," at least when applied to the situation of what some once called Third-World Americans, involves four fundamental components: (1) The racial group's entry into the dominant society is forced and involuntary. (2) The members of the dominant group administer the affairs of the suppressed or colonized group. (3) The culture and social organization of the suppressed group are destroyed. (4) Racism exists—that is, "a principle of social domination by which a group seen as inferior or different in terms of alleged biological characteristics is exploited, controlled and oppressed socially and psychically by a superordinate group."[66]

Although not all social scientists agree that economic interests play the most important role in bringing about and maintaining prejudice and discrimination, many have found that the intergroup conflict continues in large part because of the gains—both material and psychological—that are realized by assuming an attitude of superiority and enforcing social distance between one's own group and others.

Early studies of "social distance" suggested that the principal basis for differential ranking of ethnic groups is the desire to maintain or enhance one's social position by associating with groups considered to be of high status and by disassociating from those low in the prestige hierarchy.[67] Since the 1940s investigators have consistently found anti-Semitism and anti-black sentiments to be most common among people dissatisfied with their own economic position or among those whose status has declined.[68] And, as has been recently shown, the rhetoric of resentment over difficulties in breaking out of desperate situations has led some to blame other, more successful minorities, Jews, Asians, etc., for their continued failure to move out of poverty and into the mainstream of society.[69] Of course, such blame-placing for being stifled economically is psychologically significant as well. It functions as a means of displacement.

Psychological Interpretations

In 1945 Bruno Bettelheim and Morris Janowitz documented the relationship between downward mobility and increased antipathy toward Jews and African Americans.[70] In *Social Change and Prejudice,* a volume published years after the initial study, they summarized the findings of various national sample surveys conducted to reexamine the relationship.[71] In their original investigation Bettelheim and Janowitz suggested that from among the 150 young veterans they interviewed in Chicago, those enjoying moderate upward mobility were more tolerant than those who had experienced no change in status, those who were rising very rapidly, or, especially, those experiencing downward mobility. In explaining these differences the authors said that "one can argue that, given American values which legitimate social mobility ... the moderately upwardly mobile person is likely to have relatively effective personal controls." This theme of effective controls was crucial to the revised theoretical orientation of the investigators. In their more recent work they place heavy stress on new developments in ego psychology in which the person is viewed as part of, not apart from, his wider social milieu. In these terms prejudice is no longer seen as a reflection of an inherently weak ego straining against unacceptable inner strivings (as many psychologists have long contended); rather the emphasis is on the protective shield prejudice affords to those whose identity is threatened, as in the case of those experiencing sudden changes of status.

In societies such as our own, where prejudice is a "normal" rather than an "abnormal" fact of social life, Bettelheim and Janowitz once asserted that it must be understood in functional terms. Put simply, prejudice helps to pump up the egos of those who feel deprived or threatened; it reduces anxiety about one's own status; it adds in the assertion of superiority. "Unless other means of ego support are found for the person seeking identity and fearing its loss, prejudice can be expected to exist in one form or other."

The notion that prejudice may prove advantageous to certain individuals is something that bigoted demagogues and militant minority leaders have long known. This idea also has long been explored by social scientists. In the 1930s in his classic study of race relations, *Caste and Class in a Southern Town,* John Dollard examined the functions of prejudice. Dollard was particularly impressed with the level of "social inertia," the reluctance to change traditional patterns mainly because of the gains accruing to those middle-class whites who maintained the institutions of segregation.[72] Among the advantages he saw were those in the spheres of economics, sexual activities, and ego gratification linked to what Dollard called "prestige."

The psychological advantages of prejudice can be demonstrated more clearly in Freudian than in Marxian terms. Some writers have explained prejudice as a means of deflecting aggressions created by personal frustrations.[73] The thesis develops as follows: One goes through life seeking gratification for felt needs and, although many such needs have their origin in the organic structure of the individual, there are others that are culturally determined. These are learned early in life and are channeled and directed toward certain goals. When goal-directed behavior is blocked, hostile impulses are frequently created in the individual who, unable to determine the real source of his frustration but in an attempt to overcome it, manifests "free-floating aggression."[74] Such undirected aggression finds a "legitimate" point on which to focus that becomes a substitute for the actual frustrating agent. Usually the target is weak and unable to strike back. This process is well known: the boss berates his employee, who takes it out on his wife, who in turn berates the children. And so it goes.

Free-floating aggression is often directed toward a minority group or out-group whose status in society puts it in a vulnerable position. One observer has made the point in graphic—though extreme—terms: "The rich take to opium and hashish. Those who cannot afford them become anti-Semites. Anti-Semitism is the morphine of the small people.... Since they cannot attain the ecstasy of love they seek the ecstasy of hate. The Jew is just convenient.... If there were no Jews the anti-Semites would have to invent them."[75] (Today, one might substitute the word *Muslims* for *Jews* in the same scenario.)

When aggression is displaced in this manner the target is a *scapegoat.* In sociological parlance, scapegoating is the expression used to describe the psychological mechanism of displacing aggression. It refers to placing one's own "iniquities" or "sins" upon others. The scapegoat is therefore a whipping boy for the frustration-invoked hostility of the individuals or groups who use it. And, as Albert Camus once suggested, anyone and anything can become a scapegoat: "We are all exceptional cases. We all want to appeal against something. Each of us insists at all costs that he is innocent even if he has to accuse the whole human race and heaven itself."[76]

The reader who examines these economic and psychological explanations of the basis of prejudice may ask what predisposes certain individuals to attempt to exploit others or to seek scapegoats upon whom they can transfer their own inadequacies. One attempt to answer this question was made by a group of behavioral scientists who hypothesized "that the political, economic, and social convictions of an individual often form a broad and coherent pattern as if bound together by a 'mentality' or 'spirit' and that this pattern is an expression of deep-lying trends in his personality."[77] This statement is taken from a now classic study of *The*

Authoritarian Personality, which, in 1950, presented a new approach to the investigation of prejudice. The major concern of this large-scale research, conducted in the United States during and after World War II, was to understand the "potentially fascistic individual, one whose structure is such as to render him or her particularly susceptible to antidemocratic propaganda."[78]

Both quantitative and qualitative research techniques were employed in this investigation. Questionnaires administered to groups of college students (and later to others) provided background information about the respondents. Stereotype-laden questions were used as bases for the development of scales of anti-Semitism, ethnocentrism, politico-economic conservatism, and fascism. Two types of interviews were administered to the extreme scorers on these scales: one, nondirective, aimed at getting at basic ideology; the other, clinical-genetic, designed to elicit case history material. Analysis of data thus obtained suggested that antipathy toward minorities and ethnocentric thinking—called "social discrimination" by the authors—is part of a generalized ideological system pertaining to groups and group relations. Highly prejudiced individuals were found to possess the following personality characteristics: glorification of power; the tendency to view people as good or bad, and things as black or white; deep concern with status and toughness; repression of sexual feelings; conception of the world as a jungle; cynicism about human nature; the proclivity to blame others rather than themselves for misdeeds and trouble. Out-group hostility was especially prominent among the defense mechanisms of the "authoritarians." Concerning these extreme scorers, the authors wrote, "The basically hierarchical, authoritarian, exploitative parent-child relationship is apt to carry over into a power-oriented, exploitatively dependent attitude toward one's sex partner and one's God and may well culminate in a political philosophy and social outlook which has no room for anything but a desperate clinging to what appears to be strong and disdainful rejection of whatever is relegated to the bottom."[79] Put in other words, the study concluded that many, perhaps most, highly prejudiced persons are mentally disturbed.[80]

This conclusion no doubt holds for many individuals of "rigid personality," including at least some of the leaders of extremist hate movements and, perhaps, quite a few of their followers.[81] But these all-weather bigots are hardly representative of the vast number of Americans who harbor racial and ethnic prejudice and discriminate against minority groups. In fact, follow-up studies of hypotheses presented in *The Authoritarian Personality,* using similar or identical research instruments (especially the "F [for fascism] scale"), report that prejudice and discrimination characterize the attitudes and behavior of many "normal" people.[82] Moreover, careful testing of the hypotheses of the pioneering work suggests that bigotry is by no means confined to politically conservative or reactionary individuals, and that authoritarian personalities are to be found among both the right and the left segments of the nation's citizenry.[83] Given the fact that these patterns are widespread, adequate sociological explanation of prejudice and discrimination cannot be confined to psychological deviation alone. Prejudice and discrimination constitute a major social problem precisely because most of their practitioners *conform to established beliefs and values.*

Socialization and Social Conformity

Rather than conceiving of group prejudice as an inborn tendency or a rent in one's basic personality, most sociologists today view it as a social habit. This thesis derives from the general proposition that cultural traits are learned. In the process of learning the ways of their groups—the process of socialization—individuals acquire both self-perceptions and images of others. If the teaching is effective, the individual internalizes (in substantial measure, but never fully) the sentiments and customs of his social milieu—including the "appropriate" prejudices. As sociologists MacIver and Page once wrote, "The individual is not born with prejudices any more than he is born with sociological understanding. The way he thinks as a member of a group, especially about other groups, is at bottom the result of social indoctrination, in both its direct and its indirect forms, indoctrination that inculcates beliefs and attitudes, which easily take firm hold in his life through the process of habituation."[84]

An old southerner put it this way:

> I grew up just 19 miles from Appomattox. The teaching I received both in school and from my parents was hard-core South, with no chance of insight into the thinking and ways of other peoples. I was taught to look down upon Negroes, tolerate Jews (because we had to do business with them) and ignore Catholics.
>
> We celebrated Jefferson Davis's birthday, but ignored Lincoln's; the name Robert E. Lee was spoken with reverence and Appomattox was a shrine. The Golden Rule only applied to others who were either Methodist or Baptist, white and without a foreign-sounding name....[85]

The acceptance of various prejudices does not require direct contact between the learner and the members of groups held in low esteem. If the agents of socialization—parents or peers, teachers, preachers, or community leaders—are themselves prejudiced people, they are apt to be effective conveyers of group antipathies whether the objects of their attitudes are immediate neighbors or distant out-groups.

The lessons learned in this "natural" process of enculturation constitute a serious problem for those educators and other persons who attempt to make more realizable the values of the American ethos. They are competing with the home, playground, and, sometimes, the mass media, which for many people represent the normal and desirable way of life, a way of life that all too often is inconsistent with and disruptive of ideals of freedom, social equality, and unhampered opportunity. This situation is aggravated by the fact that group antipathy has been found to exist not only among individuals of high socioeconomic status but also among those in the rank and file.

Culture and Institutionalized Racism

Many contemporary writers and most militant minority group leaders consider institutionalized racism to be the principal source of prejudice against nonwhite peoples (or those treated as a "racial" group, like Jews in Nazi Germany). Their explanations find expression in many forms—from academic rhetoric to the argot of the street—but the theme remains more or less the same. The core argument is that a belief in their own superiority is deeply ingrained in the minds of those in the dominant sector (in our country this means white people) and in their social mores. They have internalized the same views as those promulgated by the early anthropologists and perpetuated by those who, for several centuries, claimed to be lifting and carrying "the white man's burden." The late Whitney M. Young put it succinctly when he wrote that "racism ... is the assumption of superiority and the arrogance that goes with it."[86]

As noted earlier, many southerners found scientific racism a justification for the exploitation of Africans during the first half of the nineteenth century, a time when the institution of slavery was being severely challenged. Increasing evidence suggests that others shared their views but, instead of putting down the blacks, they put them out, out of their minds. Joel Kovel, for example, in his psychohistory *White Racism* contends that in this country racism is still manifest in efforts to control (or what he calls the pattern of "dominative racism") or to avoid ("aversive racism").

He explains, "In general, the dominative type has been marked by heat and the aversive type by coldness. The former is clearly associated with the American South, where, of course, domination of blacks became the cornerstone of society; and the latter with the North, where blacks have so consistently come and found themselves out of place. The dominative racist, when threatened by the black, resorts to direct violence; the aversive racist, in the same situation, turns away and walls himself off."[87]

To pursue the point one step further, it is interesting to note that, like Alexis de Tocqueville long before him, Kovel asserts that aversive racists have been more intense in their reaction than their dominative countrymen. As long ago as the 1830s, Tocqueville had suggested, "The prejudice of race appears to be stronger in the states that have abolished slavery than in those where it still exists; and nowhere is it so intolerant as in those states where servitude has never been known...."[88] In the years following the order to end legal segregation in all regions of the United States, the observations of Tocqueville became quite apparent. White northerners who long overlooked what was happening in their midst while condemning southerners for their racial prejudice, began revealing that they were by no means immune to racism themselves.

Institutionalized racism pertains to discriminatory practices reflected in customs and laws and practices engaged in, even by those previously called "reluctant discriminators," and the rules surrounding what is required, what is expected, what is forbidden—and with whom. This is the principal subject of the next chapter on discrimination and institutionalized racism. But, before going there it is well to consider the most recent body of thought on the general subject. Much of it falls under the broad rubric "Critical Race Theory."

Critical Race Theory

Based on an assumption that "most people understand that 'race' as it is used in our society is a social construction not a biological truth [the fact remains] that race remains with us as a compelling myth that has real consequences."[89] It is, according to law professor Richard Delgado, the sine qua non of "Critical Race Theory."[90] Delgado and other writers on the subject contend that, far more than class or region, "race" has been and remains at the very nexus of inequity in the United States and that discrimination based on assumptions about race (as socially defined) persists not only in custom but, in many places, including the Constitution, in law.

Delgado and his coauthor, Jean Stefancic, summarize the basic tenants of the approach by noting that in our society (1) "racism is ordinary, not aberrational"; (2) "white over color ascendancy serves important purposes, both psychic and material"; and (3) "race and races are products of social thought and relations."[91]

Much of the writing of those who place themselves (or are placed) in the camp of the Critical Race Theorists frames arguments in language that highlights many of the explanations of prejudice and its effects cited in the preceding sections of this chapter. For example, Delgado and Stefancic's propositions clearly reflect ideas of some of those scholars and activists we have just discussed: who hold to cultural explanations, claiming that we should worry not only about the bigots but the "gentle people of prejudice," those who are social conformists; we should understand the functions of prejudice according to those who offer both Marxian and Freudian (and other psychological) arguments relating to material advantages and psychic rewards of power over others—and the disadvantages of those whom they exploit and victimize; and be mindful of a leitmotif that appears again and again throughout this volume, the idea that race, as it is generally used, is a social construction. But the Critical Race Theorists break new ground in their emphasis on racism itself, particularly, but not exclusively, in its embeddedness within certain influential institutions, most especially the legal and educational systems.[92]

Often the words of the Critical Race Theorists seem to echo Gunnar Myrdal's observations about the very real distinctions he and his researchers noted between professed beliefs and actual conduct, between "creed" and "deed." Many go further, following one of their pioneers, the Harvard Law professor Derrick Bell, who suggested that even the creed itself is biased. He noted that our guiding document, the US Constitution, favors property over justice, reinforcing the tendency to maintain the status quo ante. He and others claim that whites, even those (or, perhaps, especially those) who are strict constitutionalists, like many liberals, rarely support efforts to redress grievances of African Americans or other minorities unless it is in their own self- or group interest to do so. (We will return to this argument in discussing reactions to the Black Power Revolt of the 1960s and 1970s in Chapter Nine.)[93]

Other Critical Race Theorists such as Kimberlé Crenshaw,[94] Mari J. Matsuda,[95] and Lani Guinier[96] contend that the whole legal system must be changed in order to avoid the persisting pitfall of failing to move forward. Social policy as well as the actual structure of a representative democracy must be reformed to enhance the expansion of rights in an agenda that emphasizes the equality of outcome instead of the traditionally restrictive idea (deeply rooted in our legal philosophy) of an equality of opportunity. A common theme in their writings is that it is almost impossible for those who are handicapped at the starting gate to run an equal race. Thus, if the law is to be used as a means to fight prejudice and its effects, it must start by addressing its own inherent weaknesses.

Related to such a critique of the legal system is one that has to do with the nature of research itself. A number of Critical Race Theorists, many of whom are members of various "minority" groups, argue that much of what is written about the character of prejudice, discrimination, and racism in America comes from the pens and computers of those who have never endured the stigma of being "second class" themselves. Richard Delgado, for example, calls for far more appreciation of the perspectives of victims of oppression to fully comprehend the impact of socialization and social conformity in American society.[97]

In a way, it raises an issue that has long been both an epistemological and a political debate in the social sciences: Who is the better judge of thoughts and actions—outside "observers" or inside "members"? To this author, as argued in a paper on the subject in 1978,

> The sociological perspective calls for providing a framework within which to understand what is being studied, what is being read, the larger picture of the systems in which people live and work and play and suffer, the context in which to indicate and text the variables that relate to human affairs everywhere.
>
> I now feel very strongly that the work of the sociologist is like that of the Japanese judge in Rashomon, the one who asks various witnesses and participants to describe a particular event as seen through their own eyes. Like the judge, neither teachers of sociology nor students can be allowed to get off the hook. We must analyze the disparate pieces of evidence and then try to figure out how they fit together.... Then perhaps we will be better able to know the troubles others have seen and be better able to understand them.[98]

Conclusion

Prejudice, as we have seen, has been attributed to basic economic interests, to authoritarian personality structure, to reactions to frustration, to social conformity, to poor education. There are, of course, other interpretations: for example, the emphasis upon the symbolic significance of the presence of a particular minority in a certain area;[99] the idea that contact with certain minorities under certain circumstances increases rather than decreases prejudice;[100] and what Allport has called "earned reputation"—the notion that individuals react to ethnic traits that are in fact menacing and threatening and therefore evoke realistic hostility.[101]

Each of these interpretations possesses more than a kernel of truth, and each may help to explain prejudice of a particular sort. Group prejudice is not a one-dimensional phenomenon. Although we have not exhausted the various explanations for its occurrence, one thing appears certain: prejudice is learned, not inherited.

Notes

1. Rudyard Kipling, "We and They," in *Debits and Credits* (London: Macmillan, 1926), pp. 327–328. By permission of Mrs. George Bambridge, the Macmillan Co. of London and Basingstoke, the Macmillan Co. of Canada, and Doubleday and Co., Inc.

2. Ibid. See also Ronald Takaki, *A Different Mirror: A History of Multicultural America* (Boston: Little, Brown & Co., 1993).

3. William Graham Sumner, *Folkways* (Boston: Ginn, 1906), p. 13.

4. Robert Louis Stevenson, "Foreign Children," in *The Works of Robert Louis Stevenson* (New York: Walter Black, Inc., 1926) (originally published in 1883).

5. Margaret Mead, *And Keep Your Powder Dry* (New York: William Morris, 1965), p. 11.

6. See, for example, P. Zeligs and G. Hendrickson, "Racial Attitudes of 200 Sixth-Grade Children," *Sociology and Social Research* (September–October 1933), pp. 26–36.

7. Judith Andre, "Stereotypes: Conceptual and Normative Considerations," in Paula S. Rothenberg (ed.), *Racism and Sexism* (New York: St. Martin's Press, 1988), pp. 257–262.

8. Ibid., p. 259.

9. As reported in Vincent Parrillo, *Strangers to These Shores,* 4th ed. (New York: Macmillan, 1994), pp. 501–502. The findings were discussed on *Nova,* in a program called "The Pinks and the Blues," on Public Broadcasting, 1982.

10. Parrillo, *Strangers to These Shores.*

11. See Mark Snyder, "Self-Fulfilling Stereotypes," in Paula S. Rothenberg (ed.), *Racism and Sexism* (New York: St. Martin's Press, 1988), pp. 263–269.

12. Sigmund Freud, *Group Psychology and the Analysis of the Ego* (New York: Boni and Liveright, 1950), p. 55.

13. Catton and Hong have found that "after social dominance has been taken into account, the appearance of ethnocentrism in minorities is a further factor in the development of majority hostility." William R. Catton Jr. and Sung Chick Hong, "The Relation of Apparent Minority Ethnocentrism to Majority Antipathy," *American Sociological Review,* 27 (April 1962), p. 190.

14. Joseph G. Gittler, "Man and His Prejudices," *The Scientific Monthly,* 69 (July 1949), pp. 43–47. See also Herbert Blumer, "Race Prejudice as a Sense of Group Position," *Pacific Sociological Review,* 1 (Spring 1958), pp. 3–7.

15. Daniel Wilner, Rosabelle Price Walkley, and Stuart W. Cook, "Residential Proximity and Intergroup Relations in Public Housing Projects," *Journal of Social Issues,* 8:1 (1952), p. 45. For several classic discussions of the definition of prejudice, see Gordon W. Allport, *The Nature of Prejudice* (Cambridge: Addison-Wesley, 1954), pp. 3–16; Brewton Berry, *Race and Ethnic Relations* (Boston: Houghton Mifflin, 1958), pp. 363–371; John Harding et al., "Prejudice and Ethnic Relations," in Gardner Lindzey (ed.), *Handbook of Social Psychology,* Vol. II (Cambridge: Addison-Wesley, 1954), pp. 1021–1061; George Simpson and J. Milton Yinger, *Racial and Cultural Minorities,* rev. ed. (New York: Harper and Row, 1958), pp. 14–19; and Robin M. Williams Jr., *The Reduction of Intergroup Tensions* (New York: The Social Science Research Council, Bulletin No. 57, 1947), pp. 36–43.

16. See Bernard M. Kramer, "Dimensions of Prejudice," *Journal of Psychology,* 27 (April 1949), pp. 389–451.

17. Arnold M. Rose, "Anti-Semitism's Root in City Hatred," *Commentary,* 6 (October 1949), p. 374.

18. This is essentially the same definition used by Robin M. Williams Jr., op. cit., p. 39.

19. As reported in *Time* (September 29, 1958), p. 58. Italics added.

20. As reported in the *New York Times* (October 21, 1966), p. 28.

21. John P. Dean and Alex Rosen, *A Manual of Intergroup Relations* (Chicago: University of Chicago Press, 1955), p. 58.

22. Robert K. Merton, "Discrimination and the American Creed," in R. M. MacIver (ed.), *Discrimination and National Welfare* (New York: Harper and Row, 1949), pp. 99–126. The passages to follow are largely summary statements of Merton's thesis. Only direct quotations will be noted.

23. Ibid., p. 105.

24. See, for example, Robert O. Blood, "Discrimination without Prejudice," *Social Problems,* 3 (October 1955), pp. 114–117.

25. Merton, op. cit., p. 108.

26. Ibid., p. 109.

27. See Allport, op. cit., p. 68.

28. See, for example, E. Terry Prothro and John A. Jenson, "Interrelations of Religious and Ethnic Attitudes in Selected Southern Relations," *Journal of Social Psychology,* 32 (August 1950), pp. 45–49.

29. See, for example, Herbert J. Gans, "Negro-Jewish Conflict in New York," *Midstream* (March 1969).

30. See Peter I. Rose, "Blaming the Jews," *Society* (November/October 1994), pp. 35–40.

31. See, for example, Gerhard W. Ditz, "Out-Group and In-Group Prejudice among Members of Minority Groups," *Alpha Kappa Deltan* (Spring 1959), pp. 26–31; and Catton and Hong, op. cit., pp. 178–191.

32. Harry Golden, *You're Entitled* (Cleveland: World Publishing Company, 1962), p. 259.

33. For a more detailed discussion of various explanations of what have long been viewed as some of the causes of prejudice, see Allport, op. cit., pp. 206–216; Arnold M. Rose, "The Causes of Prejudice," in Francis E. Merrill (ed.), *Social Problems* (New York: Knopf, 1950), pp. 402–424; Arnold M. Rose, "The Roots of Prejudice," in *The Race Question in Modern Science* (a UNESCO publication) (New York: Whiteside, Inc., and William Morrow and Company, 1956), pp. 215–243; and Robin M. Williams Jr., op. cit., pp. 36–77.

34. See especially Peter I. Rose, *The Subject Is Race* (New York: Oxford University Press, 1968). Also see Oscar Handlin, "The Linnaean Web," in *Race and Nationality in American Life* (Garden City, NY: Doubleday, 1957), pp. 57–73; and Cyril Bibby, *Race, Prejudice and Education* (New York: Praeger, 1960), pp. 40–62.

35. E. B. Reuter and C. W. Hart, *Introduction to Sociology* (New York: McGraw-Hill, 1963), p. 263.

36. Robert E. Park and Ernest W. Burgess, *Introduction to the Science of Sociology* (Chicago: University of Chicago Press, 1924), p. 578. Italics added. Park later modified his position. For example, in "The Nature of Race Relations," in Edgar T. Thompson (ed.), *Race Relations and the Race Problem* (Durham, NC: Duke University Press, 1939), pp. 3–45, he wrote, "Race consciousness, therefore, is to be regarded as a phenomenon, like class or caste consciousness that enforces social distances."

37. This is the closing sentence of a resolution passed by the Fellows of the American Anthropological Association, November 17, 1961. A similar resolution was adopted at the annual meeting of the Society for the Study of Social Problems in 1961.

38. Audrey Sheuey, *The Testing of Negro Intelligence* (Lynchburg, VA: Randolph-Macon Women's College, 1958).

39. Arthur R. Jensen, "How Much Can We Boost I.Q. and Scholastic Achievement?" *Harvard Educational Review,* 39 (Winter 1969), pp. 1–123. See also *Educability and Group Differences* (New York: Harper and Row, 1973).

40. As reported in *The New Republic* (December 16, 1967), p. 7. N.B.: The answer is (c) in each case. The full text of the "test" appeared in the *Denver Post* (July 8, 1968), p. 6.

41. See, for example, Melvin M. Tumin (ed.), *Race and Intelligence* (New York: Anti-Defamation League, 1963).

42. Jensen, "How Much Can We Boost I.Q. and Scholastic Achievement?" See also Christopher Jencks, "Intelligence and Race," *The New Republic* (September 13, 1969), pp. 25–29.

43. The sharpest barb came from anthropologist Jerry Hyman, who facetiously suggested that the Association had not gone far enough. He suggested "That it is incumbent on all members dedicated to Truth to seek out and destroy any remaining copies of publications that include the views of Herrnstein, Shockley and Jensen so that our libraries and institutions of learning not be used to disseminate such unscientific and potentially damaging material. That special attention be paid to the destruction of *The Atlantic Monthly, Harvard Educational Review,* and *New York Times* in that their complicity in this deception has been more energetic and more constant than other publications. That the method of destruction shall be left to the conscience of the individual fellow or voting member but that fire is a particularly symbolic and therefore appropriate mechanism." (Quoted from *Newsletter of the American Anthropological Association,* 13 [February 1972], pp. 2–3.)

44. Jencks, op. cit., p. 29. See also H. J. Eysink, *The I.Q. Argument* (New York: Library Press, 1972).

45. Philip Green, "Race and I.Q.: Fallacy of Heritability," *Dissent* (Spring 1976); "The Pseudo Science of Arthur Jensen," *Dissent* (Summer 1976); and "I.Q. and the Future of Equality," *Dissent* (Fall 1976).

46. Philip Green, "Race and I.Q.," op. cit., p. 183.

47. Ibid., p. 184.

48. Ibid., p. 192. For another useful summary of the controversy see Berry and Tischler, *Race and Ethnic Relations* (New York: Houghton Mifflin, 1978), chap. 4, pp. 63–86.

49. Mark Snyderman and Stanley Rothman, *The I.Q. Controversy: The Media and Public Policy* (New Brunswick, NJ: Transaction Books, 1988).

50. Stephen Jay Gould, "Curveball," *The New Yorker* (November 28, 1994), p. 139.

51. Richard J. Herrnstein and Charles Murray, *The Bell Curve* (New York: Free Press, 1994).

52. Seymour Itzkoff, *The Decline of Intelligence in America* (Westport, CT: Praeger, 1994).

53. See Steven Fraser (ed.), *The Bell Curve Wars: Race, Intelligence and the Future of America* (New York: Basic Books, 1995).

54. Theodore Dobzhansky, "Comment," *Current Anthropology,* 2 (October 1961), p. 31.

55. Rose, *The Subject Is Race,* op. cit., p. 41.

56. George A. Kourvetaris, "Prejudice and Discrimination in American Social Structure," in P. Allan Dionisopoulos (ed.), *Racism in America* (DeKalb: Northern Illinois University Press, 1971), pp. 32–41.

57. George Eaton Simpson and J. Milton Yinger, *Racial and Cultural Minorities,* 4th ed. (New York: Harper and Row, 1972), p. 63.

58. Ibid.

59. Ibid., pp. 63–102 and 139–164.

60. Allport, op. cit.

61. Gordon W. Allport, "Prejudice: A Problem in Psychological and Social Causation," *Journal of Social Issues,* Supplement Series, No. 4, 1950.

62. Allport, *The Nature of Prejudice,* pp. 201–212.

63. Carey McWilliams, *A Mask for Privilege: Anti-Semitism in America* (Boston: Little, Brown, 1948).

64. Oliver C. Cox, *Caste, Class and Race: A Study in Social Dynamics* (Garden City, NY: Doubleday, 1948).

65. See, for example, Jack Forbes et al., *The Third World Within* (Belmont, CA: Wadsworth, 1972); and Joan W. Moore, "Colonialism: The Case of the Mexican-Americans," *Social Problems,* 17 (Spring 1970), pp. 463–472.

66. William J. Wilson, "Race Relations Models and Explanations of Ghetto Behavior," in Peter I. Rose (ed.), *Nation of Nations* (New York: Random House, 1972), p. 262. The definition of "racism" is from Robert Blauner, "Internal Colonialism and Ghetto Revolt," *Social Problems,* 16 (Spring 1969), p. 396.

67. See, for example, studies by E. S. Bogardus, including "Social Distance and Its Origins," *Journal of Applied Sociology,* 9 (1925), pp. 216–226; "Analyzing Changes in Public Opinion," *Journal of Applied Sociology,* 9 (1925), pp. 372–381; "Social Distance: A Measuring Stick," *Survey,* 56 (May 1926), pp. 169–170; and "Race Friendliness and Social Distance," *Journal of Applied Sociology,* 11 (1927), pp. 272–287.

68. See, for example, A. A. Campbell, "Factors Associated with Attitudes Toward Jews," in T. M. Newcomb and E. L. Hartley (eds.), *Readings in Social Psychology* (New York: Holt, Rinehart and Winston, 1947), pp. 518–527.

69. See Peter I. Rose, "Blaming the Jews," op. cit.

70. Bruno Bettelheim and Morris Janowitz, *The Dynamics of Prejudice* (New York: Harper and Row, 1950).

71. Bruno Bettelheim and Morris Janowitz, *Social Change and Prejudice* (New York: Free Press, 1965).

72. John Dollard, *Caste and Class in a Southern Town* (New Haven: Yale University Press, 1937), esp. chaps. 6–8.

73. See John Dollard et al., *Frustration and Aggression* (New Haven: Yale University Press, 1939). "When Marxists have described the dynamic human interrelationships involved in the class struggle ... they have introduced unwittingly a psychological system involving the assumption that aggression is a response to frustration." Ibid., p. 23.

74. See, for example, Clyde M. Kluckhohn, "Group Tensions: Analysis of a Case History," in L. Bryson, L. Finkelstein, and R. M. MacIver (eds.), *Approaches to National Unity* (New York: Harper and Row, 1945), p. 224.

75. Quoted by Allport, *The Nature of Prejudice,* p. 343.

76. Albert Camus, *The Fall* (Justin O'Brien, tr.) (New York: Vintage Brooks, 1963), p. 81.

77. T. W. Adomo et al., *The Authoritarian Personality* (New York: Harper & Row, 1950), p. 1.

78. Ibid.

79. Ibid., p. 971.

80. See Bettelheim and Janowitz, *Social Change and Prejudice*; and Selma Hirsch, *The Fears Men Live By* (New York: Harper and Row, 1955).

81. See, for example, Leo Lowenthal and Norbert Guterman, *Prophets of Deceit* (New York: Harper and Row, 1949).

82. See, for example, Richard Christie, "Authoritarianism Reexamined," in Richard Christie and Marie Jahoda (eds.), *Studies in Scope and Method of "The Authoritarian Personality"* (New York: Free Press, 1954), pp. 123–196. See also Muzafer and Carolyn Sherif, *Groups in Harmony and Tension* (New York: Harper and Row, 1953).

83. See Edward A. Shils, "Authoritarianism: 'Right' and 'Left,'" in Christie and Jahoda, op. cit., pp. 24–49. See also Stanley Rothman and Robert Lichter, *Radical Christians, Radical Jews* (New York: Oxford University Press, 1981).

84. Robert M. MacIver and Charles H. Page, *Society: An Introductory Analysis* (New York: Holt, Rinehart and Winston, 1949), p. 407.

85. Letter to the Editor of the *New York Times* (May 16, 1963). The letter was signed by Tom Wilcher.

86. See Whitney M. Young Jr., *Beyond Racism: An Open Society* (New York: McGraw-Hill, 1969).

87. Joel Kovel, *White Racism: A Psychohistory* (New York: Pantheon, 1970), pp. 31–32.

88. Alexis de Tocqueville, *Democracy in America* (New York: Vintage Books, 1945), Vol. I, p. 373.

89. From the brochure, *Only Skin Deep: Changing Visions of the American Self* (New York: International School of Photography, 2005).

90. For a synoptic view of "Critical Race Theory," see Richard Delgado and Jean Stefancic (eds.), *Critical Race Theory: An Introduction* (New York: New York University Press, 2001).

91. Ibid., p. 7.

92. See Joe F. Feagin, *Discrimination American Style: Institutional Racism and Sexism* (Englewood Cliffs, NJ: Prentice Hall, 1978).

93. Derrick Bell, considered by many a founding father of Critical Race Theory, has written extensively on this subject. See, for example, *And We Are Not Saved: The Elusive Quest for Racial Justice* (New York: Basic Books, 1987). A new collection of Bell's writings has been edited by Richard Delgado and Jean Stefancic, *The Derrick Bell Reader* (New York: New York University Press, 2005). Another useful volume is Kimberlé Crenshaw (ed.), *Critical Race Theory: The Key Writings That Formed a Movement* (New York: The New Press, 1995).

94. Crenshaw, *Critical Race Theory.*

95. See, for example, Mari J. Matsuda and Charles R. Lawrence III, *We Won't Go Back: Making the Case for Affirmative Action* (New York: Houghton Mifflin, 1997).

96. Lani Guinier has published several books on the subject. The one in which she makes a case for proportional representation within electoral districts is *The Tyranny of the Majority: Fundamental Fairness in Representative Democracy* (New York: Simon and Schuster, 1995).

97. See Peter I. Rose, "Nobody Knows the Trouble I've Seen: Some Reflections on the Insider-Outsider Debate," The Katherine Asher Engel Lecture, Northampton, MA, Smith College, 1978. Another version of this appeared as Chapter 10, "Insiders and Outsiders," in *They and We,* 4th ed. (New York: McGraw-Hill, 1990), pp. 213–231.

98. Rose, *They and We,* pp. 230–231.

99. See, for example, Lewis Browne, *How Odd of Jews* (New York: Macmillan, 1943); and Arnold M. Rose, "Anti-Semitism's Roots in City Hatred," op. cit.

100. See Allport, *The Nature of Prejudice,* chap. 16.

101. Ibid., p. 217.

Chapter 7

Patterns of Discrimination

Insult and Injury

> Eenie, meenie, miney, moe.
> Catch a nigger by the toe.

Not a tiger, a "nigger." Until very recently, the bit of doggerel chanted by children throughout the English-speaking Western world contained that explicit racial epithet. It may have been an "unintended indiscretion" but it was clearly an insult.

Insults are but one in a range of actions we call discriminatory. In this chapter various expressions of behavior that fall under the rubric of *discrimination,* the singling out of people for separate and unequal treatment,[1] are examined. The treatment itself is often institutionalized, an accepted part of everyday life. Examples include pejorative language, the denial of the franchise, selective hiring practices, restrictive neighborhoods, exclusive social clubs, and other forms of segregation. It may involve organized forms of intimidation and physical abuse as well.

Patterns of discrimination may be de jure, grounded in law, or de facto, that is, part of a tradition or custom. Moreover, as noted in Chapter Six, those who discriminate may do so because they believe they are superior to others or simply because they think "that's the way it is." Too many acceptors of the status quo are reluctant to change what, to them, are economically, psychologically, and socially acceptable or necessary arrangements. It is not surprising to find that many Americans are fair-weather liberals who more often do what is "expected" than what is "right," who often engage in behavior that is in fact racist.

Not so long ago many middle- and upper-class whites in the South regularly employed African American servants whose jobs involved intimate contact with the family, such as cooks, maids, even wet-nurses for the children. Despite such intimate sorts of relationship, these very same people were reluctant to allow blacks to drink from the same water fountains as whites or swim in the same pools, or go to school with their youngsters. Many northern whites, more self-righteous perhaps but equally inconsistent, were less concerned with such "pollution," yet kept African Americans from their neighborhoods, clubs, and churches. The height of northern hypocrisy was most clearly manifest each Sunday morning when loyal parishioners faithfully proclaimed the "Brotherhood of Man" in their very separate churches.

In addition to these seemingly contradictory practices, such patterns demonstrate the compartmentalized character of discrimination and the fact that large numbers of people subscribe to those forms of behavior that are acceptable according to the social and cultural definitions of the situations in which they find themselves. Relatively few are willing to cut the cake of custom, especially when they feel (or are made to feel) that their vested interests are threatened. In this way the fair-weather liberal often ends up being a reluctant discriminator.

Defamation, avoidance, threat, coercion, segregation, colonization, relocation, and annihilation describe points along the continuum of discriminatory practices. Of these practices, the present chapter deals with three distinctive modes: *derogation, denial,* and various forms of aggression.[2]

Derogation

Ethnophaulism is a technical word for a derogatory term used by the members of one ethnic group to describe the members of another. Ethnophaulisms are at the core of the language of prejudice and, when openly expressed, become a form of discrimination known as *antilocution,* a fancy word for name-calling.

The old saying that "sticks and stones may break my bones but names will never hurt me" is misleading, for articulated antagonisms may serve to define and reinforce the images we hold of others and may have serious psychic consequences for those on the receiving end. The repeated reference to the adult black male as "boy" or the married black woman as "miss," to cite examples graphically portrayed by Richard Wright, is like a stain that leaves an indelible imprint on the recipient's personality.[3]

People often fail to know the roots of common expressions they use. Some are quite innocuous. Think of "Cross my heart and hope to die" (a reference to the Christian gesture of reverence) or "Knock on wood" or "Touch wood" (both allusions to swearing on the cross of Jesus). Sometimes people are offended by words that sound like pejorative ones. A case in point is the objection of some African Americans to the use of the expression "niggardly," which has nothing to do with black people but means "stingy" or "tight-fisted."

Frequently, loaded words are used without any intent to disparage but may prove to be pernicious nonetheless. Think of such a colloquialism as "I've been gypped" (which means being cheated as if by Roma people or "Gypsies"). Or think of advertisements that say their products (stockings, adhesive bandages, etc.) are "flesh colored." Many words and phrases referring to color, religion, and gender are more explicit. Included would be such old-fashioned statements as "Free, white, and twenty-one" (to be a carefree adult) and "Jew him down" (to bargain sharply).

Although far less common than in the past, sometimes, in an attempt to indicate friendliness, a white person may still say to a nonwhite, "Believe me, I think you're as good as I am." More common these days is the sort of thing that happens when second- and third-generation Americans with origins in China, Japan, and Korea are confronted with questioners who, assuming they must be foreigners, speak to them very slowly in simple sentences and are then impressed with their ability to respond in perfect English—and say so!

Exasperated members of the groups in question often receive such testimonials as examples of not very subtle verbal discrimination. Others view them as evidence of narrow-mindedness or just plain ignorance. All of their concerns are compounded when, after correcting a speaker who makes such a blatant faux pas, he or she says, "I didn't mean to offend you; why, some of my best friends are ..."[4]

A not uncommon response is a polite acceptance of the apology together with a silent seething by those who are the object of such ignorant and patronizing remarks or of the sort of things that, they know, are being said behind their backs. Such remarks and other indications of prejudice often are paralleled by the comic caricatures of those who put them down. The terms used to describe those others are hardly kinder. And the jokes they tell frequently play up the differences between the cultures, illustrating the superiority of the minority.

Humor is found in all societies, and ethnic humor is particularly prevalent in ours. Most Americans are familiar with racial and ethnic jokes and frequently tell them with abandon—often failing to consider what they mean to those joked about. In an article pointedly titled "The Sting of Polish Jokes," philosopher and writer Michael Novak discussed the matter in some detail. One of his main points was that "Not all humor is humorous." As he explained,

> Ethnic humor is one of the great resources of this nation. There are forms of laughing at oneself and at others, usually based on the daily absurdities of mutual noncomprehension or double meaning. These are truly amusing, probably the most amusing jokes in the American repertoire. In this humor, all ethnic groups are equal; the barbs are shared by everybody at the same time.
>
> But there is a second genus of ethnic joke. It does not gain its force from that double understanding of the same word or doubly misapprehended event that characterizes multicultural perception. It is based on demeaning the character of one ethnic group, in line with a stereotype, and its function is to make the majority feel superior to the minority. Told in the presence of the minority, these jokes further require those who are their butt to acquiesce in their own humiliation, to laugh obediently, to accept their ascribed inferiority. (Nudging elbow: "No offense, friend. Only a joke.") The tactic is structurally the same as those techniques that force inmates to embrace their own degradation. Rage is not permitted. One must stand there helplessly and acquiesce.
>
> Southern and Eastern Europeans in the United States still seem subject to the last respectable bigotry.[5]

The last turn of phrase, "respectable bigotry," was popularized by Michael Lerner in the late 1960s.[6] It referred to the fact that for many years many liberal white people who "knew better" than to tell jokes about blacks and other nonwhite minorities seemed to have no compunction about telling them about Southern and Eastern Europeans.

Members of minority groups often affect accents and tell jokes that rely on others' stereotypes of what they are supposed to be like. The Irish tell "Pat and Mike" jokes; Italians tell stories about the Mafia—and, of late, *The Sopranos.* Among Jews it is not uncommon to hear stories that describe the conflict between the desire for acceptance and the ties to the ethnic community.[7] African Americans frequently joke about their low status, the difficulty of advancement, the special significance of "soul," and the white man's image of their lives.[8] Some stories stress the perverse "advantages" of marginality; others are tinged with the bitterness of self-abasement.

Such "inside" joking is also controversial. Many point to the fact that although self-derogation might relieve tension, the stories may suggest to others that there is a kernel of truth in stereotypes. This is seen in caricatures of Jews, Italians, Mexicans, Japanese, and especially African Americans offered on stage, in movies, and on television.

One of the sharpest critics of such sardonic humor notes that the stories and lampoons may have serious negative consequences for the groups themselves, especially when others become privy to what is being said within the community, and sometimes intentionally as in the commercialization of rap music and the glorification of "bad-ass" behavior of certain black entertainers. In a controversial book, *The Artificial White Man,* the African American jazz critic Stanley Crouch claimed, "Images of black youth seen on MTV, BET, or VH1 are not far removed from those D. W. Griffith used in *Birth of a Nation* [a famous film celebrating the Ku Klux Klan], where Reconstruction Negroes were depicted as bullying, hedonistic buffoons, ever ready to bloody someone."[9]

Much more recently some of the arguments about the perceptions of insiders and outsiders in using stereotypic characterizations in media have again arisen with a widely discussed performance piece called "Old Jews Telling Jokes."[10] For many Jewish Americans the portrayals are sharp and funny if exaggerated caricatures. Other Jewish Americans worry that what they can relate to and know as laughable spoofing could play directly into the hands of those who see Jews as they are represented in some of the more unflattering sketches.

The criticism is important. Still, there is little question that whatever else it does, for good or, as Crouch and others claim, for ill, in-group humor has subtle social and psychological functions, not least the reinforcement of group identity. The fact remains, however, that laughing at yourself is very different from listening to an outsider interpret "your" jokes or tell their own stories about you or the members of your group.

Over the past seventy-five years, in an attempt to deal more forthrightly with racial diversity and ethnic pluralism, a number of radio and television networks introduced comedy programs with "intergroup" themes. First there was *Amos 'n' Andy* (with its minstrelized "Negroes"), *Abie's Irish Rose, Life with Luigi, The Goldbergs,* and

The Life of Riley, each seeming to outdo the other in stereotype-laden language. Later came the considerably sanitized if not quite yet politically correct television show *Bridget Loves Bernie* (about an Irish Catholic woman married to a Jewish man) and an increasing number of sitcoms starring African Americans, including *Julia, Sanford and Son, The Jeffersons, Good Times,* and *The Cosby Show.*[11] Then there was the much more sophisticated and controversial *All in the Family.*

The show, based on an English program about working-class life called *Til Death Do Us Part,* pulled few punches. It (purposely) dealt directly with contemporary issues—the role of women, sexual deviance, and, especially, ethnic interaction.

In the 1970s *All in the Family* was one of America's most popular television programs. Millions of people put aside other things to watch Archie Bunker, the bumbling bigot who didn't trust anybody not of his creed or color; his dutiful wife Edith, who often revealed a crude but nascent feminism; their daughter Gloria, a child/woman caught between parental love, wifely responsibility, and cravings for independence; son-in-law Mike, a Polish American graduate student in sociology whom Archie called "a liberal meathead"; and Archie's neighbors and coworkers.

Archie's language was larded with sexist remarks as well as racist ones. Included in his everyday speech were pejorative words used in direct reference to minorities, words like "spic" and "greaser" (referring to Latinos), "wop" and "dago" (Italians), "jigaboo" and "jungle bunny" (African Americans), "hebe" (referring to Jews), "a-rab," and many others.

Because it was assumed that those so labeled would see such expressions as an extreme form of derogation, many critics argued that *All in the Family* served to legitimize the use of such terms. Moreover, and more important, some, including Laura Hobson, author of *A Raisin in the Sun,* argued that Archie Bunker made bigotry somehow respectable.[12] Others disagreed. Those who supported the program contended that it is healthy to make fun of such serious matters; it releases tensions and, perhaps, even creates a climate of understanding.

The few studies that were conducted for the Columbia Broadcasting System (CBS), the network that produced the show, indicated that most of those maligned by Archie Bunker appeared to *like* the program. One reason may be that minority individuals portrayed usually came out on top—and Archie Bunker seemed to learn something each time. Some of those who identified themselves with Archie said that he reminded them of what they used to be like.

Other studies of *All in the Family* came to the conclusion that a process of selective perception seems to take place when one is exposed to certain derogatory material or interracial satire. Researchers Neil Vidman and Milton Rokeach explained "nonprejudiced viewers and minority group members may perceive and enjoy [the program] as satire, whereas prejudiced viewers may perceive of, and enjoy the show for 'telling it like it is.'" They further speculated, "By making Archie a 'lovable bigot' the program encourages bigots to excuse and rationalize their own prejudices."[13] Vidman and Rokeach came close to the previously mentioned position taken by Michael Novak.

All in the Family remained on the air for many years and is now frequently seen as a rerun along with other classics such as *MASH,* a long-running series about a frontline surgical hospital in Korea in the early 1950s. Like *All in the Family,* the *MASH* crew addressed many issues of social importance, including racism and sexism, but did so in a far less "in-your-face" manner. That series was followed by others, such as *Hill Street Blues* and *NYPD Blue,* and many motion pictures during the past three decades that pull few punches in addressing the same persisting problems. The difference is that the more recent shows tend toward realism rather than comedy to get their points across, including those that involve exposing the exploitation of minorities and women. Their stock in trade is the use of strong, direct language.

Direct language is also prevalent among members of the contemporary counter-culture, best represented by numerous rap groups who spice up their songs/poems with racist and sexist words with abandon.

Erdman Palmore, on the basis of a careful study of ethnophaulisms, concluded that "all racial and ethnic groups use ethnophaulisms.... When the out-group is a different race, most ethnophaulisms express and support the stereotypes of highly visible physical differences. When the out-group is the same general racial type, most ethnophaulisms express and support stereotypes of highly visible cultural differences. The derivations of most ethnophaulisms express some negative stereotypes."[14]

Since ethnophaulisms appear to be essential to the support and spread of ethnocentrism, they provide one indication of the relationship between ideas and action. As noted in Chapter Six, the conative dimension of prejudice is that aspect of the attitude construct concerned with predispositions for behavior. There is little question that referring to people in particularly derogatory ways or portraying them in terms of negative stereotypes or caricatures heightens one's sense of animus and, if supported by "appropriate" norms, allows, even encourages, the further acting out of predispositions.

In his book *Hate Speech,* published in 1994, Samuel Walker indicated why many derogatory expressions are appropriately labeled "fighting words."[15] They are words so incendiary that they are said to exceed the constitutional protection of free speech.[16]

The use of defamatory language is often intentionally provocative, particularly in the hands of demagogues. Throughout history those wishing to find scapegoats and to teach others to use them have used trumped-up charges, distortions of social roles, and guilt by association.

The Roman historian Tacitus explained this practice as well as anyone. Describing the burning of Rome, an act that most historians (and many Romans) attributed to Nero himself, Tacitus wrote, "Heaven could not stifle scandal or dispel the belief that the fire had taken place by order. Therefore, to suppress the rumor, Nero substituted as culprits, and punished with the utmost refinements of cruelty, a class of men, loathed for their vices, whom the crowd styled Christians."[17] Tacitus then explained that the members of the sect, meaning the Christians, were convicted and punished "not so much on the count of arson but for hatred of the human race."[18]

The practice of such demagoguery is indeed very old. Examples are to be found throughout history. Parallels to Emperor Nero's anti-Christian statements are found in references to Muslims during the Crusades, Jews in the Middle Ages, and in many later eras, native peoples during periods of colonization. Modern times have hardly been immune to such phenomena.

It was in Germany during the 1930s that verbal abuse of Jews, called anti-Semitic propaganda, was refined to an "art" under the direction of Joseph Goebbels and through the pen of Julius Streicher. Although the Nazis almost succeeded in ridding their country and those it occupied of the entire Jewish population by turning their words about the unworthiness of these *Untermenschen* (subhumans) to live, this type of abusive language did not disappear with the end of the Nazi regime. In the Soviet Union, similar caricatures were presented, with one notable difference. Some of the Soviet propaganda, and, more recently, that disseminated in Iran and many Arab countries, portrayed Jews in general and Israelis in particular as Nazis, a curious juxtaposition but one that clearly serves the needs of the demagogues who use such imagery. In recent years, it has not been uncommon to see crude caricatures of Muslims-as-terrorists in many Western newspapers, magazines, and posters, and in speeches by those proclaiming the threat of Islamists in many parts of the world.

Our own country has not been immune to hateful rhetoric. In the early days of World War II several social scientists conducted a study of demagoguery in the United States. In the volume *Prophets of Deceit* they described the mind and ideology of the hatemonger. The book provides many examples of the sort of message being delivered by such anti-Semites as Gerald L. K. Smith and Father Charles Coughlin. Here are samples:

When will the plain, ordinary, sincere, sheep like peoples of America awaken to the fact that their common affairs are being arranged and run for them by aliens, Communists, crackpots, refugees, renegades, Socialists, termites, and traitors? These alien enemies of America. . . .

Hitler and Hitlerism are the creatures of Jewry and Judaism. The merciless programs of abuse which certain Jews and their satellites work upon people who are not in full agreement with them create terrible reactions.

We are going to take this government out of the hands of these city slickers and give it back to the people that still believe that 2 and 2 is 4, that God is in his heaven and the Bible is the Word. . . .[19]

Despite denials by his brother, former president Jimmy Carter, Billy Carter seemed to echo some of these sentiments—and those of the Ku Klux Klan of the period—when he claimed that Jews had too much power and influence in America, especially in what he termed "the Jewish media."[20] Others in prominent positions, including such African American leaders as Louis Farrakhan and Khalid Abdul Muhammad, made similar public utterances a few years later, signaling some resurgence of anti-Semitic populism.[21]

In 1969 Seymour Martin Lipset and Earl Raab published a political history of right-wing activities. In *The Politics of Unreason* they describe in detail the mentalities of such movements as the Anti-Masonic League, the American Protective Association of the 1890s, the Ku Klux Klan in its various incarnations, the Coughlinites of the 1930s, the McCarthyites of the 1950s, and the followers of George Wallace and other reactionary leaders in the 1960s.[22] In 2001, Neil Baldwin's book, *Henry*

Ford and the Jews, wrote of each of those eras and offered an updated examination of what, in his subtitle, he calls "The Mass Production of Hate."[23]

Summing up their views of those who listened to the demagogues and joined the movements, Lipset and Raab suggest that "the adherents of extremist movements have typically felt deprived—either they have never gained their due share or they are losing their portion of power and status. We might call these two groups the 'never-hads' and the 'once-hads.'" These deprived groups are not necessarily extremist, but extremism usually draws its strength from them.[24] When the demagogue speaks, somebody listens.

Once-hads feel outraged by the thought of newcomers and outsiders getting what they believe to be legitimately theirs; never-hads seem to be particularly incensed by what they see as people demanding privileges that, they claim, they never had. In the early days of the civil rights struggle not a few white ethnics and even more poor whites in the South and many "middle Americans" were attracted by the appeals of those who blamed the blacks not only for wreaking changes throughout society and having the audacity to make demands for equality but calling for compensatory acts to make up for their harsh treatment. Some of the sloganeering of those in the Tea Party movement of late harken back to the turbulent days of the Klan when blatantly racist words were spoken from a stump or written in *The Fiery Cross.*[25] Others linked the demands of African Americans with communist conspiracies. One of the favorite charges of the radical right in the late 1950s and early 1960s was that Daisy Bates, the president of the NAACP in Little Rock, Arkansas, who helped to bring about school integration there, and others like her, were fronting for "commies."[26] Labeling of this sort and the reintroduction of classic stereotypes often stir smoldering embers of old prejudices, foment further hate, and call people to take action against their "foes." Name-calling is a widely used and highly effective form of discrimination.

Denial

Discrimination often goes far beyond using ethnic labels, telling humorous anecdotes, engaging in poisonous oratory, and direct defamation. Words are inflammatory and, as the Nazi propagandist Joseph Goebbels diabolically demonstrated, they can have far-reaching effects, stirring masses to political action.

As noted previously, the saying about "sticks and stones" denies the fact that name-calling does hurt. Still, there are more direct means used to break bones—and spirits. Indeed, much discriminatory behavior is more than talk. It usually involves establishing and maintaining some measure of physical and social distance from minorities, either by avoiding contact as much as possible, or by "keeping them in their place" or depriving them of access or opportunities others enjoy. *Avoidance* and *segregation* are two effective techniques of institutionalizing discrimination. In many ways, they are related.

Discrimination often involves the practice of minimizing face-to-face relations with members of certain specified groups. Fundamental lessons in avoidance are learned early in life when children learn from parents or playmates about groups with whom they should—or should not—associate. In adulthood these lessons manifest themselves in a variety of devices used to avoid contact with group members socially defined as being of low repute, unpleasant, or even untouchable.

One method of avoidance is the economic boycott. In the not so distant past, stores, restaurants, and conveyances known to be owned, operated, or frequented by certain minority group members on an equal basis with those in the dominant group were boycotted as a protest against their integrated policies. Fear of this kind of protest led a number of department-store owners (many of whom were themselves fair-weather liberals) to refrain from desegregating certain facilities such as lunch counters. In turn they often became the targets of civil rights groups seeking a redress of grievances. Two techniques were used in challenge: one was the sit-in, which forced proprietors to bring in police and, ultimately, to seek adjudication in the courts; the other was a counter-boycott to discourage members of the minority from using other facilities in the targeted stores.

Discriminatory boycotts have also been used in public places such as playgrounds, parks, and beaches abandoned by those who used them in protest against new integrated policies. Frequently leading to a self-fulfilling situation, a common pattern is for certain groups to withdraw from participation or utilization of such facilities as others move in. Ultimately what is most feared takes place. The minority takes over and the initial boycotters say, "We told you so!"

In some cases such boycotting is seen as a worthwhile inconvenience ("You can always go farther up the coast to another beach" or "Nobody in his right mind would go there!"). But the beginning of an end of segregated schools created a setting for a somewhat more permanent pattern. In the urban centers of the North and in many parts of the South, white parents responded to the threat of integrated schooling by sending their children to private schools or by establishing such schools where they had not existed previously—sometimes with the tacit support of local and state authorities. The implementation of busing to achieve greater racial balance intensified the use of boycotting as a form of protest. In city after city newspapers noted the *Washington Post*'s headline of December 20, 1972: "8000 Boycott Prince George's Classrooms" (in protest against court-ordered desegregation).[27] That was only the beginning. The pattern continued in many areas throughout the decade. One of the most dramatic examples occurred in Boston, Massachusetts, where many working-class whites felt their sanctuaries were being invaded by court-ordered integration of the schools. Angry mobs and organized groups of local residents tried to disrupt the process and end busing. That failing, many simply refused to go to school, or to send their children.

The most widespread method of avoidance is flight or "white flight," panic-driven movement away from neighborhoods into which minority group members are entering. For more than a century, the ecological history of large American cities was marked by the "invasion" of residential areas by certain ethnic and racial minorities, initial resistance of earlier inhabitants, then attempts to frighten or cajole people to sell out in response to the perceived threat, and then the eventual abandonment of the block or neighborhood and the succession of the newcomers.[28]

In recent decades, once all-white areas in Northern and West Coast cities turned into predominantly black neighborhoods. Frequently the exodus of whites was prompted by the panic of those residents who would not accept African American neighbors under any circumstances.

Although the process of changing neighborhoods is far from uniform and the time sequence is highly variable—depending upon such factors as the size of the incoming group, the nature of residential mobility already under way, and the extent of prejudice—many move simply because of the perceived threat of an "invasion."[29] Others may be encouraged to go because of the scare tactics of realtors and people who intentionally move in and become "block busters." An example of this that was carefully studied by Hillel Levine and Lawrence Harmon is the transition of a stable Jewish community in the Dorchester section of Boston into an African American ghetto in the late 1960s, the root cause of which is attributed to the decision of bankers and block busters that Jews would be more receptive to integration than Italian or Irish Americans who occupied nearby neighborhoods.[30]

A theme runs through all the methods employed for maintaining distances by avoidance. It involves *action or movement on the part of the dominant group rather than the minority.* To do something about "them" means, in these cases, doing something to one's self, one's family, or one's group.

Although related, segregation differs from avoidance. *In segregation, instead of doing something to one's self or group, action is directed against others.* A variety of devices is used to set up and maintain barriers between one's own group and those singled out and stigmatized because they are considered unworthy of normal social interaction. Segregation involves restrictive and exclusionary policies established to keep minorities out of communities or sections of them, or to place and hold them in particular areas such as reservations, barrios, and ghettos. Segregation has sometimes evolved on a voluntary basis, as did the famous ghetto of Cologne, Germany, where the Jews of the thirteenth century sought and obtained permission to set up their own community within the city walls.[31] Most segregation, like that of Jews in Venice several centuries later, is not voluntary, as suggested by the term itself and by its definition as a "form of isolation which places limits or restrictions upon contact, communication, and social relations."[32] During the Renaissance, Venetian Jews—and sometimes concubines and prostitutes—were required to wear yellow ribbons, yellow handkerchiefs, or yellow medallions to signify their "otherness." This was to ensure that such people, who were often indistinguishable in manners and dress from those in the dominant group, could be instantly identified as "outsiders."

During the Nazi occupation of much of Europe five centuries later, German authorities used similar techniques of labeling by requiring Jews to wear yellow stars with the words *Jude, Juif,* and *Jood* (*Jew* in German, French, and Dutch) written across them.

With several notable exceptions—for example, the communities of Hasidim, the Amish, and several other religious sects and cults—most of the segregation practiced in the United States has been of an involuntary nature. The caste-like restrictions that applied to African Americans are the most obvious examples but there are many others. Until quite recently, one of the most common was the virtual exclusion of women from certain male bastions. Even when women began to make progress in achieving access into the inner sanctum of corporate America, a "glass ceiling" served to slow the process of getting to the top.

Segregation usually involves both spatial and social barriers. Social distance is most easily maintained through physical distance. In the past, Native Americans who survived the bullets and bacilli of the Europeans were forcibly restricted to reservations, a pattern followed much later in South Africa where *apartheid* (the maintaining of a separated society) was institutionalized into an elaborate hierarchy with blacks on the bottom with few civil or even human rights to protect them. Above them was a layer of "coloured" people (the descendants of certain "mixed-race" Europeans and native African tribal peoples, especially the Hottentots); then came Malays and Indians, many of whom came to the country as recruited laborers; and, at the top, Englishmen and Afrikaners, the latter descendants of the Dutch settlers, and, for a long while, despite its small size relative to the black African population, the strongest group politically. Restrictions of another sort were much in the news in the mid-1990s, most notably "ethnic cleansing," as Bosnian Serbs referred to their scheme for ridding disputed territory of their opponents, the Bosnian Muslims. In what turned out to be a replay of Nazi tactics of roundups and mass assassinations, in some areas it began with restrictions on movements, forced marches, and removal to concentration camps. In the first decade of the twenty-first century similar tactics were being used to isolate hundreds of thousands of rural people in the Darfur region of the Sudan.

In this country ghettos have often persisted, not only because of poverty but because there was no easy escape. At various times in American history, working- and middle-class minorities, including African Americans, Asian Americans, Mexicans, members of various European "nationality" groups, and others have been barred from purchasing homes in certain urban and suburban neighborhoods. Clearly, this physical separation served to limit interaction with members of other groups.

Residential segregation accounts for many other patterns of separation—even when these are unenforceable by law, as in the case of education where school districts tend to follow neighborhood patterns. Among the various devices used in the past to maintain America's own form of apartheid[33] were restrictive covenants and "gentlemen's agreements." The former were often legally binding contractual arrangements where buyers promised not to sell to anyone other than another white, Christian family; the latter were based on a symbolic handshake. Well into the last third of the twentieth century one could still find deeds to property with provisions such as the following:

> And, furthermore, no lot shall be sold or leased to, or occupied by, any person excepting of the Caucasian race.
>
> Provided further, that the grantee shall not sell to Negroes or permit use or occupation by them, except as domestic servants.
>
> ... shall not permit occupation by Negroes, Hindus, Syrians, Greeks, or any corporation controlled by same.[34]

Perhaps the most infamous of neighborhood policies was the "point system" maintained as recently as four decades ago for admittance to residence in highly restrictive Grosse Pointe, Michigan. Community leaders required that all prospective residents be screened and evaluated on the basis of race, religion, education, occupation, accent, "swarthiness," and other invidious criteria, and then allotted points for each "favorable" attribute. Only high scorers were allowed to purchase property. The Grosse Pointe pattern is an extreme example of an established, though declining, practice in many communities in the United States.[35]

Housing is not the only area where restrictive regulations, formal and informal, official and sub rosa, prevent outsiders from entering the circle of the dominant group. City clubs and country clubs, sororities and fraternities, lodges and service organizations have required applicants or initiates to be "members of the Christian faith," or to "believe in Jesus Christ," or to be "white and Caucasian." Not long ago many Greek-letter college fraternities went so far as to exclude Greeks.[36]

Admission to some private schools and colleges has also been limited by quota systems under which only certain percentages of the members of specified groups are considered eligible—irrespective of academic abilities. Since the 1950s, antidiscrimination legislation has prohibited colleges and universities in many states (and those receiving federal support) from requesting photographs, indications of religious preference or affiliation, or information about national origin from applicants. Still, such restrictions were sometimes circumvented through an old device, the implementation of "geographic quotas." By accepting only a certain percentage of city dwellers or easterners, for example, certain schools, particularly those in the "Ivy League," managed to keep a tight rein on the number of Jewish and Catholic students admitted, irrespective of their academic qualifications.[37]

In spite of the increasing recognition of performance standards in the world of work, some business corporations (especially smaller, family-controlled firms), professional organizations, and labor unions still continue to disqualify members of minority groups from employment or membership or limit the heights to which they may rise, severely hampering their opportunities to pursue occupations for which they are trained. The timeworn practice of hiring minorities and women last and firing them first still holds in many industries.

In a hard-hitting essay on "Inequality in America," Edna Bonacich made the following observation: "The United States is an immensely unequal society in terms of the distribution of material wealth, and consequently, in the distribution of all the benefits and privileges that accrue to wealth—including political power and influence. This inequality is vast irrespective of race. However, people of color tend to cluster at the bottom so that inequality in this society also becomes racial inequality.... it is deeply embedded in this [capitalist] system."[38]

Bonacich claimed that, professions of "all men being equal" notwithstanding, the entire American political-economic system is bound to racism because capitalism itself depends on an ideology of inequality and the exploitation of certain especially vulnerable groups to assure its hierarchies of power and privilege. Although many may argue with the starkness of the indictment and its concentration on the singularity of capitalism-as-cause, none can gainsay the fact that racial discrimination has served to keep many groups down and dependent.

The following statement from an annual official government document, *The Social and Economic Status of the Black Population in the United States,* published in the early 1970s, revealed the effects of segregation and exclusion in this country despite the powerful civil rights movement of the 1960s. "In the 1960s significant advances were made by the Black population in many fields—notably, income, health, education, employment, and voter participation. The current statistics indicate continued progress in some areas of life, although other areas remained unchanged. Blacks continued to lag behind whites in most social and economic areas, although the differentials have narrowed over the years."[39]

That pattern, African Americans behind whites, in almost every sphere—education, voting, and political participation, as well as employment and income—persisted well into the next three decades.[40] Despite gains on some fronts, such as greater access to higher education through the initiation of more far-reaching recruitment schemes to make campuses "more diverse," much of this triggered by the requirements of affirmative action rules, the overall picture, especially in the crucial areas of employment and income, offered little evidence of significant breakthroughs.

The generally sluggish economy and inflationary pressures in the mid- and late-1970s had a dampening effect on the chances of the able-bodied poor in all cohorts, white, African American, Hispanic, or Asian. As for the working class, that is, those already steadily employed, whites in the aggregate made some slight gains, blacks hardly any. Many conservative citizens believed that things could be dramatically changed if the "tired old policies of the 1930s" were finally replaced with new, innovative economic strategies (views to be echoed in the 1990s and again in the first decade of the twenty-first century). The opportunity to effect such changes came to pass with the election of Ronald Reagan, whose new administration sought "to get the country moving again," convinced that the trickle-down effects of supply-side economics would help all Americans realize the dream of a better life. Yet, even the economic boom of the 1980s had little direct impact on the hard-core sufferers, many of whom were members of minorities. In a hard-hitting statement, John Jacob, president of the Urban League in 1986, put it this way:

What columnist David Broder called the "fatal blend of ignorance and arrogance" [regarding such foreign policy blunders as "Irangate"] also describes the administration's civil rights policies. It tried to win tax exemptions for segregated schools, fought extension of civil rights laws, undermined affirmative action, destroyed the U.S. Civil Rights Commission, stacked the judiciary with right-wingers, and refused to budge from its support for South Africa's apartheid government—all the while implementing a public relations policy designed to convince Americans that we are now a color-blind, racially neutral society.

At the same time, it ignored mounting African American poverty. In place of substantive domestic policy, it substituted demonstrably false statements designed to convince the public that unemployment was no longer a problem, that the poor don't want to work, and that social programs simply compound social problems instead of helping to resolve them.[41]

There was a growing employment gap, a growing income gap, and a growing wealth gap. According to the Census Bureau, the typical white family in the mid-1980s had a net worth twelve times as great as the net worth of the typical African American family. And almost one-third of all black families had no assets at all.

Although Jacob did indicate that the gaps between rich and poor cut across racial lines, a point forcefully argued by the sociologist William Julius Wilson in his thoughtful volume, *The Declining Significance of Race,*[42] neither Jacob nor Wilson denied the persistence of discrimination—both blatant and subtle—would continue to hobble nonwhites in their effort to find a securer place in the wider society.

Many social scientists contend that although discrimination is no longer a sufficient explanation for all the problems of ghetto living—street crime, delinquency, drug abuse, unwanted pregnancies, child abuse, and "welfare dependency"—so often discussed in the press, it is surely necessary to take into account the effects of patterns of institutionalized racism so deeply woven into the fabric of this society.

Nearly forty-five years after the publication of the first of the census reports discussed above, the overall black/white gap remained very wide and remains so to this day.

Although it is true that the majority of the poor in this country are still white, it is also true that the majority of blacks and Hispanics are still poor. Much of their poverty is the legacy of discrimination.[43]

William Julius Wilson contended that this dependency was aggravated by the concentration of various populations in particular sectors of society and their isolation from the rest of the community, the lack of jobs and job opportunities in traditionally labor-intensive factories, and the fragmentation of the urban areas themselves by new roadways built over and often right through old neighborhoods.[44] The result, said Alan Wolfe, is that "The condition of the urban Black poor has deteriorated over the past quarter century to the point where it threatens all the other gains in race relations that were realized during the same period."[45] Indeed, the situation had become so bad that it was not unreasonable to speak of many inner-city ghettos as separate, deteriorating societies, cut off—and even cut loose—from their mainstream moorings.[46]

In spite of a number of positive changes in the behavior and attitudes of increasing numbers of those in the dominant sector who were coming to accept the reality of America as a multiracial, multiethnic society, the categorical disparities manifest in one area of life after another are related to long-institutionalized patterns of discrimination which, to this day, still make it more difficult for blacks (and, in many instances, other nonwhites) to run an equal race. They have known it for years; so, as numerous studies have shown, have policy makers. This last point was made abundantly clear nearly fifty years ago when, in the wake of the urban riots that erupted in city after city during the summers of 1966 and 1967, a Presidential Commission was invited to investigate their causes. Asked to find out why these outbreaks had taken place and what could be done to prevent them in the future, a group of leading citizens headed by then-governor Otto Kerner of Illinois carried out an extensive study of twenty-four disorders in twenty-three different American cities. A year later the report was published. In one version, Tom

Wicker, a former columnist for the *New York Times,* wrote a special introduction in which he focused on the central issue that constantly confronted the commissioners and the investigative staff. "In the end," Wicker claimed, "not without dispute and travail and misgiving, in the clash and spark of human conflict and human pride, against the pressures of time and ignorance, they produced not so much a report on the riots as a report on America—one nation divided."[47]

Wicker based his conclusion on his assessment of the report, which included the following summary statements about the explosive mixture that contributed to the potential for upheaval:

> *Pervasive discrimination and segregation* in employment, education and housing, which have resulted in the continuing exclusion of great numbers of Negroes from the benefits of economic progress.
>
> *Black in-migration and white exodus,* which have produced massive and growing concentrations of impoverished Negroes in our major cities, creating a growing crisis of deteriorating facilities and services and unmet human needs.
>
> *The Black ghettos* where segregation and poverty converge on the young to destroy opportunity and enforce failure. Crime, drug addiction, dependency on welfare, and bitterness and resentment against society in general and white society in particular are the result.[48]

In 1992's *Two Nations: Black and White, Separate, Hostile, and Unequal,* Andrew Hacker corroborated Wicker's earlier assessment. Segregation and poverty, Hacker concluded, had created in the racial ghetto a destructive environment totally unknown to most white Americans.[49]

Pathology for many nonwhites, which continues today, is doubtlessly still related to the patterns of life they are forced to adopt. Upheaval may be construed as a desperate cry for help; it may also be viewed as one of the few healthy alternatives to despair in a sick society. Whichever view one takes (and there is considerable controversy over this fundamental question), there is little question that the barriers erected to keep nonwhites in their place have done more than isolate large numbers of people.

> Segregation and poverty have created in the racial ghetto a destructive environment totally unknown to most white Americans.
>
> What white Americans have never fully understood—but what the Negro can never forget—is that white society is deeply implicated in the ghetto. White institutions created it, white institutions maintain it, and white society condones it.[50]

Aggression

Intimidation is sometimes subtle. Most of the time it is unconcealed. ("Just try stepping out of line!") Violence or the threat of violence has long been used to keep racial and ethnic minorities mindful of their subordinate status. Tied to both derogation and denial, there are many forms of aggressive action in which individuals or groups participate, ranging from the jeering at and threatening of little children to gang fights or organized terror and mob rule. The lexicon of racial conflict is filled with words related to violent aggression: "lynching," "pogrom," "genocide," and hundreds of others—and examples of their use are not hard to find.

Thousands of native people are exterminated to make the country safe—and profitable—for colonists.

Hundreds of Chinese are savagely attacked and many are killed by white mobs.

A synagogue is symbolically smeared with swastikas and the slogan "Hate Jews."

A young African American is shot at point-blank range for trespassing on "white man's turf."

A mosque is burned to the ground "to teach those people a lesson."

"Violence," Gordon Allport once wrote, "is always an outgrowth of milder states of mind. Although most barking does not lead to biting, yet there is never a bite without previous barking."[51] Led by the demagogue, the ardent segregationist, the fanatic patriot, the self-styled defender of a neighborhood, both crazed and solid and respectable citizens have done unspeakable violence against "them."

Even in our society of law and order the social conditions for mob violence still exist, as does the violence itself. Not long ago many southern blacks lived in terror of the lynch mob. Their anxiety was well justified for, according to the records of the NAACP, there were 5,112 lynchings between 1882 and 1939 (3,657 of the victims were African American).[52]

In the past, lynchings occurred mainly in those areas where the practice of segregation was maintained by the harshest forms of intimidation. Some social scientists have interpreted lynching as a means of venting frustrations against a convenient scapegoat. For example, it has been argued that the falling price of cotton portended an upsurge in the number of lynchings in the South. Whether one can make a causal reference from the correlation, the wide use of lynching indicates a tacit acceptance of such activity as a legitimate way to maintain the caste-like social system. The facts that lynchings were often not prevented even when known of by the authorities and that when culprits were known and apprehended they were seldom punished to a degree commensurate with the crime give ample evidence to support the contention that such behavior was condoned by those in official positions of authority.[53]

Although the number of lynchings remained relatively negligible from the end of World War II to the late 1970s, in those same years vigilantes sometimes took the law into their own hands, meting out "cracker barrel justice." The desire to fight against changes in the status quo saw a rebirth of mob aggressiveness in the South. In the 1950s, black parents attempting to send their children to schools desegregated by court decision in Clinton, Little Rock, New Orleans, and more than a score of other southern cities were met with angry crowds of white demonstrators who burned crosses, threatened them, and severely beat them. All too frequently the local authorities failed to provide adequate protection for the African American citizens. In some cities, once law and order were established or reestablished—sometimes with the aid of federal troops—segregation was maintained by whites who withdrew their children from public schools.[54]

Sit-in demonstrators who sought equal service in restaurants, kneel-in demonstrators desiring to attend integrated church services, wade-in demonstrators wishing to swim in areas restricted to whites, read-in demonstrators wanting to take books from segregated libraries, and freedom riders challenging the policy of segregated interstate transportation and separate terminal facilities met with similar outbursts of aggression and violence. In the spring of 1961, for example, a busload of freedom riders was greeted by an angry mob in Anniston, Alabama, who threw rocks, smashed windows, and eventually burned the bus. White men armed with clubs attacked another group that had gone to Birmingham, and several riders were brutally beaten.

In the early fall of 1962 an especially ugly incident in the long fight for desegregation occurred at Oxford, Mississippi, when, aided by several hundred US marshals and 24,000 soldiers, James Meredith was forcibly admitted to the University of Mississippi under a court order restraining the school from denying his admission. His presence on the campus triggered a series of riots that took several hours to quell. By the time order was restored by the imposition of virtual martial law, two adults had been killed and over one hundred people injured.

Only two weeks earlier, four black churches in rural Georgia were burned to the ground. All but one was being used for registering new voters. On September 17, 1962, the Student Nonviolent Coordinating Committee sent the following telegram to President Kennedy: "Another church burned this morning. Four churches burned in the past month, reminiscent of Nazi burning of synagogues. Imperative you investigate and apprehend arsonists. Halt the outrageous terror of peaceful American citizens. The national shame must be ended."[55] The president's own violent death a little over one year later indicated that terror remained rampant in our society. And we were to see more and more senseless killing—much of it related to racial tensions—in the years to come.

The annals of civil rights martyrdom are filled with names of young black and white civil rights workers gunned down by those who could not tolerate the changes in the status quo that they represented: among them Herbert Lee, Medgar Evers, and the Nobel Prize–winner Reverend Martin Luther King Jr., the "apostle of nonviolence."

James Chaney, Andrew Goodman, and Michael Schwerner, who were trying to encourage African Americans to vote in the summer of 1964, were brutally murdered in Neshoba County, Mississippi. Their assassins were members of the White Knights of the Ku Klux Klan, many of whom were identified as far back as 1967, but not until 2005 was the former Klansman Edgar Ray Killen convicted of the killings, forty years after the fact.[56]

In addition to these dastardly deeds, hundreds of other acts of violence continued to be perpetrated in big cities and rural towns. Crops were burned, workers were fired, and women and children were threatened. Even policemen, sworn to uphold the law, sometimes ran amuck, venting their wrath on unarmed protesters and innocent bystanders. The whole world reeled at the image of young blacks being attacked by police dogs in Birmingham and elsewhere in the South.

A headline in the December 12, 1972, issue of the *New York Times* stating "City Unit Sees Violence Pattern by Whites against Minorities" was a stark reminder that vigilantism persisted in a period many have viewed as a time of interracial progress. The article described a study conducted by the City Commission of Human Rights that revealed eleven cases in which homes owned by blacks or Puerto Ricans in New York City had been set afire or vandalized and instances of arson in churches and attacks on school buses. Blaming white gangs, the Commission wrote, "We can no longer maintain the myth that violence and pathology of Southern racism is totally absent in the North. These occurrences, while unconnected, nonetheless suggest an ominous trend that could mean that continued integration in the North will be resisted as forcefully and violently as in the South."[57]

The commentary proved prophetic. In the years that followed, America witnessed further evidence of the persistence of violent resistance along with other forms of reaction against moves toward desegregation. The major arena of confrontation was the northern school district and the basic issue was busing, the movement of black and white children to schools that were sometimes far from home in order to achieve "racial balance."

A debate has continued over the effects of such policies on attitudes and behavior relating to race relations and their effectiveness on the educational process itself. Sociologist James Coleman, an early advocate of desegregation and author of one of the most widely quoted reports on the problems of separate schooling, argued along with others that forced busing was counterproductive, especially since it accelerated "white flight," the movement from city to suburb.[58] Others said the evidence, including evidence from a later study conducted by Coleman himself, belied such claims, that, in fact, whites were leaving the cities whether busing was being imposed or not. And some continued to suggest that, although desegregation would not be accomplished by school integration alone, it still was essential to get people to know one another even if it meant requiring them to leave the neighborhood to do so.

Although the debate over techniques of breaking down what the English call "the colour bar" continued in many quarters, there were those who seemed to be little interested in weighing the issues. "Righteous racists," as some called them, sought to maintain closed communities, white bastions—often white, Christian bastions. They opposed "race mixing" in any form. Some such protesters joined the ranks of a revitalized Ku Klux Klan. Others found their ideological home in other right-wing groups.

In the late 1970s both the KKK and the neo-Nazis gained some strength and considerable publicity. Perhaps the most widely discussed case was the proposed pro-Nazi march scheduled to be held in Skokie, Illinois, a suburb of Chicago with many Jewish residents, including a number of concentration camp survivors. The Nazis sought and, through the intercession of the American Civil Liberties Union (ACLU), obtained a permit to demonstrate, speak their piece freely—blatant anti-Semitism and attacks on others they, like those whose banner they carried, deemed inferior and parasitic. The question of whether they should have been given a permit or not evoked a debate of its own and much soul-searching on the part of many civil libertarians. Although the American Civil Liberties Union defended the right to march, a number of ardent supporters of free speech (including several prominent former members of the ACLU) reminded their fellow liberals that, in the words of Chief Justice Holmes, the First Amendment does not give one the right to shout "Fire" in a crowded theater. And, they argued, calls for the expulsion, even the annihilation, of Jews were surely more than expressing opinions.[59] Although the Skokie March was finally called off, it represented a clear case of how our first concern with antilocution is (or may be) linked to the last to be discussed, genocide, the planned elimination of an entire people.

Lynchings, cross burnings, calls to arms, rallies to whip up attacks on racial, religious, and ethnic minorities in this country are painful reminders of the crimes against humanity perpetrated in Nazi Germany. Genocide was the national policy of a sovereign state not much more than half a century ago. Over nine million Jews lived in Europe before World War II. Nazi leaders were determined to eradicate this group and nearly succeeded.

Forced to carry identification papers marked with a "J" and to wear the previously mentioned identifying yellow stars with the word "Jew" across them, driven from their homes, often ghettoized, herded into concentration camps, used as forced labor, experimented upon, violated in countless ways, and ultimately murdered by firing squads or liquidated in gas chambers, the Jews of Europe suffered the most heinous of all fates that can befall a group: *genocide,* the slaughter of an entire people.

Death camp survivor Primo Levi, an Italian Jew, described his recollection of the steps taken to break the spirit of the healthier camp inmates, those who were to be used for forced labor—but would, in the end, be executed, joining the others who had been killed earlier.

> We had reached the bottom. It is not possible to sink lower than this; no human condition is more miserable than this nor could it conceivably be so. Nothing belongs to us anymore; they have taken away our clothes, our shoes, even our hair; if we speak, they will not listen to us, and if they listen they will not understand. They will even take away our name.[60]

And they did take away their names. In many camps, including Auschwitz, where Levi was finally taken, inmates were tattooed on the forearm with prison numbers, their only form of identification. They carried their numbers to the grave.

The word "genocide" emerged during the war trials at Nuremberg, where it was defined as "a denial of the right of existence of entire human groups in the same way as homicide is the denial of the right to live for individual human beings." Although the term is newly coined, the practice itself is very old. It was known in biblical times when Menahem smote Tiphsah,[61] it was practiced by the British when they destroyed the Tasmanians in the "triumph of 'civilization' over 'savagery,'"[62] and a version was used in early America when settlers offered bounty for the scalps and sometimes the heads of Indians[63] and when Lord Jeffrey Amherst distributed smallpox-laden blankets to the indigenous peoples in a concerted effort to eliminate them.

In 2003, Robin M. Williams Jr. noted that the twentieth century was the bloodiest in history.

> The statistics numb the mind. Although estimates vary widely, the tale of death and destruction is monumental: since 1900 some 115 million persons killed in battles— plus perhaps an equal number of civilian fatalities. These were mass killings in organized wars, [but].... The slaughter was not confined to wars between states, for governments have savaged their own people....
>
> Ever since World War II, the basic facts are stark. The vast majority of deaths from collective violence since 1945 have been within national states rather than between states; credible estimates say some 80 percent.[64]

In recent times violence has raged in our society—much of it based on racial hatred and ethnic rivalries. There is no evidence of such terrifying mass killing on our shores or sponsored genocide, but Americans have been witness to such acts. In the past few decades, television scenes have made us eyewitnesses to Pol Pot's murder of millions of his fellow Cambodians, the butchering of hundreds of thousands of Tutsi people by Hutus in Rwanda, the campaigns of "ethnic cleansing" by Serbs in various states of the former Yugoslavia, and the more recent slaughter of those in Darfur by the government-supported killers in the Sudan. Each of these actions falls clearly under the definition set forth at the time of the trials of Nazi leaders in Nuremberg, Germany, in the mid-1940s.

Conclusion

These cases of discrimination have been cited not to indicate how inconsiderate and brutal people can be (though such might be purpose enough), but rather to describe briefly the varying degrees of discrimination—*derogation, denial,* and *aggression.* Each, except *mass* murder, is a contemporary example of discrimination in the United States and an expression of both unwitting and willful behavior to which too many Americans, including fair-weather liberals, subscribe.

We have examined some formal and informal policies of those with majority status and some ways in which they seek to maintain it. Little attention has been paid to the reactions of those discriminated against. The following chapter examines the impact of discriminatory treatment and some sociological implications of minority status.

Notes

1. Robin M. Williams Jr., *The Reduction of Intergroup Tensions* (New York: Social Science Research Council, 1947), p. 39.

2. See, for example, Gordon W. Allport, *The Nature of Prejudice* (Cambridge: Addison-Wesley, 1954), esp. pp. 14–15 and 49–51; and Ernest Works, "Types of Discrimination," *Phylon* (Fall 1969), pp. 223–233.

3. Richard Wright, *Black Boy* (New York: Harper and Row, 1945), esp. pp. 128–129 and 163–170.

4. A good summary of the language of prejudice is to be found in John P. Dean and Alex Rosen, *A Manual of Intergroup Relations* (Chicago: University of Chicago Press, 1955), chap. 2. This chapter was written in collaboration with Robert B. Johnson and the ideas expressed are largely based on Johnson's unpublished PhD dissertation, "The Nature of the Minority Community" (Ithaca, NY: Cornell University, 1954).

5. Michael Novak, "The Sting of Polish Jokes," *Newsweek* (April 12, 1976), p. 13.

6. Michael Lerner, "Respectable Bigotry," *The American Scholar,* 38 (Autumn 1969).

7. Bernard Rosenberg and Gilbert Shapiro, "Marginality and Jewish Humor," *Midstream,* 4 (Spring 1958), pp. 70–80.

8. See, for example, Russell Middleton and John Morland, "Humor in Negro and White Subcultures: A Study of Jokes among University Students," *American Sociological Review,* 24 (February 1959), pp. 61–69. See also John H. Burma, "Humor as a Technique in Race Conflict," *American Sociological Review,* 11 (December 1946), pp. 710–715; Milton L. Barron, "A Content Analysis of Intergroup Humor," *American Sociological Review,* 15 (February 1950), pp. 88–94.

9. Stanley Crouch, *The Artificial White Man* (New York: Basic Civitas Books, 2005). The quotation is at the center of a critical review of Crouch's book by Emily Eakin, *New York Times Book Review* (January 16, 2005), p. 7.

10. See Sam Hoffman and Eric Spiegelman, "Old Jews Telling Jokes" (New York: Random House, 2010).

11. For an excellent analysis of such shows, see Henry Louis Gates Jr., "T.V.'s Black World Turns but Stays Unreal," *New York Times* (November 12, 1989), Section II, 1, p. 40.

12. Laura Hobson, *New York Times* (September 12, 1971), Section II, 1 and continuation. See also Robert Alter, "Defaming the Jews," *Commentary,* 45 (January 1973), pp. 77–83.

13. Neil Vidman and Milton Rokeach, "Archie Bunker's Bigotry: A Study of Selective Perception and Exposure," *Journal of Communication,* 24 (Winter 1974). Much more recently, Leonard Freedman discussed *All in the Family* and later programs and debates they triggered in civil liberties circles and by many members of minority groups over offensive language, free speech, and political correctness. See Freedman, *The Offensive Art: Political Satire and Its Censorship around the World from Beerbohm to Borat* (Westport, CT: Praeger, 2009), pp. 51–55.

14. Erdman Palmore, "Ethnophaulisms and Ethnocentrism," *American Journal of Sociology,* 67 (January 1962), pp. 442–445. See also William B. Helmreich, *The Things They Say Behind Your Back* (New Brunswick, NJ: Transaction Books, 1984).

15. Samuel Walker, *Hate Speech: The History of an American Controversy* (Lincoln: University of Nebraska Press, 1994).

16. The expression "fighting words" first appeared in the 1942 "Chaplinsky Decision" of the Supreme Court relating to the persecution of Jehovah's Witnesses. Walker, *Hate Speech,* pp. 64–65.

17. Clifford H. Moore (trans.), *The Annals of Tacitus* (Cambridge: Harvard University Press, 1937), Vol. IV, Book XV, p. 285.

18. Ibid., p. 287.

19. These phrases are part of a composite speech made up of actual statements by American demagogues; they serve as introduction to the study by Leo Lowenthal and Norbert

Guterman, *Prophets of Deceit* (New York: Harper and Row, 1949), pp. 1–2. Current examples of inflammatory writings are *Common Sense, America's Newspaper against Communism,* published in Union, NJ, and the *American Nationalist,* published in Inglewood, California. The support given to such publications is analyzed in an article by Hans H. Toch, Steven E. Deutsch, and Donald M. Wilkins, "The Wrath of the Bigot: An Analysis of Protest Mail," *Journalism Quarterly,* 37 (Spring 1960), pp. 173–185, 266.

20. Martin Tolchin, "President Won't Condemn Brother's Remarks on Jews," *New York Times* (February 28, 1979), p. A16.

21. See Peter I. Rose, "Blaming the Jews," *Society,* 31:6 (September–October 1994), pp. 35–40.

22. See Seymour Martin Lipset and Earl Raab, *The Politics of Unreason* (New York: Harper and Row, 1969).

23. Neil Baldwin, *Henry Ford and the Jews: The Mass Production of Hate* (New York: Public Affairs, 2001).

24. Seymour Martin Lipset, "Prejudice and Politics in America," in Charles Y. Glock and Ellen Siegelman (eds.), *Prejudice U.S.A.* (New York: Praeger, 1969), p. 18.

25. See David Cunningham, *Klansville, USA: The Rise and Fall of the Ku Klux Klan* (New York: Oxford University Press, 2013).

26. See, for example, *Common Sense* (September 15, 1958), p. 1.

27. *Washington Post* (December 20, 1972), p. C1.

28. See, for example, Charles Abrams, *Forbidden Neighbors* (New York: Harper and Row, 1955); and Oscar Handlin, *The Newcomers: Negroes and Puerto Ricans in a Changing Metropolis* (Cambridge: Harvard University Press, 1959).

29. Two early and now classic examples of the problems of "race and housing" are Morton Grodzins, *The Metropolitan Area as a Racial Problem* (Pittsburgh: University of Pittsburgh Press, 1958); and Eunice Crier and George Crier, *The Impact of Race on Neighborhoods in the Metropolitan Setting* (Washington, DC: Washington Center for Metropolitan Studies, 1961).

30. Hillel Levine and Lawrence Harmon, *The Death of an American Jewish Community* (New York: Free Press, 1992).

31. See, for example, Louis Wirth, *The Ghetto* (Chicago: University of Chicago Press, 1956), pp. 18–19.

32. Brewton Berry, *Race and Ethnic Relations,* 2nd ed. (Boston: Houghton Mifflin, 1958), p. 273.

33. See Douglas S. Massey and Nancy A. Denton, *American Apartheid: Segregation and the Making of the Underclass* (Cambridge: Harvard University Press, 1993).

34. Allport lists these and other examples of restrictive covenants, op. cit., p. 53.

35. See Benjamin R. Epstein and Arnold Forster, *Some of My Best Friends ...* (New York: Farrar, Straus and Cudahy, 1962), esp. pp. 106–139.

36. This practice has lessened in recent years, largely as a result of college administration action. See ibid., pp. 165–167. See also Alfred McClung Lee, *Fraternities without Brotherhood* (Boston: Beacon, 1955); and "A Study of Religious Discrimination by Social Clubs," *Rights,* 4 (January 1962), pp. 83–96.

37. See Jerome Karabel, *The Chosen: The Hidden History of Admission and Exclusion at Harvard, Yale, and Princeton* (Boston and New York: Houghton Mifflin, 2005).

38. Edna Bonacich, "Inequality in America: The Failure of the American System for People of Color," in Alberto Aguirre Jr. and David V. Baker (eds.), *Sources: Notable Selections in Race and Ethnicity* (Guilford, CT: Duskin Publishing Group, 1995), pp. 134, 136.

39. *The Social and Economic Status of the Black Population in the United States,* Current Population Reports, Series P-23, No. 42 (Washington, DC: Department of Commerce, 1971), p. 1.

. 40. *The Social and Economic Status of the Black Population in the United States: An Historical Overview 1790–1978,* Current Population Reports, Series P-23, No. 80 (Washington, DC: Department of Commerce, 1979), pp. 168–169.

41. John E. Jacob, *The State of Black America* (New York: National Urban League, Inc., 1987), pp. 7–14.

42. William J. Wilson, *The Declining Significance of Race* (Chicago: University of Chicago Press, 1978).

43. Sam Roberts, *Who We Are: A Portrait of America Based on the 1990 Census* (New York: Times Books, 1993), p. 189.

44. William Julius Wilson, *The Truly Disadvantaged: The Inner City, the Underclass, and Public Policy* (Chicago: University of Chicago Press, 1987).

45. Roberts, quoting Wolfe, *Bonfire of the Vanities,* p. 192.

46. See Gary Orfield, "Ghettoization and Its Alternatives," in Paul E. Peterson (ed.), *The New Urban Reality* (Washington, DC: The Brookings Institution, 1981), p. 103.

47. Tom Wicker, "Introduction," *Report of the National Advisory Commission on Civil Disorders* (New York: Bantam Books, 1968), p. x.

48. *Report of the National Advisory Commission on Civil Disorders* (New York: Bantam Books, 1968), p. 10.

49. Andrew Hacker, *Two Nations: Black and White, Separate, Hostile, Unequal* (New York: Scribner's, 1992), esp. chap. 1.

50. Ibid., p. 2.

51. Allport, op. cit., p. 57.

52. As reported in George E. Simpson and J. Milton Yinger, *Racial and Cultural Minorities,* rev. ed. (New York: Harper and Row, 1958), p. 515.

53. See Allport, op. cit., pp. 61–62.

54. For descriptions of several instances of school desegregation crises, see the following *Field Reports on Desegregation in the South,* written by social scientists and published in New York by the Anti-Defamation League of B'nai B'rith: a report on Beaumont, Texas, "College Desegregation without Popular Consent," by Warren Breed; on Sturgis, Kentucky, "A Tentative Description and Analysis of the School Desegregation Crisis," by Roscoe Griffin; on Mansfield, Texas, "A Report on the Crisis Situation Resulting from Efforts to Desegregate the School System," by John Howard Griffin and Theodore Freedman; and, on Clinton, Tennessee, "A Tentative Description and Analysis of the School Desegregation Crisis," by Anna Holden, Bonita Valien, and Preston Valien.

55. Reprinted in *New York Times* (September 18, 1962), p. 27.

56. See "Arrest Made in Notorious '64 Civil Rights Killings," *New York Times* (January 7, 2005), pp. 1, 15.

57. *New York Times* (December 12, 1972), pp. 1, 54.

58. See, for example, James Coleman, "Liberty and Equality in School Desegregation," *Social Policy,* 6 (January 1976), pp. 9–13.

59. See, for example, David Goldberg and others, "Thoughts about Skokie," *Dissent* (Spring 1979), pp. 226–230.

60. Primo Levi, *Survival in Auschwitz,* trans. by Stuart Woolf (New York: Orion Press, 1959), pp. 21–22.

61. II Kings 15:16.

62. G. P. Murdock, *Our Primitive Contemporaries* (New York: Macmillan, 1934), p. 18.

63. See Berry, op. cit., pp. 187–194. See also Alain Locke and Bernhard Stern, *When Peoples Meet* (New York: Progressive Education Association, 1942), pp. 165–170.

64. Robin M. Williams Jr., *The Wars Within: People and States in Conflict* (Ithaca, NY: Cornell University Press, 2003), p. xii.

In the Minority

The View from Outside

Henry James, the American novelist, spent twenty years of his life, from 1883 to 1904, away from his native land. Between his departure and return the country had undergone profound changes, most noticeably in the quality of urban life. When he left, it was English (or Anglo-American) in style and in sound. When he returned to New York the modest city had been transformed into a bustling metropolis, and homogeneity no longer marked the character of the social structure.

The old streets of the city had become warrens of poor immigrants, Little Italies and Little Jerusalems—polyglot enclaves even more strange than the shantytowns of the Irish who had come during James's youth, already signaling the beginning of the end of Protestant preeminence and Anglo conformity.

James was especially moved by the Jews he observed on the Lower East Side of New York City. His firsthand account of impressions gleaned from a visit to "that outpost of Jerusalem" was vivid as well as pointed. He likened the Jews to squirrels and monkeys. He was awed and repulsed by the crowded conditions in which they lived, enchanted and dismayed by their exotic ways and lively manners. He drank deeply of the summer city scene and then departed, as if from a voyage to the moon. (One is tempted to say as if from "abroad" but, more surely than not, he would have found London or Edinburgh or Paris less foreign than the Lower East Side of his own New York.)

If Henry James were to come back to life and visit Rutgers Street—or a similar place—today, he might have a haunting sense of déjà vu. To be sure, the "squirrels" and "monkeys" he would now observe scampering up and down the fire escapes of the tenements would be even darker than the "swarthy Orientals" he saw one hundred years ago. The argot of the street would be marked by a Spanish accent or "Black English" and rap talk rather than the babble of Yiddish. And the kitchen odors would be of paella and plantain or ribs and collard greens rather than the soups and pickled herrings of the "Israelites." Still, it would strike him that, once again, his fair New York was "swarming" (a favorite word) with alien elements.

Pushing this fantasy a bit further, James, if he listened carefully, might hear some outlandish proposals: demands for group rights and recognition, schemes for resisting the untenable choice of either completely conforming to the ways of the dominant society (*his* society) or continuing to be excluded. He might hear rumblings about slumlords that overcharge, politicians who take bribes, teachers who make fun of those who have difficulty with the language. He might even hear of plots to organize against the bosses, plans for greater community control within the ghetto, notions of developing local political organizations or bloc power.

There are many parallels between what was going on in James's New York at the turn of the twentieth century and in the New York almost a century later as described in Tom Wolfe's controversial novel *Bonfire of the Vanities*.[1] There are differences, too. To understand these, one must carefully examine the nature of minority status as it affected (and continues to affect) the various groups of white immigrants, who, for whatever reason, chose to come to these shores from Europe, and as it affected other nonwhite peoples like the Native Americans, African Americans, Asians, and many Latin Americans.

Minority Status

For most Europeans, migration to America was followed by successive stages of contact, competition, and some form of accommodation with the Old Settler population. For some (starting with the Protestants from Northern Europe and Scandinavia) accommodation led to gradual absorption into the dominant society, leaving but a vestige of ethnic difference. For others (including many Africans, Latin Americans, and Asians) the process stopped short of full assimilation. In spite of the fact that there has been increasing intermarriage in recent years, especially between members of various Catholic ethnic groups, between Protestants and Catholics, Jews and non-Jews, and, in the past three decades, between blacks and whites, clearly identifiable ethnic communities continue to exist. The most prominent of these are those sociologists call "minority communities." Such communities have several distinguishing characteristics, not least the fact that members are both differentiated from others and discriminated against in some fashion.

Minority status is sometimes "given"; often it is inherited. It may stem simply from the ascription of a differentiating label to a category of individuals who share certain social and physical traits deemed inferior to those of the dominant group— for example, persons with dark skin, atheists, and women. Statistical aggregates such as these are not social groups in the sociological sense of the term. They do, however, possess the potential for becoming groups or collectivities, especially when their members are categorically singled out for differential treatment.

Minority status is often ascribed to those social groups whose members have a history of patterned interaction, shared or similar beliefs and values, a sense of in-group solidarity, but who are also relegated to subordinate positions in the prestige hierarchy.[2] The two words *subordinate positions* are central, for all sociological minorities, no matter how tightly knit, share the fact that they have only limited control over their destinies.[3]

In 1945, sociologist Louis Wirth spelled out the concept of minority group in some detail and, implicitly, noted its relation to the concept of power. Stressing both its internal characteristics and the relation of the subordinate group to the wider society, Wirth wrote,

> A minority must be distinguishable from the dominant group by physical or cultural marks. In the absence of such identifying characteristics it blends into the rest of the population in the course of time.
>
> Minorities objectively occupy a disadvantageous position in the society. As contrasted with the dominant group they are debarred from certain opportunities—economic, social and political.
>
> The members of minority groups are held in lower esteem and may even be the objects of contempt, hatred, ridicule and violence.
>
> They are generally socially isolated and frequently spatially separated.
>
> They suffer from more than the ordinary amount of social and economic insecurity.[4]

Because of these attributes, Wirth felt that "minorities tend to develop a set of attitudes, forms of behavior, and other subjective characteristics which tend further to set them apart."[5]

In an earlier chapter it was noted that while Wirth was greatly concerned about the deleterious effect of the inferior status position of particular ethnic groups, he and others, such as E. K. Francis, stressed the fact that most ethnic groups, including many "minorities," frequently shared a positive sense of unity or "we-feeling," an ideology (however vague and unreflective it may be) and an interdependence of fate (whether based upon religious or political or cultural or racial characteristics). Moreover, ethnic group ties tend to be maintained as long as individuals feel bound to the community, "a community dependent as much upon the idea of communality as on actual proximity; a community one can 'feel' if not 'touch.'"[6]

One of the controversies that persists among students of racial and ethnic relations concerns the extent to which minority status is injurious to the individuals who occupy such a position and the benefits, if any, of proscribed separateness. This debate is most clearly joined in discussions of marginality, the concept that refers to those who appear to be on the edges of the dominant society.

Marginality

More than a few sociologists have suggested that those whose group identity is determined in part by external pressure, who are categorically excluded from opportunities for equal status, who are barred from assimilation and thus must live on the periphery of the dominant society, are "marginal men ... whom fate has condemned to live in two societies and in two not merely different from antagonistic cultures."[7]

Sociologist W. E. B. Du Bois offered the clearest articulation of this viewpoint in 1897 when he spoke of his people, African Americans, in the following way:

> After the Egyptian and Indian, the Greek and Roman, the Teuton and Mongolian, the Negro is a sort of seventh son, born with a veil, and gifted with second sight in this American world—a world which yields him not true self-consciousness, but also lets him see himself through the revelation of the other world. It is a peculiar sensation, this double-consciousness, this sense of always looking at one's self through the eyes of others, of measuring one's soul by the tape of a world that looks on in amused contempt and pity....[8]

Max Weber, Werner Sombart, Georg Simmel, and Thorstein Veblen all described the ambiguous role of the "stranger." Usually referring to European Jews, their prototypes also seemed both to enjoy and to suffer from the double-consciousness Du Bois used to describe the paradoxical situation of blacks in the United States. Simmel, for example, wrote of the "stranger" in the following manner: "His position in the group is determined, essentially by the fact that he has not belonged to it from the beginning, that he imparts qualities into it which do not and cannot stem from the group itself."[9]

Robert E. Park gave a new label to this phenomenon. He called it *marginality*. Park suggested that members of many racial and ethnic groups suffer from the ambivalence of values created by their longing for the old and their desire to participate in the new. Park and Everett Stonequist, author of *The Marginal Man*, described such persons as "cultural hybrids."[10] One of the results of their marginality, Park and Stonequist suggested, was personal maladjustment; another was the tendency to engage in deviant behavior.

Critics of the Park-Stonequist thesis have argued that "belonging to a minority group in and of itself does not necessarily predispose one to inner strain, personal disorientation, psychic difficulties, or various types of deviance such as crime."[11] Moreover, problems in one era do not necessarily mean groups or their members are destined to repeat them time and again. As many historians have pointed out, the well-known term "Paddy Wagon" (for police vans) originated because of the large number of once-marginal Irish immigrants who got in trouble with the police in the late nineteenth century. Today it is often said that "Paddy drives the wagon" and others ride in the back.

This does not mean that minority status is irrelevant; rather that it is often relative and many sociologists think the main problem is related to status consistency and inconsistency. Personal stability depends, in large measure, on the sense of security the individual members feel within the community as well as within the society.[12] Who one thinks he or she is and where he or she belongs are crucial matters; so, too, is the support system provided for the person growing up in a minority setting.

Challenging the conventional wisdom, economist Thomas Sowell once suggested that the differential mobility of various ethnic groups is often unrelated to the amount of discrimination they suffered. On the basis of his analysis of then-available statistical data, Sowell asserted that

Groups may be subject to very similar treatment by society at large and yet differ enormously in their economic achievements and social problems. Japanese Americans and Mexican Americans, for example, came to the United States in large numbers at about the same time (the early 1900s), settled in the same region (the Southwest), and faced discrimination in schools and on the job. Yet today Japanese Americans' incomes are almost double the incomes of Mexican Americans, and their crime rates and broken homes are only a fraction of the figures for Mexican Americans. As for how they were treated by "society," the Japanese suffered more—being legally denied citizenship and land ownership for many years, and being interned with great loss of property during World War II. They were also much easier targets for racism.[13]

Since Sowell made those particular comparisons some thirty years ago, the situation of many Mexican Americans has improved considerably and many are beginning to enter the ranks of the middle class. Still, his general findings are valid. For some groups, minority status has proved quite functional, or, at the least, a rallying point around which to mobilize. In recent years white women, an often overlooked category of marginal persons (both part of and apart from the dominant group) have found that much of what Betty Friedan once called "the feminine mystique"[14] resulted in their marginalization. Recognizing the effectiveness of using their separate and often inferior position came to be useful as a rallying point around which to raise their own and their "sisters'" consciousness and to mobilize resources to challenge the status quo ante.

Minority status repeatedly has been found to intensify already existing group identity or to create it where it has not existed prior to discrimination. Forced to live in particular areas and to associate with one another, members of minority groups frequently come to view themselves as a community, to feel a keen sense of responsibility for their fellow members, and to build institutions that contribute to the protection of individuals and to furthering the sense of fellow-feeling.[15] Such a development suggests that the concept of *marginal man* is too narrow; it may even be inappropriate for vast numbers of minority group members.

Thus, in one of the many attempts to reformulate the concept of marginality, Milton M. Goldberg, relying in large measure on the work of the anthropologist Alexander Goldenweiser and his idea of "marginal cultural areas," suggested that

If (1) the so-called "marginal" individual is conditioned to his existence on the borders of two cultures from birth, if (2) he shares the existence and conditioning process with a large number of individuals in his primary groups, if (3) his years of early growth, maturation, and even adulthood find him participating in institutional activities manned largely by other "marginal" individuals like himself, and finally, if (4) his marginal position results in no major blockages or frustrations of his learned expectations and desires, then he is not a true "marginal" individual in the defined sense, but is a participant member of a marginal culture, every bit as real and complete to him as is the nonmarginal culture to the nonmarginal man.[16]

Contrary to the views of Park and Stonequist, Goldberg (and those sharing his conception) did not see all or even most minority group members as maladjusted products of cultural ambivalence, but as adjusted participants in a marginal culture, itself a product of accommodation to differential treatment. This interpretation is consistent with the conviction that members of American minority communities manifest certain common characteristics normal to groups with similar marginal experiences, including certain traits that outsiders sometimes define as pathological. Goldberg's view jibes with others' perspectives, especially those who have examined historically marginal groups who, like Jews, Greeks, Armenians, and "overseas" Chinese and Indians, have often been traders within others' societies, at once needed and kept at arm's length. These "middleman minorities," as Hubert Blalock once styled them,[17] engaged in the professions or in risky businesses exist today. Many such contemporary middlemen in the United States have roots in Cuba, East Asia (Chinese and Koreans), and South Asia (Indians and Pakistanis). It is these groups in particular whose American experience has often been a recapitulation of the "leapfrog phenomenon"—of newcomers "moving in, up and over African Americans"—referred to in Chapter Two. It is they who have often been able to move with the greatest alacrity and who often generate pointed resentment in black communities.

While minority communities may differ from one another in racial and ethnic composition, their levels of socioeconomic status, patterns of social mobility, and local customs—those retained and those newly created—they tend to possess a transmitted remembrance of how the community developed. Everyone, of course, is ethnocentric to some degree. Moreover, spokespersons for almost every group engage in "the creative distortion of history" to emphasize their group's historical legacy and to underscore its unique contributions. Thus references are frequently made to the first members of the group to arrive and the conditions under which they came, how they were received and how they fared, the discrimination they encountered and how they coped with it, the grounds on which the community was established in this country, and the deeds of important leaders.

Many minorities have their own territorial bases, sometimes marked by physical boundaries ("the other side of the tracks," "down by the riverside," "in the hollow"), sometimes by psychological or social walls that set them apart from the larger community. In his memoir, *A Walker in the City*, Alfred Kazin explains, "We were the end of the line. We were the children of the immigrants who had camped at the city's back door, New York's rawest, remotest, cheapest ghetto, enclosed on one side by the Carnarsie flats and on the other by the hallowed middle-class districts that showed the way to New York. 'New York' was what we put last on our address, but first in thinking of the others around us. *They* were New York, the Gentiles . . . ; we were Brownsville—*Brunzvil,* as the old folks said."[18]

Today Brownsville is predominantly African American and those who now write of their estrangement often describe Kazin's people, the Jews, as the "they" who represent the Establishment.[19]

When separated from the dominant society, minorities frequently maintain their own traditional and social institutions. Some of these run counter to the ways of the larger community and are viewed by those who peer into their enclaves as deviant, mysterious, dangerous, as "un-American." One thinks of different ways various people "use" time, worship, and relax, to say nothing of the myriad differences in ways of perceiving themselves, each other, and the society in which they live.

The last point was most poignantly expressed through the research of Oscar Lewis. Here is a short excerpt from his famous essay in which his Puerto Rican respondents compare life in New York with that on the home island. The passage begins with Lewis asking, "Have you ever been in New York, Hector?"

> "Yes, yes, I've been to New York."
>
> "And what did you think of life there?"
>
> "New York! I want no part of it! Man, do you know what it's like? You got up in a rush, have breakfast in a rush, get to work in a rush, go home in a rush, even shit in a rush. That's life in New York! Not for me! Never again! Not unless I was crazy.
>
> "Look, I'll explain. The ways things are in New York; you'll get nothing there. But nothing! It's different in Puerto Rico. Here, if you're hungry, you come to me and say, 'Man, I'm broke, I've had nothing to eat.' And I'd say, 'Ay, Bendito! Poor thing!' And I'd give you some food. No matter what, you wouldn't have to go to bed hungry. Here in Puerto Rico you can make out. But in New York, if you don't have a nickel, or twenty cents, you're worthless, and that's for sure. You don't count. You get swallowed by a horse."[20]

But even such harshness of urban life is coped with by hundreds of thousands of Puerto Ricans and others who feel the attraction of places like New York where opportunities for work are thought to abound. While often disillusioned by what they find, many stay and attempt to survive. They do so in part by trying to maintain old ways or by engaging in a process that has been called *ethnogenesis,* the establishment of a new sense of ethnicity, often more pronounced in the country to which they move than the one left behind.[21]

Many who rarely think of themselves as Puerto Rican or Italian or Chinese or Mexican back home where everyone is Puerto Rican or Italian or Chinese or Mexican quickly learn that they are labeled as such by those around them and, in response, often create a new hyphenated social form that is manifest in a new identity (such as Chinese American) and in ways of behaving that reflect both acculturation and accommodation.

The street culture of Cuban Miami; the tight-knit social organization of Chinatowns in San Francisco and Seattle, New York and Boston; the ubiquity of storefront churches in poor, Puerto Rican areas; the twang of western music in Chicago neighborhood bars; the array of ethnic newspapers found on the stands of every large city, all indicate that many Americans carry on by retaining or reviving that which they once knew, which become lifelines of sorts, especially for those of the first generation. But they and their children also often create new institutions and organizations such as teenage gangs, athletic clubs, ethnically based patriotic clubs (such as the "Polish-American Veterans"), religious bodies ("African Methodist Episcopal Church"), social agencies (the "Catholic Youth Organization"), after-school schools (such as those offering Armenian, Greek, Chinese, Hebrew, Arabic, Vietnamese, etc.), and many kinds of businesses—some set up specifically for particular foods and special services.

Many members of minority groups make their living and spend much of their money within the ethnic community itself. Some, including those who have become quite successful, find themselves in what Norbert Wiley once called an "ethnic nobility trap."[22] Having chosen to make his or her way within the confines of the ethnic enclave, the individual may become locked in with a skill or specialty that is difficult to transfer to the wider world.

Wiley began his discussion of this phenomenon by reminding the readers of William Foote Whyte's famous study *Street Corner Society,* a detailed description and analysis of a working-class Italian area in the north side of Boston. There, Whyte noted, two avenues of socialization led to two sorts of "opportunity ceilings." If one was a "corner boy" he could aspire to work in local (ethnic) politics or to a high position in the rackets; if one was a "college boy" he was groomed for professional and managerial positions. Many, frustrated by the seeming remoteness of middle-class jobs, opted to follow the line of least resistance. Some of them even became big men in the local community, but they were nothing on the outside.[23]

Many members of minority groups fall somewhere between the "corner boys" and the "college boys." While some spend their entire lives inside the enclave and some break away completely, a common pattern is to make one's living away from the neighborhood. It is in the workaday world that one tends to have the greatest amount of interaction with members of other groups and with representatives of the wider society. When night falls, as the saying goes, "The WASPs return to their nests—and the others return to their own." Ethnic nests vary, of course, from old law tenements to high-rise apartments to ranch homes in wealthy suburbs that some have called "gilded ghettos."[24]

On-the-job participation is frequently quite formal and segmentalized, with each person playing his appropriate role. Those with whom he has contact often see the minority group member as an "ambassador of his people."[25] Because exposure is frequently limited to outstanding figures (such as athletes, entertainers, professionals), to workers, or to servants, and rarely involves intimate or informal exchanges, individuals in the dominant group tend to have distorted images of minority peoples and of their personal existence. Their views are frequently a combination of hunches (based on limited observation) and prejudices (which they have learned through contact with other prejudiced people).

The pattern is generally asymmetrical, however, for minorities are continually exposed to the values and norms of the dominant group through public schooling, mass media, employment, advertising, and just living. *Survival requires the ability to function in two worlds: that of the minority (the "membership group") and of the dominant "reference group."*[26]

Although it is not unusual to hear blanket indictments of the entire Establishment, members of minority groups learn fairly early in life that the dominant group itself is highly differentiated in various ways. They are surprised when they find that so many of those beyond the confines of their communities are unaware that they, too, have their own hierarchies, interest groups, leaders and followers, successful members and ne'er-do-wells, poets and preachers, artisans and laborers, professionals and provocateurs.

Like most communities in complex societies, minority enclaves consist of clusters of subgroupings, varying in socioeconomic status, occupational interest, and political proclivity.[27] Certain ethnic groups, to be sure, put more stress on one activity than on another and certain occupations hold greater prestige than others. One thinks of the role of the priesthood in a French Canadian village, of law and politics—and the priesthood, too—in an Irish community, teaching and the professions for Jews, or of business and science for the parents of Chinatown's children or many from Southeast Asia. While not every French Canadian child aspires to be a priest nor every Irish American wishes to be a "pol," there is no question that many members of their communities get a certain amount of satisfaction from seeing one of their own people become successful, especially in those areas toward which they feel particularly partial for sentimental, ideological, or practical reasons.

Even where there are relatively parallel systems of social stratification, there is no assurance that persons considered to be upper class by members of their own group would be accorded the same status by outsiders; nor does it mean that the respected members of a given minority would be held in the same esteem by those in the dominant group.[28]

Pride

Group identification is revealed in intragroup attitudes and actions; it is reflected in expressions of intergroup behavior and minority reaction to treatment by others.

Pride in one's ethnic or racial identity may be illustrated in the fellow feeling that predisposes many young blacks to identify with "brothers" and "sisters" they have never met. When introduced they may go through an elaborate handshake, signifying to one another that they are together. Members of other groups perform similar rituals to indicate their sense of identification and their group-based pride.

In a study of small-town Jews and their Christian neighbors, the author asked each Jewish participant what first came to mind when he or she read the following newspaper headline: "Mischa Goldberg Lauded for Concert Performance." The most frequent response emphasized a special sort of satisfaction in seeing a fellow Jew receive recognition. Many echoed the sentiment expressed by one of them who said, "I'm glad when it's one of ours who does well, it makes me feel good." When the same individuals were then asked their reactions to a second headline—"Max Cohen Indicted for Fraud"—the characteristic responses were vexation, embarrassment, and anger. "It's bad for us when a Jew gets in trouble."[29] When asked if they knew Mischa Goldberg or Max Cohen (names I had made up), they said, "No." Still, assuming they were Jewish from their names, they had answered in very personal terms.

When the same individuals were asked to respond to another set of fake headlines, this time with Anglo-Saxon names, as for example, "John Smith Wins Race," or "Thomas Jones Suspect in Murder Case," they looked puzzled. One after another would counter, "I don't know what to say, who is John Smith?" Or, "It sounds bad but I really don't know Thomas Jones."

Not surprisingly, many Jews, whatever their political proclivities, take special pride in the prominence of Jewish senators with names like Feinstein, Franken,

Levin, Sanders, and Schumer; Supreme Court Associate Justices Ruth Bader Ginsburg, Stephen Breyer, and Elena Kagan; media mogul and New York mayor Mike Bloomberg; and, whatever their taste in entertainment, identify with the celebrity of Steven Spielberg, Paul Newman, Ed Asner, Beverly Sills, Barbra Streisand, Aaron Copland, Leonard Bernstein, and Itzak Perlman. They also share a sense of collective embarrassment over the notoriety of the likes of convicted murderers going way back to Richard Loeb and Nathan Leopold or, more recently, David Berkowitz, and are embarrassed by the likes of Ivan Boesky, the discredited "inside-trader," and Ponzi-schemer Bernard Madoff.

In similar fashion many Hispanic Americans are still pleased to recall the champion of farm labor, Mexican American Cesar Chavez, and take special pleasure in cabinet members named Alberto Gonzales, Carlos Gutierrez, and Thomas Perez; US senators Mel Martinez and Marco Rubio; and Supreme Court Associate Justice Sonia Sotomayor. They enjoy identifying themselves with a host of baseball players, including Manny Ramirez, Juan Gonzales, Pedro Martinez, David Ortiz, and even if they have never swung a club, to boast of the accomplishments of former golf champions Lee Trevino and Nancy Lopez. And they can't help but be upset when the accused in a celebrated mass-murder case is named Juan Corona or when a star athlete named Alex Rodriquez falls from grace. Italian Americans often display similar feelings of nostalgic chauvinism when they think of Frank Sinatra, Joe DiMaggio, and John Sirica, and when they see the names of former New York State governor Mario Cuomo or Associate Justice of the Supreme Court Anthony Scalia, leader of the House Nancy D'Alesandro Pelosi, or the pop star Madonna. For Irish Americans names like Jimmy Walker and Jimmy Cagney, Senator Daniel Patrick Moynihan, commentator Andy Rooney, actress Rosie O'Donnell, Associate Justice Kennedy—and almost anyone else named Kennedy—have special meaning, even though they may have never met any of them.

Two factors are operating in all these cases: a sense of interdependence of fate with others with whom one is identified, and a vicarious connection with those in the limelight. This phenomenon is related to a broader one, referred to by Herbert Gans as "symbolic ethnicity."[30]

Symbolic ethnicity is manifest not only in feelings of identity but in ethnically specific activities, including eating traditional cuisine, participating in folk festivals, and trying to recapture lost languages, that remain important even for those who have found acceptance and are about to enter what Richard Alba once called "the twilight of ethnicity."[31] Of course, they are highly significant for those still subject to discrimination. Such groups often encourage participation and instill pride by creating new institutions. The African American celebration of Kwanzaa, created by Ron Karenga, a black political scientist and founder of an organization called "Us," is the best recent example.

During the annual festival celebrating freedom and Afro-American cultures, special foods are prepared, stories are told, and candles are lighted in ceremonies that remind others of everything from Christmas and Chanukah to Thanksgiving.

Minority group members often see themselves as part of a whole community, of those they know intimately and those they know only by sight or sign or name. The group identity is expressed in innumerable ways. Perhaps it is best expressed through the immediate response to the question many ask themselves about a stranger being met for the first time: "Is he a 'brother'?" "Is she a 'sister'?" "Is he a *Landsmann*?," "A paisano?" All subsequent social intercourse is apt to be shaped by this definitive beginning.

Self-Hatred

It has been hypothesized that "the greater the pressure of prejudice and discrimination, the greater is likely to be the feeling of interdependence of fate within the minority community."[32] While this relationship has been found to apply to many members of minority groups, it does not necessarily hold for all. Some individuals, objects of severe discrimination, may internalize the negative stereotypes held of them by others and, as a result, display little in-group solidarity. In fact, rather than drawing into the ranks of the minority, they may seek to withdraw from it.

As noted above, even those with a positive sense of group identity may feel self-conscious at the thought of "one of theirs" getting into trouble since it puts the whole minority in a bad light. Those who possess a low degree of self-esteem owing to their minority status are sometimes so anxious about their subordinate position that they attempt to disavow membership. To such persons the minority community is not a source of pride but of self-hatred.

In order to combat their inability to adjust to minority status they may change their names, deny their racial or ethnic origins, alter their appearance by changing the shape of their eyes (in the case of Asians) or straightening their hair (as have many African Americans) or having their noses made stubbier (as have many Italians and Jews) or narrower. (It is facetiously said that the African American entertainer Michael Jackson "cut off his nose to spite his race.") Some members of minorities refuse to associate with fellow group members with whom they might be identified. Others attempt to pass as a member of the dominant group.

If they still find themselves rejected, they are caught between two social worlds, suffering the plight of the original marginal man as described by Du Bois and Park and Stonequist.

Reactions to Discrimination

What sorts of individual and collective action can minority group members take to deal with or alter their social position in a society such as our own? What happens when, driven by the same norms and values as those in power, they are barred from full participation or made to feel inferior? Or, putting the point in the words of Langston Hughes, "What happens when a dream is deferred?"

What happens to a dream deferred?

Does it dry up
like a raisin in the sun?
Or fester like a sore—

And then run?
Does it stink like rotten meat?
Or crust and sugar over—
like a syrupy sweet?

Maybe it just sags
like a heavy load.

Or does it explode?[33]

Many attempts have been made by sociologists to describe the responses of minority group members to their social situation. While, to be sure, various minorities suffer greater or lesser discrimination, nonetheless, within most minorities in the United States there are those who "want in" and are willing to do anything to obtain entry, there are those who simply want to be left alone, there are those who want what they feel they are rightly entitled to. Thus, as George Simpson and Milton Yinger suggest, most discussions of minority responses consider at least the following models: those who favor "acceptance," those who seek "accommodation," and those who are "aggressive."[34] (They may be aggressively for reform to get themselves in; they may be aggressively for radicalization to get themselves out or to form something entirely new.)

While taking into consideration these three alternatives, it is suggested here that reactions to minority status might be better understood when two questions are posed. Answers to each question reveal at least four types of reaction (each paralleling Hughes's metaphors) that, as shall be shown, may be further broken down and, in some ways, represent points on a spectrum through which some individuals may pass at various stages of their lives. The questions are these: (1) Does the minority group member accept or reject the image of subordinate status imposed on him or her by the majority? (2) Is he or she willing to play a humble role as expected by those in positions of power?

Table 8.1 presents the four possible types of reaction suggested here: submission, withdrawal, separation, and integration. (The first two incorporate what Simpson and Yinger call "acceptance"—at least on one axis; the latter two only partially parallel the categories of "accommodation" and "aggression" for, as noted below, both may involve the process of detente and militant action to achieve certain defined goals.)

Before examining these types it should be noted that all of these reaction patterns are possible, and a given individual may manifest two or more of them at

**Table 8.1 Four Types of Reaction to Discrimination
by Members of Minority Groups**

Segregated Role	Dominant Image of Minority Member's "Inferior Status"	
	Accepted	Rejected
Accepted	Submission	Separation
Rejected	Withdrawal	Integration

different times or in different circumstances. Since it is the largest single minority group in the United States at present, illustrations of each type will be drawn from the experiences of African Americans.

Submission

Earlier it was noted that Malcolm X said, "The worst crime the white man has committed is to teach us to hate ourselves." There is little question that one of the first things many African Americans learn is their "place" and the roles they are expected to play in the white man's world. They learn "to be Negro" (or, in currently popular terms "to be black"). In 1929 A. L. Holsey wrote,

> At fifteen I was fully conscious of the racial difference, and while I was sullen and resentful in my soul, I was beaten and knew it. I knew then that I could never aspire to be President of the United States, nor governor of my state, nor mayor of my city; I knew that I could only sit in the peanut gallery at our theater and could only ride on the back seat of the electric car and in the Jim Crow car on the train. I had bumped into the color line and knew that so far as white people were concerned, I was just another nigger.[35]

Recognizing one's fate as "just another nigger" among whites has led some African Americans to accept their inferior status and to play the segregated roles socially assigned to them. American folklore is filled with stories of "Uncle Toms," the defeated persons who knew the score and could play the tune as well. They bowed and scraped, cracked jokes, and played dumb just to please the white folks. Uncle Toms exist in real life too.

Some minority people feel that the best way to live is to accept second-class status and do the bidding of those in the dominant positions. One such individual is described by Richard Wright in his famous autobiography, *Black Boy*. Wright tells of a black elevator operator with whom he worked in a Memphis hotel. One day Shorty needed lunch money and told Wright to watch him get it from the first white man who came along. When such a person eventually got into the elevator, Shorty said to him,

> "I'm hungry, Mister White Man. I need a quarter for lunch."
> The white man ignored him. Shorty, his hands on the controls of the elevator....
> "I ain't gonna move this damned old elevator till I got a quarter, Mister White Man."
> "The hell with you, Shorty," the white man said, ignoring him and chewing on his Black cigar.
> "I'm hungry, Mister White Man. I'm dying for a quarter," Shorty sang, drooling, drawling, humming his words.
> "If you don't take me to my floor, you will die," the white man said, smiling a little for the first time.
> "But this Black sonofabitch sure needs a quarter," Shorty sang, grimacing, clowning, ignoring the white man's threat.

"Come on, you Black bastard, I got to work," the white man said, intrigued by the element of sadism involved, enjoying it.

"It'll cost you twenty-five cents, Mister White Man, just a quarter, just two bits," Shorty moaned.

There was silence. Shorty threw the lever and the elevator went up and stopped about five feet shy of the floor upon which the white man worked.

"Can't go no more, Mister White Man, unless I get my quarter," he said in a tone that sounded like crying.

"What would you do for a quarter?" the white man asked, still gazing off.

"I'll do anything for a quarter," Shorty sang.

"What, for example?" the white man asked.

Shorty giggled, swung around, bent over, and poked out his broad, fleshy ass.

"You can kick me for a quarter," he said, looking impishly at the white man out of the corner of his eyes.

The white man laughed softly, jingled some coins in his pocket, took out one and thumped it to the floor. Shorty stooped to pick it up and the white man bared his teeth and swung his foot into Shorty's rump with all the strength of his body. Shorty let out a howling laugh that echoed up and down the elevator shaft.

"Now, open this door, you goddam black sonofabitch," the white man said, smiling with tight lips.

"Yeess, siiiir," Shorty sang, but first he picked up the quarter and put it into his mouth. "This monkey's got the peanuts," he chortled.

He opened the door and the white man stepped out and looked back at Shorty as he went toward his office.

"You're all right, Shorty, you sonofabitch," he said.

"I know it!" Shorty screamed, and then let his voice trail off in a gale of wild laughter.[36]

There are, of course, two possible interpretations of Shorty's acting the buffoon. On one hand, his behavior served to demonstrate the depth of his submissiveness, for he played his role according to his image of the white man's expectations; on the other hand, he was manipulating the white man—he got what he wanted. But even in the second interpretation, he had to pay a terrible price to do it.

For many minority group members, acceptance of subordinate status is the only way to eke out a living. The "red cap" with a master's degree and the Indian cab driver with an MD are prime examples.

In many cases, submission to the inferior status imposed by others is a rational acceptance, a seeming necessity for survival. Brewton Berry, for example, states "it is not uncommon for one to conform externally while rejecting the system mentally and emotionally."[37] Yet, there are significant exceptions to this generalization. "Contemporary sociology and cultural anthropology have shown that people can learn to adjust to, and even accept extremely diverse circumstances that seem strange, painful, or evil to those who have received different training. Standards of value by which the desirability of a given status is judged, as well as the status itself, are a product of the society. A whole group may accept what to others seems to be an inferior role."[38]

For some individuals, acceptance of such inferior roles is simply conformity to the traditions of the community in which they happen to be raised. While whites may learn that they are superior to blacks as part of a more general socialization experience, some blacks similarly may accept the standards of racial inequality. Thus, acceptance of inferior status may be seen as a conditioned reaction in a prejudiced society. Today many of their militant children and grandchildren disparagingly refer to such people as "Nee-groes," rather than using the preferred terms "Blacks" or "African Americans."

Withdrawal

One reaction to discrimination is submission to inferior status; another is the denial of identity. In this case the individual accepts the majority image of his group[39] and—because of self-hatred or expediency—withdraws from it. In rejecting the segregated roles they are supposed to play, some light-skinned "Negroes," Jews who wish to be taken for Gentiles, Puerto Ricans who claim they are Spanish, and others attempt to pass into the dominant group. Not infrequently they hold ambivalent attitudes toward themselves and others, and their conflicting allegiances are apt to induce anxiety, which is further provoked by the constant threat of exposure. Thus a fictional character asks himself, "But what if a lot of people know it already? Or can detect the Negro in me? I hear lots of Southerners claim they can do that. That man goggling at me down the car—can he see I'm part Negro? Has everybody always guessed it?"[40]

In 1945, St. Clair Drake and Horace Cayton estimated that each year at least 25,000 persons permanently left the Negro population to become assimilated into white society.[41] While one suspects that number would not be as high today, still there are innumerable individuals who pass on a part-time or segmental basis, for example, working as whites by day and returning home to the black community. In this way they avoid the strain of breaking contact completely and turning away from lifelong friends and neighbors.

"Passing," a course open to those who possess no identifying racial or ethnic characteristics or those who can mask them, is the only method of assimilation available to persons who wish to enter an environment that would reject them out of hand if their true identity were to be revealed. In some areas of society, racial identity is relatively unimportant, and individuals can withdraw from the minority community while still being associated with it by others. Black athletes who attend big universities or join the armed forces, African American artists who become expatriates or entertainers, others who engage in such illicit activities as gambling and prostitution, frequently find acceptance in the white world because of the special skills or characteristics that they bring to the situation. Many such individuals, while not denying their minority identity, prefer not to be "professional race men"; they wish to be accepted in spite of—rather than because of—their racial or ethnic background. In most instances assimilation for such exceptional members of minority groups is only partial, for when they step out of their specialized roles many Americans consider them as "just another nigger."

Separation

The reaction patterns of both submission and withdrawal used by certain minority group members presume the internalization of the inferior image held of them by the majority. Yet, accepting their plight as members of a group considered by the majority to be of lower status does not necessarily mean total capitulation to the stigma of second-class citizenship. In recent years, the vast majority of African Americans have rejected the idea that they are inferior and have attempted either to avoid contact with those "in the camp of their oppressors" or to integrate (a different sensibility than "assimilate") and take their place along with those in the dominant group.

Consider the first of these two response patterns.

For many years some blacks who attained a moderate amount of security and rose to relatively high status within their own segregated community seemed resentful of those who submitted to the indignities imposed upon them. Long ago, Hortense Powdermaker reported, "Those at the top deplore the others' submission to white assumptions of superiority and their recalcitrance to white standards of behavior. They decry the loose morality and the ignorance by which, they feel, the lower class of Negro lends credence to unfair notions about the race."[42]

Although these attitudes are still prevalent in certain circles, a qualification is in order: In rejecting white assumptions of superiority, many blacks accept pervasive "white" middle-class cultural standards and frequently establish parallel social institutions that mimic the presumed manners and mores of whites, sometimes to the extent of becoming distorted parodies. Such efforts—often exaggerated accounts of the achievements of individuals—have been described as flights of fantasy. The late E. Franklin Frazier, speaking of middle-class urban African Americans, claimed that "their escape into a world of make-believe with its sham 'society' leaves them with a feeling of emptiness and futility which causes them to constantly seek an escape in new delusions."[43]

The extent to which old Negro newspapers and magazines (some of which still exist) were imitative of white society was evidenced by the advertisements and articles that appeared in them. *Ebony, Jet, Tan,* and others used to be filled with pages of ads for skin whiteners and hair straighteners. Furthermore, stories of fancy cotillions and exclusive clubs, of expensive homes and problems with the help, were reported. The preeminence of white standards, even among those who by subscribing to such journals supported their own institutions, was manifest.

Discussing the general problem, Maurice Davie once wrote, "Avoidance is thus a protective device, a way of adjusting to ... [segregation] with the least pain and uneasiness. It may be carried to the point of almost complete voluntary segregation."[44]

What might be considered a conventional response to separate treatment, namely, the development of institutions paralleling those of the dominant society, is not uncommon, especially by middle-class members of minorities (here white *nouveaux riches* are little different from the black bourgeoisie). But it is surely not the only reaction pattern of people who reject others' views of their alleged inferiority but see little point in trying to enter their social world.

Some, most often those too poor to emulate middle-class whites or too disgusted to want to, have taken what seem to many to be more drastic measures. They not only seek to maintain separation and a sense of communal integrity, they also foster the rejection of "white" standards. This type of response is frequently an active and sometimes aggressive method of furthering the goals of the group as a group, strengthening its position, and justifying its separate existence. To combat discrimination, exponents of this reaction pattern sometimes adopt a chauvinistic doctrine of their own superiority. Rather than paralleling dominant institutions and values, they challenge them—often acting out certain stereotypes in the process. Jeremy Larner has addressed himself to this last point when he notes the tendency of certain black nationalists and their spokesmen to engage in a self-indulgent (and, to him, self-deluding) game of mirroring, particularly in playing on three common white themes: "the noble savage" (with its emphasis on creativity, spontaneity, and willingness to fight), "the hipster" (a "black Negro" to replace Norman Mailer's famous "white Negro," portrayed as a sort of nihilistic superman who is the cock of the walk), and "the Black proletariat" (who is part of the vanguard of the revolution to come).[45]

Another key concept marking separation is "soul." In the late 1960s the Swedish anthropologist Ulf Hannerz made a careful study of an African American neighborhood in Washington, DC. His observations offer one interesting view. He concluded that "soul as solidarity is a reaction to the threat of a split in the community" among those whose lives are circumscribed by the values and norms of mainstream (or wider American) society and those values more specific to ghetto living. Hannerz argued, "In order to make [the] solidarity encompass even the least privileged, it must be symbolized by those most undiluted forms of Black proletarian experience which everybody can claim as his heritage, and to give it a positive valence weakness must be turned into strength. Thus poverty, oppression, and troubled relationships are interpreted as the foundation of an endurance, which can only be appreciated by those who have passed the same way."[46] Others contend that "soul" is simply a label broadly applied to the shared perspective of all Blacks, the basis of their "cultural" character.

As shall be shown in the next chapter, at various stages African Americans have opted for revitalization through separation, through the exaltation of all that is Black and the denigration of all that is white, and, frequently, through making capital of what outsiders (and some high-status insiders) consider to be lower-class cultural traits specific to the black ghetto.

Thus, under the general heading of avoidance one must consider the paths of both parallel participation and ethnic chauvinism.

Integration

Protest is not always manifest in attempts to pull away, to go it alone. As James Baldwin indicated, however, the appeal for such action is very great.

> The brutality with which Negroes are treated in this country simply cannot be overstated, however unwilling white men may be to hear it. In the beginning ... a Negro just cannot believe that white people are treating him as they do; he does not know what he has done to merit it. And when he realizes that the treatment accorded him has nothing to do with anything he has done, that the attempt of white people to destroy him—for that is what it is—is utterly gratuitous, it is not hard for him to think of white people as devils.[47]

Despite such sentiments, and they are still widespread in certain circles, not all or even most African Americans have attempted to solve the problem of inequality by joining the cause of Black Nationalism and rejecting the possibility of eventual integration. In fact, a very large percentage seek equality without any strings. They do not want to be separate and equal or separate and superior. They want what is constitutionally guaranteed and are willing to fight to get it.

Here, as in the case of "avoidance," integrationists seem to have two options, two routes. The first is essentially integration-at-a-distance, the kind that most other minorities (namely, so-called white ethnics) long enjoyed; the second is full integration or, better stated, amalgamation.

It has been noted that those we call ethnics in this society do live in two distinct, though not necessarily antagonistic, worlds. One is that of their kith, kin, and community; the other is the broader society in which they study and work and sometimes play. The former comes closer to possessing what sociologists call an *emeinschaftlich* (or communal) character, a sense of total involvement, of real belonging or "weness;" the latter is more *gesellschaftlich,* that is, marked by secondary relationships, impersonal ties, partial involvement, and remoteness. Thus a surprising number of well-educated, well-to-do ethnics (white and nonwhite) still keep to their own neighborhoods and enjoy their own activities even when the formal barriers are removed. What they want, at least what many want, is the right to do as they please. Once they have that free choice they often opt for life with their "own people."

Now there are some members of minority groups who wish to live in a truly color-blind, ethnically neutral society, a society where no one is judged, considered, or even recognized on the basis of skin color or any other potentially invidious criterion. They differ from those in the "withdrawal" category in Table 8.1, for they desire not to leave their own group but to abolish the idea of group difference itself. In terms introduced in Chapter Six, they are the true advocates of amalgamation—the legatees of Crèvecoeur and Zangwill—and wish their children to be the best that the crucible can pour out.

In both instances militancy may mark the road to emancipation. For whether people want the right to decide whether or not to integrate at a distance or to foster fusion, they must often work to convince others that it is their choice to make, not that of others. Since both of these responses are well within the value framework of the American ideal, many of the activities of the civil rights movement were, and are, oriented toward these goals and many of the important pieces of legislation—including the Civil Rights Acts of 1964, 1967, and 1968—were testimony to the efficacy of integrationist pressure for many Americans.

Mixed Responses

There are times when those in the minority find that they cannot really go it alone (seeking separation or coexistence), nor can they abide the slowness of change as advocated by those whose perseverance is ever tempered by the call for patience and goodwill, as in the civil rights movement. Feeling stifled by recalcitrant institutions and reluctant officials, hampered by powerful opponents and anxious neighbors, some leaders have pressed their followers to push beyond the tolerance limits and have advocated radical tactics designed to force society to give in to their demands, to play not only on sympathy but also on fear of disruption, to appeal not merely to charity and righteousness but to countervailing power marshaled by those considered powerless. America has long been witness to such movements: the struggle for women's rights, the labor movement, and the Black Power Revolution. It is the last-named that concerns us here.

In the preceding section we looked at four typical ways minority peoples, including African Americans, have reacted to their treatment. We noted variations within each type, such as (1) unconscious as well as intentional (or calculated) submission; (2) partial or complete withdrawal; (3) avoidance, that is, mimicking the majority but avoiding contact, or opting for nationalism and putting emphasis on real, imagined, or created differences; (4) partial integration (or what was earlier called structural pluralism) or full integration (or amalgamation). Discounting those in the first two general categories because they accept dominant group definitions of their group's inferiority, it may be said that the third and fourth responses and their variations are permissible, even expected, within our normative structure. Like them or not, most Americans would acknowledge that people have the right to remain separate as long as they do not make trouble; to seek to integrate as long as they accept the values of others—and it does not cost too much. The trouble appears to begin when the limits are broached. Integrating a park is one thing; a neighborhood is quite another. Of course, as noted in Chapter One these limits—and the norms that define them—vary from region to region and from community to community. Still, in general, one can say that when blacks (or Mexican Americans or Puerto Ricans or Native Americans) become nationalistic, at least some white Americans approve (they may even find it quaint or amusing) so long as they do it in their own area, on their own turf. Likewise, when integrationists press to have the country honor its own ideals, to force the door open through the slow, tedious, and expensive process of litigation, well and good. Liberals applaud; conservatives complain—but generally they go along once a decision is made.

In other words, both "ethnocentric blackwardness" (sometimes called "chauvinistic nationalism") and "soulless militancy" are tolerable from the majority viewpoint, even if not warmly welcomed. (Numerous public opinion polls bear testimony to this response.) But when chauvinism is joined with direct action (even nonviolent direct action), when pride and protest are linked together, the critical balance is upset and new responses are devised.

It is instructive to consider what Table 8.1 would look like if one thinks in terms of *radical responses* to minority status. Figure 8.1 represents this view.

Of course, "Black Power" and similar derivative movements are not historical accidents. They grew out of the mounting realization that unidimensional programs—whether chauvinistic or reformist—are usually inadequate to meet the basic challenge, the challenge posed by those who have the power to control the lives of others. And the lack of power, as noted at the beginning of this chapter, is a fundamental attribute of minority status.

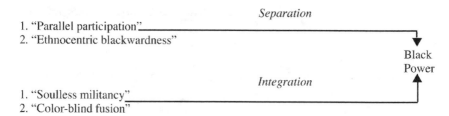

Separation
1. "Parallel participation"
2. "Ethnocentric blackwardness"

Black
Power

Integration
1. "Soulless militancy"
2. "Color-blind fusion"

Figure 8.1   Black Power in Relation to Two Typical Reaction Patterns

Notes

1. See Tom Wolfe, *Bonfire of the Vanities* (New York: Farrar, Strauss and Giroux, 1987).

2. For a more thorough discussion of groups, collectivities, and statistical aggregates, see Ely Chinoy, *Society,* rev. ed. (New York: Random House, 1967), pp. 40–43.

3. See Martin N. Marger, *Race and Ethnic Relations,* 3rd ed. (Belmost, CA: Wadsworth Publishing Company, 1994), pp. 44–45.

4. Louis Wirth, "The Problem of Minority Groups," in Ralph Linton (ed.), *The Science of Man in the World Crisis* (New York: Columbia University Press, 1945), p. 348.

5. Ibid.

6. Peter I. Rose, *The Subject Is Race* (New York: Oxford University Press, 1968), p. 71.

7. Robert E. Park, "Human Migration and the Marginal Man," *American Journal of Sociology,* 33 (May 1928), p. 891; see also Everett V. Stonequist, *The Marginal Man* (New York: Scribner, 1937), p. 217.

8. From W. E. B. Du Bois, *The Souls of Black Folk* (1903), reprinted in *Three Negro Classics* (New York: Avon, 1965), p. 215.

9. Kurt H. Wolff (trans. and ed.), *The Sociology of Georg Simmel* (Glencoe, IL: Free Press, 1950), pp. 402–408.

10. See Robert E. Park, *Race and Culture* (New York: Free Press, 1951), p. 354.

11. For example, Golovensky's study of the Jewish community contradicts many of Park's contentions. See David Golovensky, "The Marginal Man Concept: An Analysis and Critique," *Social Forces,* 30 (October 1951 to May 1952), pp. 333–339.

12. George E. Simpson and J. Milton Yinger, *Racial and Cultural Minorities: An Analysis of Prejudice and Discrimination,* 4th ed. (New York: Harper and Row, 1972), p. 186.

13. Thomas Sowell, "Myths about Minorities," *Commentary* (August 1979), pp. 34–35.

14. Betty Friedan, *The Feminine Mystique* (New York: Norton, 1963).

15. See Kurt Lewin, *Resolving Social Conflict* (New York: Harper and Row, 1941), esp. pp. 145–216; and a recent critique of Lewin's thesis, Jack Rothman, "Minority Group Status, Mental Health and Intergroup Relations: An Appraisal of Kurt Lewin's Thesis," *The Journal of Intergroup Relations,* 3 (Autumn 1962), pp. 299–310.

16. Milton M. Goldberg, "A Qualification of the Marginal Man Theory," *American Sociological Review,* 6 (February 1941), pp. 52–58.

17. Hubert Blalock, *Toward a Theory of Minority Group Relations* (New York: Wiley, 1967), pp. 79–84. See also Edna Bonacich, "A Theory of Middleman Minorities," *American Sociological Review,* 38 (1973), pp. 583–594.

18. Alfred Kazin, *A Walker in the City* (New York: Grove Press, 1951), p. 12.

19. See, for example, Candice van Ellison, "Introduction," in Allon Schoener (ed.), *Harlem on My Mind* (New York: Random House, 1968). The author's remarks were adapted from Nathan Glazer and Daniel Patrick Moynihan's *Beyond the Melting Pot* (Cambridge: MIT Press, 1963).

20. Oscar Lewis, "In New York You Get Swallowed by a Horse," *Commentary* (November 1964), p. 69.

21. See, for example, L. Singer, "Ethnogenesis and Negro Americans Today," *Social Research,* 29 (Winter 1962), pp. 419–432.

22. Norbert F. Wiley, "The Ethnic Mobility Trap and Stratification Theory," *Social Problems,* 2 (Fall 1967), pp. 147–159.

23. Ibid. Also see William Foote Whyte, *Street Corner Society* (Chicago: University of Chicago Press, 1943).

24. See Judith R. Kramer and Seymour Leventman, *Children of the Gilded Ghetto* (New Haven: Yale University Press, 1961). See also Part 1, "Jews, Gentiles and the American Dream," in Peter I. Rose (ed.), *The Ghetto and Beyond* (New York: Random House, 1969), pp. 21–97, passim.

25. See, for example, Peter I. Rose, *Strangers in Their Midst: Small-Town Jews and Their Neighbors* (Merrick, NY: Richwood Publishing Company, 1979), especially pp. 76–79. Most of the small-town Jews interviewed by the author were keenly aware of the role they were forced to play as "ambassadors to the gentiles."

26. See Robert K. Merton, *Social Theory and Social Structure* (Glencoe, IL: Free Press, 1957), pp. 290–291.

27. Edward A. Suchman, John P. Dean, and Robin M. Williams Jr., *Desegregation: Some Propositions and Research Suggestions* (New York: The Anti-Defamation League of B'nai B'rith, 1958), p. 67.

28. See, for example, E. Digby Baltzell, *The Protestant Establishment* (New York: Random House, 1964), pp. 329–334.

29. See also Peter I. Rose, "Small-Town Jews and Their Neighbours in the United States," *Jewish Journal of Sociology,* 3 (December 1962), pp. 1–17.

30. Herbert Gans, "Symbolic Ethnicity: The Future of Ethnic Groups and Cultures in America," *Ethnic and Racial Studies,* 2 (January 1979), pp. 1–20.

31. See Richard D. Alba, *Ethnic Identity: The Transformation of White America* (New Haven, CT: Yale University Press, 1990).

32. Suchman et al., op. cit., p. 198. See also Arnold M. Rose, *The Negro's Morale* (Minneapolis: University of Minnesota Press, 1949), pp. 85–95.

33. Langston Hughes, *Selected Poems* (New York: Alfred A. Knopf, 1951).

34. Simpson and Yinger, op. cit., pp. 205–233.

35. A. L. Holsey, "Learning How to Be Black," *The American Mercury,* 16 (April 1929), pp. 421–425.

36. Richard Wright, *Black Boy* (New York: Harper and Row, 1945), pp. 198–200.

37. Brewton Berry, *Race and Ethnic Relations,* 3rd ed. (Boston: Houghton Mifflin, 1965), p. 483.

38. Simpson and Yinger, op. cit., p. 251.

39. "Individuals may belong to membership groups that are different from their reference groups, and thereby manifest positive prejudice toward a social category other than that to which they apparently belong." Robin M. Williams Jr., "Racial and Cultural Relations," in J. B. Gittler (ed.), *Review of Sociology* (New York: Wiley, 1957), p. 428.

40. Sinclair Lewis, *Kingsblood Royal* (New York: Random House, 1947), p. 69.

41. St. Clair Drake and Horace Cayton, *Black Metropolis* (New York: Harcourt, Brace, 1945), p. 160.

42. Hortense Powdermaker, *After Freedom* (New York: Viking, 1939), p. 357.

43. E. Franklin Frazier, *Black Bourgeoisie* (New York: Free Press, 1957), p. 213.

44. Maurice Davie, *Negroes in American Society* (New York: McGraw-Hill, 1949), p. 440.

45. Jeremy Larner, "To Speak of Black Violence," *Dissent* (Winter 1973), pp. 76–78.

46. Ulf Hannerz, *Soulside: Inquiries into Ghetto Culture and Community* (New York: Columbia University Press, 1970), p. 157; also pp. 144–158.

47. James Baldwin, *The Fire Next Time* (New York: Dial Press, 1963), pp. 82–83.

Part IV

Power, Politics, and Pluralism

Chapter 9

Pride and Protest

Whose History?

History is often written in terms of the images people in power wish to project. American history, for example, was long recounted as if the English, Scotch Irish, and a few Dutchmen were the only ones to have had an impact on the growth and development of the country. Early textbooks and classroom lectures dealt almost exclusively with "The Anglo-American Tradition" or with "Our Christian Heritage." Throughout most of the eighteenth and nineteenth centuries, newcomers from northwestern Europe were encouraged to forget about the customs of Germany or Scandinavia and to adapt themselves to eminently superior *American* life ways. Other immigrants were often considered beyond the pale of social acceptance. In story and song, Irish Catholics, Italians, Poles, and Russian Jews—and, those who came from China or Japan—were referred to as "unassimilable aliens." Many politicians expressed serious doubts about whether such immigrants would ever have the makings of "real Americans."

In time, the majority of historians and many teachers adopted a different viewpoint. Pluralism came into vogue and school children and college students were then told that "our differences make us strong," or that "America is a multiplicity in a unity." It became fashionable to teach about the "Judeo Christian heritage." And, as if to bear public witness to such a revisionist view, the single Protestant preacher who had always intoned opening prayers at official gatherings was supplanted by a triumvirate: minister, priest, and rabbi, "representatives of our three great religions." (In time some sociologists gave expression to this new conception, a clearly symbolic recognition of the "triple melting pot" phenomenon.)[1]

In the early 1960s yet another persona stepped onto the dais—and another culture was "added" to the heritage. The figure was an African American. By mid-decade bookstores were flooded with hundreds of volumes on the Black Heritage. (By the end of the next decade the representational array of Americans would include Latinos and Asians and Native Americans in an expression of the rainbow-like character of our "multiracial and multicultural society." With the onset of the twenty-first century, especially after the attacks on New York and Washington by Arab terrorists and the clear recognition that Americans knew little about Islam, a new figure, representing those of the Muslim faith, was often also seen on the platform of public meetings.)

But the most dramatic changes occurred in the wake of the Black Power revolt of the 1960s. The textbooks that were prepared in its aftermath began to indicate that there was much more to African American history than the familiar litany: slave blocks; the old plantations; Emancipation; Reconstruction; the Hayes-Tilden Compromise; *Plessy v. Ferguson*; Booker T. Washington; race riots during two world wars; Jackie Robinson, the baseball player; Ralph Bunche, United Nations official; Thurgood Marshall, council for the NAACP and, later, Associate Justice of the Supreme Court; and that same Court's *Brown* decision of 1954. Although the new volumes continued to tell a story of the categorical treatment of those who came from Africa, readers were to learn far more about the people themselves, about *their* perspectives on the challenges created by their circumstances. For perhaps the first time, those who were not African American were exposed to the fact that, besides being victims, those long called Negroes were, like all others, parts of complex, stratified, and far from monolithic systems in which people live and work and play and suffer. They learned that, although having to respond to their particular and unique treatment, African Americans, like everybody else in the society—and in all societies—institutionalize their behavior patterns, set criteria for the conferring or denying of status, indicate the tolerance limits of accepted and expected behavior, and maintain social systems of great intricacy.

There was a surge of interest and writing about the family, occupation, politics, and stratification in various sectors of African American society. There was also a trend toward celebrating "Black History" and its heroes, heroes such as Crispus Attucks, the first "patriot" to be shot in the Revolutionary War; George Washington Carver, "the Peanut Man"; black soldiers who fought in the Union Army; black politicians in the turbulent days of Reconstruction; black troopers who rode with Teddy Roosevelt; black workers who toiled along the rail beds and in the factories and on the farms; those who were field hands; and those described by W. E. B. Du Bois, author of *The Souls of Black Folk* and political leader, a part of the "talented tenth," the Afro-American elite. They described the heady days of the Harlem Renaissance and the dark days of the Depression. And they began to concentrate on the postwar migration to the cities of the North and the expansion of the ghetto.

New publications went further, extolling the virtues of blackness and the solidarity of "soul" and exposing what was often characterized as the pallid character of Euro-American culture in contrast to that of those of African descent.

Together the factual and the fanciful, the analytically and politically oriented tracts, treatises, and textbooks, along with the various campaigns for recognition and control, served two important sociological functions: they strengthened communal ties among those celebrated and, simultaneously, taught others that those whose stories were being recounted also had a noble past and are, like themselves, a proud people worthy of respect.

Because these phenomena are so crucial for understanding the significant changes that have occurred in terms of the sociology and politics of intergroup relations in the United States in the last third of the twentieth century and the early part of the twenty-first, this chapter focuses almost exclusively on "black consciousness" and the politics of identity. Beginning with the rationale for a shift toward greater autonomy, we quickly move back in time, back to the early days of protest and the rise of the Civil Rights Movement.

The Roots of Redress

Feeling that many of the hard-won victories of the 1950s and 1960s had not made that much difference, increasing numbers of African American spokespersons began challenging a number of basic assumptions of the reform-minded civil rights advocates. First, they argued, liberal white leaders (whatever their personal goals) could rarely offer much more than palliatives that, often as not, were viewed as programs to keep their cities from erupting rather than being expressly designed for helping poor blacks. Second, they claimed that traditional black leaders rarely were much better: they were either out of touch with the people for whom they claimed to speak or were too willing to play "the Establishment game." Saying that their people had been deluded by whites who had taken up the "burden" and by "Negroes" (the term being used with more than a tinge of sarcasm) who were trying to lighten it, the new militants wanted to turn them "blackward," wanted them to have an identity that was truly their own.

They began their campaign by excoriating white liberals, "Uncle Toms" (those blacks who kowtowed to white people), and "racist Amerikkka" itself. They carried it forward with appeals to Black Nationalism. Much of this obviously had to do with two issues: identity and community.

In the early 1960s, James Baldwin wrote an essay entitled "Nobody Knows My Name."[2] In a sense, it dealt with only half of the problem. White people did not know what to call him and he did not know either. Baldwin's people—variously called African, colored, Negro, and black, and now African American—needed something to look forward to and something to look back upon. This is where the revisionist historians and sociological commentators came in. They showed that there has always been such a thing as African American culture, shared in some measure by every black person in this country. Not surprisingly, like all cultures, they noted that it was made up of many things—memories and moods and myths. What makes it different is that the memories and moods and even the myths remembered are unique: they are linked to slavery and its aftermath, the continued subjugation by those who repeatedly tried to prove that white was always right.

Not a few who focused on "The Black Experience in America," especially—though not exclusively—those collectively known as Afrocentrists, began to contend that, as a result of their unique trials and tribulations, African Americans were left with different conceptions of time and space and property—and life.

Many new studies indicated that the worlds in which black people lived, although dominated by the rules of segregation, were not simply societies of inmates, as some earlier critics would have it. The authors claimed that the hardships they endured were tempered by resilience, richness, hope, and spiritual uplift.[3] They point to the fact that these were not anomic subsocieties marked by chaos but communities with a high degree of social integration and sense of place.[4] The African American world had its own rules of conduct, its lingo, its literature, and its sound. It also had its own complex system of social stratification—and its problems; the most difficult was overcoming the barriers of segregation in the apartheid-like society.

Being frozen into the rigidity of a caste-like system and unable to become full partners in the society from which so much of their own customs, beliefs, and values were derived, what black people frequently lacked was the organizational apparatus characteristic of many other minority groups in America—the very groups with which they had long been compared and, perhaps more significantly, with which they had often compared themselves.

Segregation had long kept African Americans down and out of the mainstream. Sometimes their own leaders aided and abetted their oppressors. Early in the last century, both black preachers and white segregationists spoke of their children, both tended their flocks. Later on, the rhetoric shifted—as did the analogies—and a parallel began to be drawn between the plight of blacks in this country and that of mental patients. By that time few well-educated white people would argue that all blacks were innately inferior; they knew better—or knew better than to express such sentiments. Yet, the new conventional wisdom sounded strikingly like that of the old planters and ministers of God. Acting as if "only we know what's good for them," many viewed and treated disadvantaged black people as "culturally deprived" victims or patients in need of care and succor. And many blacks, in turn, like the inmates of mental institutions, continued to internalize the roles ascribed to them and acted accordingly. It was in this context that the late Malcolm X wrote that self-hatred was the worst of all the legacies of racist policies.[5]

Resistance and Rebellion

As indicated in earlier chapters, most efforts to redress the grievances of the past were channeled into campaigns for integration. Many African Americans believed (or wanted to believe) that, someday, somehow, color would really be overlooked. And sometimes white liberals, held in contempt by some of the angriest African American spokespersons,[6] helped to perpetuate this assumption without, for the most part, realizing what they were doing and without having very much personal contact with those they claimed to accept as equals.

The foregoing observations refer to "many" African Americans, but not to all. In there was a large cohort of blacks who had "made it"—some by the same techniques used by members of other minority groups, including the exploitation of those whose identity they shared; some by becoming athletes and jazz musicians and soul singers performing for both their own people and a wider audience; most by sheer determination to overcome the barriers of segregation, often working their way up by entering public service as postmen and clerks, secretaries and soldiers and teachers. Together, these members of what had come to be called the "Black Bourgeoisie," the "Colored Entertainers," and the "Negro Respectables," represented to many white people (especially middle-class whites) living evidence that African Americans could succeed if they tried hard enough and were willing to thicken their skins against whatever abuses the system and its agents meted out.

Since the late 1960s black people who had grown up in the days of blatant segregation have taken pride in the progress of those with whom they are most identified and, for all their difficulties, represent exemplars of middle-class respectability: friendly, hardworking, religious, and community-minded. Many of the children of such successful blacks who entered college in the mid-1960s had different memories. They remembered more of the failures of the civil rights struggles to achieve true integration than the significant gains from which they, themselves, frequently benefited. They, and not merely the poor residents of Watts or Harlem, felt they really knew what nationalist spokesman Ron Karenga meant when he cried, "There are only three kinds of people in this country: white people, black people, and Negroes. Negroes? They are black people that act like white people."

Black college students, particularly in northern schools and the larger southern ones, knew that part of Karenga's rhetoric was addressed to them and their parents. ("Which side are you on?") Ironically, it was often those who had suffered least from the stigma of color who began to feel the strain the most. Many reacted by forming Afro-American organizations on campus or by going "home" to Harlem or Hough or Hattiesburg (often places they had never been) to work and teach and organize.

Some, to resolve their race/class schizophrenia, joined ranks of the most militant members of the black community. Stressing both poverty and race, those who lived in the urban ghettos became their cause. With the poor, they argued, they could put to use some of the direct and fringe benefits of a college education. And for them they could try to uplift their spirits and offer a new and different view of the Americans who came from Africa.

The new orientation had a long prehistory. Like most social movements, it was the culmination of years of struggle and crisis during which an oppressed people was trying to come to grips with its situation and the constantly thwarted attempts by those who sought to become full-fledged Americans. In one context after another, political, social, and religious leaders claimed they wanted nothing more but nothing less. Among the various techniques of protest they had used in the past, and that were finally to be joined, two were most prevalent from the time of Emancipation to its centennial. One centered on black people themselves and was concerned with "uplift"—the learning of useful skills, the instilling of pride in self and neighbor, and emphasizing such puritan virtues as thrift and practicality. The other focused on integration and the gaining of civil rights. In the first instance, the underlying notion was that African Americans would show others that they were responsible, upright, and talented citizens and that, in time, they would be ready to take their place beside anyone. In the latter case the argument was that the problem was not the blacks' at all but the whites' and the system they controlled: both should be made to change.

Uplift

The first sustained challenge to Jim Crow laws and the entire system of segregation was to come from highly educated and remarkably well-integrated northern blacks. Men like Monroe Trotter and W. E. B. Du Bois challenged what they saw as the tendency of southern blacks and their leaders to acquiesce and accept their second-class status. A prime target was Booker T. Washington, who, before the turn of the present century, had sought to come to terms with the problem of black alienation. Washington, born a slave, saw the hope of his people—at least in a southland of deeply rooted segregation—in the development of pride and self-esteem, and in the learning of skills of the honest tradesman. A speech of his, delivered at the Atlanta Exposition in 1895, has been branded as a classic in acquiescent thinking.[7] The implication was clear: black people were not ready to take their place beside whites.

What Washington and others saw, however, was not simply the "Uncle Tomism" his critics such as Trotter and Du Bois claimed. Rather, it was, to some at least, a sort of live-and-let-live pluralism. As Washington himself put it, "In all things that are purely social we can be as separate as the fingers, yet as one in hand in all things essential to mutual progress."[8] He also said, in the same speech, that "the wisest among my race understand that agitation of questions of social equality is the extremist folly, and the progress in the enjoyment of all the privileges that will come to us must be the result of severe and constant struggle rather than of artificial forcing."[9] It was Washington's unwillingness to advocate direct action that won for him contempt in the minds of several generations of radical leaders. Yet, there is little question that Washington did begin to come to terms with two of the most serious problems plaguing African Americans: self-reliance and the question of communal solidarity, especially in the economic arena.

At the Tuskegee Institute, which he established, Washington sought and in many ways succeeded in implementing his plan. For a time he became the idol of millions of blacks and to this day he remains a symbol for some blacks and many whites (especially older school teachers) of the "responsible and reasonable Negro." Today, few young African Americans share these sentiments, although a growing number have reverted to the argument of self-help and, in some instances, even to the fingers-of-the-hand policy Washington promulgated.

Washington's famous theme of seemingly subservient accommodation turned toward one of more intentional separatism for some lower-class African Americans, especially those in the urban centers. They joined the ranks of Marcus Garvey's "Back-to-Africa" movement in the 1920s, followed Daddy Grace and other charismatic evangelists in the 1930s, and joined the Temple of Islam (the Black Muslims) more recently. All such actions were, in their own way and time, challenges to the status quo ante. In their expression, often stridently self-assured and sometimes confrontational, especially taking on other members of the black community, activists were very different from those who first followed Washington. Yet the members of each group, including the Muslims, were—and are still—participating in uplift organizations, in bodies that give a sense of identity to downtrodden followers, a measure of importance, lessons in proper decorum, and, above all, a purpose for living.

In a very real sense, what the astute observers August Meier and Elliott Rudwick said in the beginning of the days of the dramatic sea change in attitudes and actions still obtains: "Booker T. Washington's separatist ideology functioned both as a mechanism of accommodation to American racism and as a device for overcoming it."[10] Yet, until very recently, the latter point was not at all apparent or, at least, acknowledged by Washington's critics who saw accommodation and separatism as blind alleys that merely gave support to segregationist sentiment.

The Burden of Responsibility

Washington's most vocal early adversary was W. E. B. Du Bois, Harvard graduate, professor of sociology at Atlanta University, and cofounder of the then quite radical Niagara Movement, an all-black organization that he and sympathetic colleagues tried to set up explicitly to oppose Washington and his program. Taking an entirely different tack, the radicals argued that the burden of redressing grievances was "not the Negroes' problem but the whites' and *they* should be made to change." (Although at odds about approaches, on certain issues Du Bois and Washington did agree. Both believed firmly in the idea of racial solidarity. Indeed, Du Bois, whom many saw as the quintessential integrationist, went considerably further than Washington in proposing a pan-African movement to unite black people everywhere.)

Washington and his followers were able to stop the Niagara Movement of 1905 from getting started. They were unable to do the same with its successor, the National Association for the Advancement of Colored People (NAACP), founded in 1909, with the announced goal of "fighting for the Black man's constitutional rights and the undeclared aim of curbing Booker T. Washington's power."[11] The NAACP, like the Urban League, established a year later, was an organization of black and white progressives who sought to fight the battle for justice and civil rights through education, politics, and, later, and most significantly, litigation. Closely associated with the organization was its Legal Defense and Education Fund (LDEF), the result of the efforts of what was known as "The Committee of 100," established in 1943 and initially chaired by a former NAACP board member, the Edinburgh-born William Allan Neilson, former president of Smith College in Northampton, Massachusetts.[12] The LDEF, supported by the general membership, brought numerous suits against various parties accused of violating the Constitution through adherence to state and local statutes upholding segregation.

The lawyers were skilled and persistent and, in time, one barrier after another was to fall as the Supreme Court ruled in favor of the complainants. The culmination of the legal movement came in 1954 when, in a unanimous decision, the high court overturned the old *Plessy* ruling and proclaimed that separate could never be equal. Many black and many white integrationists believed that the critical point had been passed and that rapid compliance with the court's mandate for "desegregation with all deliberate speed" would toll the death knell of segregation in the United States. They were wrong.

As far back as the 1920s a number of black intellectuals had begun to question the advisability of following the slow and deliberate course of taking cases up through the courts while, as they saw it, African American people were suffering without relief. Some, even then, questioned any piecemeal approach of attacking one institution—for example, the educational system—instead of trying to alter the entire social order. A resolute few, such as A. Philip Randolph, president of the Brotherhood of Sleeping Car Porters, and several outspoken socialists, branded popular leaders like Du Bois—who, as noted, was in his day considered a radical—as "handkerchief heads," "hat-in-hand Negroes." In *The Messenger,* which Randolph edited, the NAACP was attacked as a bourgeois organization and an alternative, workingman's movement, was advocated.

With capitalism defined as the enemy of all poor people, Randolph sought to rally blacks and whites to the cause of socialism. He did not succeed. His ideological rhetoric was too much for many blacks to accept; his integrationist appeal was too much for many white workers to stomach.[13] (There is an ironic twist to all this. In the later years of his life, Du Bois moved increasingly to the left and became a member of the Communist Party in Ghana where he had gone to live, and where he died at the age of ninety-three. Randolph, still alive in the 1970s, found himself branded as a "handkerchief head" by militant young blacks for holding to the notion of a unified—black and white—attack on the system.)

Randolph never reached the urban masses to which he appealed. But Marcus Garvey did. The Jamaican founder—in 1914—of the Universal Negro Improvement Association (UNIA), Garvey claimed that the integrationists were naive for seeking to win concessions from a society that was and would always be racist.

Instead he favored the development of separate institutions in the United States and, in time, a return to Africa, the "Black Zion." He and his followers opposed miscegenation and extolled everything that was black. One sociologist noted the attractiveness of this movement as follows: "The Garvey movement was based on good psychology. It made the downtrodden lower class Negro feel like somebody among white people who said they were nobody. It gave the crowd an opportunity to show off in colors, parades, and self-glorification."[14] For a time the UNIA had great appeal, but neither Garvey nor his followers ever got to Africa. He was eventually denounced by prominent leaders of the black community, barred from bringing his people to Liberia (which was seen as the African Zion), and finally indicted and sentenced to a prison term for using the mail to defraud in selling shares of stock for his "Black Star Ship Line."

What had once been an important movement of Black Nationalism ended when Garvey was deported in 1927 as an undesirable alien.

But Garvey left a rich legacy. In fact, his banner of red, green, and black was flown anew in the late 1960s and through the next decade, especially by the cultural nationalists who, in addition to Afro hairdos, dashiki shirts, and other symbols of their African roots, frequently sported buttons with the three colors—the first represents life's blood; the second, hope, and, some say, the green hills of "home"; and the third, "the color of our skin."

The Civil Rights Movement

In the 1930s new organizations emerged, many of these seeking to find alliances with New Deal agencies that were more favorably inclined to the plight of African American citizens than their predecessors had been. Again criticism of the NAACP arose. Young leaders such as Ralph Bunche, who later became the deputy secretary-general of the United Nations, felt that the organization was not sufficiently militant to deal with the pressing needs created by the Depression and the persistence of discrimination throughout the country.

During World War II two new movements arose that presaged what was to come in the following decade. The first was A. Philip Randolph's March on Washington movement, which pressured President Roosevelt into issuing the famous Executive Order 8802, establishing the first federal Fair Employment Practices Commission. As Meier and Rudwick explained, "even without enforcement powers, the FEPC set a precedent for treating fair employment practice as a civil right. The short-lived March on Washington Movement prefigured future trends in three ways: (1) It was an explicitly all-Black organization; (2) It based its strategy on mass action by the urban slum dwellers; (3) It concentrated on economic problems."[15]

The second significant movement of the era was the Congress of Racial Equality (CORE), the first of several innovative civil rights organizations that gained prominence through their efforts to accelerate desegregation by means of nonviolent direct action. CORE began in 1942. Bayard Rustin and James Farmer, members of the pacifist Fellowship of Reconciliation both heavily influenced by the teachings of Henry David Thoreau,[16] the nineteenth-century poet and pacifist, suggested the founding of an organization devoted to the use of "relentless noncooperation, economic boycotts and civil disobedience," to fight for racial equality. A sit-in at a Chicago restaurant that same year led to the founding of the Chicago Committee on Racial Equality. Out of that organization CORE was born.

In the late 1940s radical-pacifist CORE was sponsoring sit-ins and freedom rides in the North and in Virginia, North Carolina, Kentucky, and Tennessee. And it was CORE that sponsored the integrated bus rides into Alabama in 1961 that ended in the beating of many of the participants. Those trips may have been a turning point, for, in the years to follow, CORE, an organization that had prided itself on its color-blindness, a civil rights group whose membership was for a long time two-thirds white, turned away from the course of integration and toward the building of racial consciousness. In time its founder, Farmer, was succeeded by Floyd McKissick, who, in turn, was followed by the more nationalistic Roy Ennis, who completed the process of purging the membership of whites and, in the process, lost considerable political and financial support. By the end of the twentieth century, CORE was but a shadow of its former self, riven with dissensions and doing little to aid the cause of desegregation or ghetto improvement.

A third new civil rights organization, perhaps the best known, arose from the highly successful bus boycott in Montgomery, Alabama, in 1956 initiated by Rosa Parks on December 1, 1955. Parks, secretary of the Montgomery chapter of the NAACP and active member of the Women's Political Council, had refused to give up her seat and move to the back of the bus as was the rule. Soon afterward a young minister named Martin Luther King Jr. founded a support group called the Southern Christian Leadership Conference (SCLC). Within a few years he became the most important leader and spokesperson for nonviolent direct action in the United States. He and his followers, including fellow Protestant ministers Andrew Young, Jesse Jackson, and Ralph David Abernathy (who would become King's successor) took their campaign from community to community. People from many parts of the country joined in marches on the bastions of segregation, marches designed to prove African Americans could walk with pride even in the face of strident opposition. These committed young men and women followed their leader and turned the other cheek and, all too often, got their skulls cracked open.

In 1960 a fourth organization informally began at a lunch counter in Greensboro, North Carolina, when a group of black students decided to defy the proprietor who refused to serve them. The sit-ins of young people spread from town to town and, with the backing of the Reverend King and the coordination of Ella Baker, the peer-centered collective action movement soon became institutionalized as the Student Nonviolent Coordinating Committee (SNCC). Its early leadership included Stokely Carmichael, coauthor with Charles V. Hamilton of the book *Black Power,* which some saw as a manifesto of the new movement,[17] and James Forman, who would later write *The Making of Black Revolutionaries,* the story of a critical era.[18]

In its early days SNCC led a door-to-door campaign to register voters and helped to organize "freedom schools." Unlike many of the other groups, it relied heavily on the voluntary efforts of women activists. Within a year, however, SNCC severed ties with SCLC, claiming that the parent organization was too cautious. Within five years, some critics cynically would say that the meaning of the letters in the acronym SNCC (pronounced "Snick") no longer had meaning because so many members had turned away from their previous stances of nonviolence and integration in favor of aggressive separatism. It, too, was a portent.

But, in the late summer of 1963, before the break was complete, the old guard and the new—including A. Philip Randolph, Roy Wilkins of the NAACP, Whitney Young Jr. of the Urban League, James Farmer of CORE, Martin Luther King Jr. of SCLC, and some but not all of the SNCC leadership—joined forces to lead a massive march on Washington. To many, it was the culmination of years of struggle. To most of those who were there, it was a time of rededication, a time of hope, a time of dreams fulfilled—or about to be.

From the steps of the Lincoln Memorial, in a powerful and impressive voice, Martin Luther King Jr. gave his oft-repeated speech, which ended with that now-familiar refrain,

I have a dream that my four little children will one day live in a nation where they will not be judged by the color of their skin but the content of their character....

Dr. King concluded his oration with the following words: "When we let freedom ring, when we let it ring from every village and every hamlet, from every state and every city, we will be able to speed up that day when all of God's children, Black men and white men, Jews and Gentiles, Protestants and Catholics, will be able to join hands and sing in the words of that old Negro spiritual, 'Free at last! Free at last! Thank God Almighty, we are free at last!'"[19]

Shortly before he was assassinated, Dr. King was asked how much progress had been made through the campaigns of nonviolent direct action, court decisions, and new legislation, and what the next step would be. He replied it was to accomplish the task of true integration. A commentator recently noted that to achieve King's goals black Americans would need to address "the continuing social and economic disparities between white and black communities, and work constructively in an 'Operation Bootstraps' to improve conditions to close the gap."[20]

Affirmation

By the time of Emancipation's centennial (and, for some, before), it was becoming increasingly evident to many—outside observers and workers in the movement— that neither chauvinistic nationalism nor a soulless militancy, that is, a militancy devoid of a distinctive "black" content, could, by itself, turn the tide of racism, so deep did it flow.[21] Since there was little likelihood that they could really go it alone and even less that they could (or would) ever turn white, a rising generation of African American leaders argued that their people had to learn (or relearn) to take pride in themselves *and* to become political activists. They had to hark to what Frederick Douglass had prescribed a hundred years before the Student Nonviolent Coordinating Committee was born:

> Those who profess to favor freedom yet deprecate agitation are men who want crops without plowing up the ground; they want rain without thunder and lightning. They want the ocean without the awful roar of its many waters.... Power concedes nothing without demand. It never did and it never will. Find out just what any people will quietly submit to and you have found out the exact measure of injustice and wrong, which will be imposed upon them, and these will continue till they are resisted with either words or blows, or with both. The limits of tyrants are prescribed by the endurance of those whom they oppress.[22]

Black Power did, in fact, begin as a movement of words, impassioned words, exhorting poor sharecroppers to exercise their franchise. But it was not enough. Intimidation and threats had raised the ire of the civil rights workers and turned many black pacifists into soldiers and turned away many white allies. The pacifist codes of Henry David Thoreau and Mohandas Gandhi (an idol of Martin Luther King Jr. and many of his followers) were replaced by the "eye for an eye" law of Hammurabi—much as Frederick Douglass had suggested.

For years, black leaders and their white allies had counseled patience and fortitude. And for years their authority went unchallenged, for it was widely felt that these liberal integrationists were on the right path. The civil rights campaign in the late 1950s and early 1960s, and the bills passed by Congress in their wake, seemed, to some at least, positive proof of the efficacy of their Gandhian tactics. But, as many of the victories proved hollow; as tensions mounted between those, mainly black, civil rights workers who saw radical pacifism as a pragmatic device and those, mainly white, integrationists for whom it was an ideology; as the Vietnam War siphoned off funds that (it was said) would have been earmarked for social programs; and, most of all, as the relative deprivation of African Americans became more apparent, the climate shifted. The movement went sour and the old coalitions began to break apart.

Unquestionably, urban riots in a dozen major cities were also an exacerbating factor. Many whites in the general population who had begun to feel some sense of sympathy with the embattled civil rights workers or who, at least, were talking of "giving Negroes their due," grew increasingly fearful—and hostile—as they saw the flames of Harlem and Rochester and Detroit and Watts in central Los Angeles and the section of Cleveland known as Hough on their television sets or, in some cases, from their upstairs windows. There were charges and countercharges, cries of duplicity on one hand and of corruption on the other, shouts of "Burn, Baby, Burn" and "Get the Honkies" mixed with "Send them back to Africa."

Given the disillusionment, the uncertainty, and the persistence of institutionalized segregation, and, especially, given the fact that little was being done to satisfy those poorest blacks whose expectations had suddenly begun to rise, it is not surprising that "We Shall Overcome" was replaced—literally and figuratively—with the call for "Black Power."

A new mood began to reach out and envelop the unorganized black masses, particularly in the northern ghettos where few meaningful communal institutions existed around which people could rally and where even the oratory of Martin Luther King Jr. had not been able to stir people into action. Now the focus began to shift away from integration and toward the more basic matter of "getting it together."

Half a century earlier the black sociologist E. Franklin Frazier said that "if the masses of Negroes can save their self-respect and remain free of hate, so much the better. But ... I believe, it would be better for the Negro's soul to be seared with hate than dwarfed by self-abasement...."[23] Once again it was being argued that there was a psychological need for black people to call the white society to task rather than to accept and internalize second-class status and all that it meant. At the time, William H. Grier and Price Cobbs suggested that, among African Americans, there had long been an almost desperate need to find a sense of both positive self-hood and meaningful people-hood.[24] To accomplish these goals meant that the leadership would have to change. Whites had to be eased or pushed out of positions of dominance to make room for those who could more easily identify with, and be identified with, the black masses. And in a very few months, they were.

As groups such as the Black Panthers—a name used by several different groups, some of which were engaged in such mainstream activities as voter registration, others involved in highly charged revolutionary politics—gained notoriety, those in the traditional organizations changed too. SNCC had already become more separatist; CORE was turning away from its original stance of integration in favor of black membership and black consciousness and also what many African American women would later criticize: masculinity and male assertiveness. Even the members of the Urban League and the NAACP sounded more revolutionary though they tried to walk the tightrope to maintain the fragmenting ties with white liberals. (The NAACP was later to abandon such a policy in the early 1990s, when its short-lived director stressed the fact that he welcomed all "brothers and sisters" regardless of ideology. By forming an alliance with the outspokenly anti-Semitic Muslim leader, Louis Farrakhan, NAACP President Benjamin Chavis lost much of the remaining white liberal support. In 1994 Chavis was forced out of office, partly for his alliances but mainly because of financial difficulties in the NAACP. Since his departure, his successors—Myrlie Evers-Williams, the widow of the slain civil rights leader Medgar Evers, and former activists and congressmen, Kweisi Mfume and Julian Bond—each tried to stabilize the situation and win back old allies. In recent years, the NAACP has turned a considerable amount of its energy to strengthening African American communities and addressing the crises of poverty and anomie in the inner cities.)

The Southern Christian Leadership Conference continued fighting its battles for jobs and freedom but also began forming coalitions with other organizations, including those representing other embattled minority groups. Despite differences in symbol (the clenched fist or the double bar of equality), in slogan, and in style, pride and protest were joined and, for many, it had become a time to be "Black."

Black Studies, White Responses

The struggle was waged in many parts of the country, in small towns and big cities, North, South, East, and West. But it was almost invariably the university campus that was the seedbed and most frequent scene of some of the most extreme tactics. In response to mounting pressure, college officials, often less liberal than their faculty members who were often sympathetic and sometimes supportive of the challengers to the status quo ante, tried to hold the line. They called for the establishment of ad hoc committees to consider the changes sought through petition. But the protesters, undeterred, steadily increased the pressure—and upped the ante. In the face of mass demonstrations and intimidating actions including the takeover of college buildings or student unions,[25] many administrators not only capitulated, they helped to legitimate and found the funds to support the demands. On campus after campus they agreed to increase the recruitment of minority students and faculty members, underwrote ethnically specific political organizations such as Black Student Alliances, provided facilities for cultural centers and, in some places, separate dormitories, and introduced African American programs and curricular innovations geared to the special needs of black undergraduates and, in time, other students "of color."

From among the welter of proposals and pronouncements requesting or, as often, demanding such programs, one message came across loud and clear: the tactics were working. The protagonists had seized control and, sometimes dressed in revolutionary garb, even with bandoleers of bullets and intimating weapons (as happened at Cornell University),[26] they told their teachers and fellows students, and the rest of the world through the media, whose representatives were following the events with considerable interest, "We will be *Negroes* no more." There is little doubt that this mood, seized on by increasing numbers of minority students, including many from middle-class and liberal backgrounds, signaled the end of an old era and the beginning of a new phase in racial and ethnic relations in the United States.

One of the most tangible signs of the success of the student uprisings was the establishment of Black Studies programs at many universities across the country, and, soon on their heels, Chicano, Puerto Rican, Native American, and Asian American Studies programs in appropriate geographic areas. Some institutions, particularly those on the West Coast, placed several such programs under a single roof, creating departments of Ethnic Studies or of Comparative American Cultures. Whether separate or united, the newly—and often quickly—created programs and departments were, from the start, staffed by a mixture of highly trained academics who specialized in the study of ethnicity, race relations, history, and literature; activists whose professional skills were frequently far more organizational than analytical; and assorted instructors whose main claim to expertise was their status as members of the group being studied and whose main staying power depended on the support of student claques. Not surprisingly, the arguments over whether or not Black (and other sorts of) Studies had a place in the academy gave way (once it was a fait accompli) to debates over what was being taught and by whom.

Several studies were conducted that examined these questions. One of the most comprehensive was that carried out by C. Wilson Record. Record's research and his findings provide a still-useful paradigm for understanding reactions to the even more controversial subject of "multiculturalism" today.

With grants from the Metropolitan Applied Research Center and the American Philosophical Society, Record moved around the country visiting seventy campuses and interviewing 209 black and white sociologists who "at the time or in the previous few years considered race and ethnicity as a teaching or research field."[27] Among this admittedly limited sample, Wilson found that reactors to his questions could be grouped under four rubrics: (1) the *Embracers,* those who welcomed the innovation of ethnically specific courses and programs (although they were rather sharply divided as to the rationales for doing so); (2) the *Antagonists,* those who openly opposed Black Studies as a separate field and resented the tendency of its supporters to exclude them from participation or dismiss their prior contributions; (3) the *Accommodators,* those who reluctantly accepted what they saw as inevitable and tried to make the best of a dubious situation; and (4) the *Dropouts,* those who withdrew from the field under the fire of black militants.

Each group had a diverse array of members. The first, the "Embracers," although dominated by critics of the Establishment, also included conservatives who saw Black Studies as a device of both containment and decompression (much in the way that urban police forces had set up "human relations units" in the wake of the riots of the previous decade, and then went about business as usual). And there were those who saw Black Studies courses as a needed challenge to the traditional ways sociologists and others had addressed themselves to studying "The Black Experience."

The "Antagonists" were also a heterogeneous group, but at their core were a number of white integrationists (and some blacks) who saw themselves as part of the solution not the problem. It was this subgroup more than any other that was caught between the rock and the hard place. For years, many had studied race relations and tried to implement policies that would serve to make society more sensitive to discrimination and more tolerant of diversity. Many had been civil rights activists who were also frustrated by the slowness of change and saw the necessity for African Americans and other minorities to become more assertive. What they hadn't expected was that they would become targets and, in many cases, scapegoats for those who saw them as establishment-types themselves.

Some reacted to attacks upon them by pointing to the ideological rigidity of the promoters of the new programs. Said one "antagonist" interviewed by Record, "They read Fanon but not Rustin; Malcolm X but not Kenneth Clark; Angela Davis and LeRoi Jones but not Roy Wilkins; the latter-day Du Bois but not Booker T. Washington; Marcus Garvey but not the mature Frederick Douglass. And a lot of time they don't read anything."[28]

The third category, "Accommodators," seemed better able to ride the tide, many undoubtedly thinking that, in due course, it would ebb. Condescendingly they would say, "Of course it isn't academically respectable, but there are a lot of things around here that aren't—physical education, home economics, social work, business administration."[29] In other words, Black Studies was something that had to be tolerated and even legitimated as part of the general offerings of a multiversity.

"Dropouts," roughly 20 percent of the sample, were older and more bitter than most of the others, including the "Antagonists." Unlike the "Antagonists," whose members dug in their heels to fight against the separatist bent of the Black Studies supporters, those in this last category threw in the towel. Like all the others those in the dropout group included black as well as white sociologists, but particularly individuals who were often accused of being "Uncle Toms," whatever their skills or prior commitments. In fact, most seemed to have dropped out only after having had a series of confrontations with reactionary nationalists or cultural revolutionaries who publicly denounced them or barred them from speaking or blocked access to classrooms and offices.

Of course, demands for and the establishment of Black Studies programs were not the only manifestations of conflict between conservatives and radicals, integrationists and separatists. Campuses also came under increasing pressure to alter traditional standards for admission to facilitate the entry of more minority students.

Although "affirmative action" became a descriptive term for a process of targeted aid and group-based efforts during the administration of Richard M. Nixon, the idea of reaching out with special programs for minorities had deep roots, going back to the days of Franklin D. Roosevelt. The label itself came into vogue with

President John F. Kennedy's Executive Order 10925, urging federal contractors to seek and employ more minority group members. In the period immediately following his assassination, there was further recognition of the extent to which, as Jill Quadagno notes, "race … had moved from the periphery to the center. No longer a regional embarrassment, racial inequality had become a national malady."[30] In the days of FDR and JFK the emphasis was on jobs and job training, not special consideration for entry to colleges.

Such new demands seemed shocking to many who argued that they flew in the face of meritocratic principles despite the fact that advantages had long been given to certain categories of applicants: offspring of alumni, super athletes, and those from distant places, "to provide geographical diversity." Why not do the same to insure racial and ethnic diversity? That was the real question. And those who asked it had become quite skilled in pressing the point.

Designated Minorities and Affirmative Action

Responding to the change of strategy and, in turn, of policy as it was beginning to be reacted to by sympathetic power brokers, vulnerable governmental agencies, frightened managers, school boards, union leaders, politicians, and college admission boards, historian Daniel Boorstin once wrote a facetious essay. Zeroing in on college admission boards, Boorstin suggested that if the trend were to be followed to its logical conclusion, the I.Q. and other such tests would be abandoned as criteria for academic admission and would be replaced by an "E.Q.," an Ethnic Quotient.[31] This would mean that students and eventually teachers and their subject matter would have to be apportioned strictly according to background. There would be so many blacks and so many whites; so many Jews and so many Catholics—these to be further subdivided according to whether they were children or grandchildren of Italians or Irishmen, Slavs or Slovaks. (Fractional men, as Vance Bourjaily once called people of "mixed marriages" like himself, would prove difficult to judge.)[32] What, for example, would one do with an application from a modern-day Fiorello La Guardia, that half-Italian, half-Jewish Protestant mayor of New York? Boorstin offers an answer: give him so many points for each of his traits in proportion to their representativeness in the overall population and make sure, of course, that his curriculum is balanced in similar fashion! What Boorstin lampooned more than forty years ago was soon to become a very real issue, and one that went far beyond the college and university campuses.

The problems of racial inequality had migrated north and west along with the tens of thousands of blacks who left the South starting in the last decades of the nineteenth century and settled in the North. Over the decades the dichotomous— white/nonwhite (usually meaning African American)—character of southern society began to become a pervasive reality in many cities far removed from the Old South. Although some, such as Michael Harrington, author of *The Other America*,[33] tried to alert the public to the damaging effect of the deepening chasm, most public officials paid little heed until it was thrust upon them by the widely publicized activities of civil rights activists in the South and the angry outbursts of those who lived in the black ghettos of the North. Much of what became known as the War on Poverty, and, according to a number of scholars, much of the nature of the welfare policies that came in its wake, was directly related to the continuing presence of racial injustice in America.[34]

The Civil Rights Act of 1964, signed by President Lyndon B. Johnson, barred discrimination in the workplace and supported LBJ's contention that casting wider nets for employees, providing training for those who need it, and taking extra steps to insure that opportunities existed for all would enhance his goal of seeking "equality as a result." Johnson went further. Executive Order 112246 established an Office of Affirmative Action in the Labor Department. And his successor, Richard Nixon, went further still. His administration's "Philadelphia Plan" (named for building contract arrangements in that city) put in place a system of quotas.[35]

The gradual shift from a plan to insure equal employment opportunities for anyone to favoring those who had belonged to a category of persons who had been discriminated against (often referred to as "group rights") was the basis of a renewed controversy, a controversy less about goals of overcoming the impact of racism and more about the means to achieving a truly just society. It not only pitted traditional libertarians against interventionists but created coalitions of unlikely allies. For example, many of the strongest advocates of "affirmative action"—the phrase now used variously to describe the casting of wider nets for minority applicants, offering compensatory advantages to lower-scoring but still potentially qualified students, and establishing targets and goals and, sometimes, actual quotas for minorities—found it increasingly difficult to implement their new policies without triggering resistance from those who felt that such programs were designed only for certain segments of the population, which, for obvious reasons, they were. Even if what some call "benign quotas" were applied across the board, it was argued that certain groups would have to lose. Many critics saw the trend as "racism in reverse."[36] And some brought suit. In the spring of 1973 complaints were filed against several schools and universities.

The most celebrated case at the time was that of Marco DeFunis, a white applicant to the University of Washington Law School who was twice denied admission and brought suit claiming that his constitutional guarantee of equal protection of the laws under the Fourteenth Amendment had been violated. DeFunis charged that the law school used racial categories to admit less-qualified minority students on a preferential basis. In time his claim was rejected by the highest court in the state but, in many ways, the die was cast. A quite similar case, brought by Allan Bakke, a twice-rejected applicant to a University of California Medical School, eventually made it to the Supreme Court where, in an ambiguous decision, the Court ordered Bakke admitted since it appeared that the only grounds for his denial were racial. Yet, it also upheld the use of affirmative action measures in which the race of the applicant was to be one of a number of criteria admission boards might use in recruiting and selecting candidates.[37] Here is what was actually said in the brief filed by the Office of the Attorney General of the United States as amicus curiae in October 1977:

The judgment of the Supreme Court of California [which upheld the University's exclusion of Bakke] should be reversed to the extent that it forbids the Medical School to operate any minority-sensitive admissions.

The remaining question is whether respondent is entitled to admission to the Medical School. We have argued that it is constitutional in making admissions decisions to take race into account in order fairly to compare minority and nonminority applicants, but it is not clear from the record whether the Medical School's program, as applied to respondent in 1973 and 1974, operated in this manner.

The trial court found, and the University did not contest, that 16 places in the class were reserved for special admittees. The record did not show, however, how this number was chosen, whether the number was inflexible or was used simply as a measure for assessing the program's operation, and how the number pertains to the objects of the special admission program....

The deficiencies in the evidence and findings—which pertain to both the details of the program and the justifications that support it—may have been caused by the approach both parties, and both courts below, took to this case. They asked only whether it was permissible to make minority-sensitive decisions, but that it is necessary to address, as well, questions concerning how race was used, and for what reasons. The findings with respect to these latter, critical questions are insufficient to allow the Court to address them.

Accordingly, the judgment of the Supreme Court of California should be vacated to the extent that it orders respondent's admission and the case should be remanded for further appropriate proceedings to address the questions that remain open. In all other respects the judgment should be reversed.[38]

In its arguments the majority made the following points, which, to many, served as guidelines for future action: "Minority-sensitive decisions are essential to eliminate the effects of discrimination; both the legislative and executive branches of the federal government have adopted minority-sensitive programs for the purpose of eliminating the effects of past discrimination; Minority-sensitive relief is not limited to correction of discrimination perpetrated by the institution offering admission; and, Discrimination against minority groups has hindered their participation in the medical profession."[39]

Then stating, "The central issue on judicial review of a minority-sensitive program is whether it is tailored to remedy the effects of past discrimination,"[40] citing numerous cases, the Court concluded, "A program is tailored to remedy the effects of past discrimination if it uses race to enhance the fairness of the admissions process; and, There is no adequate alternative to the use of minority-sensitive admissions criteria."[41] All told, knowledge of racial group affiliation could be considered a necessary criterion, but it could not be the only one.

Many followed these cases with considerable interest. Not a few were uneasy about the pressure to right recognized wrongs by accepting a change in the ground rules for "making it" into the university, onto public school faculties, or into public service, or entering a profession. These were not merely philosophical differences. The seeming challenge to the traditional ground rules for both opportunity and advancement meant that some, no matter how hardworking or smart, might be passed over for others less qualified by conventional standards.

The problem, as Allan Sindler pointed out, is partially the differing perspectives (and understandings) of what "affirmative action" and "equal opportunity" actually mean. Sindler summed up the traditional view by asserting that

> The traditional concept of equal opportunity, when applied, say, to jobs, emphasized a fair process of evaluation among the applicants competing to be hired. This involved assessment of applicants on an individual basis by use of nongroup criteria relevant to satisfactory handling of the job in question. The result of such a meritocratic process was the selection of the persons best qualified to do the job, judged in terms of the current performance abilities of the competitors. By definition, a genuinely merito-cratic process was fair and, therefore, both guaranteed and defined a fair outcome and equality of opportunity. The elimination of racial discrimination in hiring thus represented a belated purification of the traditional concept, not a challenge to it. Hence both nondiscrimination and government enforcement of nondiscrimination have become comfortably incorporated within the prevailing notion of equal opportunity.[42]

At least one justification that embodied an alternative view of equality was the claim that, in contrast to the traditional concept, it stressed groups and outcomes, not individuals and processes. If all other things were truly equal, asserted this view, a genuinely fair and meritocratic process would result in roughly the same proportion of nonminorities and minorities gaining the school admissions, the jobs, or whatever the competition. Where disparate group proportions were the outcome, that indicated the existence of unfairness and unequal opportunity for the underrepresented groups, for which the selection process had acted simply as a "pass-through" rather than a corrective. The proper measure of fair process and equal opportunity was, then, proportional group results.[43]

Many poor and working-class whites were inclined to accept the first view, feeling (as suggested earlier) that being unlucky or not having tried hard enough could explain their failures. Few would accept the second argument, saying no one ever gave them special treatment just because they were poor even though they, too, knew the meaning and effects of discrimination.[44]

In 1980, the very beginning of the Reagan Era, the Supreme Court upheld a congressional plan that required 10 percent of federal work contracts to be set aside for businesses controlled by minorities, a clear attempt to alter the imbalance in opportunities. Although opposed by many conservatives in the new administration, such set-asides were viewed as a victory for civil rights forces that felt that without special consideration it would remain very difficult for blacks and others long ex-cluded from full participation in all aspects of the economy to break the pattern. The opponents saw the set-asides, and other schemes to increase minority participation, as "affirmative discrimination."[45] Many scholars and lawyers debated the morality and legality of programs that were not based on a specific company's acts but were intended as general ways to redress past grievances. (The arguments echoed those heard surrounding the DeFunis and Bakke cases discussed in the previous section.)

In a landmark 6–3 decision, early in 1989, the Supreme Court (still known to many as "The Reagan Court," owing to the conservative justices appointed by Rea-gan) ruled that the Richmond (Va.) City Council unconstitutionally discriminated against whites by demanding (presumably in compliance with the earlier ruling) that a contractor with any city building contract must give at least 30 percent of the value of the project to firms that are at least one-half minority-owned. Speaking for the majority, Associate Justice Sandra Day O'Connor claimed that the city had violated the Constitution because it had relied on past societal discrimination to justify the quota. "Since none of the evidence presented by the city points to any identified discrimination in the Richmond construction industry ... the dream of a nation of equal citizens, in a society where race is irrelevant to personal opportunity and achievement, would be lost in a mosaic of shifting preferences based on unmeasurable claims of past wrongs."[46]

The late Associate Justice Thurgood Marshall, one of the three dissenters and the only African American member of the high court at the time, bitterly stated that the new ruling "sounds a full-scale retreat from the Court's longstanding solicitude to race-conscious remedial efforts." He continued by claiming, "[the] decision masks a deliberate and giant step backward in the court's affirmative action jurisprudence."[47] Within several weeks the Supreme Court followed its Richmond decision with two other related reversals of prior policy. In the first, the Court set new limits on measures minorities could use to attempt to prove that they had been relegated to less desirable jobs. In the other, *Martin v. Wilks,* a case involving white firefighters in Birmingham, Alabama, who contended that they were being discriminated against because of affirmative action policies, the Court ruled in their favor. President George Bush, viewed by many as more sensitive to minority concerns than his predecessor, although claiming he believed in fairness and the protection of civil rights, did not challenge the Court's decisions in these critical cases. More recently, in an era when, for the first time in its history, a black man had become president of the United States, the Supreme Court reversed itself on some of the principal issues relating to affirmative-action policies and especially the long-upheld rules of the Voting Rights Act of 1965. In June of 2013 in a 5–4 decision the court ruled that because the goals of equal protection had been achieved, especially those relating to assuring fairness in voting, the requirement that areas with long-known practices of discrimination toward minorities must obtain government approval to change rules was no longer necessary. Many applauded this endorsement of alleged progress. Many others decried the ruling, seeing it as a major setback for the still-unfinished business of addressing slavery's legacy and the persistence of categorical discrimination against African Americans and other groups.

A contemporary example of such seemingly selective law enforcement and differential attitudes about it was revealed in two news items that were widely read and debated in August of 2013. First, a Quinnipiac University poll regarding the "stop and frisk" policy in New York—established several years before to reduce crime in the city and claimed by many to account for a sharp drop in the crime there—found that while 60 percent of white residents approved of the policy, less than 30 percent of blacks and less than 40 percent of Latinos did. It is clear that far larger percentages of those in the latter groups disapproved of the policy than did whites, presumably because of clear evidence that they were far more apt than whites to be looked on with suspicion, stopped, and searched.

Around the same time the results of the poll were released, a federal judge ruled that the "stop and frisk" policy was unconstitutional, claiming it violated the rights of minorities by engaging in unreasonable searches, a violation of the Fourth Amendment. (Instead of imposing a "cease and desist" ruling, she ordered a federal monitor to institute a reform of the policy.)

Others have long seen "stop and frisk" as a challenge to the equal-protection clauses of the Fourteenth Amendment, arguing that because the majority of those who are stopped and searched are nonwhite minorities, and because so many of them, especially blacks and Latinos, are arrested, convicted, and incarcerated even for minor offenses, this is a new form of state-sponsored segregation. Law professor Michelle Alexander calls such practices "the new Jim Crow."[48]

Is Affirmative Action a Form of Discrimination?

The issue of identity politics, usually centered on the matter of affirmative action, was to be revisited a number of times over the decades as the case was made for it, against it, and "against the case made against it," as Michael Kinsley noted in *The New Yorker* in March 1995.[49] His essay opened with the thoughtful statement that "Affirmative action is one of those controversies, like abortion, in which opponents have the advantage of moral clarity. They are defending a seemingly absolute principle, although supporters are defending something much more ambiguous."[50] They are often wont to give "on the one hand/on the other hand" responses to their critics, suggesting that, although not everything that falls under the broad umbrella of affirmative action is good, there are approaches with which all reasonable people ought to be able to agree. Among these are the casting of the widest nets possible to insure broad-based pools of applicants to schools or candidates for jobs; using minority group membership as a tie-breaker in the case of equal qualifications to enhance diversity in the academy or the workplace; and—the most common argument used today—defining "disadvantaged" in nonracial (and nongendered) terms with "class" becoming the favored variable.

As noted, affirmative action is a matter that continues to be debated and has recently become the focus of a vigorous campaign to "return to meritocratic principles" and stop "favoring minorities and women." The division of the people was most clearly evident in a California initiative petition, endorsed by the then leading Republican candidates for president, including California governor Pete Wilson, to abolish even the limited use of preference decided by the Warren Court in the case of Bakke.[51] The issue, which was initially the topic of considerable discussion in the universities, remains alive there as well. In fact, at the University of California, a gigantic institution of many campuses came under the severest attack for its policies. Berkeley was almost entirely "white" in 1964; twenty years later whites were still in the majority (around 60 percent). In 1994 slightly less than a third of the students were white (32 percent). Thirty-nine percent were of Asian background, 14 percent Hispanic, and 6 percent black. In the intervening years, several criteria had been established for admission to the highly competitive university: slightly more than half were to be admitted on the basis of grades and test scores alone, another 46 percent are welcomed under a combination of grades, test scores, essays, and background (meaning, in the instance, racial and ethnic background), and the rest, 3 percent are brought in under "the special decision of the admissions committee."[52]

Despite this attempt to satisfy a number of constituencies, it seemed to have antagonized most. Some whites, many of whom resented the whole system, joined with African Americans and Hispanics in protesting what they saw as undue advantages for Asians (long considered one of the four affirmative action categories) and called for restrictions on their "disproportional representation." The argument sounded strikingly like that used to keep Jews out of Ivy League institutions from the 1920s to the 1950s. The whole matter had become a political football and a part of the politics of resistance that has been mounting, especially among those who feel that they are forced to pay the price for something for which they claim to have had no responsibility, the discrimination of minorities.

In 1999 Philip A. Klinker and Rogers M. Smith published a retrospective examination of changes in race relations in the life course of American society. They contended that it has been an unsteady march, marked by "two steps forward, one step back."[53] What they wrote was hardly a new idea. As Hosea Williams put it on the occasion of the thirty-fifth anniversary of the dramatic events that occurred in Selma, Alabama, on March 16, 1965, "We're not where we used to be but we're not where we ought to be either." What is significant in Klinker and Smith's study, and extremely relevant for our own understanding, is the explanation the two social scientists offer for the fact that the course has been marked by short bursts of dramatic reform lasting for a decade or two, almost invariably followed by long periods of retreat, retrenchment, and a kind of homegrown nativist revanchism.

On the basis of their analysis of the politics of race, especially as practiced by those in power, the authors challenge conventional schoolroom rhetoric about the triumph of Judeo-Christian principles and the basic decency of people imbued with strong liberal proclivities upon which they are wont to act and often do. Instead, it is argued that significant advances that have been made have rarely occurred as a result of the initiatives of the pure of heart, but rather as a result of reactions of those who realized what they might lose if they failed to react to external and internal threats.

Klinker and Brown cite three principal determinants of such reactions. The first is the response to the outbreak of large-scale wars requiring extensive economic and military mobilization that, time and again, led to the reluctant but necessary recruitment of blacks. (N.B.: It is important to note, once again, that African Americans usually served in segregated units of the US Army. Desegregation was not ordered until 1948 and only implemented during the Korean War in the early 1950s.)

The second condition for change, though also pragmatic, was more reflexively ideological. At certain critical times, such as during the Revolution, the Civil War, World War II, and the Cold War, national leaders found themselves in a situation when the character of the country's enemies prodded them "to justify such wars and their attendant sacrifices by emphasizing the nation's inclusive, egalitarian, and democratic traditions."[54] They were then forced to demonstrate the efficacy of that which they professed. Minorities, including blacks, were the beneficiaries.

The third reaction is related to a different sort of threat, not one that encouraged sacrificing tradition to "nobler ends" but one that meant bowing to the force of domestic political protest movements for civil rights and access such as those described above. (The passage of the Voting Rights Act of 1965 is a good case in point.)

What is especially useful to students of race relations in their analysis is that Klinker and Smith put flesh on the bones of their history. The core chapters, presented in chronological order, offer in-depth ethnographies of the national political, economic, and social climates in eight distinctive eras, beginning with "Slavery, 1619–1860" and ending with "Post–Civil Rights America, 1968–1998." Each is a critical assessment of the behavior of principal actors and their shifting positions, which frequently reflect more calculated compassion than genuine commitment to the ideals of equality and justice. Hundreds of illustrations of such politically motivated concessions and compromises are offered and explained. Among them are such cases as the severe shortage of fighting men that lead to the recruitment of blacks after the disastrous winter at Valley Forge; the melding of racism and opposition to slavery's expansion to enhance recruitment to the new Republican party in the 1850s; and President Eisenhower's decision to call in federal troops to restore order around Central High School in Little Rock, Arkansas on September 24, 1957, in reaction to the mounting risk of domestic discord, a looming constitutional crisis, and international embarrassment.

All told, the researchers see ample evidence to suggest that events and actions, provocations and publicity, rather than goodwill, triggered reactions that proved beneficial to the cause of desegregation and mobility for African Americans, taking them—along with other minorities—"two steps forward." In the next chapter another type of action provoking reaction, that often referred to as "backlash," is examined.

Notes

1. See Will Herberg, *Protestant-Catholic-Jew* (New York: Doubleday, 1955).

2. James Baldwin, *Nobody Knows My Name: More Notes of a Native Son* (New York: Dial Press, 1961).

3. See, for example, James Baldwin, *Go Tell It on the Mountain* (New York: Knopf, 1952).

4. See Henry Louis Gates, *Colored People: A Memoir* (New York: Knopf, 1994).

5. *The Autobiography of Malcolm X* (New York: Grove Press, 1964), pp. 169–190.

6. See, for example, Eldridge Cleaver, *Soul on Ice* (New York: McGraw-Hill, 1968), p. 46.

7. Booker T. Washington, "The Atlantic Exposition Address, September 1895," from *Up from Slavery* (New York: Doubleday, Page and Company, 1901), pp. 218–225.

8. As reprinted in August Meier, Elliott Rudwick, and F. L. Broderick (eds.), *Black Protest Thought in the Twentieth Century,* 2nd ed. (Indianapolis: Bobbs-Merrill, 1971), p. 6.

9. Ibid., p. 7.

10. August Meier and Elliott Rudwick, "Radicals and Conservatives: Black Protest in Twentieth-Century America," in Peter I. Rose (ed.), *Old Memories, New Moods* (New York: Atherton, 1970), p. 124.

11. Ibid., p. 125.

12. See Peter I. Rose, "Making a Difference," in Peter I. Rose (ed.), *The Dispossessed: An Anatomy of Exile* (Amherst: University of Massachusetts Press, 2005), pp. 120–121.

13. Ibid., p. 127.

14. Maurice Davie, *Negroes in American Society* (New York: McGraw-Hill, 1949), p. 440.

15. Meier and Rudwick, op. cit., p. 130.

16. Thoreau himself was influenced by the utopian educator Bronson Alcott. See Geraldine Brooks, "Orpheus at the Plough," *The New Yorker* (January 10, 2005), pp. 62–63.

17. Stokely Carmichael and Charles V. Hamilton, *Black Power: The Politics of Liberation in America* (New York: Vintage, 1967).

18. James Forman, *The Making of Black Revolutionaries* (New York: Macmillan, 1972).

19. Martin Luther King Jr., "I Have a Dream," *SCLC Newsletter,* 12 (September 1963), pp. 5, 8.

20. See Peter Kuryla, "Ralph Ellison, Iriving Howe and the Imagined Civil Rights Movement," *Society,* 50:1 (January–February 2013), p. 10.

21. See, for example, James Farmer, *Freedom—When?* (New York: Random House, 1965).

22. The quotation is from a West Indian emancipation speech delivered by Douglass in 1857. It appears in Carmichael and Hamilton, op. cit., p. x.

23. Richard Wright also expresses this most poignantly. See his "Foreword," in St. Clair Drake and Horace Clayton, *Black Metropolis* (New York: Harcourt, Brace, 1945).

24. William H. Grier and Price M. Cobbs, *Black Rage* (New York: Basic Books, 1968), esp. pp. 152–167.

25. See Cushing Strout, *Divided We Stand: Reflections on the Crisis at Cornell* (Garden City, NY: Doubleday, 1970).

26. Ibid.

27. C. Wilson Record, "Responses of Sociologists to Black Studies," in James Blackwell and Morris Janowitz (eds.), *Black Sociologists: Historical and Contemporary Perspectives* (Chicago: University of Chicago Press, 1974), pp. 368–401.

28. Ibid., p. 381.

29. Ibid., p. 386.

30. Jill Quadagno, *The Color of Welfare* (New York: Oxford University Press, 1994), p. 4.

31. Daniel Boorstin, "Ethnic Proportionalism: The 'E.Q.' and Its Uses," in *The Sociology of the Absurd* (New York: Simon and Schuster, 1970), pp. 25–35. See also Martin Mayer, "Higher Education for All? The Case of Open Admissions," *Commentary,* 45 (February 1973), pp. 37–47; and "An Exchange on Open Admissions," *Commentary,* 45 (May 1973), pp. 4–24.

32. Vance Bourjaily, *Confessions of a Spent Youth* (New York: Dial Press, 1952). See, especially, the chapter, "The Fractional Man."

33. Michael Harrington, *The Other America* (New York: Macmillan, 1962).

34. See Quadagno, op. cit., pp. 4–5; also pp. 10–15.

35. For an excellent thumbnail summary of the history of, and controversy generated by, affirmative action programs, see Nicholas Leman, "What Happened to the Case for Affirmative Action?," *New York Times Magazine* (June 11, 1995), pp. 36–43, 52–62, 66.

36. See, for example, Pierre van den Berghe, "The Benign Quota: Panacea or Pandora's Box?" *The American Sociologist,* (June 6, 1971); Murray N. Rothbart, "The Quota System, in Short, Must Be Repudiated," *Intellectual Digest* (February 1973), pp. 78, 80. See also Earl Raab, "Quotas by Any Other Name," *Commentary* (January 1972), pp. 41–45; Bart Barnes, "Reverse Bias Alleged in College Hiring," *Washington Post* (March 5, 1973). See also Nathan Glazer, *Affirmative Discrimination* (New York: Basic Books, 1978).

37. See Allan P. Sindler, *Bakke, DeFunis and Minority Admissions: The Quest for Equal Opportunity* (New York: Longmans, 1978).

38. *The Regents of the University of California, Petitioner v. Allan Bakke,* Brief for the United States as *Amicus Curiae,* 76–811 October Term, 1977, pp. 28–29.

39. Ibid., pp. 30, 33, 38, 41.

40. Ibid., p. 50.

41. Ibid., pp. 55, 63.

42. Sindler, op cit., p. 12.

43. Ibid., pp. 14–15.

44. See Ralph Levine, "Left Behind in Brooklyn," in Peter I. Rose (ed.), *Nation of Nations* (New York: Random House, 1973), pp. 335–346.

45. See Nathan Glazer, *Affirmative Discrimination* (New York: Basic Books, 1975).

46. This quotation appeared in the *New York Times* and in Associated Press releases on January 24, 1989.

47. Ibid.

48. See Michelle Alexander, *The New Jim Crow: Mass Incarceration in the Age of Color Blindness* (New York: The New Press, 2010).

49. Michael Kinsley, "The Spoils of Victimhood," *The New Yorker* (March 27, 1995), pp. 62–69.

50. Ibid., p. 62.

51. Leman, op. cit.

52. See Peter Applebome, "Gains in Diversity Face Attack in California," *New York Times* (June 4, 1995), pp. 1, 22.

53. See Philip A. Klinker, with Rogers M. Smith, *The Unsteady March: The Rise and Decline of Racial Equality in America* (Chicago: University of Chicago Press, 1999).

54. Ibid., p. 3.

Social Physics

Action and Reaction

One of the basic laws of physics is that every action has an equal and opposite reaction. The laws of society are not that simple. Yet, it is safe to say that in "social physics" (a label Auguste Comte, the "father" of sociology, wanted to use for his new discipline) there are numerous examples of changes provoking reactions. This is certainly the case in the area of racial and ethnic relations. It was evident in the responses of nativists to the increasing flow of immigrants into "their" country. As noted in the last chapter, it was clearly evident in the growing militancy among the ranks of minority groups who had grown restive as they waited for the nation's institutions to uphold its own ideals. It was seen again in the response to *their* demands by many other Americans, particularly those who had come to be called "white ethnics," in the wake of the new policies wrought by the consciousness-raising movements of the 1960s and 1970s. It is evident today in reaction to what some have called the "declarations of independence" by those who continue to feel excluded by institutional racism. The resurgence of militant black nationalists and their less strident but equally determined brothers in the Million Man March on Washington by African American men in the fall of 1995 gave new voices to such old and deep-rooted sentiments. Now, two decades later, and in the wake of a highly controversial finding of "not guilty" for the killing of a black teenager, Trayvon Martin, tracked by a neighborhood-watch member in Sanford, Florida, those voices are still being heard, this time joined by millions of protesting whites who decried the seeming miscarriage of justice, especially the failure to fully take into account the circumstances leading up to Martin's death. If nothing else (and there was much else), the case reminded

216

Americans that our country still has far to go in addressing the stain on the fabric of our democracy: racism.

The "Unmeltable Ethnics"

In a book with an intriguing title, *The Rise of the Unmeltable Ethnics,* published in 1971,[1] social philosopher and commentator Michael Novak claimed to speak for many children and grandchildren of Eastern and Southern Europe whose relatives left the Old Country to seek a better life in the new and often found it. They also found that they were outsiders and, in many ways, were to remain so despite the fervor of their patriotism and their willingness to prove it. To many, they were "peasants"; looked down upon not only by white Protestants who saw them as socially, religiously, even racially inferior, but also by more than a few intellectuals of varying backgrounds who depicted them as unwashed, uneducated, uncouth—in general, culturally inferior.

> [Those] ... who appear most willing to sacrifice time and effort in a "good" cause, whatever the cause, prove invariably to be those who can retreat to upper middle class sanctuary and rejoin the "establishment" whenever the need arises. Such [individuals] seem either unable or unwilling to recognize a simple truth; that people considerably lower (although not the lowest) in the class structure, lack a similar sense of mastery and freedom, but rather are fighting desperately to achieve the sense of economic and social security which these [people] accept as their birthright.[2]

In corner bars and coffee shops working-class ethnics remonstrated about "the squeeze," about the insensitivity of the people uptown. Then, after decades of public silence, spokespersons for increasing numbers of angry, frustrated, and self-styled "abandoned" people began to express their feelings more publicly. They did so by supporting conservative candidates for local and national political offices; by organizing neighborhood associations, which some observers saw as northern equivalents of white citizens' councils; by playing on the growing resentment that others were feeling. Not only did all Americans hear what was being said, they began to read about their sentiments in a spate of articles and books on ethnic Americans (an interesting counterpoint to the raft of books on nonwhite minorities that had also begun to appear at the same time).[3]

Common themes ran through many of these writings: The earlier immigrants faced great difficulties and obstacles, but they accepted the challenges and internalized the values of the wider society, values that were often quite alien to their own heritages. They knew camaraderie of kin and countrymen, their own people who understood them, respected them, and stood by them when others failed to do so. Indeed many had become more prideful of being Irish or Polish or Italian or Greek than they had been "back home."[4] They knew what it meant to be helped by others in similar straits and how to use certain public institutions to advantage, especially the schools, political machines, and, eventually, the civil service. But what they also knew, and this is perhaps the most persistent theme, was that one could not ask for special favors because of background or by pleading "special conditions." (Most failed to indicate that, whatever the dire circumstances of the previous lives of their forebears, the vast majority of them—or their parents or grandparents—had come to America voluntarily, not in the chains of slavery or under conditions of some form of indenture.)

Given the sentiments of having had to find their own ways, many white ethnics reacted with astonishment at the seeming capitulation being made to demands by blacks and other nonwhites for group rights and privileges. "Who do they think they are?" They began to ask, "Why can't they be like us?" A growing resolve to get their own share arose. A sense of righteous indignation at being put down by those above them to satisfy the demands from below them in the pecking order became more and more apparent and more and more annoying. Many argued that they were loyal, decent, hardworking, God-fearing, and patriotic Americans who had had nothing to do with slavery or with segregation but were being forced to pay for the sins of other peoples' fathers. Many were especially upset by the fact that the authorities seemed too willing to buy urban peace at their expense.

Much of the animosity was directed at the members of the more affluent liberal community, those, they said, who seemed to love the poor (often at a distance) and champion the underdog but condemned white ethnics and middle Americans for "their complacency," "their ignorance," "their lack of compassion."[5] They grew equally impatient with the "radical chic" displayed by many celebrities who appeared to kowtow to militants. The comments of a steelworker, Mike Fitzgerald of Cicero, Illinois, interviewed by Studs Terkel, are illustrative:

> *Terkel:* Does anger get you, bitterness?
> *Fitzgerald:* No, not really. Somebody has to do it. If my kid ever goes to college, I just want him to realize that when I tell him somebody has to do it, I just want him to have a little bit of respect, to realize that his dad is one of those somebodies. This is why even on (muses)—yes, I guess, sure—on the black thing ... (Sighs heavily) I can't really hate the colored fella that's working with me all day. The black intellectual I got no respect for. The white intellectual I got no use for. I got no use for the black militant who's gonna scream about 300 years of slavery to me while I'm busting my back. You know what I mean? I have one answer for that guy.... Don't bother me. We're in the same cotton field. So just don't bug me....
> It's very funny. It's always the rich white people who are screaming about racism. They're pretty well safe from the backlash. You ever notice it's always: go get the Klansman, go get the Hunkies, go get that Polack. But don't touch me, baby.[6]

People like Mike Fitzgerald felt—and expressed—a backlash sentiment most strongly. Although of a variety of backgrounds themselves, many had begun to move up and away from seeing themselves solely in terms of their ethnic identity. Since such people were often the first to be affected by the new policies, a forceful reactive assertion of ethnicity occurred in many communities, even at the expense of class-based allegiances. Nathan Glazer and Daniel Patrick Moynihan noted in 1970 that "ethnic identities have taken over some of the task of self-definition and in definition by others that occupational identities, particularly working-class identities, have generally played. The status of the worker has been downgraded; as a result, apparently, the status of being an ethnic, a member of an ethnic group, has been upgraded.... Today, it may be better to be an Italian than a worker. Twenty years ago, it was the other way around."[7]

The following year, the sociologist Andrew Greeley wrote, "the new consciousness of ethnicity [among white ethnics] is in part based on the fact that the blacks have legitimated cultural pluralism as it has perhaps never been legitimated before."[8] This new reality significantly altered a number of other aspects of American life. For the last five decades, policies for dealing with recognized—and, sometimes, institutionalized—diversity has been one of the most hotly debated issues in government circles, in the universities, in the journals of opinion, and, in very direct ways, in the streets of America's cities.

Even as the debates were heating up, there were many who, despite certain misgivings, believed that the resurgence of ethnicity among those no longer viewed as minorities was highly functional for our society because, after all, Americans must appreciate that this is a kaleidoscope of separable pieces of a complex if ever-changing social structure.[9] Some went further. They argued that not only would African Americans benefit from their newfound sense of consciousness, but so too would other minorities, white as well as nonwhite, who had suffered far too long under the cultural domination of "the WASP Establishment."[10] Their prescience was noteworthy; within a few decades, the most prominent beneficiaries of this would turn out to be members of various Latino communities who would soon become the largest minority cohort in the nation.

Other observers contended that reality was simply catching up with the dreamers who were convinced that ethnicity was rapidly becoming a thing of the past. Irving Levine and Judith Herman, for example, claimed that their data indicated that Glazer and Moynihan were wrong. There had not been as much change as they suggested. What was different was that the strains and divisions that had always existed were now being recognized and validated.

> In most of the cities where the white working class is ethnic—in the Northeast and Midwest particularly—common origin is reflected in distinctive neighborhoods. People tend to live near one another according to ethnic background, even "unto the fourth generation." For some, the choice is a conscious one, influenced by the presence of such institutions as the church. For others, the ethnic neighborhood is a convenience, maintaining some features of the extended family, lost (but yearned for) in more heterogeneous neighborhoods.
>
> Even suburbanization has not diminished the intensity of many ethnic neighborhoods. In many cases, what looks like an economics-based blue collar suburb is in reality a community consisting of several ethnic enclaves. For instance, Long Beach, a Long Island town, has been described as "three worlds," Italian, Black, and Jewish—though to the outsider it may seem a "typical lower income suburban community."[11]

Two disclaimers, each dealing less with the substances of the analyses and more with the sympathy expressed for the tendency to support or even advocate further mobilization or separation along ethnic lines, were offered. The first, briefly touched on in the last chapter, was a "class" rather than "ethnic" argument that stated too much attention was being given to cultural and nationalist feelings and too little to the sense of alienation of all who are relatively powerless in the context of the larger society. Their contention was that fostering the ethnicity of any group serves mainly to keep the separate entities from uniting into a coalition of opponents to a repressive economic system. Foremost in the ranks of those who took this stand was Bayard Rustin, who opposed both black nationalism and white ethnic revivalism. Rustin wanted the people to have power collectively and believed that they would not achieve it by putting their special, separate interests above more basic social and economic needs.[12]

The second critique came from liberal integrationists who had long stood firm against the winds of change, if for somewhat different reasons than those of Bayard Rustin. Most notable among them was Harold Isaacs, who condemned what he saw as a "retribalization."[13] Reviewing Murray Friedman's volume, *Overcoming Middle Class Rage,* which sought to explain backlash politics and ethnic insularity, Isaacs wrote,

> The two themes—on the Middle American as a harassed man and as an ethnic—are presented . . . as if they harmonize. They are in fact tunes beaten out by separate drummers who march down quite different roads. In effect, the appeal here to the Middle American is to depolarize on social issues and to repolarize ethnically.[14]

Referring to the older pluralists, particularly Horace Kallen and Randolph Bourne and their imagery of symphonic harmony, Harold Isaacs warned against too high expectations, for modern symphonies often resound with disturbing dissonances. "This [repolarization along ethnic lines] may make beautiful music in the heads of some of these composers, but it has to be played out loud to hear what it actually sounds like."[15]

Isaacs was prophetic. In subsequent years the orchestra did began to sound less and less polyphonous and more and more cacophonous. Some found the raucous "polyrhythms," as the performance artist and playwright Andrea Hairston[16] calls them, quite exciting. Others thought them highly disruptive—and they meant it in a more than symbolic sense. They contended that the new players were the vanguard of a movement that could disunite the country. The "either-it-is-good-or it-is-bad" dichotomy is what grabs the headlines and the attention of talk show hosts.

However, to characterize all differences of opinion about such matters as so sharply polemical is to minimize the importance of a large center cohort of Americans baffled by what was going on in the post–Civil Rights Era and quite ambivalent about how to react to it. Leaders in the different camps, sensitive to this reality, often exploited it, vying for the support of those not already polarized into extreme positions. One side did so by attacking what they saw as the failures of the civil rights campaigns to right historic wrongs; the other by claiming that the successes of those campaigns led to excesses and to escalating demands.

Not surprisingly, as the American political parties became more like those of Europe, that is, working under far more ideologically consistent guidelines, the question of "One America—or Many?" was raised again and again. It was also answered in a series of policy decisions that altered previous practices quite dramatically. The changes were not only structural. They were "climatic" as well—affecting the social atmosphere and the civic culture in rather profound ways.

During the years of the Carter administration, the president from the Deep South had rekindled the spirit of "welfare-minded" Democrats from the New Deal days of Franklin Delano Roosevelt through the Kennedy-Johnson Era; lent his weight to a variety of programs to assist the poor, especially those in racial minorities; and vigorously advocated human rights at home and abroad. But Carter, an outsider to the Washington, DC, establishment, had difficulty in a variety of other spheres. Not least was his inability to curb mounting inflation (which reached double-digit heights before he left office) or to quell the feeling of serious malaise throughout the country, a sentiment that he sometimes expressed himself. By the time of the presidential election of 1980, it seemed to many that America was in deep trouble and needed a change.

Carter's opponent, Ronald Reagan, had campaigned on a "Get-America-Moving-Again" and "Get-the-Government-Out-of-Private-Life" ticket and won handily. Once in control, he moved to keep the promises made during the campaign. Through a variety of economic strategies, including a massive increase in spending for defense, inflation was reduced, as was the percentage of Americans unemployed. In addition to those on the right (both political and religious), many middle Americans—now including numerous white ethnics—felt that at last there was someone in the White House who understood their plight and was not only willing to articulate it but was acting to stop the drift of the "welfare state."

Watershed

Under the first Reagan administration hundreds of programs designed to aid the poor were disbanded, thousands of conservative judges were appointed to federal courts, and millions of dollars were diverted to matters other than human services. The curtailment of the role of the US Civil Rights Commission as both arbiter of interracial conflict and as a dynamic force for the advocacy of fairer practices sent a very clear message across the land: "Activists for group rights: Beware!"

In many ways the representatives of the Reagan administration and their sympathizers were returning to what the sociologist Michael Lewis aptly named the "individual-as-central sensibility."[17] Those who took such a stance argued that responsibility for success and failure is highly personal, not collective. They contended that, in America, one must always be encouraged to strive to be the master of his or her own fate—that too much reliance on others, particularly on the institutions of government, threatens the moral fiber and weakens the whole conception of a true meritocracy.

Although emphasizing the work ethic and praising individual initiative, the proponents of Reagan's policies also stressed the importance of patriotism and the idea that "We are all Americans." Not inconsistently, given the interplay of individualistic and nationalistic themes, many opposed (openly in some cases, more circumspectly in others) affirmative action policies. These, it was argued, were not only unfair but, perhaps, unconstitutional—because they gave special advantage to the "designated minorities," contributing to a fragmentation of the polity.

All told, those in positions of the greatest power seemed determined to move minority demands low down on their list of priorities—and did.

Many civil rights advocates were troubled but not surprised. They had seen the handwriting on the wall. Still, not a few predicted that the anticipated retrenchment would trigger new outbursts of protests from the quarters of those who seemed to be losing the most from new federal action as well as inaction. In fact, the response was not as explosive as many had expected. When it came, very late in the decade, it took rather unexpected forms.

For almost ten years those still concerned about continued discrimination against racial and ethnic minorities watched in sadness but did little to attempt to stem the erosion of the federal commitment to redress legitimate grievances. There is little doubt that the lack of vigorous response was related, at least in part, to the failure of the civil rights movement's aging leadership to replace itself. There were far fewer spokespersons for integration, and those who were there were hardly the charismatic leaders of the earlier era.

As America entered the 1980s, schools, although far from being truly integrated in their student bodies, had curricula that had begun to more accurately reflect the true nature of America's checkered history and the heterogeneous character of its people. Factories, although not yet realizing parity of placement and achievement, were beginning to respond to the pressure of federal requirements first imposed during the Nixon administration and supported by the moral suasion of those in Carter's administration and the more progressive labor leaders. Political parties and local organizations clearly showed the effects of the struggle for enfranchisement, recognition, and a share of the spoils. The gains in the political arena were the result of challenges to the old system, the growing strength of African American and other minority blocs, and anxiety among the once-dominant forces about their own vulnerability. The last factor undoubtedly led to many concessions to stave off disruption.

Black consciousness, black mobilization, and black pressure—and similar developments among those in some other minority communities—appeared to have paid off in two realms: one highly personal, the other, political. Psychologically, those who had been seen, and often saw themselves, as second class, increasingly rejected such imagery and took increasing pride in who they were. That pride undoubtedly gave impetus to the outward expressions of a unified sense of peoplehood. As members of a group, now seen as an ethnic group and not just a social category, more and more African Americans sought to use their collective consciousness to get their piece of the action. In many instances they succeeded. But in other arenas, especially the economic and the social, the record was far more mixed.

On the one hand, many African Americans with sound educational credentials—and some with rather marginal ones, as critics of certain new policies were quick to point out—benefited dramatically from mandated efforts to improve employment opportunities. Not a few came from the already well-established "black segment" of the working class (an often neglected part of the population). But, as William Julius Wilson has shown, many who were "eligible" to make it were ready and willing and often able to move. And move they did.[18]

By 1978 a far larger percentage of college students; graduate students; foremen (and women); junior managers; and local, state, and federal government officials were from minority groups than ever before. But as the decade ended, the country entered a period of stagflation, a time when recession and inflation simultaneously threatened all Americans, taking a heavy toll on those in the precarious position of having just entered the middle-class technocracy. Moreover, as Department of Labor statistics revealed, those in the lower class had even less hope of breaking out of their dependency. They remained as unemployed and as unemployable as did so many of their older siblings and parents ten, twenty, and thirty years before.[19] That situation still persists in many parts of the society.

In many ways it might have been expected that the presidential campaign of 1988 would have been the context for contending parties to put forth their ideological positions on such issues as the character and direction of intergroup relations in America. Race, class, and gender were thought to be prominent among them. Yet, with the exception of the powerful voice of Democratic candidate Jesse Jackson, this did not prove to be the case. Such matters were among the most significant issues buried under Republican rhetoric about good times brought on by peace and prosperity and Democratic rhetoric about helping the little guy access the system. When race was raised, it was by innuendo—such as the Bush campaign's celebrated exploitation of the decision of Governor Michael Dukakis's administration to furlough the convicted murderer Willie Horton, a black man who then committed violent crimes while on leave. The Democrats' counterattack was weakened by reluctance, until the waning days of the campaign, to take strong, identifiably liberal stands.

Waving the Flag

Both parties used patriotism to rally support, with American flags being more common icons of the 1988 election than bumper stickers or lapel buttons. The Republicans claimed that things had never been better; the Democrats promised (with clear echoes of the campaigns of Adlai Stevenson in the 1950s) greater tomorrows. Although acknowledging that there were still unsolved social problems, neither of the chosen candidates seemed willing or able to specify how he would address the needs of millions of Americans who had not only failed to benefit from the vaunted boom of the Reagan Era but had fallen further and further behind. Nor was either specific in speaking to the realities of homelessness, teenage pregnancy, drug trafficking and substance abuse, the ills of the elderly, and continued racial unrest in our cities.

The election itself proved to be a mandate for continuity as the majority of Americans appeared to be more willing to rally to a team that, to them, had brought stability than to the vague promises of the Democrats. And, in the beginning, stability seemed to be what they got.

However, almost immediately upon his inauguration, George H. W. Bush began to send out signals that, in favoring what he called "a kinder, gentler nation," he would be reaching out to those generally ignored, including the members of racial minorities. His words were applauded by many Democrats, including a number who had supported the unsuccessful candidacy of Jesse Jackson in the primaries and who now suggested the possibility of some shifting of party allegiances if Bush began to deliver on his newly proclaimed promises.

Still, most advocates of minority rights remained skeptical of the new administration's ability to do so, particularly with its continued commitment to avoiding the imposition of new taxes or other means of revenue enhancement—as well as its position on those previously mentioned Supreme Court decisions that signaled a continued erosion of hard-won gains relating to improving opportunities for minorities to gain access to the social, political, and economic systems.

The first Bush administration inherited a number of old, unresolved foreign policy problems, some of which had indirect if not direct bearing on ethnicity—and ethnic politics—in this country. Most critical were relations with the Soviet Union and the matter of the opportunities for emigration for Jews, Armenians, Pentecostalists, and ethnic Germans; the then-forty-year-old Arab-Israeli conflict and the effects of the Palestinian uprising in the occupied territories on the future of the area, its people, and those who supported them here; the much older civil and religious war in Northern Ireland, fought in the streets of Belfast and Londonderry but also the source of tension in the homes and community centers of Irish Americans; the powerful impact of the Japanese on the American economy and the growing resentment it engendered in many parts of the country, especially in the industrial sector; the continuing conflict with Iran, greatly exacerbated in the winter of 1989 by the violent reaction throughout the Muslim world to the publication of Salman Rushdie's controversial novel *The Satanic Verses* and some prominent Muslim clergymen who ordered the killing of its author for blaspheming against Islam; the Gulf War and persisting conflicts in Central America and the outflow of persons from Nicaragua, Guatemala, and El Salvador who sought asylum as refugees—the same status that was more easily obtained by those fleeing Indochina, Cuba, the USSR, and (after the violent suppression of the prodemocratic demonstrations in the late spring of 1989 in Beijing) China; and the general matter of immigration from Latin America and from across the Pacific. Many of these issues also became points of contention in the next presidential campaign when, after a series of bruising primary battles in the Democrats' camp, Bill Clinton was nominated to run against George Bush in 1992.

Clinton's victory in November of that year was hardly a mandate. The independent candidacy of the millionaire electronics entrepreneur, Ross Perot, siphoned considerable votes of traditional Republicans as well as many conservative Democrats. Clinton won the popular vote with a narrow plurality but succeeded in securing his success in the Electoral College. Although the Democrats did manage to control both houses of Congress, and though a number of liberals were elected (more minorities and females than any time in history), many feared the victory would prove Pyrrhic. In many ways, it did.

Despite a good deal of rhetoric about getting America back on course, solving social problems, controlling spending, and dealing more forcefully with racial issues, only part of the Democratic agenda was realized. Various explanations have been given for the failure. One of the most persuasive is that, for all the talk of commitment to change, for all the involvement of minority representatives, for all the meetings and hype about sweeping reforms of health care and welfare, the Clinton administration did not know how to buck the continuing tide of resentment over what was seen as special treatment for special interests. Actions relating to health and welfare were seen by many as litmus tests of the willingness of the new government to temper its "Big Brother" approach and hew more closely to the campaign-based sloganeering about giving the power back to the people (a theme that ran through the materials put out by all the candidates, including Clinton).

Old Agendas, New Alignments

Toward the end of his own second year in office, Clinton, who, despite significant moves to bring the country together had never firmly established himself as a unifier, became the principal target of the Republicans. In 1994 they swept into office in one of the greatest routs in modern American history.

Led by the new speaker of the House of Representatives, Newt Gingrich, and the new majority leader, Dick Armey, the House Republicans tried to implement the very conservative "Contract with America" on which they had campaigned with such obvious success. Not long in office, they threatened—and, in many cases, succeeded in—the dismantling of a raft of social programs that had been hallmarks of Democratic governments and accepted by Republican ones since the days of the New Deal. Among the many that were targeted for extinction or, at the least, drastic curtailment by House committees on Labor, Health and Human Services, and Education were such federally supported activities as job training, assistance to homeless youth, and a variety of educational programs at every level, primary, secondary, and tertiary. Also included in the list of what were construed by many as superfluous bodies or those that were anathema to the ideological stances of the majority party and many of its members was the Corporation for Public Broadcasting. It was all part of what Norman Podhoretz, a neoconservative sympathizer with many of the ideas of the new leadership, called a true "counterrevolution."

Although some of the recommended changes were to move specific funding from the federal government to bloc grants for states, where statewide and local authorities who were closer to the scene would determine spending priorities, opponents worried that, with states already burdened with increasing costs of social services, their administrators would divert funds to pet projects. Furthermore, it was argued, when the grants ran out, there would be a natural inclination to close down programs that seemed too expensive. The losers in all such moves would doubtless be those least able to care for themselves. This category of often unemployed and, even more often, only marginally employable people would clearly be disproportionately Native American, Puerto Rican, and African American citizens and millions of newcomers, mostly from Asia and Latin America. Here again, the plight of old minorities and new Americans seemed to hang in the balance.

To many observers the Republican sweep seemed to signal the solidification of a party of reactionary white males (and many white females too), a cohort that numbered in its ranks not only many white Protestants from every part of the country, including the once solidly Democratic South, but also increasing numbers of Catholic conservatives, many of whom had voted for Reagan and retained local loyalties who were now shifting allegiances across the board. The Democratic Party seemed to be so crippled as to hardly serve as the bastion of succor and support of the nonwhite minorities it had generally championed. Many surviving members, especially in the House of Representatives and in many state governments, found themselves worried about being seen as too "pro-minority" and began to echo the sentiments of the Republicans relating to such issues as affirmative action for minorities; the treatment of newcomers, legal as well as illegal; and the sharp rescission of entitlements even for those called "the deserving poor."

In the third year of Clinton's first term, there was increasing talk of disillusion with the major stances of both major parties. Many commentators noted that, although there was a wide chasm between the hard-line conservatives and old-fashioned liberals, the disaffected middle was searching for a home. What was apparent to those who examined the socioeconomic character and the political views of that vast center was that there were at least two very different constituencies. Journalist Michael Lind summed up the differences. He called one the "moderate middle" and the other the "radical center" (a label first used by sociologist Donald Warren).[20]

To Lind, the moderate middle consists of those sometimes known as "Eisenhower" or "Rockefeller Republicans" and others sympathetic to their highly pragmatic and Progressive views. Well educated and well-heeled, living in better urban neighborhoods (many of them in gentrified homes in downtown areas) or in the suburbs, members of the moderate middle are fiscally conservative and critical of many government programs that they feel are based on outdated as much as misguided policies, but take strong libertarian stances on such hot-button issues as abortion and gay rights. They are also internationalists, centrists of the left.

Their opposite numbers were more apt to be alienated Democrats, the sort of Populists of the right who abandoned their party before: to vote for George Wallace in the 1960s and Ronald Reagan in the 1980s (and, later, for George W. Bush in 2000 and, again, in 2004). They hated big business and big labor and big government, too. And, although far more apt to wear the flag on their sleeves like other conservatives (who would soon be wearing theirs on their lapels), their attitudes toward foreign policy had more to do with maintaining trade sanctions than keeping the troops at home. As for civil rights and matters of affirmative action, there was a further crossing over of attitudes.

The Progressives, most of whom had come from Republican backgrounds, tended to be more supportive of mainline Democrats; the Populists, most of whom grew up as Democrats, were more likely, like Mike Fitzgerald, quoted earlier, to sound like conservative Republicans: opposed to "special favors."

The election of "Bush II," George W., in 2000 seemed to capitalize on the splits witnessed in the late 1990s. It had been an extremely close race, marked, as had all recent elections, by sharply divided ideologies and an increasing amount of political and personal mudslinging. Clinton's vice president, Albert Gore, who campaigned as a Progressive, won the popular vote but lost in a highly contested struggle over the electoral process in Florida. The Republican's victory was assured only by a decision of the Supreme Court of the United States.

The new president appointed a cabinet that, even more ethnically diverse than that of his predecessor, Bill Clinton, reflected in appearances and in surnames a true composite of "American types." There were whites and blacks, Asians and Latinos, in strategic positions. What they had in common was a commitment to a very conservative agenda, one that, ironically, would hardly serve the most basic needs of many with whom they, at least the nonwhites, were identified. Reflecting more of the rhetoric of his father, George H. W. Bush, George W. spoke of his desire to bring the country back together, but not at government expense. He fostered "compassionate conservatism" and advocated more private initiatives, faith-based charitable activities, and the desire to stay out of foreign entanglements. And he wanted to impose a huge tax cut to bolster a flagging economy through the same sort of "trickle-down" economic policies that Ronald Reagan had instituted—and that critics of both administrations argued could not succeed. George W. Bush had entered the White House with a huge surplus and did implement a huge tax cut, one that gave a big boost to millionaires but did little for the middle and working classes and left everyone with a burden that would set the treasury in arrears for years.

The new president, who seemed to have little interest in other lands or peoples prior to his election, was also critical of the interventionist practices of his predecessor, particularly in the Balkans when he tried to stem the tide of "ethnic cleansing." President Bush saw no reason for Americans to be involved in peacekeeping or nation-building abroad. However, many Democrats and a number of journalists and scholars were concerned about the seeming influence of a group of people inside and outside the administration known as "neoconservatives," who were bent on asserting America's power throughout the world, especially in oil-rich countries, and, to some, seeking to complete the first President Bush's battle with the Iraqi dictator, Saddam Hussein. Then, on September 11, 2001, the day suicidal hijackers forced pilots to fly their planes into the World Trade Towers in Manhattan and the Pentagon in Washington, many things began to change.

Within a month, American forces were attacking targets in Afghanistan, then ruled by the militant Islamic regime of the Taliban and said to be the home base of Al Qaeda, the terrorist organization headed by the Saudi expatriate Osama Bin Laden. Claiming that Iraq, too, was a sanctuary for anti-American terrorists with links to Bin Laden, as well as having a large arsenal of weapons of mass destruction (despite claims to the contrary on both charges by numerous United Nations' inspectors and a number of prominent Americans), the president persuaded Congress to back him in a preemptive war against Saddam Hussein. He and his advisers argued that it would be a quick fight and that the masses of Iraqis would welcome our forces and those of our allies (to become known as the "Coalition of the Willing") as liberators. Then, presumably, together American "liberators" would help to rebuild the society, its infrastructure, and its oil business. But, as is well known, it did not work out that way.

The war in Iraq was one of the principal matters in heated debates during the campaign season of 2004. But other issues, some of which echoed those of the previous three campaigns, became flashpoints. Not least were those related to "moral values," including "a woman's right to choose" (to have an abortion) and homosexual marriage. Rarely did the spokespersons for the president, nor did he, speak with conviction about the treatment of prisoners in American prison camps at Guantanamo Bay in Cuba or in those in occupied Iraq by our own forces. Nor was there much said about values of tolerance for those of different faiths and ethnic backgrounds. Indeed, there was an underlying linkage in much of the arguments of those in power that implied in some instances and contended in others that they, along with members of the "Christian Right," were keeping America safe from the scourge of Islamic fundamentalism.

Bush's opponent, Senator John F. Kerry, who had voted for the resolution to go to war and then became one of its biggest critics (though he was unwilling to say that, had he known when he voted what he claimed to know during the campaign, he would have opposed it), seemed to waffle on many cutting-edge value issues. He went down to defeat in November 2004.

As the second inauguration of George W. Bush approached, a new crisis confronted the nation: the gigantic tsunami, or tidal wave, that rolled across the Andaman Sea and the Indian Ocean killing over 150,000 people in Indonesia (the country with the world's largest Muslim population). This time, after a slight delay, the administration pledged $350 million, joined forces with other nations, accepted the titular authority of the United Nations, and, perhaps as important, deployed thousands of American troops to assist in the rescue and reconstruction efforts. Some thought the prime motivator was the opportunity to offer a different face to other countries, such as Indonesia, with its huge Muslim population. Others, less cynical, chose to see this as a true change in orientation, but one that seemed to be in keeping with earlier views of compassionate commitments.

A second matter also raised questions about motivation. The subject was immigration, especially from Mexico, and the growing concern across the country that illegal entrants were overwhelming the United States. A survey conducted in May through August of 2004 with a nationally representative sample of 1888 respondents eighteen years of age and older by the NPR/Kaiser/Kennedy School Poll, offered some interesting findings. Among them:

> The public's views on immigration are significantly less negative than they were in the months after the Sept. 11 terrorist attacks. [By October 2004, 41 percent said that they thought immigration to the U.S. should be decreased; a much lower figure than the 59 percent that CBS and the *New York Times* found when they asked the same question in December 2001].... Although attitudes are less negative than they have

been in years, many negative attitudes toward immigration persist.... The public is divided on whether the large influx of recent immigrants has been good or bad for the country, with 30 percent saying good, 39 percent saying bad.... Americans express ambivalence, if not downright unease, about the cultural impact of immigration. Many nonimmigrants believe immigrants are changing American culture and values when they ought to be adopting them.... Generally, native-born Americans with higher levels of contact with immigrants have more positive views of immigrants and immigration than those with less contact.... The public is concerned about il-legal immigration and wants the government to crack down.... Immigration is not a particularly partisan issue, and the president's proposal to deal with it draws stronger opposition than support.[21]

The report further noted that, although those in the two major political parties do differ in some of their attitudes about immigration, the differences are far less than on other issues. However, there was widespread concern about two proposals, mainly focused on would-be migrants from Mexico: President Bush's suggestion that would allow some illegal immigrants currently in the United States to legally stay in the country for several years as long as they hold jobs that no US citizens want, and the establishment of a renewed *bracero*-like "guest worker program" that would insure a cheap labor supply for growers in the factory farms of the South-west. Without saying so, many in the administration seemed to believe that if they were to impede the flow of migrant workers to the factory farms of the Southwest and the restaurants and other service industries in big cities across the nation, all dependent on cheap labor, the "food and fiber industry" would collapse.

Whether true or not, the pollsters learned that three out of four of their respon-dents believe that, once allowed to stay or admitted on short-term contracts, most workers will never go home. Even among supporters of the guest worker initiative, 61 percent doubt that workers would go back.[22]

A third major issue, and one that would most affect those, including many mi-norities, in the lower third of the nation's hierarchy of income levels, was what to do about Social Security. Here the president was pushing hard for a reform package that would move in the direction of privatization of retirement benefits by allowing individuals to invest a certain portion of their money in hopes of future growth.

George W. Bush's presidency was marked (some would say marred) by the ways in which he handled foreign policy, including waging wars in both Afghanistan and Iraq—wars in which thousands of Americans and tens of thousands of others were killed and millions and millions of dollars were spent. The wars and their proponents and detractors served as a further wedge between those once called "hawks" and "doves." The growing groundswell of hard-line conservative candidates who opposed almost every even mildly progressive program shook the Republican party, which seemed to respond by echoing the views of the rightists rather than challenging them. This seriously exacerbated the divisions between the parties, nullified many possibilities for comity, and led to polarization and deadlock not seen in many decades. The divisions continued long after the second Bush had left the scene. And it was not eased by the election of a man known to many as a pragmatist rather than an ideologue, Barack Obama.

The 2008 presidential election was even more significant than that of John F. Kennedy's in 1960, when he became the first Catholic president. The inauguration of the first black president, Barack Obama—a constitutional lawyer and former community organizer and US senator, born in Hawaii to a Kenyan father and an American mother—seemed to many to signal a sea change in race relations in this country. After all, here was a person who embodied so much of what civil and human rights advocates had been struggling for.

For many Americans both white and nonwhite, Obama was "everyman"—and some thought he could do anything. For others, especially those who felt the struggles of minorities were far from over, he was too much of an icon and too little of a true leader. While he tended to say the things that liberals, especially, wanted to hear, he seemed tone deaf to the members of congress, even those in his own party who urged him to be more aggressive, "more like Lyndon Johnson, the arm-twisting consummate politician."

Persisting Issues

Parallel to the political debates mainly centered on the role of government in addressing and redressing age-old social problems, including health and welfare, employment and Social Security, and the lingering effects of discrimination taking place at the highest levels of government, others had their own thoughts about these and other matters.

Going back once again to the late 1960s and 1970s, in the ranks of what was left of the old race relations community—which still included the remnants of the civil rights movement, a number of mainstream politicians, and several prominent social scientists—an old issue much discussed in the turbulent 1930s (and again in the 1960s) became the focus of deliberation once again. In the present decade, the issue has been revived. Some call it the race-versus-class debate.

In its earlier manifestations, it tended to be an either/or matter. Some argued that racial oppression was a unique phenomenon, relating to particular attitudes toward those viewed and treated as different from themselves ("the white man's burden"), and was therefore almost immutable. Others contended that racial oppression was hardly unique but was instead a clear example of capitalist exploitation and that "difference" was being used as a mask for privilege.

The sociologist William Julius Wilson attempted to put it in perspective. In his 1978 book, *The Declining Significance of Race,* referred to previously,[23] Wilson argued that, as traditional barriers were removed or lowered as a result of the political, social, and economic activities of the Civil Rights Era, they were replaced with a new set of problems, problems that, with what now turns out to have been considerable prescience, "may prove to be even more formidable for certain segments of the Black population."[24] Among the most significant were the lessening need for unskilled workers (the traditional road to stabilization if not instant success), extreme poverty and deprivation of the basic amenities of living, the anomic conditions of home environments and decaying neighborhoods, the lack of middle-class role models, diversion from conventional paths by drugs and other means of escape (most of which give but short-term gratification), and increasing dependence on a welfare system that, many have long argued, undercuts incentives.

Wilson noted that "whereas the old barriers bore the pervasive features of racial oppression, the new barriers indicate an important and emerging form of class subordination."[25] Those being left behind are what he and others have come to refer to as "the truly disadvantaged."[26]

Wilson's claim of an expanding gap in "Black America," and, by extension, in other minority communities, was widely acknowledged, but his seeming unwillingness to place the principal blame for difficulties faced by African Americans and other nonwhite members in one basket labeled "Racial Discrimination" rankled many critics. Indeed, the Association of Black Sociologists, a group to which Wilson had belonged, attacked him for downplaying what, to them, remained the principal issue: institutional racism.[27] They contended that, despite the changes in law and practice, it remained true that, although most poor people in the United States were (and are) white, a disproportionate percentage of African Americans and Hispanics in the country were (and continue to remain) poor—and that unemployment rates among such cohorts had hardly changed in four decades. Moreover, they pointed to the resegregation of society (usually citing the increasing number of all or mostly black schools in northern cities, a function, in large part, of "white flight" to the suburbs) as evidence of the narrowness of Wilson's arguments.[28]

Furthermore, Wilson's use of the term "ghetto underclass" to describe those inner-city dwellers most disadvantaged served to increase criticism of his overall thesis. Although many saw it as an apt descriptor, others saw it as an unfortunate use of language, as something akin to "outcaste." Yet, some went further, asserting that it is a pejorative label, or put-down. More critical than its usage was the persistent implication that the concept "underclass," itself, reified the socioeconomic thesis at the expense of its "racist sources." Stephen Steinberg, for example, offered the following commentary:

> The first thing that needs to be said is that the very existence of a ghetto underclass is evidence of institutionalized racism. That is to say, if the cumulative disadvantages that ensue from past racism leave many blacks without education and skills to compete for the better jobs, we are left with patterns of racial exclusion and inequality even if employers are not personally motivated by racial prejudice. That less than half of black men of working age are part of the labor force speaks for itself. This is a measure of the extent to which American labor markets are perpetuating patterns of racial inequality.[29]

Steinberg went on to note that black workers are being discriminated against to a far greater extent than Wilson allowed. Commenting on Wilson's claim that a large and growing black middle class was relatively immune from racial stereotypes and acts of overt discrimination was not really germane, it only shifted the nature of stereotyping, even further isolating those who live in the inner city.

> Instead of blanket stereotypes that once applied to all blacks, whites have learned to discriminate between those respectable blacks who are reasonably tolerated, and

those other blacks who bear the stigma of the ghetto and are still objects of racial
stereotyping, fear, and scorn. This elaboration of a once monistic system of beliefs
may well be part of a long-term attenuation of racist ideology, with parallels to other
ethnic groups (as when lace-curtain Irish were distinguished from shanty Irish, uptown
Jews from downtown Jews, and so on).[30]

Peter Kwong made a similar point in distinguishing between the "Downtown
Chinese" who live in the crowded and often poorest sectors of Chinatown and the
"Uptown Chinese" who are increasingly exempt from the traditional stereotypes
and patterns of discrimination that still plague those left behind.[31] In fact, as he and
others suggest, the success of some reinforces the image of the failure of others.

The matter of the character and vulnerability of the "underclass" is also the
concern of other social scientists.

Taking a position very different from Steinberg, others have long linked the Race/
Class Debate to another one, that of "ethnic background and social values." Writers
such as Thomas Sowell[32] pointed to the differential success of those whose groups
faced severe bigotry—including clearly race-based derogation, denial, and even
violent acts—but were, nonetheless, able to rise and even flourish in the system,
suggesting that the critical variable is culture and adaptability, not discrimination.
Citing Jews and several Asian groups, Sowell also singled out fellow blacks, namely,
West Indians,[33] as exemplars of what others have called, in a related context, "model
minorities." Sowell's argument, and that of others who support the position, stated
that those raised with values that emphasize self-control, delayed gratification,
respect for education—and the belief that it has a double benefit, one aesthetic, the
other highly instrumental—and norms that support family togetherness, achievement, and its rewards, have a better chance in a modern, industrial, and capitalist
society like that of the United States than will those who come from cultures and
subcultures more fatalistic or hedonistic or collectivistic in orientation.

In point of fact, the situation is always more complicated. Considering West
Indians, for example, Suzanne Model has suggested that they may be more successful than other blacks in the United States because they are a "positively selected
population, i.e. those most prepared for life in a society like the United States are
more apt to migrate to it."[34] Orlando Patterson, in an article about Colin Powell
and other Jamaican Americans, corroborates this and notes that "Those left behind
tell a different story: Jamaican family life today is in even greater trouble than is
African American."[35]

The debates about culture and character almost inevitably turn to proclivities
for or resistance to dependency on public assistance.

Another issue, that of "welfare dependency" in the United States, has been the
basis for considerable criticism and vigorous reassessment. Among the central issues was a questioning of traditional, and mainly Democratic, approaches to care
for the indigent, the elderly, the infirm, and those single parents with dependent
children. Increasing numbers of those who favored considerable direct government
involvement have begun to rethink the efficacy of programs that seemed to prolong
rather than eliminate dependency, programs their more conservative critics had

always claimed, "paid people more not to work than to get a job." Although such claims were generally off target, since they failed to allow for the special needs of many who were not only unemployed but often also unemployable, they did raise questions about the overall system. More and more people came to espouse "workfare," a program where the able-bodied poor would be required to do community service in order to earn their allotments.

In actual practice, the workfare programs that were instigated varied widely. Most effective seemed to be those most sensitive to the conditions under which those in need came to be dependent. Understanding both the problems and the "culture" of poverty, the programs altered outmoded and outrageous stipulations that limited access to certain programs (for example, accepting a family into the program with the father present even when it was almost necessary to be husbandless to obtain Aid to Families with Dependent Children [AFDC] benefits) and provided two very necessary services: childcare and training.

The "Welfare versus Workfare Debate" symbolized in concrete terms the more widespread reassessment of various long-entrenched social policies and practices, many of which focused on services for racial and ethnic minorities. It also led to the realignment of advocates, contributing to—and accelerating in a number of dramatic ways—a process that had already begun to take shape in the late 1960s and throughout the 1970s when many liberals, who in the aggregate were consistently the staunchest supporters of minority causes, became critical of certain trends that deeply disturbed them.

For example, close connections between the Jewish and African American leadership began to come unstuck as a result of strains dating back to the end of the Civil Rights Era when whites, many of whom were Jews, found themselves rejected by former allies in the struggle. It was exacerbated by disagreements over certain aspects of affirmative action programs and by diverging political attitudes, especially toward the warring factions in the Middle East (most Jews, even those critical of "West Bank" policies, continued to support Israel while increasing numbers of African Americans sided with the Arabs).[36] These were not the only strains in old alliances.

Labor movement leadership, traditionally at the forefront of the struggle for human and civil rights, found itself under increasing pressure from rank-and-file members to resist the kind of categorical imperative required by the advocates of "affirmative action" programs. Those in small businesses also raised questions about the fairness of policies that seemed to be discrimination in reverse.

Today such matters are daily fare on political talk shows and in op-ed essays in prominent newspapers. For example, in June 2013 the columnist David Brooks, referring to a Supreme Court decision that had just been handed down (sharply limiting the terms of the 1965 Voting Rights Act, imposing much stricter standards on affirmative action practices, and signaling the end of explicit race-based attempts to redress grievance), noted several things. First, he explained, while many blacks had benefited significantly from affirmative action, they did so at the expense of others, sometimes other minorities, such as Asian Americans. As importantly, he noted that, according to many economists, "economic inequality is now trumping racial inequality as the chief source of disadvantage," that the ethnic makeup of the country has become far more complex than when the initial program was instituted. Third, because we are living in an "age of data," it is far easier to get a more personalized look at disadvantage."[37] Brooks's call is not for the rejection of special programs to help those most in need, but for more narrowly tailored criteria. These factors likely will be central to discussions of the matter for the foreseeable future.

The Immigration Debate Revisited

By the end of the 1980s, in addition to the debates about class versus race, the realignment of confederates in various civil rights struggles, the matter of the legality and significance of "affirmative action" and "set-asides" off the campuses and on them, and the meaning of foreign policy matters for those in various interest groups in the United States, the ever-smoldering immigration debate was fanned afresh by the increasing presence of new "foreign elements" on American soil. Immigrants, legal as well as "undocumented," came to be seen by many as an undue economic and social burden and by some as a cultural and political threat. They also were to become convenient scapegoats for some who needed a new "other" to blame for their own misfortunes.

As the numbers increased to over 750,000 per annum (it is now double that), including refugees, old nativist sentiments began to resurface. There was talk, once again, of the dangerous influx of "foreigners." This time, however, others' views were added to the more traditional opponents of immigration. The new opponents argued that, until American society takes care of its own, it should not allow others to enter. Some of the neorestrictionists, whose most effective lobbying organization was called FAIR, for the Federation of Americans for Immigration Reform, were white ethnics; others were members of American minority groups: African Americans, Puerto Ricans, Native Americans, and some Mexican Americans, too. Sometimes their leaders and spokespersons expressed the view that it is they who would have to pay the highest price for assistance to immigrants and for refugee relief, a contention made by labor economist Vernon Briggs.[38] They claimed that whatever scarce government funds there are they were likely to be diverted to more appealing causes. They also contended that their constituents were at a disadvantage in the job market since "immigrants will do anything" and will often do it for well below minimum wage. Both points sounded strikingly similar to what was said by Anglo-Americans in the mid-nineteenth century about the Irish; what the Irish said about the Italians and Southern and Eastern Europeans; and what those now labeled "white ethnics" have been saying about African Americans and other "preferred" minorities more recently.

To help the newcomers overcome the problems they faced, two matters took center stage: the familiar issue of Americanization and a newer one—bilingualism. The former is, to many civil rights advocates and pluralists, an old code word used by many who believed firmly in the idea that forced assimilation into Anglo-American molds was the only way outsiders could ever be accepted. Critics once again argued that Americanization would be responsible for turning ethnic pride into self-hatred and for leaving many immigrants in the unenviable position of being cast adrift without a firm anchor, the sort that the ethnic group so successfully provides. Supporters of the program, by contrast, expressing the ideas of early assimilationists, voiced the opinion that only when foreigners cast off their alien skins and forget the customs of their "homelands" can they really be absorbed. To be sure, they admitted, the immigrants would have to give up a great deal, make tremendous sacrifices; but, they argued, "Think of what they are getting."

Bilingualism is a more modern concept. In the nineteenth century, many European immigrants retained their native languages. There were areas where German was the *lingua franca,* others where Norwegian, Swedish, and other languages predominated. However, with the increasing influx of Southern and Eastern Europeans toward the end of the century, a campaign was mounted to see that everyone spoke English. It became a part of the Americanization process.

Despite ambivalences and insecurities, most newcomers accepted the idea that learning English was critical in order to move into society. Their children learned it in school "sink-or-swim" style and, highly motivated, many swam. Some of the adults also attended night schools where they studied English, sometimes with those who knew nothing of their culture or native languages, sometimes with those who, in perhaps the first instance of bilingual education, taught them English as a foreign language. In order to prevent their offspring from being totally immersed in the new language and culture, some immigrants set up and maintained private language after-school schools. Some of these still exist.

The migration of large numbers of Spanish-speaking Puerto Rican Americans to the New York area in the late 1940s and early 1950s, prompted by the economic boom of the post–World War II period and the availability of cheap and fast air service, changed the culture and the character of the city, brought about vigorous resistance to assimilation, and more formally introduced the idea of bilingualism. As indicated previously, some sociologists have speculated that clinging to their Latin heritage was one way Puerto Ricans could separate themselves from African Americans with whom they were often being grouped. Others say that easy access to Puerto Rico made acculturation less necessary or desirable.

The latter argument also came to be used to explain the reluctance of some Mexican immigrants to Americanize. The closeness of the motherland meant that one could be in one world (that of the United States) although in a sense living in another (Mexican). Whatever the reason, the result was that many Mexican Americans, like many Puerto Ricans, felt they should be allowed to retain their ways and their language. Some argued that their children should have instruction in Spanish and that their home language should be used as a transitional vehicle for moving along the road to learning to use English in everyday life. (In 1974, in the case of *Lau v. Nichols,* the Supreme Court ruled that being taught in a language they did not understand was discriminating against Chinese-speaking students of San Francisco. Schools were required to find bilingual teachers to work with these students.) Others claimed that even such a strategy was too "assimilationist," that they—and other non-English speakers—ought to be encouraged to maintain their own language, even to the extent of having it as a recognized option to English in all public matters, following the pattern in Francophone Quebec.

Because Hispanics make up the largest linguistic minority in the United States, debates about bilingualism have tended to revolve around the teaching of Spanish and the provisions for bicultural as well as bilingual programs for them. However, Latinos are not alone in this controversy. Other groups began pressing for similar opportunities and many have received them. There were schools in Virginia, near Washington, DC, and in metropolitan parts of New York, and in other states where fifteen or more bilingual programs were running simultaneously. In Massachusetts, for example, the success of such a campaign is evident, and controversial. At the end of 1995, any school with twenty or more children of a particular language background is offered some instruction in their native tongue. In a most extreme case, in Boston young people whose parents came from Cape Verde, where Portuguese, and not the Creole spoken at home, is the official language and the language of instruction, are taught in Creole—from primers with newly constructed grammar.

The reaction against bilingualism, and what were seen as its excesses, increased quite dramatically in the 1980s, culminating in a campaign to establish the rule of "English Only," not only proclaiming but mandating that Americans have a single official language: English. The effort soon led to the passage of laws in fifteen states, and more battles are expected in the years ahead. One ironic twist in the controversy is that some of the most fervent supporters of English Only—the result of whose campaign imposes severe hardships on those who must fill out forms for medical assistance, welfare, further schooling, and employment—also argued that once the singularity of "our" language is established in law, we can then encourage the teaching of other languages to "enhance the understanding of others."

Americanization and bilingualism were not the only issues that occupied policy maker members of the public concerned about the status and impact of new Americans. Others include questions about how assistance is offered and given to newcomers and the extent of control service providers should have on their settlement in this country, especially refugees who receive support from federally funded programs. Should refugees be allowed to cluster, to form and maintain enclaves where they might find security through familiarity, or should they be scattered to encourage their early absorption into the mainstream?

If past history were any indication, it would seem most logical to allow people (indeed, to assist them) to form ethnic communities, thereby easing the transition into the American scene from often totally alien cultural milieus. Although some immigrants and refugees, especially those with higher education and familiarity with the language and customs of this country, have successfully moved into dominant communities with little difficulty, the evidence suggests that, for many, the acculturation process is painful and often prolonged. The support of compatriots who have traveled the difficult road from "foreigner" to "American ethnic" has always been a boon to newcomers.

In recent years and, especially, during the administration of George W. Bush, immigration again became a controversial issue. To be sure, some of it had to do with "homeland security" and the desire to do a better job of patrolling the borders to prevent acts of sabotage and terrorism, but most of it has to do with a feeling among many that Americans (mainly white Protestants) are losing their birthright.

As noted, the language of many critics of recent immigration policies is familiar, especially concerns about "unassimilable aliens," a phrase often used in regard to the Irish in the mid-nineteenth century and, later, to the Jews and Poles, Italians, Greeks, and Slavs. It was prejudice against such groups that, in the 1920s, led to the most restrictive legislation against "foreign invasion." In his book *Assimilation American Style,* Peter Salins indicates that those old worries proved unjustified. Over several generations after rocky starts, millions of immigrants (almost exclusively European) were accepted into the mainstream of American society. It wasn't always easy, but a belief in "The Dream," a commitment to full participation in the civic culture, and effective use of their ethnic "bloc power" helped to get them *into* the system. But Salins sees such a movement as more problematic today, not so much because of greater discrimination against recent immigrants (though there is considerable resistance to their presence) but because too many have fallen under the spell of "multiculturalism," a group rights counter to the melting pot ideology, strongly rooted in Black Nationalism.[39]

Salins rightly argues that "since the birth of the republic, black Americans have been the great exception to its assimilation paradigm" but he doesn't think "ethnic federalism" is the answer to the persisting racism that has kept those least foreign of all American minorities so alienated; nor does he favor its emulation by other nonwhite minorities, many of them recent immigrants from Asia and Latin America.

Salins was not alone in his concerns. A broadside attack on the new immigration, in particular the immigration of those from Latin America, is Samuel P. Huntington's *Who Are We?: The Challenges to America's National Identity,* published in 2004.[40] Huntington's arguments continue to echo through the country, especially in states where the numbers of Americans from Mexico and other "Latin" countries have been increasing in recent years.

Although couching his concerns in learned language, Huntington expressed sentiments that were not far from those of old nativists. The message is a familiar one: There are strangers at the gate, and strangers within the gate. And, once again, they are seen as a threat to "real Americans." In yesterday's lingo, in addition to the racial slurs, the outsiders were also called "un-American dissidents," "communists," "anarchists"—and "moochers"; in today's they are "destabilizers," "disuniters," "deconstructionists"—and "welfare queens."

Huntington's book offers a very personal commentary on what he saw as the beginning of the end of *his* tormented tribe. His thesis is, in many ways, an argument claiming that something must be done to reverse course and reinvest power and privilege to those most deserving, that is, his fellow ethnics and coreligionists, those he calls the "Anglo-Protestants." In making his case, Huntington appealed to those who, like himself, see themselves as "victimized minorities in a country that once was theirs," clearly reviving what John Higham once called "the central apotheosis of a tribal spirit."[41]

Huntington's book begins with the following "observation" about "the low salience of national identity" before September 11, 2001.

Among some educated and elite Americans, national identity seemed at times to have faded from sight. Globalization, multiculturalism, cosmopolitanism, immigration, subnationalism, and anti-nationalism had battered American consciousness. Ethnic, racial and gender identities came to the fore. In contrast to their predecessors, many immigrants were ampersands, maintaining dual loyalties and dual citizenship.... The celebration of diversity replaced emphasis on what Americans had in common. The national unity and sense of national identity created by work and war in the eighteenth and nineteenth centuries and consolidated in the world wars of the twentieth century seemed to be eroding.[42]

His observation ends with a bit of sarcastic hyperbole. "By 2000, America was, in many respects, less a nation than it had been for a century. The Stars and Stripes were at half-mast and other flags flew higher on the flagpole of American identities."[43] And it gets worse. So harsh are some of his words and judgments that many parts seem as if they were written in 1904, a time when other notable scholars were terribly worried about alien and subversive threats to a very precious way of life, instead of 2004.

In language that might have been written by some of the outspoken xenophobes mentioned in Chapter Three, Huntington asserts that "immigrants become citizens not because they are attracted to America's culture and Creed, but because they are attracted by government welfare and affirmative action programs."[44] It is again being argued that immigrants—legal and illegal—imperil the system with their questionable pedigrees; their foreign ideas and bad habits; their subversive intentions; their willingness to toil for low wages, which undercut those of hardworking Americans; and their dependence on handouts from kindly almoners and public agencies when they can't find work.

Huntington had little empathy for anyone who would disagree with his mono-culturalism. Put differently, for Huntington there was only one culture. His.

In a thoughtful *New Yorker* review of *Who Are We?* Louis Menard called the book "as blunt a work of identity politics as you are likely to find.... [It is] against foreigners and their threat to the very fabric of our society, echoing in its language and reasoning diatribes written a century earlier." Menard suggested that Huntington "is not interested in values per se; he is interested in national security and national power. He thinks that the erosion or diffusion of any cluster of collective ideals, whatever those ideals may be, leads to weakness and vulnerability."[45]

Menard may have been correct in his assessment, but it must also be said that, because the members of the Old Establishment feel they have lost considerable influence, economic clout, and social standing over the past three or four decades, Huntington and those of his ilk seem to have reverted to old, simplistic arguments to hang on to the vestiges of their proclaimed entitlements while reverting to the practice of scapegoating on a grand scale. Today, instead of the unacceptable Irish, or the Chinese of the "Yellow Peril," or the Jews and Italians and Slavs, or the Afrocentrists, it is now a frightening "Brown Wave" of Mexicans coming across the Rio Grande who are poised to destroy American civilization.

In a critical chapter called "Fault Lines Old and New," Huntington minces few words in creating, or trying to create, a self-fulfilling prophecy: "The most powerful stimulus to white nativism is likely to be the threat to language, culture, and power that whites see coming from the expanding demographic, social, economic, and political roles of Hispanics in American society."[46] One can almost hear the voice of John Rowland once again: "And the one thing we can do right now is to lock and bar the gate."[47]

In the arsenal of Huntington's cant are expressions that have recently been heard in debates across the country: righteous indignation coated with cloying religiosity, the protective posturing, and the assertion of how different and right and better are "real Americans" in contrast to those with the audacity to challenge them. Like George W. Bush, Huntington encourages a return to nationalism and patriotism with fighting words about defending the *culture* (and "the homeland") and protecting *the people.* Not surprisingly, he highlights the Arab-Islamic threat post–September 11, 2001.

Although it may well be argued that there is a need for better screening of outsiders and for greater surveillance of those in suspect populations, even worry about organized terrorists entering through the porous southern border does not explain the near paranoiac concerns Huntington and his sympathizers have about our neighbors to—and from—the south, the Mexicans. In what is perhaps the most substantive—and telling—chapter, "Mexican Immigration and Hispaniciza-tion," Huntington offered his view on what he predicted would be an increasingly bifurcated society. These pages are filled with statistics and charts that show rising numbers of immigrants, rising costs, and rising concerns about the political clout of the Mexicans. Like Sam Roberts, the author of *Who Are We Now?*,[48] Huntington pointed to the huge growth of population in the United States in the 1990s and the fact that much of it is attributable to increasing rates of immigration, especially from Mexico.

Samuel Huntington's book does raise a number of legitimate points about the character of that flow and the failures of the Amnesty Bill of 1986 to stem it. It highlights some important differences between Mexicans and other large groups of immigrants in the past, not least the fact that, save for the indigenous Ameri-cans, Mexicans are the only people whose lands had been forcefully incorporated into the United States—in the 1830s and 1840s. Huntington notes the continued proximity of and easy access to Mexico today, which provides a constant cultural counterpull to assimilationist entreaties. He says that in the not-too-distant future (many say it will be before 2050) non-Hispanic whites in the aggregate will repre-sent a minority across the country, as they already are in California, and that there are "Hispanic advocates" who reject the idea of a single national community and cultural homogenization as they "seek to transform America as a whole into a bilingual, bicultural society."[49]

But Huntington failed to look carefully at the increasing numbers of studies that indicate most Mexican Americans are following a course similar to that of other economic migrants from across the seas (described in Chapter Three), who came in the nineteenth century, drawn to America's shores by opportunities said to abound in the United States. Some of those were also "birds of passage," who moved back and forth, like so many Mexicans today, but eventually stayed, learned English, and became Americans, even as they retained some significant vestiges of the old culture. Once again, the findings of the NPR/Kaiser/Kennedy School Poll on immigration issues are enlightening.

In questioning some 784 immigrants, the researchers learned that there were sharp differences in their own attitudes and other perceptions of them. For example,

> Immigrants are more likely than non-immigrants to say that immigrants strengthen the country because of their hard work and talents, rather than be a burden on the country; they are more likely to say immigrants work harder than other Americans, less likely to believe that they take jobs away from Americans. Moreover, the findings clearly show that while immigrants keep some ties to their home country, it is not as much as many believe.... And, perhaps, not surprisingly, children of immigrants have views more like native-born Americans than like those in their countries of origin.[50]

There is little evidence that Samuel Huntington and other prominent critics of immigration in general, and Mexican immigration in particular, were moved by what the immigrants themselves had to say.

When Huntington's opening salvo was first published in the journal *Foreign Affairs,* there were many critical responses. They showed that surveys of Mexican Americans demonstrated a high degree of patriotism, an eagerness to participate in the society, and more than a willingness to learn English, as clearly indicated in the work of Richard Alba and Victor Nee. In the recently published *Remaking the American Mainstream: Assimilation and Contemporary Immigration,* the authors point to the fact that in 1990 more than 95 percent of Mexican Americans between the ages of twenty-five and forty-four who were born in the United States could speak English well.[51] In another new book that is far more nuanced than Huntington's, *Impossible Subjects: Illegal Aliens and the Making of Modern America,* Mae Ngai and her colleagues make points similar to those of Alba and Nee. Various contributors to the book explain the reasons for the dramatic increases in border crossings by both legal and undocumented Mexicans.[52] Had Huntington looked at these studies and a number of others, his fears of a pending demographic debacle might have been calmed. But, from the start, he seems to follow that old saying, "My mind is made up, don't confuse me with the facts."

But critiques of Huntington's arguments notwithstanding, a difficult question remains: If everyone who wants to come to the United States for whatever reason cannot be allowed to do so, who should be admitted? At a conference held in the late 1980s on "The Acculturation of New Americans," sponsored by the Institute on Pluralism and Group Identity of the American Jewish Committee, one participant, an economist, asked the assembled corps of policy makers—representatives of major volunteer agencies that work with immigrants and refugees, members of several ethnic organizations, and some foundation personnel and academics—a similar question: How many would favor unlimited immigration to the United States?[53] Not one said he or she would. But the experts could not, or would not, say whom they would admit and whom they would exclude.

Some members of minority groups who were at the meeting later commented that most Americans would probably be willing to continue to welcome as many

Indochinese as wanted to come, as well as any number of anticommunists from Europe, including Soviet Jews and Pentecostalists, but would balk at large-scale requests from Africans or Latin Americans. They called this "racism," pure and simple. Others, also speaking off the record, argued that it was not racial prejudice per se but political and cultural bias, a preference for those fleeing left-wing dictatorships and those thought to have the skills or the "potential" for developing skills necessary for a modern industrial society.

The issue reached the halls of Congress when, in the last year of the Reagan administration, the Kennedy-Simpson Immigration Bill was introduced. (It was passed overwhelmingly in the Senate, failed in the House, and was resubmitted a year later.) The bill sought to alter certain provisions of the 1965 Immigration Act by including reductions in the family reunification system and the addition of an independent category of some 50,000 visas allocated on the basis of a point system that favored those with high educational levels, professionals over unskilled workers, and English language ability. The bill was denounced by many Hispanic and Asian representatives because of the favoritism shown to English speakers. They also opposed it because it would eliminate visas for married brothers and sisters under what is known as the "fifth preference," used mostly by Hispanics and Asians to bring in relatives. Others from all over the world objected to the proposed elimination of "sixth preference" visas, those issued to unskilled workers who are in demand in the US labor market.

Much of the controversy over the proposed legislation reflected deeply felt sentiments in our society. For some there was continuing concern about the changing character of American culture (being directly linked to debates about Americanization and bilingualism), a feeling—later to be spelled out in detail by Samuel Huntington—that "they" are so different from "us" that things will never be the same, and that a limit has to be imposed on what seems like a threat of inundation. For others, the threat was not that the newcomers were so different but that, whatever they are today, tomorrow they will be too similar: skilled competitors in a society in which ethnic ties remain a primary basis for group cohesion and for social action. The latter sentiment seemed especially to underlie the concerns of those who object to the high rate of emigration from Asia.

Debates about acculturation paradigms aside, as Ellis Cose has noted, "Congress had ended up with a most expansive result—one ensuring that an already steady stream of strange people knocking on America's door would swell into a torrent, heightening not only the potential for ethnic enrichment but also for ethnic turmoil."

The last five words highlight an old and familiar problem that, in recent years, has taken on renewed urgency, that is, finding a way to reconcile diversity—the most recent flow of immigrants contains the largest influx of nonwhites of any time since the peak years of the slave trade—with the renewal of group-based competition and further black alienation so characteristic of the years of the Great Migration and their immediate aftermath.

Some of the recent tensions between new immigrants and old minorities, especially African Americans, in cities across the land are pointed indicators of the sorts of conflicts Cose feared.

Notes

1. Michael Novak, *The Rise of the Unmeltable Ethnics* (New York: Macmillan, 1971).

2. Ralph Levine, "Left Behind in Brooklyn," in Peter I. Rose (ed.), *Nation of Nations* (New York: Random House, 1973), p. 342.

3. See, for example, Ben Halpern, "The Ethnic Revolt," *Midstream* (January 1971), pp. 3–16.

4. Nathan Glazer and Daniel Patrick Moynihan have pointed out that, in many ways, the American ethnic groups are a new social form, having no counterpart anywhere. See *Beyond the Melting Pot,* 2nd ed. (Cambridge: MIT Press, 1970), p. 16.

5. Michael Lerner, "Respectable Bigotry," *The American Scholar,* 38 (Autumn 1969), pp. 606–617.

6. Studs Terkel, "A Steelworker Speaks," *Dissent* (Winter 1972), pp. 12–13.

7. Glazer and Moynihan, op. cit., pp. xxxiv–xxxv.

8. Andrew Greeley, *Why Can't They Be Like Us?* (New York: Dutton, 1971), pp. 13–19.

9. See Lawrence Fuchs, *The American Kaleidoscope: Race, Ethnicity and the Civic Culture* (Hanover, NH: University Press of New England, 1990).

10. See Peter Schrag, *Out of Place in America* (New York: Random House, 1970); and Michael Novak, op. cit.

11. Novak, p. 290. The reference is to Bob Wyrick, "The Three Worlds of Long Beach," *Newsday* (October 18, 1969), p. 6w.; *Dissent* (Winter 1972), pp. 278–285.

12. See, for example, Bayard Rustin, "'Black Power' and Coalition Politics," *Commentary,* 42 (September 1966), pp. 35–40; and "The Failure of Black Separatism," *Harpers,* 240 (January 1970), pp. 25–34. See also Orlando Patterson, *Ethnic Chauvinism: The Reactionary Impulse* (New York: Stein and Day, 1977).

13. Harold Isaacs, "The New Pluralists," *Commentary,* 53 (March 1972), pp. 75–79. See also Robert Alter, "A Fever of Ethnicity," *Commentary,* 53 (June 1972), pp. 68–73.

14. Isaacs, p. 75.

15. Ibid.

16. Andrea Hairston, "Polyrhythm-Wise: No More Bad Guys in Black Hats," in Peter I. Rose (ed.), *Professorial Passions* (Northampton, MA: Smith College, 1998), pp. 49–58.

17. See Michael Lewis, *The Culture Inequality* (Amherst: University of Massachusetts Press, 1978).

18. See William J. Wilson, *The Declining Significance of Race* (Chicago: University of Chicago Press, 1978).

19. See section "Social Indicators of Black Progress" in Vincent Parrillo, *Strangers to These Shores,* 4th ed. (New York: Macmillan, 1993), pp. 379–387.

20. See Michael Lind, "The Radical Center or Moderate Middle," *New York Times Magazine* (December 3, 1995), pp. 72–73.

21. NPR/Kaiser/Kennedy School Poll, *Immigration: Summary of Findings,* as reported on NPR.com, October 7, 2004, pp. 1–4.

22. Ibid., p. 4.

23. Wilson, op. cit.

24. Ibid., p. 1.

25. Ibid., p. 2.

26. See William Julius Wilson, *The Truly Disadvantaged* (Chicago: University of Chicago Press, 1987).

27. See Anthony Gary Dworkin and Rosalind J. Dworkin (eds.), *The Minority Report,* 2nd ed. (New York: Holt, Rinehart, and Winston, 1988), p. 125.

28. Ibid.

29. Stephen Steinberg, *The Ethnic Myth: Race, Ethnicity, and Class in America,* 2nd ed. (New York: Beacon Press, 1989), p. 288.

30. Ibid., pp. 288–289. See also Stephen Steinberg's more recent study, *Turning Back: The Retreat from Racial Justice in American Thought and Policy* (Boston: Beacon Press, 1995).

31. Peter Kwong, *The New Chinatown* (New York: Hill and Wang, 1987).

32. Thomas Sowell, *Ethnic America: A History* (New York: Basic Books, 1983).

33. For a testing of these assumptions, see Suzanne Model, "West Indian Prosperity: Fact or Fiction?," *Social Problems,* 42:4 (November 1995), pp. 535–553.

34. Ibid.

35. Orlando Patterson, "The Culture of Caution," *The New Republic* (November 27, 1995), p. 26.

36. See Paul Berman, "The Other and the Almost-the-Same," *The New Yorker* (February 1994). Also Peter I. Rose, "Blaming the Jews," *Society,* 31:6 (October/November 1994), pp. 35–40.

37. David Brooks, "Speed of Ascent," *New York Times* (June 25, 2013).

38. Vernon M. Briggs Jr., *Mass Immigration and the National Interest* (Armonk, NY: M. E. Sharpe, Inc., 1992).

39. Peter D. Salins, *Assimilation American Style* (New York: Basic Books, 1997).

40. Samuel P. Huntington, *Who Are We?: The Challenges to America's National Identity* (New York: Simon and Schuster, 2004).

41. John Higham, *Strangers in the Land: Patterns of American Nativism, 1860–1925* (New Brunswick, NJ: Rutgers University Press, 1953), p. 123.

42. Huntington, op. cit., p. 4.

43. Ibid., p. 5.

44. Ibid.

45. Louis Menard, "Patriot Games," *The New Yorker* (May 17, 2004).

46. Huntington, op. cit., pp. 316–317.

47. John Rowland, "A Connecticut Yankee Speaks His Mind," *Outlook,* 136 (March 1924), pp. 478–480.

48. Sam Roberts, *Who Are We Now?* (New York: Henry Holt, 2004).

49. Huntington, op. cit., p. 316.

50. NPR/Kaiser/Kennedy School Poll, op. cit., pp. 4–7.

51. Richard Alba and Victor Nee, *Remaking the American Mainstream: Assimilation and Contemporary Immigration* (Cambridge, MA: Harvard University Press, 2003).

52. Mae Ngai, Gary Gerstle, and William Chafe (eds.), *Impossible Subjects: Illegal Aliens and the Making of Modern America* (Princeton, NJ: Princeton University Press, 2004).

53. See *The Newest Americans,* a report of the American Jewish Committee's Task Force on the Acculturation of Immigrants to American Life (New York: American Jewish Committee, 1987).

Part V

The Meanings of Multiculturalism

Chapter 11

E Pluribus Unum or *E Pluribus Plures?*

Celebration

After a decade of refurbishing, the hundred-year-old immigration facility at Ellis Island was rededicated in 1992. Americans of different backgrounds and from different shores—European, African, Asian, and Latino—came to New York to pay homage to all those things that that portal to America was said to represent: shelter, opportunity, liberty, justice. One person after another extolled the wonders of "the world's oldest democracy"; "our haven in a stormy sea"; "the land of the free"; "the world's only truly multicultural society." It was heady stuff, the sort of imagery that makes one proud to be an American.

Yet, social scientists, journalists, and leaders of various minority communities who attended the festivities and many more who heard the speeches on radio or television found the commentary somewhat overblown. They readily acknowledged the fact that there had been remarkable advances in intergroup relations in the century that had just passed, especially the integration of the children and grandchildren of the "tired and poor and tempest-tost" who came through Ellis Island in the years between 1892 and 1954 (the year the center was closed). They pointed to the acculturation of successive waves of newcomers, the sort of process so many foreign observers had noted when they wrote of the marvelous achievement of taking so many disparate Europeans, most of them impoverished and parochial, and making them into good, productive, and participating Americans. They further affirmed that most such people were, today, living proof of the notion that ours is a nation in which hyphens connect instead of separate, where having a name like Cohen, Cuomo, or Kennedy, Celusniak, Dubinsky, or Papadopoulos, whose forebears came through the very same gates at Ellis Island, meant being Americans, too—as American as an Adams or a Cabot, a Bush or a Clinton. And going further, they recognized and applauded marked successes in the realm of legal rights for all citizens, increased opportunities resulting from campaigns for civil rights and the implementation of affirmative action policies, and growing evidence of greater tolerance among most white Americans toward minorities. But they also reported that just across the harbor—and throughout the land—there were struggles that belied the lofty rhetoric of acceptance, inclusion, and unity. Now, twenty years later, there still are.

Wretched slums not all that different from those that existed when the reception center was first dedicated still pock the cityscape. These days, however, instead of the babble of German, Italian, Polish, Yiddish, and brogue-heavy English, so confusing and offensive to the ears of many old Americans who felt they were being overrun by foreigners in the late nineteenth and early twentieth centuries, many urban centers resound in Spanish, Chinese, Creole, Arabic, and "black" English. What many of those who speak in such languages and dialects face—racism, poverty, alienation, rivalry with others in similar straits, and envy for those who have managed to escape—has a depressing familiarity, particularly to those close at hand.

City councilors, police authorities, social workers, schoolteachers, factory managers, storekeepers, journalists, bail bondsmen, welfare mothers, gang members, local residents, and nearby neighbors know that the nation's poorest communities are still seething caldrons of competition and intergroup tension.

There are still "in-groups" and "out-groups." Despite the many reasons to celebrate the success of so many in moving from the margins into the mainstream of American society; despite the growth of a significant middle class in almost every ethnic group, including those of African and Mexican Americans; despite far greater visibility of minorities, and not just those of European background, in positions of power and influence—and celebrity, including the first black person to occupy the White House—barriers still exist. Many of these barriers are rooted in a prejudice that is nurtured by still-extant institutionalized practices of discrimination, and manifest in persistent scapegoating and differential treatment. And although the effects are evident in many sectors of society and at many levels, those who suffer most are those farthest removed from the arenas of social intercourse between groups, especially the ghetto poor.

In those neighborhoods so geographically close to Ellis Island and the Statue of Liberty and in other parts of urban America such as Washington, DC, Philadelphia, Chicago, and Los Angeles, as well as in many rural regions, large segments of the population are hardly better off than they were a decade or two ago. In many places they are in worse shape. The plight of too many Puerto Ricans, Dominicans, Mexican Americans, recently arrived refugees from Haiti and Somalia, and African Americans has been further aggravated by intergroup rivalry, a shortage of jobs—many the result of the disastrous economic recession that occurred in the late 2000s—an increasingly polarized polity, a deterioration of communal structures, a sharp rise in levels and technology of violence, and, in too many circumstances, a growing desperation born of anomic conditions marked by the collapse of social institutions and a cutting back on public assistance for healthcare as well as welfare. Without major changes in ways those in positions to influence social conditions act, the outlook for a reversal of fortune is not great. In a number of communities social entropy, a disease manifest in the breakdown of communal spirit as well as the social structure, is viral. Many feel that unless means of healing the many affected by it and ways of preventing its further spread are implemented, there will be ever-greater alienation on the part of many who constitute the poorest, weakest elements. Again, echoes of the dichotomy between "they" and "we." *They* are the folks with the disease; *we* are the ones who will suffer if it is not cured! But what is the cure?

It is not that no one cares about the urban poor. From New Deal days to the present, efforts have been made to address their needs. But few have found a way to effect major changes without doing things that would mean unacceptable alterations in the political economy and/or too much personal sacrifice on their own parts. Even when good-intentioned attempts have been made to stimulate change, they frequently have been instigated without full comprehension of their consequences, and then greeted with horror when things seem to go awry.

Aaron Wildavsky once described the risks of such misunderstandings: "Promise a lot; deliver a little.... Lead people to believe they will be much better off, but let there be no dramatic improvement.... Feel guilty about what has happened to black people; tell them you are surprised that they have not revolted before; express shock and dismay when they follow your advice." He called it a "minus-sum game," one in which all players are losers.[1]

Revolts have occurred. Some, such as the riots in Watts in the 1960s and in South Central Los Angeles in the 1990s, have been violent and dangerous. Many others have been less raucous but also disruptive, shaking not only the social order but the conscience of the public. The Black Power Movement was one clear expression of such a revolt. Its more recent incarnation, expressed in such singular activities as the Million Man March on Washington twenty years ago and the much broader campaign to challenge "Eurocentric hegemony," a central theme of the new multiculturalism, are two others. For the participants in most such activities, then as now, there is an underlying theme: a desire to lift the burden of oppression, to take charge of one's own destiny. For the others there is a very direct message, something expressed long ago in Richard Wright's telegraphic admonition, "White man, Listen!"[2]

Different Drummers?

Referring to the riots that occurred in South Central Los Angeles in 1992, the black scholar Cornel West offered a thoughtful commentary on the divisions that persist in this society and in the continuation of the "they and we"—or what he calls "us versus them"—mentality that seems, he says, to prevail over a consensus about the common good. West suggested that a dialogue on the real meaning of race in America is long overdue.

It must begin not with the problems of black people but with the flaws in American society—flaws rooted in historical inequalities and longstanding cultural stereotypes.

How we set up the terms for discussing racial issues shapes our perception and response to these issues. As long as black people are viewed as "them," the burden falls on blacks to do all the "cultural" and "moral" work necessary for healthy race relations. The implication is that only certain Americans can define what it means to be American—and the rest must simply "fit in." The emergence of strong black nationalist sentiments among blacks, especially young people, is a revolt against this sense of having to "fit in."[3]

To many commentators, the kind of revolts West described are potentially more disruptive than urban riots. They can also have much more far-reaching effects, especially so if led by those

who can situate themselves within the larger historical narrative of this country and world, who can grasp the complex dynamics of our peoplehood and imagine a future grounded in the best of our past, yet attuned to the frightening obstacles that now perplex us. Our ideals of freedom, democracy and equality must be invoked to invigorate all of us, especially the landless, propertyless and luckless. Only a visionary leadership that can motivate "the better angels of our nature," as Lincoln said, and activate possibilities for a freer, more efficient and stable America. . . . Either we learn a new language of empathy and compassion, or the fire this time will consume us all.[4]

The Reverend Louis Farrakhan and his companions who organized the Million Man March on Washington had been acutely sensitive to the feelings of the "landless, propertyless and luckless." Indeed, it was for them and for the working class and their families that, Farrakhan claimed, black *men* would be marching on October 16, 1995.

Before it was to take place, a number of African American leaders were asked to comment about its significance, especially in light of the fact that it had been called by the controversial Muslim leader, Farrakhan, and that he extended his invitation only to black males. Some, such as Jesse Jackson, said that, despite concerns about the leadership, they would attend—and did. So did a number of others who had attended the integrated March on Washington led by Martin Luther King Jr. some thirty-two years earlier.

But there were those who refused to participate, among them Congressman John Lewis, a former chairman of the Student Nonviolent Coordinating Committee, who had been beaten almost to death by an angry mob of white racists in the early 1960s. In a lengthy statement Lewis explained the basis of his decision not only to forego the then still forthcoming Million Man March but also to oppose its premise. He began with a reflection on the earlier march that took place in 1963: "In the sea of humanity before me, I saw blacks and whites. Protestants, Catholics and Jews. I saw people in my organization . . . wearing buttons with a black hand shaking a white hand—and that became our symbol. We really did believe in integration and in the creation of what we called 'the beloved community.'"[5]

"Thirty years ago I thought we would be further down the road toward an integrated society by now," Lewis said. But he had not given up. Although acknowledging that its general goal of "encouraging African American men to be responsible is sound," he said he wouldn't attend the Million Man March because "it goes against what I have worked for—tolerance, inclusion. ..."[6]

After the march a number of those like John Lewis, who had opposed it, had some second thoughts. This included a number of black women as well as many male and female white Americans, especially some who called themselves conservative. (Said one commentator, "Many of the themes of the Million Man March are echoed in Republican rhetoric: family values, self-sufficiency, the power of market economics.")[7] Although decrying the bigotry of the organizer and its message of separation, a number of skeptics now said they recognized the empowering character of so disparate a cross-section of African Americans gathered together to foreswear despair and rededicate themselves to the support of kith, kin, and community. They hoped such efforts would make a difference both in the way African Americans saw themselves and in the views of others.

What they thought was also reflected in the sense of those who were there. David Ruffin, editor of *Focus,* the monthly bulletin of the Joint Center for Political and Economic Studies, reported that for months before he had been getting hints that "something big was building."

> I'd heard expressions of enthusiasm about joining the event from younger men with blue collar jobs who tended to be disconnected from politics. [But] many of the middle-class, college educated men over forty I know had strong reservations about the march, because of the discomfort with its principal organizers or with the fact that women weren't invited. ...
>
> I predicted ... that most who would show up in Washington on October 16 would be nonprofessional men in their late teens and early twenties who had never been politically active. I was wrong.[8]

David Ruffin's report was accompanied by a statistical profile based on a survey conducted by Howard University and the Wellington Group. In addition to the demographics and the answers to questions about political affiliation and ideology and candidate preference, the study—and Ruffin—revealed that, contrary to the assumptions of many that the "messenger" was the magnet, it was the "message" that energized the participants. Ruffin claimed that "Attending the march was an expression of black unity and a way to affirm what is best among African American men"[9]—a sentiment corroborated by most other participating observers.

Whether intended or not, the March became at once a counter to the Ellis Island jubilee celebration as well as, ironically, its functional equivalent. Both gatherings were assertions of pride and purpose: pride in past achievement, calls for further unity. But each was also a symbol of two rather different "takes" on American society, the one showing how far we have come, the other saying how far we have yet to travel.

Cornel West, John Lewis, and other prominent African Americans, including Shelby Steele, Toni Morrison, Angela Davis, Stanley Crouch, and Henry Louis Gates, had been drawn into the debates not only about the March, but about other then-current controversies, not the least of which was the matter of multiculturalism and what came to be known more broadly as "the Culture Wars." Although the conflicts over these latter issues were to take place in the universities, they were not purely academic. To appreciate them, it is important to understand the social topography of the battlefields and the character of the disputed turf—much of it intellectual but all of it highly political.

Trends on Campus

Two decades after the tumultuous 1960s, colleges and universities that had reeled under the constant strain of political polarization and confrontation seemed quite oblivious to the debates that were still so central to social scientists. In fact, across the country, the onset of the Reagan Era seemed to have signaled a return to the 1950s and a final break from the 1960s. Group-oriented activism gave way to self-centered personalism characterized best by the materialistic, style-setting "yuppies"—young, urban professionals. The change was noticeable in course enrollments and the choice of majors, especially in the social sciences. Sociology, which had flourished in the heyday of civil rights and antiwar protest, lost students; economics gained them, and business administration thrived with a new respectability. (Of late, doubtless related to the recent disastrous downturn in the economy and the slow recovery, there has been somewhat of a trend back toward sociology and the policy sciences.)

In the later years of the Reagan presidency, things began to change yet again. According to Shelby Steele, two phenomena led to a heightening of tension and, in many places, even sharper divisions along racial and ethnic lines.[10] The first was the result of the successes of the group rights campaigns of the 1960s and 1970s, which had made even the most elite of universities far more open to the enrollment of individuals from very different backgrounds, far more diverse in student composition than ever before. The second was the result of the additional measures taken to further ensure that the trend toward the integration of the schools did not abate, even when those minorities best qualified to compete were able to go where they wanted. It was not enough to remove the color bar; the affirmative action policies on college and university campuses, though increasingly under attack, were in fact expanded and more carefully monitored.

In spite of the significant increase in the presence of nonwhites (which soon included many Asians) on campuses—or perhaps because of it—in the middle of the 1980s "race" again became a topic of concern. In some places it was a subject for positive action, most dramatically characterized by coalitional campaigns to demand that regents of public institutions and members of boards of trustees of private ones divest themselves of stockholdings in companies doing business in what was still a white-dominated South Africa.

But in many places it was not apartheid abroad or segregation in their hometowns that brought out the protesters: it was both the social and academic aspects of life on campus. The first had to do with patterns of interaction where students of color sometimes followed the mechanism of minority adaptation known as defensive insulation, while simultaneously challenging what they saw as persistent biases in the standard curriculum. (A similar charge was made regarding "sexist biases" and parallel demands were made to revamp courses and programs to address the contributions and roles of women.)

Beginning in 1986, at colleges from New England to California, there were ugly racial incidents ranging from name-calling and graffiti writing ("Niggers, Spics, and Chinks: If You Don't Like It Here, Go Back To Where You Came From") to cross burnings and direct physical violence. Minority students, especially African Americans (who were most often the targets), responded with petitions, marches, rallies, sit-ins, and takeovers of administrative offices. One campus observer noted that "much of what they were marching and rallying about seemed less a response to [the] specific racial incidents than a call for broader action on the part of the colleges and universities they were attending."[11]

Many who had been involved in or had firsthand memories of the campus turmoil of the 1960s viewed the incidents as a seeming replay of an earlier scenario. Black students were again making demands: more African American faculty members, more courses on "The Black Experience," more attention to the issue of diversity. (In many places across the country, most notably on the West Coast, these demands were matched by those of Asian and Latino students.) Yet, for all the similarities, there were differences between the protests of the earlier period and the more recent ones.

> Those undergraduates involved in the new debates were born after the passage of the 1964 Civil Rights Act. They grew up in an age when racial equality was for the first time enforceable by law. This too was a time when African Americans suddenly appeared on television, as mayors of big cities, as icons of popular culture, as teachers, and in some cases even as neighbors. Today's black and white college students, veterans of Sesame Street and often of integrated grammar and high schools, have had more opportunities to know each other—whites and blacks—than any previous generation in American history. Not enough opportunities, perhaps, but enough to make the notion of racial tension on campus something of a mystery....[12]

Shelby Steele suggested that the mystery might be partly explained by recognizing that the new problem became how to live in an atmosphere of equality instead of the old context of inequality. "On a campus where members of all races are gathered, mixed together in the classroom as well as socially, differences are more exposed than ever."[13] Minority students often found themselves caught on the horns of a dilemma. If they seemed to accept the newfound openness that did exist on many campuses, they were seen by some of their more militant "sisters" and "brothers" as sellouts. But if they maintained a kind of separate existence, in special houses and cultural centers, they would be betraying what had been fought for so diligently in the Civil Rights Era: true integration.

At American universities many involved in new movements for group solidarity also wanted recognition and representation. Their spokespersons argued that, although they may be engaged in "the politics of difference," their goals were to enhance inclusion and try to alter the structures of society and the character of the universities for the benefit of everyone. In a seeming replay of the demands of those engaged in campus demonstrations in the 1960s, some again began calling for separate facilities for their own group meetings, financial and administrative support for lecturers and other visitors who would present "alternate" views, shifts in departmental and program priorities, and curricular changes that would "begin to neutralize the hegemonic cabal of dead, white males." Included in the newer proposals were those for new courses of study that would include other perspectives and, more pointedly, "the perspectives of others."

Many white students were puzzled by what they perceived as the desire for self-segregation on the part of minority students. Public opinion data clearly indicated that, having grown up in a period when the acceptance of diversity was far more actively promoted than in the past, most were quite prepared to encounter people different from themselves and were far more open to meeting them than many in the minority communities believed to be possible. The suspicions of those who resented what they saw as racism in reverse may have been compounded by the tendency of many universities to offer special orientation programs for minority students—programs intending to ease their way into the new environments but that, intentionally or inadvertently, reinforced notions of how different they were from those in the dominant group. In certain cases, first-year students and transfers from other schools were told, often by peer leaders, how to prepare themselves for slurs and snubs, how to organize to fight racism, and the importance of bonding with others in similar straits.

Such activities often proved to be self-fulfilling prophecies. Many of those who had come from quite integrated environments felt alienated when told they would feel alienated. They looked more at examples of negativity and rejection on the part of others (that *were* still to be found on many campuses) than at the increasingly pervasive signs of acceptance.

The programs to socialize minority students and prepare them for potential hostility had their parallels in the cases of women—white and nonwhite—and of those sometimes called "lifestyle" minorities, especially gays and lesbians.

In the case of all these groups, the deliberations increasingly shifted from social activities to more academic ones, and especially to the character of what was being taught, and how. Sometimes those who belonged to none of the "minority" cohorts called themselves "allies" or some variant and joined forces with them. Students organized to demand some restructuring of the curriculum to make it more inclusive and balanced, to introduce perspectives that, they claimed, had always been overlooked or deliberately underplayed. They sought supporters and faculty advocates among the social scientists who had been the principal partners in the struggle of the 1960s and now those in the Humanities, where many battles were waged in the waning decade of the twentieth century.

In a forceful essay on the debate over the demands to make core curricula less "Western" and to include in the basic canon the works of minority writers and women, Henry Louis Gates Jr. suggested that much of the conflict had arisen as new voices with significant representation on the campuses began to challenge what he calls the "antebellum esthetic position ... when men were men and men were white, when scholar-critics were white men and when women and people of color were voiceless, faceless servants and laborers, pouring tea and filling brandy snifters in the boardrooms of old boys' clubs."[14] Those leading the campaign to reshape the character of traditional education, challenging the assertions of the new cultural right, began to use the collective strength of newly present groups to assert their critical theories.

Many of the demands were met as colleges and universities adopted policies that led to greater appreciation for the varieties of human experiences and expressions, as, once again, they sought to increase the numbers of minority faculty members and students and devoted more money to the general cause of multicultural education. In a number of places, "distribution requirements" came to include courses on diversity. Although the civil rights of all were an underlying issue, the main thrust of the new programs and curricular innovations seemed to be on the cultural side, that is, to highlight the contributions of nonwhite minorities in world and American history. Most positive was a shift from an almost exclusive focus on "victimology," or what has been done to this group or that, to a "celebration" of how its strength has been enhanced by certain styles and experiences, and how much others benefit from knowing about this. It was a central part of the new movement called "multiculturalism."

From Adjective to Ideology

As every reader of this book must surely know by now, throughout American history a variety of terms has been used to describe the United States. Many have to do with the *multicultural* character of the country. Even without using the adjective, it was implicit in the images conjured and discussed in earlier chapters: to Walt Whitman, ours is a "nation of nations"; to Horace Kallen, a "symphony"; to John Kennedy, "a nation of immigrants." More recently, Lawrence Fuchs used the metaphor of a "kaleidoscope" with its multicolored and variegated parts.[15] In each instance, the emphasis was a play on the theme of the motto *E pluribus unum,* "Out of many, one."

Toward the end of the twentieth century the descriptive adjective "multicultural," by the addition of a short suffix, "ism," was turned into an ideology. *Multiculturalism* came to be used by some and seen by many as a term to describe resistance to such traditional views and to offer an alternative. It was in reaction to what was felt to be a failure of integrative pluralism to recognize or appreciate the rich contributions of the widest variety of America's people to the common good.

Some critics saw the neglect of the culture, literature, and music of certain mainly nonwhite minorities as a clear reflection of persisting racism. And even those who saw less malevolence in what they came to call "Eurocentric biases" noted that, by seeing minorities only as victims, villains, superjocks, entertainers, fools, or menaces, those in schools and universities and in the media were still contributing to the perpetuation of stereotypes of many fellow citizens.

The move toward a greater appreciation for the contributions of those of non-European background had a long history dating back to the Harlem Renaissance in the 1920s when the expression of musical, artistic, and literary forms that were to form the core of the most important yet least credited aspects of what the world knows as "American popular culture" were germinating. It was revived again in the late 1960s with the rise of Black Power and its counterpart, the ethnic consciousness movement, which led to expansion of affirmative action programs and the emergence of cultural centers and departments of Afro-American, Latino American, and Asian American Studies and many related programs on a number of college campuses. The main difference was that, in previous times, the principal rationale of those who pushed for these was to enhance access and to fill the void in their own education. Although there was discussion of the importance of such augmentations of regular offerings, many administrators and traditional faculty members saw them as "caving in," acquiescing to the militancy of minority students. Others, more sympathetic, would sometimes explain their agreement as "giving *them* their just due."

More recent campaigns have had a somewhat different focus. And the message is even more complex. Many want multiculturalism to be the instrument of the education and enlightenment of those who are ignorant of their own ways or those of their people, a means of opening the minds of those both inside minority communities and outside them who have been too narrowly grounded in a single tradition (Western civilization) and "need liberation from their provincialism." Others, from radical feminists to Afrocentrists, went much further, offering not only information but also new ways of thinking and interpreting and of defining the principal goals of affirmative action.

Among those who anticipated this new development was Milton Gordon, the sociologist who had written so insightfully about cultural and structural assimilation. Sensitive to the growing frustration of the "never-hads," particularly those in minority communities, thirty years ago Gordon predicted there would be an upsurge of demands for *group* rights and a new "corporate" form of pluralism as an alternative to the earlier "liberal" version.[16]

Gordon further argued that deciding which approach to pluralism to adopt, or which path to follow, would become an issue not only for scholars of American culture but for the society as a whole. Resolving this "new American dilemma," as he referred to the problem, "will have much to do with determining the nature, shape, and destiny of racial and ethnic relations in America in the twenty-first century."[17] He proved to be most prescient.

In the early 1990s, the historian Arthur M. Schlesinger Jr. angered by what he felt was undermining the liberal agenda on which he had committed much of his work, suggested that the time had already come to make the choice. He posited the problem as a challenge to the inclusive trend of American democracy by "multicultural separatists." In a lengthy attack against "the ethnicity rage in general and Afrocentricity in particular," Schlesinger saw such movements as serious threats that "not only divert attention from the real needs but exacerbate the problems."[18] "The recent apotheosis of ethnicity, black, brown, red, yellow, white, has revived the dismal prospect that in happy melting pot days Americans thought the republic was moving safely beyond a society fragmented into ethnic groups. The cult of ethnicity exaggerates differences, intensifies resentments and antagonisms, drives ever deeper the awful wedges between races and nationalities."[19]

Schlesinger's major thesis, expanded in the last two chapters of *The Disuniting of America,* was that the multiculturalists were the vanguard of those who would reverse the course of history to the point where the country would see itself "as composed of groups more or less indelible in their ethnic character."[20] "Are we," he asked, "to let the *pluribus* overrule the *unum?*" In other words, a future description of the United States could become *E Pluribus Plures* ("Out of many, many") instead of "Out of many, one."

This question, raised early in the twentieth century by many who, like Theodore Roosevelt, opposed any sort of "hyphenation," was being asked again. Although in the old days the debate was between the "assimilationists" and the "*cultural* pluralists," it became one between those who wanted to go way beyond the basic premises of the old pluralists and their view of many peoples bound together by a common set of civic and moral values and those who advocated a much more narrowly conceived sense of competing sensibilities. It is not enough to celebrate the diversity of backgrounds, they argued, it has to involve recognition of fundamental differences.

It is hardly necessary to state that members of minority groups, especially nonwhite ones, were then and are still well aware of the difficulty of erasing their "indelible" ethnic character because of the persistence of those who have prevented their full integration. On the contrary, many feel that they have too often been forced to succumb to others' definitions of their cultures and their conditions. Those who are the most ardent defenders of multiculturalism noted that Schlesinger and many others in his camp admit that "American history has long been written in the interests of white Anglo-Saxon males" but seek a kind of absolution for whatever sins have been perpetrated by such biases by noting their own solid liberal credentials and the fact that they rarely fail to discuss slavery, the harsh treatment of native peoples, and the exploitation of immigrants.

The historian Ronald Takaki, a leading figure in the movement to broaden the horizons of all Americans through multicultural education, pointed out that such a "discussion on racial oppression is perfunctory and parsimonious," and that such writers still devote the bulk of their attention to the defense of traditional approaches—and stances.[21]

What happens, Takaki asked, when minority peoples try to define their own histories and conditions? To Schlesinger and other opponents, whatever they called themselves, those who attempt this are seen as subversive particularists. Those opposed to the wide-ranging array of people grouped together as "multiculturalists" often argue that *they* cannot be trusted, for *they* will be ethnocentric, telling lies, exaggerating things in their own favor. Just imagine, they say, "When cohort membership becomes the *sine qua non* of identity and power, extremists will claim that Columbus was an intruder, not a discoverer; that Jefferson was a participant in activities that denied the very spirit of the Declaration of Independence; and that FDR was a racist!" (It must be noted that all of these accusations turned out to be quite accurate!)

The critique was clearly a counter to assumptions that "since only we know what's good for them, only we can assess their reality"—the kind that reminds those with a different sense of history than, say, Schlesinger's, of political cartoonist and writer Jules Feiffer's pointed commentary on an earlier stage of the struggle for access and recognition by African Americans and other minorities. One of his cartoon characters, a white, presumably liberal man appropriately dressed in suit and tie, says to his clone, "Civil rights used to be so much more tolerable until the Negroes got into it."[22]

Writing about the alchemy of race, civil rights, and the legacy of racism, Patricia Williams puts this sentiment in poignant perspective. Speaking of "something as rich, soulful and sonorously productive as black depression," she said, "For blacks ... the battle is not deconstructing rights, in a world of no rights; nor of constructing statements of need, in a world of abundantly apparent need. Rather the goal is to find a political mechanism that can confront the denial of need."[23]

Schlesinger and others of his persuasion argued that any acceptance of the demands of the multiculturalists would be the first steps down a slippery slope leading the country toward its ultimate disintegration. This extreme view was not widely shared. However, the issue on which Schlesinger and his allies focused, often spoken of as the "strain toward balkanization," and its many ramifications is being debated in many places today.

The debates tended to center on three often overlapping issues: the meanings and relevance of multiculturalism; what should be taught and what belongs in the "literary canon"; and the relationships between civil rights and individual liberties, most clearly expressed in discussions of "political correctness" and academic freedom.[24]

With some notable exceptions, the stances of the antagonists in all the debates on multiculturalism and the related topics were and are not only philosophically significant; they are also sociologically interesting, for they are frequently related to group membership (meaning, in the instance, class, status, power, gender, age, and, especially, ethnic/racial group membership). Not surprisingly, those who have become successful, particularly but not exclusively the old white ethnics and their children, favor what Gordon called the liberal approach—Diane Ravitch called it "pluralistic multiculturalism" as opposed to a more "particularistic multiculturalism"[25]—and see the other one less as a means of enhancing the richness of the society than as the vehicle for its disintegration. On the other hand, those who are still on the outside, who have suffered discrimination generally greater than that ever conferred upon the others, want to use collective action to satisfy a desire for acceptance on their own terms.

The African American sociologist and leader W. E. B. Du Bois's famous statement (first referred to in Chapter Five) that "one ever feels his twoness, an American, a Negro" is followed with a desire: "He simply wishes to make it possible for a man to be both a Negro and an American, without being cursed and spit upon."[26]

If African Americans can achieve this still relevant twin goal, then the marches in the streets and messages conveyed in classrooms will have been triumphant. The victories will be theirs but they will also be those of a society in which what George Frederickson calls the peculiarly American "arrogance of race"[27] will have been finally put to rest.

This may still take a while, as Benjamin Jealous, president and CEO of the NAACP, asserted on January 19, 2013, the day before the first black president in American history was to enter his second term. Jealous noted that too many African Americans were still struggling to make it and attributed this to two factors: persisting racism in many parts of the society and, clearly related, past discrimination, which kept so many far removed from the networks of access that made it easier for others to climb the ladder of success. A third factor, mentioned earlier, is the lack of jobs, especially for those who are unskilled.[28]

Of late there has been increasing discussion that many of the problems of nonwhite minorities, especially in inner cities, have been made even worse by the disappearance of opportunities for blue-collar employment caused by the decline of heavy industry, the outsourcing of such forms of manufacturing as garments and shoes, and the new demands of an increasingly technical society. Especially for formerly steadily employed workers in factories that required little education and taught on-the-job skills, the problem of coping with the overwhelming reality of being laid off and then bombarded by more responsibilities than they can handle makes it hard to accept the frequently offered argument that moral degeneration underlies their unhappy placement in their new and sad estate. This state of affairs is not unique to African Americans. Many immigrants, especially nonwhites, have had their mobility hobbled by such critical economic factors.

Pathways to Immigration

Many concerned with revising America's immigration policy have focused on the jobs debate—not the least of those are people who feel opening the gates more widely or, even more critically, offering pathways to citizenship to "illegals" only increases the number of competitors, many of whom, willing to work for very low wages, undercut the labor market. It is an old argument. Yet in recent years there has been a clamor to redress the concerns not only of workers but also of more than ten million undocumented immigrants, including those brought to this country as children to grow up in the limbo of feeling American but not being recognized as such.

For years, Barack Obama and many members of his Democratic Party favored immigration reform through a "DREAM Act" that would, among other wide-sweeping changes, adjust the status of those brought to the United States at early ages. The road toward such new legislation had been very rocky, but a singular factor made the hoped-for change one of the most important bipartisan efforts in recent years. It was the election of 2012, when citizens of the fastest-growing ethnic group in the United States, Latinos, gave the Republican candidate, Mitt Romney, less than 30 percent of their votes and the members of his party realized that, without far greater Latino support the GOP was facing increasing decline.

Within a few weeks of the second inauguration of Barack Obama in January 2013, a bipartisan committee of eight senators, led by New York's Charles Schumer, a Democrat, and including Arizona's John McCain, Obama's rival in the 2008 presidential race, proposed a broad-spectrum change of policy. While making it clear that border security is a priority, the group weighed the benefits of the proposed changes and addressed some of the costs.

Not long afterward, even some of the most conservative members of the Republican Party began to change their positions, favoring some sort of arrangement to accommodate the millions of undocumented immigrants in this country. Whether this was a true change of heart or a calculated move to try to win the votes of many Latinos who failed to support their party, it changed the dynamics and there seemed little question that immigration reform is going to take place.

Perhaps as striking as the change of heart of many in Congress was a decision of the American Federation of Labor–Congress of Industrial Organizations (AFL-CIO). The union coalition, with deep roots in the anti-immigrant populism of the late nineteenth and early twentieth centuries, had long opposed "guest worker" programs that would permit temporary migrant laborers to be contracted for work in this country, arguing they undercut the American labor market—particularly in agriculture, construction, and service industries—by accepting lower wages. But early in 2013 the AFL-CIO joined with its longtime nemesis, the national Chamber of Commerce, in support of a new type of guest worker program with strict controls on employers and an unprecedented allowance for those who would come under the guidelines of the program to petition for citizenship. The new program would begin slowly, with some 20,000 visas in 2013, and be allowed to rise to 200,000 within the decade.

While some may live for the present, many of today's immigrants are following the old pattern:

> Europeans who settled America gave their lives a slingshot shape. They pulled back so they could shoot forward. They volunteered to live in harsh conditions today so their descendants could live well for centuries. The pioneers who traveled West did the same thing. So has each generation of immigrants—sacrificing the present for the sake of the future.[29]

The strength of most immigrants' commitment to the values that Americans assert are the true measure of good citizenship (something akin to the Boy Scout law, which includes the words *trustworthy, loyal, friendly, courteous, kind, thrifty, clean, brave,* and *reverent*) is important (making them model citizens as they augment the labor force); some make more significant contributions to the arts, the sciences, and the economic well-being of the country. Consider these comments, published during recent debates about the efficacy of immigration reform:

> From 1995 through 2005, immigrants founded 25 percent of the venture-backed startups in the U.S., and nearly 50 percent in Silicon Valley. In 2011, immigrant entrepreneurs were responsible for more than one in four new U.S. businesses and immigrant businesses employ one in every 10 people working for private companies. Immigrants and their children founded 40 percent of Fortune 500 companies.

To these facts and figures, the reporter Dean Garfield added, "Immigration is innovation. Every day that goes by without immigration reform is another day when new jobs and new industries start in foreign countries instead of on American shores."[30]

However, before true reform is assured, there will be much wrangling over what is meant when "balancers" (those who favor regularizing the status of illegal immigrants while assuring better surveillance of the national borders) speak of "enhanced border security." Critics like the sociologist Douglas Massey worry about this. Favoring a much freer circulation of people, especially in the "NAFTA zone" (that of the North American Free Trade Agreement with Mexico and Canada), they argue that "not since the days of slavery have so many residents of the United States lacked the most basic social, economic and human rights."[31]

The Dream of Martin Luther King Jr.

August 2013 was the fiftieth anniversary of the famous March on Washington for Jobs and Freedom. It was a time for stock taking, for reviewing how far the country had moved from the time Dr. Martin Luther King Jr. spoke his dream of an America where character would trump pigmentation, where comity would replace conflict, where none would any longer have to sing "We Shall Overcome," because all would be free to do whatever they could without reference to race, creed, or color.

In reviews and assessments, many Americans, mainly whites, took to podiums and airwaves to say how far we had come. Others, mainly blacks, spoke of how far we still have to go. Among those in the first group there was much talk about the Civil Rights Act of 1964 and the Voting Rights Act of 1965, of the achievements of black entertainers and ball players and business people and politicians, particularly the election of Barack Obama as president of the United States. In the ranks of the second group were many who spoke of the riots that followed the great march, the beatings of protesters, the persistence of categorical discrimination, and the disproportionate numbers of African Americans still in poverty and in prison.

Two incidents that occurred in the first half of 2013 highlighted the nature of the continuing debate. The first was the Supreme Court's decision to rule as unconstitutional certain sections of the Voting Rights Act of 1965, which assured fairness at the polls for those long discriminated against. The 5–4 majority concluded that, given the many successes in breaking down barriers to voting and providing access to all, such protections were no longer needed. Supporters of the decision pointed to the number of African Americans serving in Congress, as mayors of cities, and, of course, to Barack Obama as proof of our progress.

The decision came less than a month before the acquittal—on the grounds of self-defense—of a pistol-carrying "neighborhood watcher" named George Zimmerman who pursued, confronted, and (in an altercation that he initiated) shot to death a black teenager, Trayvon Martin, who was passing through the predominantly white community where Zimmerman lived. This may have been the only decision possible given the very limited options presented by the judge, but to many it was a miscarriage of justice. Those who spoke out in protest argued that from the start it seemed to be a clear case of racial profiling that caused the killer to pursue and confront the young African American, even when the police told Zimmerman to let them handle it. In surveys taken in the immediate aftermath of the trial and "not guilty" verdict, white people of varied backgrounds were somewhat divided in their opinions of the decision—many argued that the jury had no option given its instructions, while others claimed the matter of why the teen was suspected and followed in the first place should have been taken into account. African Americans were nearly unanimous in decrying the whole matter and were outraged that the killer could go free. They immediately evoked memories of the lynching of the fourteen-year-old Emmet Till in Mississippi in 1955 and the killing of a number of civil rights workers in the 1960s and 1970s.

In an essay called "A Different Kind of Division?" written on the occasion of the celebration of the fiftieth anniversary of the March on Washington, *New York Times* columnist Ross Douthat offered his perspective on the state of black/white relations. He said that while we are hardly in the "postracial era" that many had hoped would be signaled by the election of Barack Obama, there is far less vicious separation of races in the United States than in years past, when there seemed to be almost no common ground between them. Instead, he noted, "the threat of white identity politics running through the Obama-era conservatism is just that—a sense of resentment and grievance, not supremacist ideology reborn." This is progress, but we are far from King's Promised Land.[32]

Addressing America's Original Sin

Throughout this book on racial and ethnic relations in the United States, there has been an emphasis—some readers might say an undue emphasis—on the plight of African Americans. In Chapter Four there is a long section on "unique Americans"; in Chapter Eight, responses of African Americans are used to illustrate "reactions to discrimination"; in Chapter Nine, "Pride and Protest," it is *black* pride and *black* protest that are highlighted. Although the topic is "multiculturalism," this chapter also focuses more on the disputes between those in the dominant groups and African Americans than on others. The reason for this distinction is based on a fundamental truth: *Tocqueville was right.*

A quarter of a century before the Civil War, Alexis de Tocqueville predicted that, even with the emancipation of the slaves, the racial situation in the United States would be a continuing source of domestic unrest. Writing in the 1830s, Tocqueville expressed the fear that the majority of whites would never overcome their views of the innateness of their own superiority and that the majority of blacks would never lose their enmity for the humiliation and suffering they had experienced.[33] Tocqueville claimed that what we now call "racism" would "perpetually haunt the imagination of Americans, like a painful dream."[34]

Some seventy years later W. E. B. Du Bois claimed that "race" would be *the* problem of the twentieth century. The Swedish observer Gunnar Myrdal, writing in the middle of World War II, a war in which the racist policies of the Third Reich threatened to wipe out an entire people and nearly succeeded, claimed that "the Negro Problem" was America's main dilemma.[35] And just a few years ago, looking back over all that his people had been through, and all they had achieved in persistent struggles against the inequities of institutional racism and various forms of segregation, the widely recognized "Dean of Black Historians," John Hope Franklin, sadly concluded that as we face the new millennium, race is still our number-one domestic problem. He was correct. Now, well into the twenty-first century, the legacy of slavery lingers.

Blacks remain apart and their destinies are still too much in the hands of others. Even Nathan Glazer, a previous opponent of affirmative action, which he saw as a state-supported reinstitution of a form of discrimination, came to believe that "thirty years of effort, public and private, assisted by antidiscrimination law and a substantial rise in black earnings, have made little effect on this pattern."[36] The pattern to which he refers is the one rooted in slavery and the caste-line of harsh segregation that is different from that even of other "colored" minorities.

For Hispanics and Asian Americans, marked in varying degrees by race, it is largely a matter of choice, their choice, just how they will define their place in American society. We see elements in these groups who, in their support of bilingual education and other foreign language rights, want to establish or preserve an institutional base for a separate identity that may maintain some resistance to the forces of assimilation.... But the difference that separates blacks from whites, and even from other groups "of color" [that] have a [unique] history of discrimination and prejudice in this country is not to be denied.[37]

It is owing to this history that Glazer believes controlling more of their own destinies to be "the most powerful force arguing for multiculturalism and for resistance to the assimilatory trend of American culture and American society."[38]

What has been missing most for too many African Americans have been options freed from those hat-in-hand dependencies that allow them but grudging entry to the big, white world.[39] Now many resisters to such a form of assimilation are, in fact, trying to assert alternative means to their goals. The motivation for their actions, and the language of their spokespersons who articulate it, are reminders of Babylonian-born Hebrew sage Hillel's famous questions, first asked over 2,000 years ago.

If I am not for myself, who will be for me?
[But] if I am only for myself, what am I?
And, if not now, when?

Notes

1. Aaron Wildavsky, "Recipe for Violence," *New York* (May 1, 1968), p. 36.
2. Richard Wright, *White Man, Listen!* (Garden City, NY: Doubleday, 1957).
3. Cornel West, "Learning to Talk of Race," *New York Times Magazine* (August 2, 1992), pp. 24, 26.
4. Ibid.
5. John Lewis, "Why We Marched in '63," *Newsweek* (October 23, 1995), p. 33.

6. Ibid.

7. Howard Fineman, "Grappling with Race," *Newsweek* (October 23, 1995), p. 32.

8. David C. Ruffin, "Inside the Million Man March," *Focus* (October/November, 1995), p. 7.

9. Ibid.

10. Shelby Steele, "The Recoloring of Campus Life," *The Atlantic* (February 1989), pp. 47–55.

11. Ibid., p. 47.

12. Ibid., p. 48.

13. Ibid.

14. Henry Louis Gates, "Whose Canon Is It, Anyway?" *New York Times Magazine* (February 26, 1989), pp. 44–45.

15. Lawrence Fuchs, *American Kaleidoscope: Race, Ethnicity and the Civic Culture* (Hanover, NH: University of New England Press, 1990).

16. Milton M. Gordon, "Models of Pluralism: The New American Dilemma," in Milton M. Gordon (ed.), *America as a Multicultural Society. The Annals of the American Academy of Political and Social Science,* 454 (March 1981), pp. 187–188.

17. Ibid.

18. Arthur M. Schlesinger Jr. *The Disuniting of America: Reflections on a Multicultural Society* (Knoxville, TN: Whittle Communications, 1991), p. 2.

19. Ibid., p. 58.

20. Ibid., p. 2.

21. Ronald Takaki, "Battleground or Meeting Ground?" in Peter I. Rose (ed.), *Interminority Affairs in the U.S. Today: The Challenge of Pluralism. The Annals of the American Academy of Political and Social Science,* 530 (November 1993), p. 115.

22. The Jules Feiffer cartoon, from Robert Lantz, Candida Donadio Literary Agency, Inc., appears with permission in Peter I. Rose, *They and We,* 2nd ed. (New York: Random House, 1974), p. 79.

23. Patricia Waters, *The Alchemy of Race and Rights* (Cambridge: Harvard University Press, 1993), p. 152.

24. See Paul Berman (ed.), *Debating P.C.: The Controversy over Political Correctness on College Campuses* (New York: Dell, 1992).

25. Diane Ravitch, "Multiculturalism: E Pluribus Plures," *The American Scholar* (Summer 1990), as reprinted in Berman, *Debating P.C.,* op. cit. pp. 271–298.

26. W. E. B. Du Bois, *The Souls of Black Folk* (1903), as reprinted in Three Negro Classics (New York: Avon Books, 1965), p. 2.

27. George Frederickson, *The Arrogance of Race: Historical Perspectives on Slavery, Racism and Social Inequality* (Middletown, CT: Wesleyan University Press, 1988).

28. See Peter I. Rose, "Systemic Angst in a Polarized America," an essay on Charles Murray's *Coming Apart: The State of White America, 1960–2010, Social Science and Modern Society* (November–December 2012), pp. 554–547.

29. David Brooks, "For Too Long, America Hasn't Put Future First," *New York Times* (February 12, 2012).

30. Dean Garfield, "Immigration Reform Will Propel the Economy," *San Jose Mercury* (February 13, 2013), p. A12.

31. As quoted in John Carroll's "A Surrender in Gridlock," *International Herald Tribune* (August 12, 2013).

32. Ross Douthat, "A Different Kind of Division?," *New York Times* (August 26, 2013).

33. See Peter I. Rose, introduction to Peter I. Rose, Stanley Rothman, and William J. Wilson (eds.), *Through Different Eyes: Black and White Perspectives on American Race Relations* (New York: Oxford University Press, 1973), p. v.

34. Alexis de Tocqueville, *Democracy in America,* trans. Henry Reeve, text revised by Francis Bowen (New York: Vintage Books, 1945), Vol. 2, pp. 391–392.

35. Gunnar Myrdal, *An American Dilemma* (New York: Harper, 1944).

36. Nathan Glazer, "Is Assimilation Dead?," in Peter I. Rose (ed.), *Interminority Affairs in the U.S. Today: The Challenge of Pluralism. Annals of the American Academy of Political and Social Science,* 530 (November 1993), p. 135.

37. Ibid., pp. 135–136.

38. Ibid.

39. See Mary Waters, *Ethnic Options* (Berkeley: University of California Press, 1990).

Chapter 12

Perspectives on "Others" at Home and Abroad

The House We Live In

In 1939, when the United States was rife with various forms of white-supremacist ideology, when segregation was still legal, and "America Firster" sloganeering dominated the media, outside observers would be struck by a paradox. For all the ranting and raving about those who were not "real" Americans (meaning that they weren't white, Anglo-Saxon Protestants), the United States was already quite unique among the nations of the world. It was clearly, as Walt Whitman had so eloquently put it, "a nation of many nations," a society where those "of every hue and caste ... of every rank and religion" were represented. That diversity was the theme of a stirring cantata, written and sung as a counter to the homegrown racist bigots. Called "Ballad for Americans," it was made famous by the great African American singer and civil rights champion Paul Robeson.

> What's that, lady?
> Am I an American?

The singer responds to his own question by saying,

> I'm just an Irish, Negro, Jewish, Italian,
> French and English, Spanish, Russian,
> Chinese, Polish, Scotch, Hungarian,
> Litvak, Swedish, Finnish, Canadian,
> Greek and Turk and Czech and double-check American.

And that ain't all, I was baptized
Baptist, Methodist, Congregationalist,
Lutheran, Atheist, Roman Catholic,
Orthodox Jewish, Presbyterian,
Seventh Day Adventist, Mormon, Quaker, Christian Scientist
And lots more.[1]

Those lines alone offered a lyrical description of the demographic diversity that existed in pre–World War II America. It was also a pre–Martin Luther King Jr. template of comity for our country—and for the rest of the world. Five years later a near-parallel ballad was composed by Earl Robinson, this time in collaboration with lyricist Lewis Allan, and made popular by a very young Frank Sinatra. It was called "The House I Live In." But instead of asking, "Am I an American?" the singer asks, "What is America to me?" He then answers his own question:

What is America to me?
A name, a map, or a flag I see?
A certain word, "democracy"?
What is America to me?

The house I live in, a plot of earth, a street
The grocer and the butcher, and the people that I meet
The children in the playground, the faces that I see
All races and religions, that's America to me.

The place I work in, the worker by my side
The little town or city where my people lived and died
The "howdy" and the handshake, the air of feeling free
And the right to speak my mind out, that's America to me

The things I see about me, the big things and the small
The little corner newsstand and the house a mile tall
The wedding in the churchyard, the laughter and the tears
The dream that's been a-growin' for a hundred and fifty years

The town I live in, the street, the house, the room
The pavement of the city, or a garden all in bloom
The church, the school, the clubhouse, the million lights I see
But especially the people
That's America to me.

At the time the first of these two ballads was written the country was on the brink of World War II and despite resistance from isolationists—the label given to those who wanted to keep us "free of foreign entanglements"—after the attack on Pearl Harbor on December 7, 1941, almost all Americans rallied to the cause of uniting to "bury the Axis," the three enemy nations: imperial Japan, Nazi Germany, and fascist Italy.

After the allied victory in 1945, the United States, while still rent with various forms of intergroup tensions and still highly segregated (we have to remember that the US military would not be integrated nor school segregation ruled unconstitutional until the 1950s), suddenly became something that it had never been before—not just a beacon for those Emma Lazarus had called "the tired and poor and tempest-tost" way back in 1883, but a *superpower.* As such it was in a position to influence the lives of millions and millions of people. In addition to helping facilitate the establishment of the United Nations, those in the American government made the decision to assist the country's former foes rather than punish them as had been done in the aftermath of World War I. Many saw the next great threat as being from the Soviet Union and its communist ideology and urged the development of an economic and ideological counter to serve as a bulwark against it—and developed generous programs to maintain American power and influence. What became known as the Marshall Plan for Europe (named after the statesman and general George C. Marshall) and a somewhat similar program for the democratization and reconstruction of Japan (under the leadership of General Douglas MacArthur) were both highly successful. Our former adversaries were not only given massive assistance and guidance to develop into full-fledged democracies, but their citizens also became enamored of many aspects of our culture.

Not surprisingly, by the 1950s it could be said that the twentieth century was "the American century." And for the next five decades, few could refute that description. During that same period, in no small measure as a result of American aid, Germany and Japan and several other nations devastated by the war underwent an incredible metamorphosis. They were not only rebuilt, but became industrial giants once again.

Within a few decades the countries of Europe that had been ravaged by war were modernizing at such a rapid clip that they became magnets for labor from many parts of what was then called the Third World and, soon, from countries of the former Soviet bloc as well. For perhaps the first time in recent history many members of nations that had long prided themselves on their homogeneity and monocultural character, and often felt especially comforted by the dominance of their own state religions, were forced to face the reality of ethnic pluralism within their borders and to address their own dilemmas of diversity. For many it was—and remains—a huge quandary. The growing multicultural character of their societies was countered by the feeling on the part of many that they were being invaded by foreign ways and ideologies. Such sentiments would lead one after another European nation to experience their own form of isolationism and resurgent nationalism.

Some were quick to exploit such anxiety and use the "outsiders" as convenient scapegoats for the growing pains of nations undergoing rapid changes. In many places the trauma of war, the recovery and then the boom in the economy, and the presence of large numbers of foreigners on their soil began to affect standards for behavior and the things people considered most important—that is, norms and values. These changes would become the subject of many new studies by sociologists, political scientists, and economists. Often the United States would be the template against which they would measure their own changing national characters.

Such introspection had long been a preoccupation of many who wrote about the United States, which was, for some foreign observers and many American social scientists, a living laboratory—and no wonder. In the words of the political sociologist Seymour Martin Lipset, ours was "the first new nation."[2]

American Value Orientations

One of the first major reports on American folkways and mores was written not by an American but by a French observer, Alexis de Tocqueville, who came to visit in the 1830s. In his book *Democracy in America,* he wrote extensively about what was then still a very new nation.[3] His commentaries on the culture and character of the fifty-year-old country were both perceptive and prophetic. In addition to predicting that the scourge of slavery would long haunt the collective psyche of Americans, he noted many contradictions in the way Americans saw themselves and the way they acted, such as the favoring of individualism at the same time they clung to group-based identities of kith and kin and former countrymen, often becoming "faces in a lonely crowd."

Over the next century others came from abroad to visit, explore, and write what some saw as exposés about the United States. Additionally, many Americans would offer their own assessments of our social system and culture. Some, such as David Riesman and his collaborators Nathan Glazer and Reuel Denney, would even use some of the imagery evoked by Tocqueville more than a century earlier. The best example is their book *The Lonely Crowd* (1950),[4] in which they stressed the tendency of middle-class Americans in the years immediately following World War II to eschew traditional commitments to religion and even to forgo opportunities to strike out on their own, preferring conformity to rebellion. To Riesman and his collaborators, many Americans favored going along to get along. They called such people "other-directed." As a former student of the author once succinctly described this trait, "In this country today, one might say, 'I am what I think others think I am.'"

A year after *The Lonely Crowd* was released, Robin M. Williams Jr. published an even more detailed and comprehensive sociological analysis of the United States: *American Society.* Williams identified and sought to explain the many contradictions between our lofty creeds and the actual conduct of the American people. He highlighted then laid the groundwork for examining many value conflicts that many more scholars would write about and pundits and politicians would discuss in the years ahead.

Williams noted how deep were the roots of our values and, also paying homage to Tocqueville, noted that almost all of the characteristics he would highlight had been first noted by the French visitor.[5]

Discussing "major value orientations" in American society, Williams listed such familiar blocks in the foundation of our collective nature and the deep-rooted subjects of our early socialization, inculcated by our families and our teachers: achievement, success, activity, work, efficiency, practicality, progress, material comfort, science and rationality, external conformity, and nationalism-patriotism. In addition, he discussed several that were sometimes contradictory. One of these is the heavy emphasis Americans place on "humanitarian mores," the unselfish willingness, even eagerness, to aid and comfort those in dire straits, including people we hardly know.

Modern-day examples include the incredible outpouring of concern and money by private citizens at the time of the great tsunami that killed nearly 175,000 people in countries around the Andaman Sea and Indian Ocean in late December of 2004, and the response to the Haitian earthquake in 2010 and to many other disasters since then. Williams contended that such a value is rooted in the humanitarian and communitarian thinking of the French Enlightenment, which contrasted sharply with an English philosophy that bore a French name, laissez-faire, which did not stress man's relationship to his fellows but rather to the acquisitive instinct, reflected in many of the values listed earlier, especially efficiency and practicality.

Then Williams mentioned "equality," a value that requires that "the individual must feel guilt, shame, or ego deflation when he acts in inegalitarian ways."[6] Equality, Tocqueville had noted long ago, is often connected to the idea of freedom, but they are clearly quite different and, in some ways, opposing concepts. The former implies some sort of leveling of the playing field (often defined as fairness); the latter refers to the license to do one's own thing, even to fly in the face of tradition. The insightful Tocqueville said that America had sooner or later to face a conflict of values described as a contradiction between the principle of freedom and the principle of equality. We have not yet addressed the full implications of the distinction recognized nearly two centuries ago.

"Democracy" is a concept and a value we hold especially dear. As Tocqueville— and, later, Williams and many others—pointed out, it encompasses not only the system of our government but also the character of the civic culture itself. It may be something we take for granted but, as we have learned time and again (most recently in Iraq, Afghanistan, and Egypt), it is a most difficult thing to export and an even harder thing to impose on others.

Democracy consists of a congeries of variables: "along with majority rule, representative institutions, and the rejection of the monarchical and aristocratic principles under which [American] society began, early American democracy stressed the reservation of certain 'inalienable rights' as unalterable by majority rule."[7] Almost all Americans proud of this value orientation may want to ask themselves how it jibes with another set of values, highlighted by Williams: those relating to racism and related group-superiority themes, matters we have been addressing throughout this book.

One contemporary writer, Pierre van den Berghe, has contended that for much of US history, many in the government as well as those in the majority of the populations operated under the double guise of a "Herrenvolk democracy." The German word *Herrenvolk* literally means *the people* but was used by the Nazi leadership for those they defined as belonging to the "master race." (They called Jews *Untermenschen,* subhuman.) In other words, van den Berghe argued that America was a democracy for some but not for others—namely, African Americans.

The New France

The highly cosmopolitan Thomas Jefferson (who, as a slave-owner but "man of the people," in many ways embodied what van den Berghe described), is reported to have said, "Every man has two nations, his own and France." The reference was to that powerful, worldly, sophisticated, and cultured Gallic society whose political system, refined tastes, and general joie de vivre seemed so appealing.

In the aftermath of World War II, around much of the globe the United States became the new France; for good or bad reasons it became everyone else's primary reference point, a fact that still persists in many parts of the world.

Even today, well into the second decade of the twenty-first century, the United States is seen by many in other lands as freewheeling, open, and innovative. It is not at all surprising that others, especially those in totalitarian societies (many recently freed from the yoke of Soviet rule, and some trying to loosen the shackles of various forms of political and religious fundamentalism) are envious. They want what we have, not the least of which are our freedoms. Even those who decry many things about America often seem to be drawn to some aspects of our culture.

These days there is ample evidence that in spite of diatribes against everything from our continuing economic and social problems at home to our still-too-powerful global economic and political influence on others, people in every part of the world remain taken with the myriad manifestations of American spirit and enterprise, the popular culture, and the techno-wizardry. They may decry the aggressive openness and roughrider manners of the "Yank" (not infrequently used as a four-letter word in anti-American graffiti) but remain mesmerized by them. They may laugh at the proclaimed piety of our politicians and denounce reports of American fetishes relating to sexuality and guns even as they are titillated by the former and intrigued by the latter. And, although criticizing the treatment of minorities in the United States, many will acknowledge that most such people have many more chances for moving into the mainstream of society than those starting out in similar positions in their homelands. This is particularly true of those who come to their countries from foreign lands.

This love-hate relationship with the United States has been the subject of a number of post–World War II studies and commentaries following that of Robin M. Williams Jr., including books with provocative titles like the 1972 volume *Without Marx or Jesus*,[8] by the French writer Jean-Francois Revel; *American Exceptionalism*, by Seymour Martin Lipset, published fifteen years later;[9] and more recent volumes such as *The Eagle's Shadow*, by the journalist Mark Hertsgaard.[10]

Revel mapped out what he saw as the new American revolution. Lipset had viewed it as a double-edged sword. Hertsgaard implicitly highlighted a number of Revel's ideas and then made a point-by-point critical examination of American values written about earlier by Riesman, Williams, Lipset, and many other sociologists, political scientists, and historians, but in a much more reportorial and even folksy manner.

For students of sociology, *The Eagle's Shadow* is an engaging and informative commentary on America's image abroad, based on its American author's two decades of encounters and reflections while living overseas, and a six-month Earth-girdling excursion that spanned the time surrounding September 11, 2001. In his journeys he spoke to political leaders and ordinary people in every part of the globe. His book is a revealing report on others' views of American society and everything associated with it just before and immediately after the attacks in New York City and Washington, DC. It is also something more: a critique of our society by those outside it, complemented by Hertsgaard's own running commentary on how *he* sees the United States.

Using the advantage of having been away for so many years Hertsgaard scrutinizes the scene with the eyes of an outsider as well as those of an insider. And, as the writer Henry James, who had been away from the United States for two decades 100 years before, Hertsgaard expresses displeasure with what he found on his return.

Hertsgaard suggests that he was struck by the fact that the worldview of too many Americans seemed anything but worldly. Even more troubling than such insularity, he reports that people "not only don't know about the rest of the world, [they] don't care." Hertsgaard also captures the other side of the coin, the mixed and often confusing presumptions of those who see us from afar and often through Hollywood-tinted glasses, and he offers an array of explanations why—as his subtitle succinctly states—"America fascinates and infuriates the world."

His book, completed before America became engaged in two of its most prolonged wars—those in Iraq and Afghanistan—is organized around a number of dialogues relating to sets of generalized images, all starting with the words "America is" and followed by such descriptors as "parochial and self-centered; ... rich and exciting; ... a land of freedom; an empire; ... hypocritical and domineering; ... [a land of] philistines; ... a land of opportunity; ... self-righteous about its democracy; ... only out for itself." These assumptions, beliefs, and values are interwoven throughout the text.

The author visited many places on both sides of what he calls the "rich/poor divide." One of the last excursions he writes about started in South Africa, where his thirty-two-year-old driver, Malcolm, told him that every black township in South Africa has "two street gangs named for your country: 'The Young Americans' and 'The Ugly Americans.'" The former "dress like Americans"; the latter "shoot like Americans." Wealthy and dangerous, stylish bullies: that is how many there saw us. And these are the views of our admirers! Others described how ignorant Americans are, how wasteful, how corrupt—and corrupting—and yet even they tended to echo the words of the former environmental minister of the Czech Republic, Bedřich Moldan, whom Hertsgaard quotes: "You may like the United States or dislike the United States but you know it is the future."[11]

America and the Wider World

In the six decades since Williams first published his assessment of American value orientations, and in the much shorter period since Hertsgaard's book was released, many things have changed in this country and abroad. At home, as has been noted previously, there has been a dramatic demographic shift in the character of the population. In the not-too-distant future, white Protestants, who were not only the statistical majority *and* the dominant group in American society when Williams published his treatise, will have lost both titles and will have to reconcile themselves with living in a country where they are in the minority and those of other identities will play an increasing role in the polity. Overseas, even more rapid changes have taken place: the end of European colonialism and rise of new nations; the development of the European Union; the fall of the Soviet Union and its reversion to fifteen independent states where many not only rejected communist ideology but replaced it with traditional religious fervor—much of it Eastern Orthodox Christianity, much of it marked by Islamic fundamentalism; the end of federated Yugoslavia and the Balkan wars among its former states, which would give "ethnic cleansing" a whole new meaning; and the steady rise of the People's Republic of China. More recent have been the "War on Terror"; the "Arab Spring," marked by uprisings in Tunisia, Libya, Egypt, and Syria; the rapid resurgence of old racial, religious, and tribal rivalries in decolonized states; and an acceleration of migration caused by both "push" and "pull" factors—the former affecting groups forced to flee, the latter referring to the continuing lure of a better life in other, richer lands. On top of this is the reality of new modes of near-instant communication that have contributed to the breakdown of barriers through the spread of ideas and innovations, many still emanating from the United States. The new media has also been used to rally demonstrators on all sides, often heightening tensions between countries and within them.

If the twentieth century was America's, many observe that, while our country will still have great influence, the situation today is far more fluid. Owing to the power of the Internet, increased uses of "offshore" labor (where workers in countries with far lower wages than those in the United States and Europe, like China, India, Bangladesh, and some African and Latin American countries, produce the bulk of goods for American and European markets), the widespread influence of international corporations, and the unprecedented movements of people across borders, the twenty-first century is proving to be one of global interaction—and tension. Much of this has had to do with reactions to the accelerating movement of people from poor countries to richer ones, to pressures on generous welfare systems developed during the boom in industrial growth in many of the latter countries, and to cultural and religious rifts between "natives" and "newcomers." Referring to the mounting conflicts between Western-dominated religions and ideologies and radical Islamists, Samuel Huntington predicted the new century would also be an era marked by a "clash of civilizations."[12] His phrase, while debated by some, seems today to have been most prescient.

On Global Interaction—and Conflict

While many critical observers see much merit in what is currently referred to as globalization, usually referring to the dispersion of goods and services and the breakdown of artificial barriers drawn by politicians in the Age of Empires, others are more skeptical. The sociologist Robin Cohen addressed this in his 1997 book *Global Diasporas*.[13] He began a critical chapter, "Diasporas in the Age of Globalization," by first stating the rather upbeat characteristics of the new world order as enumerated by Andrew McGrew and his colleagues in their book *Global Politics*. He noted their view

> that the claims of the Enlightenment—proposing that human beings are essentially similar and have similar needs and aspirations—have now been embraced by most political leaders and by democratic movements in most countries; that there is now worldwide financial, economic, technological, and ecological interdependence and a growing perception, aroused and confirmed by the satellite pictures from space, that "planet Earth" is a single place. Moreover, with the collapse of the Soviet Union, the bifurcation of the world—one part democratic, the other communist—no longer exists; and the "Third World" has all but disappeared as a coherent category. There is, they argue, now only one world. Goods, capital, knowledge, images, communications, crime, culture, pollutants, drugs, fashions, and beliefs all readily flow across territorial boundaries. In sum, we are on the road to the first global civilization, a discrete world order with shared values, processes, and structures.[14]

But are we?

Cohen says that, while it all seems reasonable at first blush, at least five major caveats need to be considered: First, that a number of writers on the subject, such as Andrew McGrew, "slip uneasily between description and prediction"; second, that there are very different theories about what globalization is all about—from the "voluntarist" view of mutual accommodation and coexistence to the more traditional one of dominance and the fateful impress of the capitalist world economy on everyone else. As a third point, Cohen further indicates two strongly divergent theses about the future of nation-states: one claiming that they are in the process of dissolution in the face of global pressures and the other asserting that nation-states are adapting to the new pressures by changing their functions. In the latter case, it can be argued that "while the nation-state no longer crystallizes and organizes domestic capital, it still continues to police inward labor flows and seeks to galvanize, although with diminishing capacity, a single identity around a national leadership, common citizenship and social exclusion of outsiders." Cohen's fourth point is directly related to the last sentence. Finally, he writes that theorists of globalization tend to ignore "powerful hegemonizing forces at work." He suggests that there are a number of countertendencies to globalization, not the least of which is the fact that "whatever the future of the nation-state, there is no doubt that nationalism as a force and as an ideology is on the increase." And, he rightly adds, "*As with nationalism and ethnicity, so too with religious fundamentalism, racism, sexism and other forms of social exclusion, all of which also seem to be on the increase, despite globalization.*"[15]

Cohen's admonitions about buying at face value the almost kumbaya words of McGrew and others, written nearly twenty years ago, were to prove most prophetic.

In recent years, there have been many changes in the world economy, in the forms of international migration, in the development of "global cities," and in the growing gap between cosmopolitan and local cultures. All these are happening along with two almost contradictory trends: first, the assertion of chauvinistic nationalism; and, second, what some call the deterritorialization of social identities in many places, especially those whose borders were artificially drawn by colonial powers, leaving ethnic groups on either side of the lines. (One of the best examples of the latter point is the place of Kurds who dwell in both Iraq and Turkey.) Such movements have been serious challenges to "the nation-state's claim to make an exclusive citizenship a defining focus of allegiance and fidelity in favor of overlapping, permeable and multiple forms of identification."[16]

While in one way the American reader might feel some sense of familiarity in reading the last quotation, he or she, thinking twice about it, would realize that there is a major difference between the situation in the United States and in many other places. Even the early assimilationists who advocated "Anglo-conformity" recognized that they were dealing with multiple forms of cultural, religious, and national identity and had to adjust to that reality. For most, the integration of ever more diverse newcomers was symbolized by the motto *E pluribus unum* and most of those eager to move from the margins to the mainstream found it a compelling idea. (Even at the height of the Black Power movement, the majority of African Americans, when asked what they wanted, said they wanted to find acceptance, respect, and equal treatment in *their* country, the United States.)

More often than not, pluralism—even the sort of corporate pluralism advocated by many African American and Latino spokespersons and tied to interest-group politics—has meant something quite different to many in European, Middle Eastern, African, and Asian nations than it does in this country. Moreover, often political identities are not like those in the United States, where, as discussed earlier, "hyphens connect instead of separate," where like spokes on a wheel, various ethnic and religious groups are coupled to a common hub. (Again we have the idea of "many peoples, one nation.) A result of the persistence of maintaining social distance, sometimes in law, often in practice—as was long the case in our own sordid history of segregation—is almost an institutionalization of "they" and "we" distinctions, frequently accompanied by the demonizing of those who are not of the "proper" party, faith, tribe, or clan—or color. Such attitudes toward others, especially suspicion about them, remind one of Rudyard Kipling's poem "The Stranger."

> The stranger within my gate,
> He may be true or kind,
> But he does not talk my talk—
> I cannot feel his mind.
> I see his face and the eyes and the mouth,
> But not the soul behind.
> The men of my own stock,
> They may do ill or well,
> But they tell the lies I am wonted to,
> They are used to the lies I tell;
> And we do not need interpreters
> When we go to buy or sell.[17]

In this country many have held such sentiments about others. Such prejudicial thinking is also rampant well beyond our shores.

The Threat of the Stranger

Discrimination and intolerance are widespread today, particularly against immigrants as well as people of recent migrant background who are often treated as foreigners even in countries where they are both natives and citizens.

This is the summary statement of the findings on the situation *in Europe* drawn up by a group of eminent persons—diplomats, parliamentarians, and scholars from a number of different countries—and headed by the former German foreign minister, Joschka Fischer, for the Council of Europe. The final report, "Living Together: Combining Diversity and Freedom in 21st-Century Europe," written by the distinguished British journalist Edward Mortimer and published in May of 2011, boldly states that there are eight specific risks in Europe today: rising intolerance; rising support for xenophobic and populist parties; discrimination; the presence of a population virtually without rights; parallel societies; Islamic extremism; loss of democratic freedoms; and a possible break between "religious freedom" and freedom of expression.

The Council of Europe document contains the following passage most relevant to the previous discussion:

> The report holds firmly that identities are a voluntary matter for the individual concerned, and that no one should be forced to choose or accept one primary identity to the exclusion of others. It argues that European societies need to embrace diversity, and accept that one can be a "hyphenated European"—for instance a Turkish-German, a North African–Frenchwoman or an Asian-Brit—just *as one can be an African- or Italian-American.*[18]

As in the case in the United States, while some newcomers are refugees fleeing persecution or trying to avoid being caught in the cross fire of conflicts in their homelands, the vast majority of those who move to Europe are economic migrants searching for work and a better way of life for themselves and, especially, their families.

Through a series of accords—collectively known as the Schengen Agreement—to which almost all nations in the European Union are signatories (exceptions being the United Kingdom, Ireland, Romania, and Bulgaria), those who legally enter the "Schengen area" come into a territory where the free movement of persons is guaranteed, where all internal borders have been abolished in lieu of a single external border, and common rules and procedures are applied with regard to visas for short stays, asylum requests, and border controls.

This often means that legal migrants entering countries of southern Europe may stay there or move on to Switzerland, Austria, Germany, or any other signatory country. In recent years, most of those taking advantage of this quite open system have been coming from North Africa, the Middle East, the Balkans, and the former Soviet bloc.

Despite the agreement, some "Schengen states" have tried to set up barriers to prevent certain groups from crossing their borders. Those targeted are usually but not always those without proper papers; they are referred to as "undocumented." This put increasing burdens on countries such as France after the Tunisian uprising, when many sought refuge there, and, more recently, on Malta and Italy, where thousands of undocumented Africans from Libya and as far away as Somalia (after first moving overland to the coast) crossed the Mediterranean seeking asylum. Their presence and that of others arriving in these as well as other lands on Europe's periphery and eager to move north has created increasing rifts within the European Union, especially in countries where there are already strains on the welfare system and where authorities are increasingly being challenged by extreme nationalists to keep out specific foreigners.

Many refugees as well as more conventional migrants are Muslims and their growing presence has been accompanied by an upsurge of religious intolerance throughout Europe. The sentiment of many can be summarized in that singular expression mentioned in an earlier chapter: "Islamophobia." It is a word combining the faith of millions with the Greek word for fear.

Something similar, if not quite so blatant, has happened in the United States. Prior to the attacks on New York and Washington, DC, on September 11, 2001, most Arab, Asian, and African Muslim migrants to the United States, and their offspring, were accepted with considerable equanimity, perhaps even more so than African Americans who converted to Islam and were often referred to as "Black Muslims." While some non-Muslims found the "Arabs'" ways full of mystery and sometimes spoke of followers of the Islamic faith in terms of crude stereotypes, there was little talk of danger coming from their ranks. But with what will forever be known as "9/11" the situation changed dramatically. More than one Arab American noted that they had to prove they were not terrorists, but that doing so is something akin to proving the null hypothesis.

In the immediate wake of those attacks, many Muslim Americans and civil rights advocates worried that the horrendous events in which thousands of lives were lost owing to the demonstrable work of militant Islamists would result in a repeat of what happened after December 7, 1941, when the Japanese attacked Pearl Harbor and more than 110,000 Japanese Americans (which constituted almost the entire population of that group at the time) were incarcerated in internment camps. Government officials were quick to dispel rumors of any such action, and no large-scale roundup of Muslims living in the United States took place. However, violent incidents such as the bomb attack during the 2013 running of the Boston Marathon, coupled with conflicts in many Muslim countries, have created an ongoing sense that havoc might be wrought at any time by potential terrorists—this has become far more focused than resentment of the "invading Mexicans." In other words, in recent years Americans have tended to separate what some perceived as a long-term economic and cultural threat from an immediate, existential one.

Today, in European societies many (but far from all) newcomers are of the Islamic faith and are often perceived as part of a siege that is at once economic ("They only want the benefits of the generous welfare states"), cultural (the old argument about disrupting traditional ways), and highly political. Writing in the *Middle East Quarterly* a few years ago, Esther Ben-David noted that

> Beginning in the mid-twentieth century, European countries have changed from net sources of emigration to attractive destinations for immigration. These days Muslims,

many from rural traditional areas, comprise a significant cohort of non-European immigrants to Europe. Even those who have settled in cities retain a village mentality and are seen as backward by the business and cultural elites in their home countries. Moroccans who settled in the Netherlands and Belgium, for example, are mostly Berbers from the Rif mountains, not the Arab cultural elite from Casablanca, Rabat, or Fez. These immigrants came to Europe in order to build railroads, work in the coal mines, clean streets, and do the jobs that Europeans did not want to do.[19]

Later in her article, Ben-David explained,

Immigration is a personal decision. However, once many people make the decision to leave their home country, the flow of immigrants takes on a life of its own. This immigration dynamic is hard, if not impossible, to stop. Immigrants choose to go to destinations with which they are acquainted and about which they have heard from friends and relatives who immigrated previously. Such destinations provide informal support structures and social networks. This leads to a situation where immigrants from a certain home area all congregate in a certain area in the host country, thereby leading to immigrant ghettoes. In the United States, for example, Minneapolis–St. Paul has become an unlikely immigrant ghetto for Somalis, and Los Angeles—"Tehrangeles"—is an immigrant destination for Iranians.[20]

A similar pattern exists throughout Europe. In every country on the continent, and in almost every major city, new ethnic enclaves have grown up. Some are in the inner cities, but many are in working-class suburbs that ring them. And many are replete with infrastructures of their own. Most prominent among these are in France, a country with many peoples from Algeria and other former colonies in North Africa, and Germany, with a current population of three million Turks (of roughly seven million foreigners, the largest number of any country in Europe), most of whom came as "guest workers" during the economic boom that began in the 1960s, and stayed. Never fully integrated into the society, many young members of the Turkish community in Germany—a country that now recognizes dual citizenship, but only for those with roots in countries that belong to the European Union—face a dilemma. Because Turkey is not yet a member of the Union, upon reaching the age of twenty-three, according to a law passed in 1999, all German-born Turks—many of them third generation—must decide whether to be German or Turkish. If they choose the latter they immediately lose their German passports. Experts feel that putting them in such a bind hinders rather than enhances their integration. Young people who are proud of their Turkish heritage feel they are being forced to renounce it in order to be accepted into the society in which they have long lived, in whose language they are fluent, and by whose laws they have abided. A few years ago, a bold headline in a German newspaper said it all. "After Decades, German Turks Still Feel Like Outsiders."[21] This sentiment was corroborated by a major survey conducted by Harris International for the *International Herald Tribune* in the United States and Europe. The survey posted questions about whether the number of legal immigrants in the respondents' countries was too high, how successful the integration of legal immigrants has been, what rights recent immigrants who did not have citizenship should be granted, and what measures governments could put in place to help better manage immigration. The survey's major findings are summarized as follows:

Asked the general question, "Is immigration a good thing?" nearly two-thirds of Americans said it is, in contrast to roughly half of Germans and French and only 45 percent of Britons who responded that way. Sixty-seven percent of those in Britain and 55 percent of Italians surveyed thought there were too many *legal* immigrants in their countries. This was true of only 35 percent of Americans and 32 percent of those in France.

When asked whether policies should be put in place to aid legal immigrants' transition to their new cultures, 56 percent of French respondents were favorable but seven in ten in the United Kingdom were not.

According to the *Tribune* writers, the survey also uncovered strong feelings on the stage at which immigrants should be entitled to benefits. An overwhelming majority in all of the countries believed that immigrants should only have access to benefits once they have citizenship.

Perhaps even more telling is that, in contrast to the United States and Canada, the majority (between 52 and 56 percent) in all European countries surveyed felt that immigrants have not been successfully integrated into their societies. And roughly six in ten of those in the United Kingdom, Germany, and Italy said "yes" in answer to a question about whether undocumented (illegal) persons should be expelled.[22]

Those who conducted the study did not control for levels of education, social class, or age, which usually are critical variables regarding both attitudes and behavior. Those better educated, better off, and younger are generally more progressive in their attitudes than those who have less schooling, are working class or poor, and are older. But this is not always the case. Consider the situation in the Netherlands.

New Realities in Europe: A Case Study

After World War II new migrants came to many countries of Western Europe, including the Netherlands. In the first wave there were many Dutch-speaking "repatriates" from former Dutch colonies such as Surinam and Indonesia. Then others, mostly "guest workers" from North Africa and the Middle East, mainly from Morocco and Turkey, were encouraged to come to do the heavy lifting in a growing economy. Political asylees came, too, first from Vietnam and later from Somalia, Bosnia, and other war-torn states. The presence of these foreigners would soon challenge the resurgent spirit of hospitality and welcome and lead to unprecedented intergroup tensions.

Other European countries have had somewhat similar recent histories, particularly with regard to the presence of both economic migrants and asylum seekers from North and sub-Saharan Africa, Turkey, the Balkans, South Asia, and the Middle East.

Studying the situation in many of these countries, and especially in the Netherlands, one cannot help but think of what the French sociologist Emile Durkheim called *anomie,* a shorthand term for a breakdown in the social order often provoked by dramatic changes for which members of society are unprepared.

Such a breakdown happened in many places over the century since *anomie* first entered our vernacular: the chaos in Europe following World War I, the worldwide Depression, the effects of Nazism and Fascism on millions, the disorientation of displaced persons after the war, and the upheaval that began in the mid-1960s when rebellious young people challenged the establishment on both sides of the Atlantic. In the last instance, the parents of the rebels, who were finally experiencing a semblance of normalcy and increasing affluence, hardly knew how to react. Their confusion and anxiety were particularly dramatic in the Netherlands, where, reeling from unanticipated challenges to the status quo, many leaders in government, the academy, and the industrial sector acquiesced to the demands for a more open society and often for direct participation in decision making at every level by those known as "Provos" (short for provocateurs). They had successfully undermined many aspects of the well-known Calvinist, Catholic, and secular/humanist pillars that were the principal supports of Dutch society. (Somewhat parallel phenomena were occurring in France and Germany at the same time.)

In many ways, the cultural revolution the Provos unleashed resulted in a sea change in the normative order. It was even more dramatic than what many called our own cultural revolution. The Dutch nation officially became more accepting of diversity, and many experiments in a freer, more open system became institutionalized. Soon the Netherlands gained fame (or, to its critics, notoriety) for becoming the most liberal nation in Europe. Best known, of course, were its legalization of prostitution, decriminalization of the use of soft drugs, acceptance of the practice of euthanasia, and open-mindedness in regard to homosexuality. Less celebrated was the nominal acceptance of multiculturalism.

In recent years the Netherlands experienced another challenge. This time the matter did not start with the rebellious progeny of old Dutch *burgers* and working-class conservatives, but rather with the offspring of non-Dutch migrants, increasingly referred to by the invented and, initially at least, neutral word *allochtoonen* (meaning something like "newcomers" but often used today as a pejorative term for "outsiders").

Most of the Dutch Provos, like many of those who joined Students for a Democratic Society and the Free Speech Movement in the United States in the 1960s, had been middle-class insiders who had sought to break loose from the confines of their seemingly smug, self-righteous, and stratified society where people took pride in minding their own business—and in many ways they succeeded in their attempts. Forty years after their appearance, those who challenged the status quo and upset many members of society were part of a generation whose parents had migrated to the Netherlands from North Africa eager to work and hoping to enjoy the rights, privileges, and welfare benefits the old Dutch bourgeoisie had come to take for granted. In certain ways, they were not disappointed. Whatever anxieties they felt, most seemed grateful for the chance to start life anew in a freer society than the ones they had known before. Others, even when disillusioned, tended to feel and behave as if they were guests in someone else's home.

Often too old to learn the ways and difficult language of the new society—like millions of immigrants who came to the United States during our early history as a nation, at the time of the "Great Atlantic Migration," and again after 1965—they frequently sought out others like themselves. Many found housing in "changing" neighborhoods, "dish cities" that redefined the urban landscape. (They were so named because of the numerous satellite dishes set on rooftops and used to get better TV reception from their countries of origin.) Whether working or unemployed, those of the first generation found their personal solace in family, faith, and links to homelands. Few had the energy or time for politics.

Those of the second generation frequently found themselves in a triple bind, first caught by parental hopes (usually for *them*); then by parental fears, especially about being enticed by what they saw as rampant permissiveness; and then frustrated by the official promise of equality contrasted with the reality of increasing resentment from the society in which they were growing up and being educated and upon which they were often dependent for support. Fluent in Dutch, and attuned to the world beyond that of their kith and kin, many felt betrayed by their immigrant fathers and infuriated about the seeming hypocrisy of their prejudiced hosts. In many ways they became modern exemplars of those, more than eighty years ago, Robert E. Park referred to as "marginal men"—"those whom fate has condemned to live in two societies and in two not merely different but antagonistic cultures."[23]

Within the ranks of those no longer foreign but still alien—and increasingly alienated—a number of Muslim youth in the Netherlands, like many of their counterparts in other European countries, sought to resolve their frustration and their persisting estrangement by seeking a sort of redemption in ethnic pride and religious fervor, especially in Islamic fundamentalism. In a very real sense, they sought to turn the negativity of their marginality into a functionally positive response. Like those undergoing the "ethnogenesis" of many African Americans in this country in the 1960s and 1970s as they increasingly stressed their own cultural uniqueness and the "racialization" of Latinos who adopted a stance of distinctiveness as *nonwhite Hispanics,* many young Dutch Muslims began to take increasing pride in their differences from those in the majority. Some, influenced by charismatic and persuasive religious leaders known as imams, underwent true born-again conversions, renouncing their "errant" and "decadent" Western ways, celebrating their Islamic heritage, and becoming more orthodox than their parents. This was manifest in many ways, including the denouncing of those in their ranks who fraternized with non-Muslims, a rise in attendance at mosques, and sometimes in the manners of dress by men who donned traditional garb paralleling the women with their headscarves, and, sometimes, veils and full-body burkas.

Within the host society, growing anger at the seemingly ungrateful behavior of some second-generation *allochtoonen* and their perceived radicalization often turned from ethnocentric insensitivity to outright hostility, even among those who had been socialized to avoid expressions of nationalism or racism and to cap their real feelings about the "outsiders." For a time, right-wing parties gained traction and votes as they mounted increasingly vitriolic attacks on the *allochtoonen,* particularly after the murder by members of the Muslim community of two flamboyant and incendiary anti-immigrant leaders, one a member of parliament, Pim Fortuyn; the other, Theo van Gogh, the grand-nephew of the celebrated Dutch painter.

The perceptive Dutch writer Ian Buruma, seeming to echo Kipling's thoughts about "the stranger within the gate," put it this way:

> Tolerance has its limits even for Dutch Progressives. It is easy to be tolerant of those who are much like ourselves, whom we feel we can trust instinctively, whose jokes we understand, who share our sense of irony.... It is much harder to extend the same principle to strangers in our midst who find our ways as disturbing as we do theirs, who watch fearfully as their own children, caught in between, slip from the paternal grasp into a new and bewildering world.[24]

In his book *Murder in Amsterdam,* about the issues surrounding the killings of Pim Fortuyn and Theo van Gogh, Buruma quoted the Iranian-born Muslim professor at the University of Leiden in the Netherlands, Afshen Ellian. "Citizenship of a democratic state means living by the laws of the country. A liberal democracy cannot survive when part of the population believes that divine laws trump those made by man."[25] This is a most reasonable argument and few can deny its truth. But one wonders if a truly liberal democracy can survive when, by the same token, racial purists and anti-minority bigots feel they have unbridled license to cry "fire!" in that proverbial crowded theater, saying and doing whatever they want, distinguishing membership from citizenship in a society in which they alone claim ownership, and encouraging many to be intolerant of tolerance in the name of protecting the natives from those outsiders, those *allochtoonen*. Somehow such actions—reminders of the arguments of Nazis about their primary nemeses, the Jews—have an all too familiar ring.[26]

The Resurgence of Ultranationalism

In recent years the tensions illustrated by the case study of the Netherlands have manifest themselves in every country in Europe, in many places with even greater vehemence. In reaction to the presence of foreigners, political parties, all stressing what in the United States would be called "nativism" but is generally expressed as *ultranationalism* overseas, have been gaining strength from the British Isles to Greece and from the Scandinavian countries to Italy. While not yet dominant in most of those countries and sometimes somewhat neutralized by members of liberal factions who, in coalition with those in migrant communities, elect representatives of minority groups (such as Ahmed Marouch, a member of the Dutch social-democratic labor party),[27] populism's backlash across Europe is widespread and the few members of parliaments of different backgrounds from the dominant groups remain vulnerable to both blatant and insidious attacks. For example, as recently as August 2013, the first and only black minister in the Italian government, Congo-born physician and politician—and Italian citizen—Cécile Kyenge, was called an orangutan by a parliamentary colleague and well-known neofascist. In a public arena she was told to go back to her own country.

During that same month, an Italian winery brought out a new lot of varietals with Nazi-themed labels, including pictures of Adolf Hitler in full salute, and members of his inner circle. It was reported that bottles with such labels quickly became the winery's best sellers.

While the agendas of most ultranationalist groups have slight variations, most of their party platforms contain two solid planks: *national sovereignty* and *xenophobia,* generally expressed in anti-immigrant, often anti-Muslim, and, of late, increasingly anti-Semitic terms. Much of the rhetoric heard at rallies and seen in broadsides and on banners outlines schemes for mobilization and echo, in almost an uncanny way, the sort of American bigotry discussed in earlier chapters and the calls to maintain white supremacy and racial purity, keep foreigners out, and put tight controls on those who somehow managed to enter what others defined as their God-given turf. And, closer to their homes, many proponents of such resurgent nationalism sound strikingly like those of the Nazi demagogues who railed against the Jews and whipped up citizens into a patriotic and murderous frenzy.

While none call themselves National Socialists (the actual title of the Nazis), some come close with such patriotic titles as *Front National* of France, the British Nationalist Party, *Danskfolkeparti* (Danish People's Party), True Finns, *Vlaama Belang* (Belgium's Flemish Interest), Germany's *Pro-Deutschland,* and Italy's *Lega Nord* (Northern League). Others use less chauvinistic, more innocuous names such as Sweden Democrats; Norway's Progress Party; and Freedom Party, the title used by extreme right-wing parties in the Netherlands, Switzerland, and Austria. One of the newest and most violent of them all is Greece's Golden Dawn, which some describe as a fascist mafia. Each of them blatantly evokes the onset of a hoped-for new era or a return to the status quo ante, that is, "The way it used to be."

While almost every one of those mentioned has latched on to the language of Islamophobia, Hungary's nationalist, anti-Semitic, and anti-immigrant party, *Jobbik,* which in 2013 held 20 percent of the seats in parliament, also specifically targets Roma people, those often referred to as Gypsies, the one non-immigrant group that the Council of Europe report "Living Together" cited as being discriminated against in many parts of the continent.

As significant as their names and symbols (which also frequently evoke images of those of the recent past, including variations on the design of the swastika, the Nazi's principal logo) is the influence that these parties exert on the populaces of their homelands, often by telling stories and spreading false rumors about those, such as Jews, Roma, and Muslims, they see as "the strangers in our midst." By doing this they rely on stereotyping and various methods of agitation to gin up mass hysteria, as discussed in Chapter Seven.

As was the case in the highest peaks of anti-foreign sentiment in the United States, while the majority of citizens do not accept the full contentions of the most brazen and outspoken leaders (those sociologist Robert K. Merton once referred to as "all-weather bigots"), many come to accept the persuasive arguments that the ills of their societies have something to do with those "damned foreigners." *Scapegoating* and *the displacement of aggression,* two concepts introduced in an earlier chapter, are often useful tools in the arsenal of mobilization. When under stress, as are many in economically depressed Europe, skillful agitators seek to convince fellow citizens that "the outsiders" are the real enemy. And, as was the case in Germany and Italy after the Great Depression, demagogic nationalists are often able to rally even those in two cohorts discussed in Chapter Six: "the gentle people of prejudice" (those who harbor hatreds but rarely act), and the "fair-weather liberals" (who know what's right but tend to follow the crowd).

One need only consider the implications of the fact that in April 2013, the Euro Zone (a bloc of twenty-three countries that use the Euro as its currency) had the highest average rate of unemployment since the common market was founded. It was 12 percent. In Greece and Spain it exceeded 25 percent. The anxiety of trying to "care for our own" provoked by such dire statistics played into the hands of people eager to blame the "damn foreigners" for their plight and attack not only those already in their countries, but those seeking to enter. Of late, new concern has focused on those in poverty-ridden sectors of Romania and Bulgaria who, now granted full access across European labor markets and eager to move into Western Europe and to the United Kingdom, are viewed as threatening to exacerbate an already volatile situation.

Even people one might think would be the most welcome, such as those coming from former colonies, are hardly immune. In 2013 the British government imposed a discriminatory policy on migrants coming from six such places—Nigeria, Ghana, India, Pakistan, Bangladesh, and Sri Lanka—requiring the posting of a bail bond of approximately $4,500, lest they overstay their visas. This is something never required of other visitors. It was argued that such a procedure was necessary because of the evidence that people coming from those societies enter on temporary visas with the intentions of staying in the United Kingdom and "adding to the welfare burden."

The presence of people from other lands has provided needed hardworking laborers and enriched cultures of staid European societies, but they have also provided easy targets for displacing frustration when the economies falter—and the demagogues know this. Many, even when knowing the truth, exaggerate the dangers and inflate statistics such as the number of foreigners in the country. And this is relatively easy to do because many are quite ignorant of the facts.

According to historian Caroline Brothers, "Perceptions of the impact of migration in some countries are so distorted that citizens estimate that there are as many as three times the number of immigrants living there than is actually the case." She reports that the International Organization for Migration warns that misinformation fans "harmful stereotypes, discrimination and xenophobia." For instance, "The actual percentage of migrants in Italy in 2010 was around 7 percent, the report said, 'yet polls showed that the population perceived this percentage to be around a staggering 25 percent.'"[28]

Are there countertrends?

In the midst of all the nationalist fervor in many European countries, there are some signs of accommodation and attempts at coexistence if not true integration. Not surprisingly, they are most often found in bazaars and markets where folks from different backgrounds sell their fruits, vegetables, and crafts. One such example is in the city of Rome. Locals, those from rural areas, and those from other places, especially Romania and Albania, Morocco and other places in North Africa, and

South and East Asia (especially migrants from China) are all hawking their wares to Romans eager to buy their produce and products. This is positive pluralism and, to some, a hopeful sign in the face of persisting and still pervasive racism. This sort of thing is surely necessary to kindle the flames of real change, but it is hardly sufficient. Without stricter and strongly enforced laws against discrimination, hate mongering, hooliganism, and vigilante-like campaigns, it will be a long time before most nations of Europe can call themselves "nations of nations."

In an effort to distill available data on ways of moving toward greater understanding, acceptance of diversity, and improving the conditions for minorities in many countries—most specifically, Britain, Canada, France, Germany, and the United States—under the aegis of the Dahrendorf Programme on the Study of Freedom at St. Antony's College at Oxford University, Timothy Garton Ash, Edward Mortimer, and Kerem Oktem offered some useful lessons. Although doubtlessly more difficult to implement than to specify, and while those nations to which the guidelines are addressed might well have different ways of implementing them, each is worthy of consideration for those studying immigration issues as well as those setting government policy related to it. They are as follows:

- *The importance of citizenship*: All long-term residents in a democratic state should be able to become citizens of that state.
- *The acquisition and obligations of citizenship*: New citizens must be made welcome in their new country, and be willing to contribute to it.
- *Dual citizenship*: Citizenship of another country should not prevent people being citizens of the country where they live.
- *Education*: Schools must have the curriculum and resources to perform their vital function of preparing pupils for life as active citizens in a free society.
- *Labor markets and the workplace*: Employers and colleagues must give migrants and post-migrants equal opportunities, and help them integrate socially as well as economically.
- *Cities and local communities*: Towns and cities have a unique role to play in creating a sense of shared community and common purpose.
- *Representation in the media*: Minorities must be fully represented both in the media and by the media.
- *The duty to speak out*: Public figures, and people with a significant presence online, should challenge stereotypes and misleading generalizations about any group.
- *Politics*: Active steps need to be taken, notably by political parties, to ensure that minorities and their members are fully represented through established democratic institutions.
- *How attitudes are changed*: For everyone in a diverse society, the feeling of belonging together depends crucially on the social and cultural signals sent and received every day.[29]

At the present time, how many national and regional leaders will heed the admonitions and suggestions the Dahrendorf group put forward remains highly speculative.

Faith Under Fire and the Fire of Faith

Because it represents one of the most critical flashpoints of conflict in the world, it is well to briefly return to one of today's principal issues, religious intolerance, or what Martha Nussbaum calls "the new religious intolerance."[30] There is ample evidence to indicate that persecution over beliefs within and between societies is once again on the rise, and this includes both a resurgence of anti-Semitism in many parts of the world—even those such as in Hungary and other Central European countries where, because of the Holocaust, few Jews still reside—and the even wider-reaching Islamophobia.

Steven Lee Myers, discussing an annual government report of the state of religious freedom, concluded that "bigotry and sectarian violence are spreading, while religious rights are in retreat."[31] Using the example of the political turmoil in Turkey, Myers notes that the longtime prime minister Recep Tayyip Erdoğan has increasingly inserted anti-Semitic tropes into speeches aimed at increasing and maintaining the support of Islamic fundamentalists. Matching such statements are those used by the opponents of the Islamic hard-liners, who often include all Muslims in their diatribes, regardless of their marked differences of attitude, belief, and social organization. Here we see a conflation of many of the issues addressed in earlier chapters, especially relating to prejudice and discrimination as expressed in the United States.

Studies of such demagoguery have been quick to note that some of the caricatures of Jews in yesterday's Europe and Muslims in today's have striking similarities. Comparisons are often made between the propaganda of those who reduced Jews to vermin and posters in various parts of Europe showing Muslims, or Arabs, as rats. Some of the most graphic were seen in Switzerland, showing rodents in "Muslim" garb gnawing on a big piece of cheese embossed with the Swiss flag.

Not since the 1930s and 1940s has there been such an uprising of targeted animosity toward those of different faiths both within and between societies. Many feel that religious warfare on a global scale is in the offing. Such thinking is not without justification and it is important to recognize that what the social psychologist Gordon Allport once called "earned reputation" is still a factor to reckon with.

Many conflicts now extant are related to attachments to traditional groups whose members have primordial ties to those of tribe and clan; claims to specific turf; and, especially, membership in a particular religious group, sect, or faction, even when the members are part of some overarching faith. They are sometimes carried abroad and are serious threats to stability.

When Westerners raise their hackles in horror reading of persisting tensions between Kikuyus and Luos in Kenya, of the simmering disputes between Tamils and Sinhalese that still exist in Sri Lanka, of the struggles between Pakistanis and Indians over Kashmir, and of the bitter feuding between Sunnis and Shiites in Iraq and many other Muslim countries, it is important to reflect on the age-old conflicts that long existed between Christians and Muslims dating back to the Crusades and on the much more recent conflict between Protestants and Catholics in Northern Ireland. (The latter, while currently in check under the terms of a special peace accord, still simmers in the cities and towns of that part of the United Kingdom.) Still, such reflection does not gainsay the fact that some people are bent on imposing their version of God's—or Allah's—will on others, often by rallying to the cry of converting or killing the "infidels."

In the late days of the Roman Empire, the exclamation was *Nobiscum deus* (God with us). Centuries later Teutonic knights, and later still Prussian soldiers, used the same slogan, in a German version: *Gott mit Uns*. The words were embossed on the helmets of German soldiers in World War I and on the belt buckles of those of the *Wehrmacht* in World War II. Variations on this are a worldwide phenomenon, as we Americans ought well be aware. Our coins and bills are marked with the slogan, "In God We Trust," implying, some critics say, that others don't!

Given the daily fare on the television and computer screens showing pitched battles in the streets between religious and political factions, especially in what is sometimes called "the arc of instability" that stretches from Syria through the Middle East and curves back across North Africa, it is understandable how easily such conflicts can be exploited by those who use the same arguments to defend what they do in other languages.

Those conflicts are real. And, given the instantaneous exposure everyone has to what is going on in almost every corner of the world, they are there for all to see. But are they simply what sociologist Robin M. Williams Jr. called "the wars within,"[32] dangerous enough in their own right, or are they part of much larger regional, even global struggles?

A classic example is what has happened in the wake of the Arab Spring, the overthrow of dictatorial regimes in Egypt, Tunisia, and Libya and the subsequent upheaval in Syria. Many Western governments and the United States found themselves on the horns of a dilemma. Should they support those who see themselves as "freedom fighters" or defend their longtime allies (perhaps "clients" is a better word), helping them to stem the tide of forceful takeovers by well-organized and well-funded Islamist jihadists, many of whom favor a worldwide war against non-Muslims and the return of the Caliphate of old, who might well push aside progressive secularists once the first part of the revolution is over? The jury is still out. But, as *New York Times* columnist Roger Cohen explains,

> Poisoned by colonialism, stymied by Islam's battle with modernity, inebriated by oil, blocked by the absence of institutions that can mediate the fury of tribe and ethnicity, Middle Eastern states turn in circles. Syria is now the regional emblem, a vacuum in which only the violent nihilism of the jihadi thrives.
>
> Just two and a half years after the Arab Spring, talk of the future—any future—seems preposterous. Countries build futures on the basis of things that do not exist here: consensus as to the nature of the state, the rule of law, a concept of citizenship that overrides sectarian allegiance, and the ability to place the next generation's prosperity above the settling of past scores.[33]

It is a true dilemma for those in power, but an existential tragedy for those bewildered, frightened, and trapped people caught in the line of fire. They are especially wary of the rigid rules of conduct often demanded by those who gain control of neighborhoods, states, or whole countries—whether secular or religious. They are the people I had in mind when I wrote the following poem, "To Die For."

To die for what?
The cause.
The *Volk.*
For *Lebensraum.*
For glory.
For a shortcut to Paradise.

To die for whom?

The emperor, the czar,
The king, the country.
For Christ's sake.
Or Allah's
In crusades to rid the world of infidels.

Ours.
Theirs.

Obscenity begets obscenity.
And the orphans cry, "Stop the killing!"
But none pay heed.
They are true believers.
They just rattle their sabers and exclaim,
"Gott mit uns."[34]

A Conundrum Revisited

American sociologists who study racial and ethnic relations in the United States have long examined often-lopsided face-offs based on unfounded prejudices, entrenched patterns of discrimination, and many other matters discussed in this and previous chapters, and now find themselves doing so on a more global basis, making comparisons to how we see ourselves and how we see others. Much of it has to do with a close reading of unfamiliar histories and unfamiliar cultures, with data gathering and analysis. It also has to do with values and value judgments.

In the earliest pages of this book, I posed a conundrum. I suggested that a moral judgment, no matter how much one may agree with it, cannot be a substitute for the systematic study of why people do what they do. But I also pointed out that the subject of this book, racial and ethnic relations, is generally studied because those who examine it are concerned about human rights and their abuse. It is a concern with what some call social evil. Now, at the end of this introduction to racial and ethnic relations, the conundrum remains.

A recent book, *Evil,* by the noted French sociologist Michel Wieviorka, offers a most interesting take on the matter and all that we have been examining in this study of insiders and outsiders in our country and elsewhere in the world. Wieviorka points out that, usually perceived in religious discourse, from the social science perspective "evil is the outcome of human action and implies degradation, destruction, negation, in any event a challenge to the physical, mental, or moral integrity of certain people or groups, directly or indirectly."[35] Examples cited are particularly pertinent to this construction: *racism, terrorism,* and other forms of *violence against a targeted group*—often a scapegoat. Here the author infers that what is really happening is the labeling and demonizing of others—and the solidification and often the institutionalization of those age-old distinctions between "they" and "we."

The contention is that evil, like one of its most insidious manifestations, racism, is a social construction. Because it is "man-made" and not the product of some external factor or divine expression, it is therefore within the power of humankind to address what is often calculated malevolence, that is, behavior destructive to its targeted victims and, in the end, counter to any reasonable and honorable comity among peoples.

It is difficult to legislate morality, but it is possible to assert that human rights and the dignity of all people are worth supporting, and that to do so there must be not only the will, but ways that will protect the victims from their victimizers. In this country, while we clearly have a long way to go, we have made considerable progress by not only passing antidiscrimination laws but also developing modes of action to enforce them, with severe sanctions for violation.

In the 1930s there was a debate among social scientists over "cultural relativism"—that is, the claim that people had the right to do whatever their cultures required. Even if this meant favoring men over women, causing harm by body mutilations, and waging tribal warfare, it was not for outsiders to say such things were wrong. Sometimes called "national character," it was argued that while "we certainly wouldn't do such things, it is not for us to judge others." This was before many relativists broke with those who took such a stance. Especially after the rise of Nazism and the brutality of the Holocaust, others began speaking forcefully of universal human rights, of the dignity of all men and all women, of the protection of the weak and the poor, and of an end to intergroup conflict.

Agreeing with Michel Wieviorka's definition of evil is no sociological transgression. It is an affirmation of human rights.

Figure 12.1   Demonstration for Fairness to Migrants, Ceuta, Spanish Morocco

Photo by Peter Rose, 2006.

Notes

1. "The Ballad for Americans," text by John Latouche, music by Earl Robinson, 1940, copyright renewed in 1967 by the Robbins Music Corporation.

2. See Seymour Martin Lipset, *The First New Nation: The United States in Historical and Comparative Perspective* (New York: Doubleday Anchor Books, 1967).

3. Alexis de Tocqueville, *Democracy in America* (New York: Vintage Books, 1945 edition).

4. David Riesman with Nathan Glazer and Reuel Denney, *The Lonely Crowd: The Changing American Character* (New Haven: Yale University Press, 1950).

5. See Robin M. Williams Jr., *American Society: A Sociological Interpretation* (New York: Knopf, 1951).

6. Ibid., p. 411.

7. Ibid., p. 433.

8. Jean-Francois Revel, *Without Marx or Jesus: The New American Republic* (New York: Delacorte Press, 1972).

9. Seymour Martin Lipset, *American Exceptionalism: A Double-Edged Sword* (New York: W. W. Norton, 1997).

10. Mark Hertsgaard, *The Eagle's Shadow: Why America Fascinates and Infuriates the World* (New York: Farrar, Straus and Giroux, 2002).

11. Ibid., p. 175.

12. See Samuel P. Huntington, "The Clash of Civilizations," *Foreign Affairs,* 72:3 (Summer 1993), pp. 22–49.

13. Robin Cohen, *Global Diasporas* (London: UCL/Routledge Press, 1997).

14. Ibid., p. 155. The reference is to Andrew McGrew et al., *Global Politics* (New York: Wiley, 1992).

15. Cohen, *Global Diasporas,* pp. 156–157. Italics added.

16. Ibid.

17. Rudyard Kipling, "The Stranger," *Morning Post* (April 1908).

18. Council of Europe, "Living Together: Combining Diversity and Freedom in 21st-Century Europe," Report of the Group of Eminent Persons of the Council of Europe (May 2011). Italics added.

19. Esther Ben-David, "Europe's Shifting Immigration Dynamic," *Middle East Quarterly* (Spring 2009), pp. 15–24.

20. Ibid.

21. Henry Chu, "After Decades, German Turks Still Feel Like Outsiders," *Los Angeles Times* (December 9, 2013).

22. Survey results announced in press release by *International Herald Tribune* based on study by Novatris/Harris/France 24 on May 25, 2007.

23. See Robert E. Park, *Race and Culture* (New York: Free Press, 1951), p. 354.

24. Ian Buruma, *Murder in Amsterdam: The Death of Theo van Gogh and the Limits of Tolerance* (New York: Penguin Press, 2006).

25. Ibid.

26. Much of the text in this "case study" of the Netherlands is excerpted from a review-essay by the author. See Peter I. Rose, "Minus-Sum Games in a Land of Guilty Memories," *Congress Monthly* (January–February 2007), pp. 3–7.

27. See Ian Buruma, "Parade's End: Dutch Liberals Get Tough," *New Yorker* (December 7, 2009), pp. 36–41.

28. Caroline Brothers, "Perceptions of Migration Clash with Reality, Report Finds," *New York Times* (December 5, 2011). See also Christopher Caldwell, *Reflections on the Revolution in Europe: Immigration, Islam, and the West* (New York: Doubleday, 2009), especially Chapter 4, "Fear Masquerading as Tolerance," pp. 82–107.

29. Timothy Garton Ash, Edward Mortimer, and Kerem Oktem, *Freedom in Diversity,* a report of the Dahrendorf Programme for the Study of Freedom at St. Antony's College (Oxford: Oxford University, 2013), p. 3. The report is also available online (www.sant.ox.ac .uk/esc/freedomanddiversity.html) and as an ebook.

30. Martha C. Nussbaum, *The New Religious Intolerance* (Cambridge: Belknap Press of Harvard University Press, 2012). For further discussion of this topic, see Humayun Ansari and Farid Hafez (eds.), *From the Far Right to the Mainstream: Islamophobia in Party Politics and the Media* (Frankfurt and New York: Campus Verlag, 2012), pp. 7–28.

31. Steven Lee Myers, "Persecution over Beliefs Is on the Rise," *International Herald Tribune* (May 21, 2013).

32. See Robin M. Williams Jr., *The Wars Within: Peoples and States in Conflict* (Ithaca, NY: Cornell University Press, 2003).

33. Roger Cohen, "The Middle East Pendulum," *New York Times* (October 14, 2013). See www.nytimes.com/2013/10/15/opinion/the-middle-east-pendulum.html.

34. Peter I. Rose, *Postmonitions of a Peripatetic Professor* (Amherst: Levellers Press, 2013), p. 226.

35. Michel Wieviorka, *Evil: A Sociological Perspective* (New York: Wiley, 2012), p. 11.

Epilogue

Throughout the pages of this book, the focus has been on the nature of often-strained relations and competition based mainly, if not exclusively, on social definitions of race and ethnicity—concepts grounded, often as not, on misperceptions of others. The "they versus we" motif has been a constant in a volume that touched on many subjects—prejudice, discrimination, actions, reactions—all couched in a framework of a Humanistic Sociology, a sociology that demands both rigor in the assessment and analyses of social interactions and empathy for those involved. This duality underscores the entire enterprise: learning about root causes of intergroup tension and current problems; getting to know *all* the players, those in positions of dominance and those called minorities—and those often caught in the middle; coming to terms with one's own values while learning "to see ourselves as others see us." This last idea, succinctly conveyed in a closing stanza of the Kipling poem quoted in the beginning of Chapter Six says it all.

> If you cross over the sea,
> Instead of over the way
> You may end by (think of it!) looking on We
> As only a sort of They.

What the poet said is rather easy to grasp intellectually. But to internalize such a sentiment and make it truly a part of one's own worldview is quite another thing. In many ways it is the hardest lesson that those of us who conduct research and teach about intergroup relations try to convey.

When I first started offering courses on race and ethnicity in America, I was convinced that the only way to really come to grips with the issues was through direct involvement. You had to leave the ivory towers and go into the streets, becoming, as it were, at once a participant and an ethnographer. But I soon learned that one doesn't need to leave the classroom to at least start "crossing over the sea."

Over the nearly sixty years I have taught such courses, that realization was re-inforced on innumerable occasions, but never quite so dramatically or poignantly as one time not so long ago.

Two days earlier, I had said to my students, "The next time we meet we will be discussing integration." I began that next session by asking them what *they* thought the concept meant.

An African American sophomore spoke up immediately. "Well," she said, "speaking as a black woman...." Before she could finish her sentence, a white student interrupted. "Forgive me, but I'm sick and tired of having every comment by some of those here prefaced by the line 'Speaking as a black woman.' I don't begin every sentence with 'Speaking as a white woman!'" I started to intervene when an angry voice boomed out of the back of the room. "You don't have to!"

The tension was palpable. Most of the black students were clearly upset; so, it appeared, were many of the other nonwhites in the class. The target of the sharp rebuke sat there stoic but clearly shaken. Most of the other white students looked almost as uncomfortable.

Although more edgy than most, what we had all just witnessed was not, to me, an unusual exchange. But, somehow, I was especially dispirited by it that day.

Once things had calmed down a bit, I tried to use the incident itself as a basis for a conversation about what had just happened. It was tough going in the beginning but, once the ice was broken, it proved to be one of the best discussions we had all semester. Nearing the end of the period, I again asked if anyone could offer an explication of the term "integration." There was a pregnant silence.

Perhaps, I thought to myself, I've pushed them too hard and they need a breather. Then, with the hands on the clock moving toward the end of the fifty-minute ses-sion, a rather shy white student who had always seemed very engrossed but rarely spoke in class said she thought she could define it.

"When she," pointing to the black student who had first spoken out, "can do the things I take for granted, then we will have integration."

A simple truth—and, I think, a fitting coda to this overview of racial and ethnic relations in the United States and in lands beyond our shores.

Index

About the Author

Peter I. Rose, a sociologist and writer, is Sophia Smith Professor Emeritus and Senior Fellow of the Kahn Liberal Arts Institute at Smith College. He has held visiting professorships at Clark, Wesleyan, the University of Colorado, UCLA, Yale, and Harvard; served as a Fulbright professor in England, Japan, Australia, Austria, and the Netherlands and as a member of the faculty of the Salzburg Global Seminar; and been a resident fellow at centers and institutes in Beijing, Jerusalem, Oxford, Bellagio, Bogliasco, Honolulu, Harvard, and, most recently, Stanford University.

In addition to *They and We,* he is the author of *The Subject Is Race, Strangers in Their Midst, Mainstream and Margins, Tempest-Tost, Guest Appearances and Other Travels in Time and Space, With Few Reservations,* and *Postmonitions of a Peripatetic Professor.* He is also editor of a number of other books on sociology, American culture, intergroup relations, ethnic history, and immigration and refugee policy, including *The Study of Society, The Ghetto and Beyond, Americans from Africa, Working with Refugees,* and *The Dispossessed: An Anatomy of Exile.*